Sometimes
a Shining Moment

Sometimes a Shining Moment

The Foxfire Experience

ELIOT WIGGINTON

ANCHOR PRESS/DOUBLEDAY
GARDEN CITY, NEW YORK
1985

Copyright © 1985 by Brooks Eliot Wigginton
All Rights Reserved
Printed in the United States of America
First Edition

Library of Congress Cataloging in Publication Data

Wigginton, Eliot.
  Sometimes a shining moment.

  Includes index.
  1. Wigginton, Eliot.   2. High school teachers—Georgia—Biography.   3. Foxfire—History.   4. Georgia—Social life and customs—Study and teaching (Secondary)—Georgia—Rabun Gap—Case studies.   5. Country life—Georgia—Study and teaching (Secondary)—Georgia—Rabun Gap—Case studies. I. Title.
LA2317.W49A38   1985   373.11'0092'4   85-19967
ISBN 0-385-13358-8

Contents

I tell you one thing, if you learn it by yourself, if you have to get down and dig for it, it never leaves you. It stays there as long as you live because you had to dig it out of the mud before you learned what it was.

—Aunt Addie Norton

Introduction

I am a public high school English teacher.

Occasionally, on gloomy nights, my mood shifts in subtle ways, and familiar questions rise in my throat; in social situations, confronted by those whose lives seem somehow more dramatic, an implication in the air is that I will have little of interest to contribute to the conversation; many people with fewer years of formal education make more money. Then the mood passes, for I know that surface appearance is deceitful and salary is a bogus yardstick of worth.

If you pick up this book when it is published in the fall of 1985, your interest will coincide with the beginning of my twentieth year in the profession. And actually, if the truth be told, it is only rarely that I wonder why I am still teaching. I know why. I teach because it is something I do well; it is a craft I enjoy and am intrigued by; there is room within its certain boundaries for infinite variety and flexibility of approach, and so if I become bored or my work becomes routine, I have no one to blame but myself; and unlike other jobs I could have, I sometimes receive indications that I am making a difference in the quality of people's lives. That, and one more thing: I genuinely enjoy daily contact with the majority of the people with whom I work. Our disagreements are Frost's "lovers' quarrels."

I'm not saying that teaching is the only field in which such benefits exist, and I'm not saying that I will stay in the profession for the rest of my working days. If I do begin looking for a new job, however, I'll cross my fingers and hope to find one with a similar profile.

I began writing this book years ago. Its first draft was privately printed in 1975. It was called *Moments: The Foxfire Experience.* The audience it was directed toward was those teachers who had written me to ask how and why I had integrated the publication of our magazine, *Foxfire,* into my language arts curriculum, for many of them were interested in trying the same thing. This book is the second draft. Its audience is still teachers, but it is an audience with broader questions—questions I encounter whenever I am with a group of public school people—questions like, "Given our limited resources and our sometimes medieval working environment, how can we do a better job without pushing ourselves into a state of nervous exhaustion in the process?"

I began with the self-imposed, rather youthful and naive determination to make this the best book ever written for that audience. Years later, the goal is more realistic: the questions are still there, and I just want to take my shot at answering them as best I can, at the same time encouraging those who have the questions to continue asking them of themselves, their students, and others for as long as they stay in the field. For I have found that it is the constant, unrelenting examination and revision of approach—not a package of answers to packaged questions—that makes the better teachers among us the best.

The book is divided into three parts. The first is the Foxfire story: how and why the first issue of *Foxfire* magazine was put together, what happened in the years between its publication and the appearance of the *Foxfire Book* in 1972, and the immediate aftermath of that event. The narrative then jumps to 1984 and to the structure and purposes of the organization that evolved out of the chaos of 1972 and 1973. The leap forward is jarring but intentional, for the purpose of this book is not to tell our whole story but to relate those parts of it that might be most applicable and useful to the intended audience. (Most of you are far more likely to find yourselves facing the situations I faced in those earlier years than you are to find yourselves in the midst of simultaneous contract negotiations with Doubleday and E. P. Dutton, for example.) Besides, there's a question of space.

While I'm on the subject of the first section, there is one more thing I must note: I've chosen to use excerpts from a few of my journals and letters so that you can share with me exactly the thoughts that were going through my mind in those early days, asking you to remember that when they were written, this country was in the midst of a time when John Kennedy, a man I and many of my peers revered, had been killed; when "Negroes" were being jailed for having the audacity to try to purchase a cup of coffee; when Peter, Paul and Mary and Bob Dylan and the Beatles made most of the music we listened to; when the threat of having to serve in Vietnam for a cause that was questionable at best had many of us torn between loyalty to country and loyalty to conscience; and when $3,500 a year was a living wage.

Things were different then, but I learned, and I grew; and in relation to the job I had, much of what I distilled out of those years makes up Part II. The lessons—especially those having to do with how one treats other people, no matter what their age or race or ability, and what school is (or should be) for—are lessons that inform all that I and my staff members continue to do today, and they are lessons that are just as valid and applicable now as they were then. They are principles—touchstones—that are never outdated; a fact that is made even more convincing by reading the works of philosophers like John Dewey, who foretold my questions and answered them years before I began asking them. So how come, when I was learning how to teach, the work of these individuals was not emphasized and memorized and internalized? Was it because my instructors believed that I would have to learn all the old lessons by myself in order to internalize them, or because they had decided that they would just throw us all to the wolves? How come I had to do all that work and am still having to fight because I understand some of those philosophers so imperfectly? Having to reinvent the wheel may have some perverse merits, but when I think of the inefficiency of that system and the number of talented classmates I had who dropped out of teaching in premature frustration, I have to wonder about the wisdom of such a system if, in fact, it exists by design.

Part II, therefore, is a recitation of those touchstones, *not* because I believe I am the first to discover them and must hasten to relay them to a waiting world, but because of the number of teachers I meet who, in workshops I conduct, persist in saying for reasons I have stopped trying to fathom, "Wait a minute. I don't understand that one. Explain that again. I may have heard that before, but I've forgotten it." They are, in other words, just like me: sometimes peering out from under piles of obligations and navigating with a compass that seems to have no needle.

Part III is an attempt to show the philosophy outlined in the second section at work in several actual twenty-five- to thirty-pupil courses being offered within the constraints of fifty-five-minute periods inside our traditional public high school. The directions for producing a magazine like *Foxfire* are not there, for that is a specific activity that only a minority of teachers will find useful, and there are other books available already that describe the process for those who want them (see Bibliography). Rather, a sample grammar/composition course is described; also included are suggestions for bringing the content of other courses in the curriculum more in line with a philosophy that is like an overarching umbrella, beneath which hundreds of expressions—among them the production of a magazine—are equally valid.

So much has been left out, and good friends are going to be disappointed. Many of them, for example, have taken some of our ideas and applied them in ways more exciting than I could ever have imagined ten years ago (like Paula Palmer, whose students' work in Costa Rica has culminated in a social studies text that is so culturally appropriate that the Ministry of Education there has printed and distributed it to every secondary school in the country; or Jan DeWeese, whose newly immigrated Southeast Asian students in Portland, Oregon, have produced a book that is one of the few things they can truly call their own in a strange country;

or Malcomb Smith and Rich McConnell, who applied the philosophy successfully with a group of residential high school students in a psychiatric institution in the Midwest). But these examples are not lost. These and hundreds of others will appear in a set of pamphlets and course guides that I and my staff members are writing at this moment, and those of you who are interested may find further information in the Bibliography.

Meanwhile, there is this thing called teaching. We all have our own methods, our own answers. That's fine, and maybe even essential. Survey any random group of high school graduates and you will find that some of them responded most positively to a traditional teaching style and others to a more freewheeling one.

But fundamental common denominators remain. They always have and they always will. They are the talismans around which this book is built, attention to which helps keep me, at least, from going forth into this world of teaching and getting absolutely lost in its complexities.

This is the book I wish I had had twenty years ago.

                                                                BEW

Sometimes
a Shining Moment

Prologue: Excerpts from a College Journal

Prodded by an English teacher who believed in the keeping of journals, I kept one intermittently in both high school and college. On reading them years later, I was so embarrassed by the naïveté and the brash, shrill adolescent tone of so many of the entries that I destroyed most of them. They had accomplished their purpose. They had taught me something of the discipline required in the craft of writing, and they had taught me to be somewhat introspective and reflective. Best, they had taught me not to simply let life wash over me like a wave, but to examine my actions and motivations and attempt, however unsuccessfully, to make some sense out of the world around me; to keep in mind that life, as a gift, is finite—at least on this earth; to keep in mind an obligation to others besides myself; to keep score.

A few brief excerpts from those journals that survived follow. I include them here with the thought that the reader may find them interesting from a purely historical standpoint in terms of what eventually happened in Rabun County, Georgia. Being at Cornell in the sixties, of course, with John Kennedy as our President, made an enormous difference. Had I gone to college in the seventies, I feel reasonably sure that none of the events recounted in this book would ever have happened.

[APRIL, 1963, AS A PRE-MED STUDENT]

I don't mind the [college] work so much. It's just this feeling of guilt twenty-four hours a day—guilt that I didn't do everything I *could* have done. Discouraging. I feel an almost total lack of fulfillment and direction, and that hurts—not just on the surface, but deep inside.

A train whistle is blowing. Sounds very forlorn at two A.M. Funny how something like that can become the symbol of loneliness and discouragement. Easy to see why, though. Gives you goose bumps just to hear it. Makes you chilly, too, the way it pierces the air.

What a strange, unearthly feeling it is to be suspended in air, with the feeling that at any minute, something will happen that will change the course of your whole life. You're very susceptible to change, hanging like that. It's as if you were swinging on the end of a rope hung from a crane. A wind can swing you any way, and when the crane drops you, you simply fall in the direction the wind has been blowing. So helpless. There are so many winds— so many influences—and 360 degrees' worth of direction for them to choose from.

I have no right to flatter myself into thinking that I have talent worth developing [in writing] and yet I *feel* that something is there. I feel a push. An urge. I only hope it is not youthful impetuosity, or an ill-meaning wind blowing me in the wrong direction. And yet what if I don't take advantage of it?

[DURING SUMMER OF 1963, WORKING IN A HOSPITAL]:
The woman Mrs. Johnson and I saw brought into emergency was scheduled for OR next day, so we set up two bloods on her. The day of the operation came. She died on the table. That afternoon, I saw the cards from her blood bottles in our wastebasket—all that remained to show that she had been there.

[OCTOBER, 1963, AFTER DROPPING PRE-MED]:
The biggest question: Who do you live for? Yourself, or the fulfillment of the expectations of society? The older one gets, the more of these little expectations there are to bind one down.

It's almost as if each "duty" was a Lilliputian with a silken thread. One is not enough to hold you down, but the longer you stay in one place, the more time you give the rest to arrive on the scene.

Society is sometimes like a bad movie—you paid your admission fee, and now, despite the fact that you hate the damn flick, you're too cheap to walk out. You *know* what the end is, but you can't leave. You just sit and watch— maybe eat some popcorn along the way.

[NOVEMBER, 1963, FOUND IN RILKE'S Letters to a Young Poet]:
"If your daily life seems poor, do not blame it; blame yourself that you are not poet enough to call forth its riches; for to the Creator, there is no poverty."

[DECEMBER, 1963, AS AN ENGLISH MAJOR AND PRESIDENT OF MY FRATERNITY]:
My graduation from college will be a severing of all old ties. Friends will become vague memories; responsibilities at college flitting shadows. Thus graduation will be a rebirth. A chance to start anew. I must be the master of my own fate. Life is short, and at the day of death, I want to say, "World, I

leave you happy. Life has been mine. I have held it in my palm and found it good."

One must have an income in this world today—only a small one is needed. Only a small one is to be desired! But an income, nevertheless. Teaching English may be the key . . . Perhaps I will teach while writing.

[JULY, 1964, IN THE MIDST OF A SUMMER-LONG TRIP ACROSS COUNTRY, ALONE, CAMPING, DOING ODD JOBS FOR SPENDING MONEY, AND TAKING ADVANTAGE, FROM TIME TO TIME, OF THE HOSPITALITY OF FRIENDS. THIS, WRITTEN WHILE IN RABUN COUNTY EN ROUTE TO NEW ORLEANS]:

I spent the afternoon with Richard Norton looking for arrowheads. We found two or three good ones . . . and I again got the old desire for a huge museum devoted to Georgia and North Carolina Indian culture . . . Idle dreams probably never destined to bear fruit.

The evening saw conversation with Richard, who was in rare form. From it I was able to remember only the following snatches. How I wish sometimes my mind was a tape recorder:

"You know, people sells old clocks for $1,400 around here to rich folks who buys 'em and puts 'em on their mantel pieces and says they was passed down for generations in the family. Laws, that old clock in yonder—I bought it thirty years ago for five dollars and hit had been running seventy-five years before that, and hits in perfect shape 'cept for the chimes. I tore them out. That thing rang every half hour and was so loud you could hear it acrost the road. I'd be in bed of a night and just be gettin' t'sleep and that dang thing'd strike out again. I just tore 'em out. Body couldn't never sleep with them things blazin'.

"When the Government took over these woods, they was an Indian chief and some boys that hid out in these woods 'stead a'goin' to Cherokee. My grandfather took 'em bread and used to stay with 'em for a week or so. Took 'em an old hog rifle, too. The chief used it—wouldn't let them boys get their hands on it. He had a bullet mold, too. Used to mold 'em up a whole load of bullets and take up there, and waxed rags that he used to load with, and them boys could *hunt*. He used to tell me how they was just like half dog. Ate half-raw meat all the time—made 'em strong. One time a bear killed his dog and he didn't have no dogs less they was all spunk. Made them Indian boys so mad they swore they'd have that bear by sundown next day. They did, too. He went with 'em, and they tracked just like dogs. Said he couldn't see no trail at all, but they'd catch a broken grass no bigger 'n a matchstick and know where he was headed—through which gap and all—and they got it, too. Pretty soon they took off and he heard that gun twice down by the branch—took four of 'em to carry it out. They bound his legs with hickory bark and carried it up the hill on a pole just a'pantin'.

"When the Government bought up land in here, they wouldn't listen to the old folks. Had to see for theirselves. You know what they done? They ringed all the hickory trees to kill 'em, then made this place a game reserve. But a lot of the game ate hickory nuts and stuff, don't you see? And then those dead trees got the worms started—'bout killed these woods. And the old folks used to burn the woods over. Now we've got mosquitoes, worms, and all kinds a'insects; half of 'em I never seen before. Never used to have them.

"Many's the day I spent out there on Nantahala or Standin' Indian huntin'. We'd build a shack out of poles and long bark strips two feet wide and spend weeks up there. Time was I could find my way through all them woods at night. Now they's places I can't crawl through. I tell you, it sure wasn't like this then. They just wouldn't listen to the old folks that knew by experience."

Night was coming on then, and he had to go milk with Margaret, so I left. The cat led the way, as it did every night, hoping he'd "shuffle the corn" and scare out a rat or two. And they'd always give it a cup of milk.

And before I left, I looked back at those mountains, dark, and shrouded in fog—still as wild and rough as when the Indians were there—still filled with rattlesnakes, copperheads, foxes, bobcats, deer, bear, etc.—and I shivered a little and thought how glad I was that I was not lost in their depths.

[FALL, 1965, IN GRADUATE PROGRAM LEADING TO A MASTER OF ARTS IN TEACHING DEGREE, WHILE DOING A SEMESTER OF PRACTICE TEACHING IN BINGHAMTON, NEW YORK]:

These junior high students have stimulated me into being more creative and active than I have been for a long time now, and I appreciate that simple fact after so many years of non-producing at Cornell. Finally I am doing something that seems to me really meaningful and satisfying.

Of course there are problems. Students everywhere at this age level are constantly "trying out" their teachers to see how much they can get away with, and teachers everywhere must constantly redraw the proverbial line. And certainly everywhere exist the problems of slow learners, students who cheat, students who skip school, students who fail because of their environment and their crowd, and students who leave you breathless with their intelligence. And certainly everywhere young teachers such as myself have a problem of identification and of teacher-student relationships. I, for example, am made acutely aware of the fact that I am less than ten years older than most of these kids, *look* five years younger than that, and am even still in school. When they ask me to join in one of their football games or chaperon one of their dances and dance with them I am unsure as yet how to handle the situation. And when my first-period class comes in with a necktie for me at the end of the first marking period and starts clapping, I don't know whether to feel like a success or a failure. And when I walk down the street and a hundred kids I've never seen before say, "Hi Mr. Wigginton," I'm a little at a loss as to how to conduct myself. And when they say they like me as a teacher, I don't know whether it's because of something I've done or something I haven't done. Maybe I'm making universities out of one-room schoolhouses—but the line we tread between like out of respect and like out of familiarity, success versus total failure, is often a thin one indeed. But teaching is a good deal. The kids are so enthusiastic and fresh—a welcome relief from college cynicism and people who become defeatist, give up trying anything and just lie back on the heap of manure they have accumulated around themselves by choice and mutter at everyone and everything until they die by choking finally in their own bile.

Not everything about teaching is great, but I'm playing someone else's game now, and I didn't write the rules, and I'm hardly in a position to rewrite them. Not yet.

[MARCH, 1966, BACK IN CLASS AT CORNELL]:

Today I sent out seven letters of application to various school systems. One went to Colorado Springs, another to Palm Beach, another to Martha's Vineyard, and the rest to California. I have also applied to Rabun Gap, Cleveland, and Glen Cove. Now I guess I sit and wait. At this point, all I know is that I think I want to teach either in the New York City or the San Francisco area. Boston would also be nice. Something keeps saying Georgia (as always, it seems) but at this point, that remains an outside chance. If I'm going to write, I now know I can't split it with teaching. And since it looks like I'm going to teach, I might as well go whole hog teaching for several years, then write a book and quit.

Found out today that I am currently number one in the ed school. Out of all the interns, I was the only one to receive an A for my practice teaching. Fired with new determination, I went to the library to do the newly assigned Ed Psych readings only to discover, to my dismay, that I just couldn't get anything out of them. I'm going to have to teach flying by the seat of my pants.

What a strange point in my life all this is. I was also told by my adviser that I would probably be drafted within the next six weeks, and so perhaps I'd better enlist on my own. Vietnam hangs over everyone's head like an ax. It's changing people's lives to an unbelievable extent. People are planning (or not planning) whole careers—whole futures—around it. I rebel at the idea of enlisting.

[MAY 10, 1966]:

At this point in time, I am relatively safe from the draft with a 1-Y and have mixed feelings about the whole thing, but am much more glad than not.

Last night, Rabun Gap called and definitely offered me a job—ninth- and tenth-grade English and one class of geography—all for $4,280 per year. One-hundred-forty-plus kids, so I won't have time to write. They want me to live at the school. The worst part of the whole thing is that I think I just may take it. For a year, it might not be so bad—see what things are like down there as a teacher. I might really like it. I know I like the country anyway.

I talked with Archie Ammons about it for a long time. He's one of the few professors here I feel I can talk to. He knows I've got job offers from Cleveland, New York, etc.—but he says go to the mountains. My father doesn't want me to—it's less money, less security, less prestige, less chance for real success and advancement; but I'm still young. I can afford to take a flyer. I think I'll try it.

Book I

1

A Job in the Mountains

I went to Rabun Gap to teach because I wanted to live in Rabun Gap. That's all. No great sense of mission or purpose as far as a school and its students were concerned. No grand scheme playing like a symphony on a tape loop over and over in my mind. I wanted to live in that part of the country and teaching was a legitimate way to get there and support myself.

I had been there many times as a child and, later, as a college student. Our home was 83 miles south in Athens, Georgia, where my father was a professor of landscape architecture at the University of Georgia. We used to go there together frequently, and some of my earliest, best memories are centered on hunting for arrowheads in the cornfields beneath those mountains and hiking in those woods. That—and the people. People like Margaret and Richard Norton and Jack and Dean Beasley and Edith and Claude Darnell—most of whom you can meet in the pages of the *Foxfire* books—and Mrs. Jay Hambidge, who presided over a 710-acre place called The Jay Hambidge Art Foundation, a place where many of the people I've mentioned worked, and where (after I returned to Rabun County) I lived for a while until she died, and where *Foxfire* was partly born —but all that's another story—another book. If I get off onto all that, we'll never get out of here.

Shortly before graduation from Cornell, I wrote a letter to the superintendent of schools in Rabun County inquiring about the possibility of working for him as an English teacher. As there were no openings in the larger county high school, he referred me to the Rabun Gap–Nacoochee School (RGNS)—a semiprivate high school I had passed on the highway dozens of times but had never really noticed. There was an opening there, but when the principal, Morris Brown, asked me to come down for an interview, I was stuck. It's a long, long way from Cornell to Rabun Gap, and I just couldn't do it. As a compromise, I suggested he talk instead to some of the people I knew in the county. He agreed, and did that, and called back several days later with a statement that went something like: "Well, Margaret said it's okay, so I guess you can come."

In August of 1966, I drove to Rabun Gap.

2

"To Read Out Loud
Is Like Ordering
a Big Fat F"

The centerpiece of the school's campus was—and is—the classroom building, a long, two-story red-brick affair with columned central porches, white trim, a slate roof, and a bell tower. It had been placed on top of a hill that rose above the main highway, and clustered around it among dogwoods and oaks were other red-brick buildings: two dormitories, a dining hall, a gymnasium, a recreation center, a woodworking shop, dairy barns, and a faculty apartment building for those teachers who wanted to live on campus. Surrounding the buildings stretched hundreds of acres of rolling bottom land which in turn were surrounded by mountains. Looking for all the world like a small, immaculate, prosperous junior college, it was a stunning setup.

The school had been founded at the turn of the century by Andrew Ritchie, a Rabun County native who had pulled off the absolutely unheard of feat of attending—and graduating from—Harvard University. He returned to a county when those public schools that did exist, dotted around in tiny valley communities, were primarily one-room affairs that were only in session during the worst winter months because of the necessity of having everyone in a family turn to during the growing and harvesting season and concentrate on the business of survival.

Ritchie, in the tradition of all great educators, tailor-made his approach to the needs of the clientele. Because there were no paved roads or automobiles, making daily travel to and from a central school a near-impossibility, he built over thirty small but comfortable satellite homes on campus, each with its own barn and farm acreage. A family with children would move into one of those homes and live there for as long as its children were of school age leaving its own farm in the care of relatives or friends. When the last of the children graduated, the family would return to its own farm, thus vacating the home for another family. Rent and tuition were paid in the form of upkeep on the satellite farms and the requirement that parents and children help with the maintenance and smooth running of the school as a whole; there was ground to be plowed with teams of mules, crops to be planted and harvested and canned for the school's dining hall; dairy and beef cattle to be attended to; feed and fodder to be raised and gathered; hay to be baled and laid by; and sorghum molasses to be boiled down and bottled. The curriculum of the school was geared to the immediate needs, and to the longer-range physical, spiritual, and mental uplifting of the families involved. Much of what was learned in the classroom or on the job was immediately applied by the students on the school farm itself—and presumably at their own homes. The addition of dormitories made it possible to reach additional local students who would live on campus during the week and return home on weekends and holidays.

By the time I reached the school, it was still in the thick of a long-standing identity crisis of gigantic proportions. Many of the original needs the school had been founded to serve had evaporated like mist from the valleys. Highways and cars and industries and the government had arrived. A central public high school and three elementary schools had been built—complete with school buses and attendance laws and cafeterias with USDA soybean patties. The public Rabun County High School (RCHS) had burst its seams, however, so the school board leased the Rabun Gap facility for a dollar a year to educate those 140 or so local students in the northern end of the county who simply wouldn't fit into RCHS. Meanwhile, new dormitories had been built on the campus, and they now housed nearly a hundred out-of-town boarding students, many of whom came there from unfortunate family situations.

And so the school to which I arrived was really neither fish nor fowl. During the school day, it was regarded as a public school, and so it had a state-paid principal and teachers, with state and county supplements for the school lunch program and educational materials. After the school day, it reverted to a private facility with a president, a dean of students, houseparents, and all the other typical financial and recreational and moral burdens of such an institution. Dorm students all worked off a portion of their tuition expenses, the amount depending on their individual needs, at various jobs around the school campus. These included, in much diminished fashion from the early days, raising and cooking vegetables and livestock for the dining hall, attending to the dairy (which collapsed not long after I arrived under the accumulated weight of financial problems and government regulations), and general maintenance of the buildings, machinery, and grounds. The farm family program had earlier disintegrated as the needs of the area had shifted, and many of the houses were now occupied by faculty members with families, or farm and maintenance supervisors. With the uneasy alliance of both local and out-of-town students, most of whom came from totally different backgrounds (country versus city, by and large), it was a school in search of a successful unifying theme.

Having been a high school student at both a public (in Athens) and a private boarding school (the Hill School in Pottstown, Pa.), I was amazed that it held together at all. Just for starters, imagine creating a situation where a hundred adolescents are jerked out of a home situation that more often than not had been urban, fast-paced, and permissive, and plopped down in the middle of what to many of them seems a deathly quiet, maddeningly dull rural wasteland. Now complicate things further by making them adolescents who (not totally, but for the most part), because of various family situations, have not only not had a lot of pretty important attention but have also been allowed to have—or have demanded and taken—advantage of all that a permissive society has offered and so are perceived as being primarily in need of that discipline which parents have been unable to provide. To meet this need, you create a school filled with rules and regulations governing every aspect of the students' lives, from dress and hair length to the time they get up in the morning (7 A.M.) and the time they go to bed at night (10 P.M.), and, with the exception of an infrequent respite, you require that they remain on campus. Now make it co-ed. Add to this a religious emphasis that determines not only where you advertise for staff help (religious publications) but also dictates that you forbid certain kinds of behavior (smoking of cigarettes, dancing, holding hands). Now figure out how you're going to enforce it. And just to make things interesting, add 140 adolescents from the community and put them in daily classes with your captive population, and let them brag openly about their hangovers, the dates they had the night before and what they did on (or to) those dates, and what time they got to bed. Twist things a little further by making them country kids who deer hunt and squirrel hunt, dress funny, talk funnier, and don't cotton to what your residential group brags about in retaliation: pot and Day-Glo posters and Janis Joplin and what it used to do before it was put in prison in this hick town. Set the school campus astride a couple of public county roads so the local kids can ride through at midnight and toss a few beer cans around and cut a few "doughnuts" (put their '56 Chevys into circular skids that leave rings of black rubber on the pavement). And now, just for fun, set all this pot of stew abubble right in the middle of the historical and sociological and cultural context of the sixties. Now tell me what you've got.

The job that I was given was to teach English to all the ninth- and tenth-grade students in the school. I was also given one section of geography. That amounted to six classes a day—no free periods—for a state salary of less than $400 a month. The upstairs classroom to which I was assigned was a spacious, high-ceilinged one with pastel plaster walls, the obligatory chalkboard and bulletin board, and something over thirty sturdy desks that I was thankful were not bolted to the oak floors—floors that had been varnished and buffed so enthusiastically they looked as though they belonged in a gymnasium. One entire wall was windows that stretched from my waist to the ceiling, could be opened to let in fresh air, and afforded a pretty satisfactory view of most of the campus. In retrospect, it was one of the most pleasant classrooms I've ever had.

Conveniently located across the hall from my room was a bathroom and lounge, complete with daybed and easy chairs, which I assumed was for all teachers to use, and so I used it until that day a sign appeared on the door that read, THIS ROOM IS RESERVED FOR WOMEN TEACHERS. Males, it turned out, were relegated to a closet-size lavatory downstairs.

In addition to my teaching duties, I was asked to be an assistant houseparent at the boys' dorm. What that essentially meant was that I would live part-time at the dorm in an upstairs room. Whenever the houseparents were off duty, which was usually on weekends, I moved in that Friday following class and stayed until they returned on Sunday. If they left during the week, I stayed over on those days instead, and then I helped run recreation programs on the weekend. It amounted to no days off, and my salary was supplemented by the school, but since I had to pay rent for the room in the faculty apartments where I stayed for that part of the week when I was not in the dorm, and since I had to pay for any meals I ate in the dining hall (which was most of them, since neither of my rooms had a kitchen), there wasn't much left over. I wanted the job badly enough, though, that when Mr. Brown offered me the additional responsibility of driving one of the school buses on weekday mornings and afternoons, I would have taken it had I not been so fearful of the responsibility. There's nothing like coming off an icy mountain in the middle of January with a bus loaded with forty-six children to teach one indeed about religion. I declined.

Meanwhile, I began a steady stream of letters to one of my closest friends in college, Howard Senzel. Copies of most of those letters survived, somehow. In addition, I saved bits and pieces of in-school memos and directives. Some of these memos and excerpts from some of these letters follow in an attempt to give you a feel for the situation in which I found myself at the end of the summer of 1966:

September 16, 1966

Dear Senzel,

Your recent letter is demanding—perhaps too much so—but I will see what I can do to fill your requests. Detailed *and* sensitive [analysis of the situation]? Yeah.

At the moment, I am sitting at a desk in the boy's dorm. [The dorm] houses 50. The normal houseparents have fled the scene for the entire weekend, leaving me in charge of the roost. Quite frankly, I am going slowly mad. At the moment, while sitting at this desk, I am also being interrupted every thirty seconds by one of my charges. This is one of the reasons why your request for a sensitive analysis will be so incredibly difficult. I'll save that part for later, and now try to tackle the "detailed" part which I can conceivably handle in the midst of chaos.

First of all—the problem immediately at hand. In the last twenty-four hours I have put salve on two bee stings, Mercurochrome on five cuts, given pills out for eight colds; worked one set of algebra problems, drawn a paramecium, a euglena, and a diagram of the earth's two motions; rung the dorm bell twenty-two times for various reasons (bedtime, get up time, get laundry time, movie time, mealtime, etc.); broken up a fight, refereed a boxing match; reported one case of glue sniffing and one case of aspirins and Coke; and smashed a dedicated plot to wake up half of the boys in the dorm at one A.M. telling them it was 6:30 (get up time on Saturdays)—and so it goes. I have a ring with almost thirty keys on it, and I only know what six of them fit—the others are merely ballast to aid my wadings through a sea of sniffling young humanity—some members of which, by the way, look ten years older than me while being six younger.

Let me now jump to another front. I am trying to get down all the information that I can that doesn't require concentration. I have enclosed a Ditto which may interest you. It is the result of a sunny September 8 when I led my classes outdoors one at a time and made each of my 146 (the number is not a typographical error) pupils sit quietly and alone in front of a plot of ground for the entire class period. While sitting, they had to tell me what they saw, describing it [using colors, similes, etc.]. From many of the themes, I took one phrase which caught my fancy and put them all together on one sheet to make a composite description of the day, which I think is not bad. Reads almost like poetry at times.

Outdoor descriptions:
—a huge spider web that serves as some spider's estate
—brave little red ants coming to spy on the intruders
—a house with the floor dirt swept clean by the busy cricket family

—the smells of smoke from a trash dump

—a jar fly that sounds like a rattlesnake

—hot and sweet pepper field

—walnuts about ready to open

—spider web; a transparent power line stretching from Death Valley to Mt. Ranier

—a gnat crawling around on a leaf, swaying in the wind

—leaves turning brown and red in the autumn sun and breeze

—brown dead grass—fallen lumber

—dew—a diamond

—a spider's web with dew drops—when the sun shines on it it looks like all the colors of the rainbow woven together

—ants in a line—they look like a train

—a feather, deep blue with black tips

—caterpillars with black fuzzy antlers that make them look like they have ribbons tied on their heads

—a caterpillar that moves like a wave

—a wasp with all the long black wire extending from her stomach: she is drilling into the wood with all the strength she can muster

—a bright blue flower, bluer than the sky

—the bark of a twig—brown, green, dark and light gray, pink, black, white, and red

—dull green moss like seaweed—feels like steel wool

—a mushroom, like a rust-colored umbrella with its top turned wrong side out

—Queen Anne's Lace, like a snowflake magnified a million times—like skyrockets exploding

—sweet clover tastes like bitter lime, or lemon mixed with milk

—a spider—salt-and-pepper colored

—a bug's wing—like polished mahogany

—lichens—greenish, grayish, bluish

—a bee with a stinger like a straight pin

—a spider as red as the inside of a watermelon

—a bee, its tail moving up and down as it edges forward, the tip of its tail a tangerine color

—a mushroom, the inside like reddish-brown velvet or bat's hair, smells like pecans

—gnats like dive bombers circling a target

—a caterpillar that moved like an accordion

—a spider web in a dogwood tree—thin and wispy like the entrance to a wonderful fairyland: frail mosquito trapped in the beautiful but deadly web

—a spider with its nest built in a hickory nut shell sitting on some eggs.

—a white moth that laid two eggs on Doug's finger

—two squirrels fighting over a nut—they both lost it

—leaves of grass that move easily when the wind hits them

—mushroom with a stem that is cloud white and a top as red as raw hamburger
—cows grazing in green pastures
—boy and girl sitting under a tree, their laugh carried in the wind
—flower—a canopy—mint green leaves
—a red barn
—hickory nut—smells bitter—oval, green, smooth

In addition, here are some selected mistakes which I have painstakingly gleaned from the same assignment as I thought you might enjoy them. Most were on the outdoor description bit. (These are all direct quotations, untarnished by correction): a spator web/big green creaters/wasper—yellow stripes—it can sting / now I see 2 grandaddys. Whats this. Ah, those previlaged charters. They're making out / bird making a sound like a record that has hung up / put your arm in that thorn bush and it'll come out festerin' / pine combs / a white musaroom / mushrum / bee getting pollen from a flow / I moved a rock and saw a few crickets and a smell / mother nature's deadly weapon poisy ivy / cricket with horns on the rong end / a musring worm / bee getting the surpy out of flowers / mushroom—it can't be tasted unless you are sure its not poisonous / lathindar flowers / Skipper [a girl's name]—nice leges, soft, smoove / a hicker nut.

At this point in this letter I was interrupted by a kid, age sixteen, who said, with tears in his eyes, "Mr. Wigginton, I feel just awful." He then turned on his heel, ran to the bathroom, and lost about a gallon. Turned out he had gulped about twenty Excedrin tablets for a kick and had gotten just what he asked for—right in the gut. I called the dean of students (amid cries of anguish from his confederates who were sure they would get in plenty of trouble) and the hospital, and we took him in and got him pumped out and calmed down and brought him back. Then I had to sit up with him half the night and watch him puke the rest of his stomach lining out.

The time now is 8:40 P.M. on Sunday. I was just interrupted by the arrival of the houseparents returning from their weekend. I filled them in on all the news, including information about one sickness that I allowed to miss church this morning. This afternoon he went to the local burger emporium and I assumed him well. The head resident told me to go and check his room right now and see if he had skipped evening vespers which are going on now. I just did. He wasn't in his room. So I went into mine and there he was on my bed watching a television set which I recently acquired for the general entertainment of any and all. He hadn't told me he was going to skip or anything—his comment "Oh! I thought you knew." Sent him to his room and told him that if he came out I would behead him without blinking. Then went and told the houseparent, whose comment was, "Well, things seem to be running true to form. I forgot to warn you about that one."

Now I'm back. But so are the marching men from vespers. *Yee haa!!* This latter exclamation just added by one of the more forward of the marching men.

Another interruption—a shaving cream fight just broke out that completely coated one whole room in icy white frosting. The houseparent called me out of my room where I had retreated turning the whole dorm situation over to him in relief, and told me to call the dean and get him down here right away. The dean came (for the third time this weekend), witnessed the scene of the Waterloo, and fled in disgust and dismay. I assume he has had just about enough and will kick someone out—will keep you posted.

I'm about ready to say the hell with it. The letter, I mean.

Another interruption. Look. This is not going to work at all, and I want to get this in the mail to you tomorrow so that you do not think I have died. Everything I have said in this letter, and the order of events, is fact, and so you can see why it has taken me so long to get this thing off the ground.

I will fill you in on other details later. As a parting shot, and since you want to know about the school, and since the work of the kids themselves is more descriptive than I could ever be, I give you their reasons for disliking English [a composition I asked them to write when they told me in class they were going to hate this subject no matter who the teacher was].

"To read out loud is like ordering a big fat F."

"I don't like Englas becan the senter are tolong and they. Englan can be breant. Becase you repent over the same think over and over. And some day you have tomuch homework."

"I do not like English because it never has agreed with me."

"Because I don't have the brain for taking in English. Last year we had a rotten teacher which made hat ever worst."

"I hate English because the grammar part give me trouble. And makes it hard for me to learn."

"I hate English altogether, but I have no reason to feel that way about English Literature, In fact I love it!"

"I don't like English because most of the time it doesn't make any sence, and sometimes the teachers that teach doesn't express things the right way for you to learn."

"I hate to study Julius Caesar and Macbeth. Anything that's got anything to do with Shakespeer. Forget it!!!"

And from the geography notebooks:

"Geography is the land and study of the land and ever what helped to build the land."

"The two movements of the earth are 'rolation' and 'revelotin'."

And with that parting shot I temporarily say adieu.

All

bew

* * * * * *

ATTENTION: ALL STAFF, FACULTY AND FARM FAMILIES

Mr. Tatum killed a rabid fox on his porch Friday. Dr. Harris says there are many mad fox coming into this area from Tennessee. Dr. Harris himself was bitten by an infected animal and is now taking rabies shots.

If you have a dog that has not been inoculated you should have this done at once or get rid of it. This is a dangerous situation for a mad animal will attack children and other animals even cows and horses.

Jack M. Smoot, Business Manager

JMS/wb

* * * * * *

October 4, 1966

Howard,

As I correct my first set of student journals, I submit for your approval choice excerpts that may both tickle your fancy and further give you an idea of the flavor of life here—

"Today I am disappointed in almost everything. I shall try to correct this situation but I believe all my efforts to be feudal."

"85% of the grade school kids in Georgia have hook worm."

"A boy got stopped for cutting a doughnut. I think the sheriff let him go. He was drunk."

"After game went to dance. It wasn't worth nothing. After that we drug town. We left a few black mark before we went home. When I got in bed I thought I had had a good time."

"We killed a fair size rattler after the man that was with us nearly stepped on it."

"After lunch a group gathered and had a mouth running contest."

"I got a spotlight for my father to use when he went coon hunting."

"Blowed a wiskle on the bus."

"Our buss driver told Mr. Brown we were cutting up on the bus, but he just plain told a lie. He said we were hallowering at him and all that bunch of lies. We yelled at him one time because he didn't let some children off where they lived instead he took them all the way to the post office (about 1/2 mile) and made them walk home on the highway."

"_____told me again what I already knew, that Mom was pregnant but he also told me something I didn't know that the baby to come doesn't have the same father as I do. I still love my mom though."

"5:30 A.M. Toilet tissue zig zag all across both downstairs hall and top stairs hall. We're restricted to dorm till someone tells who did it."

"_____hit _____in boob everybody saw it."

"_____went home with a physical, mental, and emotional problem."

"_____had a miscarriage first or second week of school."

I am quickly finding that one of the hardest things about this job is being asked to enforce rules I can't agree with because of my own background, knowing that the students will always find ways around them anyway, and in the process will simply escalate the levels of paranoia and suspicion. They get caught and punished, and additional rules get created to cover the new varieties of infractions, and the whole thing goes on and on in a never-ending spiral that, in the end, just winds up hurting people who should never have been hurt, for what are usually all the wrong reasons.

Let me illustrate the point I was trying to make. One of the rules here is that no students will be seen anywhere on campus holding hands or coming in contact with each other at all physically unless they are of the same sex and carrying on a contact sport of some sort. The other day a boy was sent from the table (breakfast) for jokingly caressing some girl's hand that passed him the toast. His name appeared on the punishment list the next day as "holding hands at breakfast," and I thought I'd split. *Finally* the school let up a little and said that when students were on a Sunday hike under faculty supervision they could hold each other's hands, but only while staying in the group (escorted front and back by a teacher). So the dorm students spend half their time trying to figure out ingenious ways of getting together with each other. Last night, for example, four boys left the dormitory (they dropped out of the second-floor windows onto the ground) and skirted briefly around the girls' dorm during the study hall. Really crazy—had they been caught it would have been curtains. The other day four girls came up missing—they had pulled the same stunt but after lights—they were all caught and sent home the next day.

At the last faculty meeting, one of the older women took up forty-five minutes of our time by instigating a discussion of dubious merit on the fact that several students had been seen together in the corridors that run perpendicular to the one main hall. She initiated her discussion with the following gem: "Well you *know,* far too often I have seen students *courting* in the halls at the lockers before school. I've always made it a point to go past and *look* at them right *strongly* but I never knew whether I was *really* right or not. It just didn't seem right to *me* don't you know; I mean courting right in school like that out in plain view." She was roundly applauded for her Herculean efforts to save mankind from itself, and the upshot of the whole thing was that students were banned from the "cross halls," with the result that many cannot get to their lockers. Very wise. Naturally, with characteristic good taste, I managed to crack up at just the wrong time and earned a couple of well-placed "strong" looks from the women. My reputation stands on tottering foundations. You really have to watch yourself in such an atmosphere.

It really is not as bad as I've made it sound. I just got carried away by several things that have happened here in the last few days. The school has great ideals, but is so obsessed with the tiny everyday workings that it cannot get above itself and jump for higher ground. It drowns in the murky waters of trivia despite and because of itself.

And at the same time I say that, I have to add that I have really seen the need for some of these seemingly trivial regulations. For example, there is a rule here that says no water fights. Now, that seems pretty minor. Yet in this activity, as in so many others that they have rules about, there is always the potential for it turning into something bigger due to the inability of people to control themselves. One water fight this weekend started out harmless, and ended up by my running a kid to the hospital with a broken nose. He got smashed in the face by some kid who got mad.

It's going to take me a long time to sort all this out. Right now I'm just tired.

bew

* * * * * *

[Each week, from each dormitory, a misconduct report was issued which detailed student infractions and the resulting punishments. A "major" was a major offense which kept the student barred from certain activities during the following weekend. Three "minors" added up to one "major." Here's what such lists looked like. A dash has been substituted for each student's name, but the offenses and their punishments are as they appeared originally]:

BELLINGRATH [GIRLS] DORMITORY
(from the week ending_____)
Restrictions in effect from_____

NAME	OFFENSE	MAJOR	MINOR
_____	Left window open		1
_____	Leaving ladder in hall all day		1
_____	Going to rec after being too sick to work	1	
_____	Talking to waitress during breakfast		1
_____	Continually leaving for school with wet hair	1	
_____	Leaving curling iron on	1	
_____	Using fire escape illegally	1	
_____	Leaving soap and shampoo in living room chair		1
_____	Talking to people in stopped car	1	
_____	Yelling out window	1	
_____	Hitting another student at another table		1
_____	Throwing ice at dining table	1	
_____	Changing tables in dining hall without permission on Saturday	1	

NAME	OFFENSE	MAJOR	MINOR
_____	Failure to hand in report card	1	
_____	Untruthful	1	
_____	Patching jeans during study hall		1
_____	Throwing cup on floor		1
_____	Bathing suit left in bathroom 2 days		1
_____	Leaving dorm with wet hair		1
_____	Smart mouth	1	
_____	Climbing out window	1	
_____	Blouse outside of window		1
_____	Putting poster on wall with tape	1	
_____	In hall after being told to go to room		1
_____	Leaving dorm without permission	1	
_____	Skipped breakfast and hid	2	
_____	Carrying soft drink into living room		1
_____	Offensive teasing		2
_____	Horseplay	1	
_____	Indecent dress on campus	1	
_____	Toothbrush left out		1
_____	Didn't sign in		1
_____	Too amorous		1
_____	Reading magazine late at night	1	
_____	Pranks causing inconvenience at dorm	1	
_____	Horseplay		1
_____	Disrespectful remarks about staff members	1	
_____	Screaming in dorm		1

*   *   *   *   *   *

COIT [BOYS] DORMITORY MISCONDUCT REPORT
(from the week ending_____)
Penalties and Privileges of this effective_____

NAME	OFFENSE	MAJOR	MINOR
_____	Not ready for bed at 10:00		1
_____	Complete inattention during vespers		1
_____	Left shoes on bathroom floor (4 times)	1	2
_____	Late for study hall		1
_____	Reading magazine during sermon		1
_____	Smartmouthing housemother		1
_____	Running in dorm		1
_____	Arm on back of pew		1
_____	Grabbing food before grace said	1	
_____	Skipped breakfast	1	
_____	Turning off bell causing study hall to start late	1	
_____	Late for breakfast		1
_____	Not wearing socks to dining hall		1
_____	Playing after lights out		1
_____	Playing cards during study hall		1
_____	Nosey		1
_____	Playing with lights after lights out	1	
_____	Sneaking Coke from machine during study hall	1	
_____	Shoes on in dorm		1
_____	Out of room when study hall bell rang		1
_____	Making unnecessary noise before bell rang		2
_____	Poor table manners		1
_____	Bad table manners		1
_____	Throwing water on others	1	
_____	Giving waitress a hard time		1
_____	Disturbing others doing a war dance at 11:45	1	

NAME	OFFENSE	MAJOR	MINOR
_____	Slapping another with wet rag		1
_____	Wet shirt left on lawn		1
_____	Left books in lobby		1
_____	Carving on furniture	1	
_____	Socks left on floor		1
_____	Disrespect to an adult on Highway 441	2	
_____	No attempt to clean room	1	
_____	Not ready for bed		2
_____	Not ready for study hall and not trying to get ready	1	
_____	Late leaving for school		2
_____	Repeatedly late leaving for school	1	
_____	Untidy room 3 days	1	
_____	Locking self in room repeatedly	1	
_____	No attempt to clean room	1	
_____	Messy room		2
_____	Extremely dirty room repeatedly	2	
_____	Extremely untidy room		2
_____	Spitting on carpet in lobby	1	
_____	Throwing Frisbee in room with lights out		1
_____	Bed linens hidden and not on bed		2
_____	Ungentlemanly conduct and language at supper	1	
_____	Taking Lord's name in vain	1	
_____	Behind bed during study hall		1
_____	Shirttail out		1
_____	Messy room	1	
_____	Loud, foul-mouth talk, and continually using Lord's name in vain	2	
_____	Too amorous		2

_____	Shoes on in dorm	1
_____	Wearing skates in dorm	1
_____	Cutting across grass	1
_____	Improper use of TV room chairs	1
_____	Wasting time in study hall and study hall disturbance	5
_____	Foul mouth (twice)	2
_____	Late for breakfast	1
_____	Late for school	1
_____	Late for study hall	1
_____	Late for breakfast	1
_____	Stringing beads during study hall	1

* * * * * *

October 29, 1966

Dear Howard,

I am continuing to have a struggle with my classes. The dorm students aren't too bad, in general. Their backgrounds don't seem to have severely blunted their abilities to study or become interested—even excited—about what they're doing in school. Some fail, but I have found many to be good students worthy of a good English class. Perhaps part of the reason is some prior good schooling somewhere along the line.

The community students seem to be another story. About a third of them are like the above, but the majority are ill-prepared and restless. School is a place where they can show off their cars, their cigarette packs, make social contacts, and a place they are required to attend by law and against their own wills. Attendance is tenuous—anything makes a good excuse for skipping—and this includes picking peppers, a broken car, a driver's test, or a hangover.

When in school, they seem only to know how to sneer. There is nothing you can threaten them with (and I mean almost nothing short of death) that can make them do anything they do not feel like doing—homework, keeping quiet in class, etc. The universal comment is, "I don't care" and they really _don't_ seem to. I have kicked them out of class and had them come back the next day even _worse._ I keep telling myself that they really _do_ care but they are just putting up a false front—bravura—and they've been so used to being knocked down that with a little encouragement they'll come along fine. That's the accepted panacea. It may be true, too, but I don't see it yet. Whatever the cause, they really do seem to be genuine in their not caring. If I could just convice them that it _isn't_ "cool" to shoot craps in the classroom, or throw all my chalk away so I can't use the board or any of a thousand other things that irritate a teacher to the point of no return. The problem is it *is* "cool"—at least here.

One class in particular grates. It has about four "A" dorm students, and twenty-four rearing community ones who can't pass a thing they are taking. They enter my class, turn off their ears, turn on their mouths, and settle down for a period of socializing. Every time I think I've gotten through to some of them, one of two things happens—either someone belches and breaks the spell, or the period ends and they are out in the free world again where the last fifty minutes evaporate like mist from dry ice. They really do *not* see why they should have English, and in a sudden revelation several days ago I suddenly realized that I couldn't see why they should have it either. Lots of them will never leave this area of the country except perhaps to go to war— they will never read or write—they will help with a gas station and love it— that's all they need. All the disciplines and beauties of English are as foreign to them as an opera, and that's the way they want it. *Any* person with a mouth could leave them with as much as I have left them with so far—and so why am I here? I keep trying to think of something that will wake them up that they may also find useful someday, and I can't. A very curious situation indeed.

A funny feeling takes over a place like this. I knock myself out doing creative lessons, running off hundreds of Dittos, etc., etc. At the end of the month I take up notebooks and find nothing in them but notes from friends. At the end of each class I find the carefully prepared Dittos stuffed into desks in wads to be discarded. I find theme papers I have carefully corrected wadded around used chewing gum, I find myself totally exhausted at the end of the day—emotionally, creatively, physically, spiritually and every other way wondering how I made it through another day, and then another week, and then another marking period, and still I go on. But always, in the back of my mind, is the unreality of the demand that I make it through a whole *year.*

Students are really funny. They aggravate the hell out of you in class, or do something behind your back that they know you don't want them to, and then come up to you two minutes later and expect you to laugh with them, joke with them, and do them favors. Amazing.

A final note. As I've said before, religion plays a major part in the life of the school—especially for the dorm students.

Fact: They have vespers every morning before class. They have an optional faculty and staff prayer meeting every Monday night. They have three religious services that are required attendance every Sunday. They have vespers every Wednesday night in the dormitories. They invite speakers from AA and from homes of dope addiction; they show films of the horrors of lung cancer. Last week three students were kicked out of school. They had made a zip gun in the school shop. How did they get the directions? From a speaker at a religious revival meeting who, before he turned to Christ, had been a member of a gang in New York City. And so it goes. . . .

Eliot

* * * * * *

RABUN GAP–NACOOCHEE SCHOOL
RABUN GAP, GEORGIA
November 14, 1966

TO THE FACULTY AND STAFF:

(1) More than 30 of the boarding students and some day students have accepted Christ during the Christian Emphasis Week. They need our prayerful support so that they might stand in their new found faith. They need our example so that they might grow to more effective Christian living.

(2) We are having fine prayer times at the weekly faculty-staff prayer meetings each Monday night, beginning at 7:00 P.M., in the Home Economics Kitchen. We are seldom there more than half an hour. If you have not been coming, we urge you to join with us. God's work moves forward most effectively when it is undergirded with prayer.

(3) The Rabun Gap–Nacoochee Club of Atlanta is putting on a sale of electrical appliances and items of all kinds at a price which is only slightly above what the wholesaler actually paid for the merchandise. The profits from this sale will go to the Rabun Gap–Nacoochee Club to be added to the Addie Corn Ritchie Scholarship Fund.

I am going to attend this sale on Wednesday, November 16, in Atlanta and will be glad to purchase items for you if you will tell Mrs. Anderson what kind of things you would like to have purchased. There will be a line of Sessions clocks, G.E. electrical appliances of many kinds including radios, televisions, etc., Norelco radios, shavers, tape recorders, items from the Sunbeam Company, and many others. If you are interested in my making a purchase or purchases for you, please let my wife know by Tuesday night for I will be calling her to get whatever orders you may have placed with her. I will pay for the items and collect from you when I return.

As we approach the Thanksgiving season, I thank God for the excellent staff and faculty that have assembled at Rabun Gap–Nacoochee School and thank Him for the challenge which He gives to each of us to be His servant in this great work.

Very sincerely yours,

Karl Anderson
President
KKA:hk

* * * * * *

TO: Parents and guardians of Boarding Students

FROM: President, Rabun Gap–Nacoochee School

During the fall we have spent many hours counseling young people who are found to be smoking. We have used a variety of ways to deter such activity. We have used suspensions, have had boys dig a grave to bury their cigarettes, room restrictions. We have called parents to the school for conferences, etc.

We believe that smoking is definitely harmful to the health of young people. Medical evidence indicates that the earlier a person begins smoking, the more they tend to smoke per day, and generally the more certain they are to run into physical problems in the future. We abhor smoking. We will not allow students to smoke. If they are found to be smoking, we will take direct action. You know that the worst thing for a young person is to see that there is a rule, but that it is not enforced.

Beginning as of Friday night, November 20, we are following this policy:

    a. The first time a boarding student is found smoking, an on-campus punishment will be meted out. For boys it will mean that they will have to dig a grave, five feet deep, four feet across, and six feet long. He will be on dorm restriction until the hole is dug and filled back. For the girls it will mean a room restriction in the dormitory. This means that the girl attends classes, takes care of her work responsibilities, attends meals and of course worship activities, but at all other times she is to be in her room. She is not to visit others and she is not to be visited. We have a room, comfortable, but spartan, without radio or record player to which the girl will move during the ten-day period.

    b. The second time the student is found smoking, he or she will be dismissed.

We do not expect to find the youngster with a cigarette in hand. Other evidence that the student has been smoking or possesses cigarettes is, we believe, sufficient. We have talked and talked. We feel we must take more definite action now.

Many students will be going home for Thanksgiving. We have endeavored to set high ideals at the school. We prohibit smoking or drinking. We do not believe it is helpful for a young person to be permitted to smoke while at home, and then have to kick the habit all over again when they come back.

We have not had much problem with drugs. One girl had used some drugs while away from school. She is receiving help for her problem at an institution which is designed to help cases such as that. We are not equipped to help those fooling around with drugs.

We will try to answer any of your questions at any time. We count on you to give us all the backing you can to help lift each of the young people here spiritually, physically, and mentally.

Yours truly,

Karl Anderson
President

               * * * * * *

December 3, 1966

Dear Howard,

    Last week a dorm student was kicked out for smoking. He had been caught and, according to the new policy in effect here, required to dig a grave to bury his cigarettes in. He had just finished digging his grave and smoothing up the sides so it would pass inspection, at which point he would fill it in. The boy was sitting on the edge, his feet dangling into the hole, looking at the finished job, when he was surprised by the dean and sent to the dorm to pack. The problem? While surveying his handiwork, he was smoking a cigarette.

Sunday I took a crew of boys out to Mrs. Hambidge's and we made her grounds look like the Ambassador's Palace. She was overjoyed. I plan to do it again this Sunday if I get the chance. The boys love it as they are away from school and doing something that is truly constructive and truly appreciated. They are fascinated by her charm—just as you and I have been before. It's an experience I am glad to give them.

Meanwhile, I think I have isolated one of my biggest problems in teaching. Students are totally unable to separate a classroom situation from a situation involving the same person outside of class. Tyrant in class, tyrant out of class. And vice versa. If the teacher is a friendly, happy-go-lucky person who kids around outside of class, it stands to reason that he will be the same in class. The latter destroys control faster than any single other thing. You correct them, and they say, "Aw, that's just old Joe. He's not mad. He's just kidding. Don't worry about it. He won't do anything. He's our buddy." Doubtless you can see where I am involved in this thing. They even carry it so far as to refuse to believe that you will flunk them if they do no work. Thirty-six people found out to the contrary this marking period just ended.

Yesterday some of the community students that I have had the most trouble with as far as scholarship goes, grabbed me and challenged me to an arm-wrestling match. I agreed, and after the first one beat me they scrambled like girls over the Beatles to get their chance at me. When their teacher came in and broke it up, I heard one of them exclaim as I left, "He's such a *great* guy!" I got invitations to weekend fox and deer hunts, and rides in their cars—the two greatest gifts they can bestow as these are their two passions. I was flattered and proud, until I discovered that in my class they had become uncontrollable. The sweat I had getting them back into order was one of the labors of Hercules. All is well now, but I immediately saw the problem one can get himself into with relative ease. As a peace offering Friday, one of the students brought in the tail of a fox he had just killed. I was glad to have it, but the next day I had to kick him out of class. Very strange problem that I have not yet learned how to cope with. Same for the dorm—I really love to get out and play football, Frisbee, take them to movies, etc., but the following day in class can be torture. By the end of the year it will be okay, I am sure. But it certainly is a problem now. The dorm boys have adopted me as their big brother, and I hope it doesn't have to turn into "Big Brother is watching you."

As far as school goes, I am still in search of the golden city—the subject area that will fascinate and involve them all. I have come close, thankfully, several times. One is an idea we're playing with for putting out a magazine which they are fervent in their approval of. Another was the teaching of poetry from Simon and Garfunkel; Cher; Peter, Paul, and Mary; and the

Lovin' Spoonful. I had all the lyrics Dittoed off (also *West Side Story*, which I taught not only from the record, but also from *Mad* magazine where it appeared as the satirical "East Side Story")—and left off the end words from many of the verses and had them supply them while listening to the songs so they could see the rhymes develop, etc. All went over fantastically well. I was even able to give them a healthy dose of Frost supplemented by a movie. The last thing that got them going was a three-day devotional—a tribute to Twain. I had two albums of the Broadway show done by Hal Holbrook and played them both. They took notes like fiends, and were rewarded not only with a superb knowledge of Twain (to set them up for reading *Huck Finn*), but also choice quotations like the following, which help take the edge off the situation here:

"There's a familiar old maxim that assures us that man is the noblest work of God. Well now, who found that out?"

"I make it a point never to smoke more than one cigar at a time. I have no other restrictions."

"I've never taken any exercise except sleeping and resting. I don't ever intend to take any. I don't see any benefit in being tired."

"My dear wife, God rest her soul, tried diligently for years to get me to give up profanity. And I tried, but I never could get over the notion that in certain desperate and trying circumstances, profanity furnished a relief. If I cannot swear in heaven, I shall not stay there. 'Course they probably won't let me in anyway. Well, maybe it won't be so bad down there. When I think of all the disagreeable people I know who have gone to a better world. . . ."

On your letter: Right. We have been given too many options; too many paths to choose from and as a result we find it hard to choose at all. "Two roads diverged in a yellow wood, and sorry I could not travel both and be one traveller. . . ." I'm not so sure that I don't like this though. It makes things very hard, but at least I *can* stop doing one thing and move on to another— that is a thing I am counting on. The hope of moving to other things besides teaching keeps me alive.

bew

3

So What *Did* I Learn in School, Anyway?

I had never been in a situation before where I was so completely confused by all that was going on around me. I wasn't panicked. Just confounded by the fact that the conventional logic I had learned to apply to times of crisis in college seemed to have no place here. It was a through-the-looking-glass world where the friendlier I was in class and in the dorm, believing that would generate cooperation, the more liberties the students took and the harder it became to accomplish anything. Both the classes and the dorm would spin crazily out of control—beyond my reach. And so I'd crack down, kicking students out of class for several days at a time, or using my grade book and my power to fail them as a retaliatory weapon ("one more word out of you and I'll give you a zero for the day"), and the mood would turn sullen and resentful and no sharing and learning would take place. They would be captives, praying for the bell to ring. And in the dorm, whenever I lashed out and punished them by restricting them from all recreational activities or confining them to their rooms, their predominantly lighthearted misbehavior took an ugly twist and became calculated and mean. It was impossible. I began to regard them collectively as the enemy—and I became the prisoner—not they. Worse, to accomplish anything of substance academically in such an atmosphere was to dream of Camelot. The thought that I would continue to work seven days a week, supposedly for *their* benefit, and at the salary I was getting, suddenly became an absurd proposition. Hell, at one point I had made double the money I was making now working part-time as a waiter in a restaurant to pay my tuition at Cornell. Nothing made sense anymore.

On one of the bleakest fall days of 1966, I walked into my first-period class, sat down on top of my desk and crossed my legs, and said, very slowly and very quietly, "Look, this isn't working. You know it isn't and I know it isn't. Now what are we going to do together to make it through the rest of this year?"

The class was silent. For long minutes we simply stared at each other. And then slowly, quietly, the talk came. Nothing of real consequence got resolved that day in terms of specific classroom activities that they might enjoy more than what I had imposed on them (I realized later how helpless many of them are to come up with brilliant suggestions when, because of the way they've been taught for so many years, they can't even imagine what the options could be; and how wrong teachers are who say, "Well, I asked them for their ideas and they couldn't come up with any good ones so we just went on with the text."). But at least we began the dialogue, and we began to look at each other in a different light.

The process of examining ourselves, English and what it's for, school and what it's for, and sampling new activities went on all year. In fact, ten years later at Rabun Gap, I and new students were still at it—still tearing things apart and putting them together in different ways. Still experimenting. Still talking. Still testing. And I still do it with my students today at Rabun County's new consolidated public high school, where I now teach. And, being a slow learner, I still haven't got it right. But I'm getting there.

Meanwhile, for purposes of this book and in the interest of coherence, I'll have to compress several months of this introspection and dialogue into a few pages. Understand that there was no Road to Damascus flash of enlightenment, so if you try the same thing with your classes, don't get discouraged if it takes years. Believe, though, that it will be worth it.

The first thing I tried was a composition assignment in which I asked them to describe, as honestly as possible, things that had happened to them in their school careers thus far that had been positive and/or negative—experiences that stood out in their minds. I asked them to talk about teachers they had had (without mentioning names). Which of them had done fine jobs, which had failed, and why. The compositions I got were a disappointment. Part of the problem may have been that we didn't trust each other yet. And I couldn't say honestly, "Don't put your names on them and write them anonymously," because they knew I could recognize their handwriting. That would have been seen as just another teacher trick.

I got much better results when I went to the English teacher who had the juniors and seniors and explained to her what I was doing. She let me come into each of her classes at the beginning of the period and enlist their help. To ensure anonymity, the students wrote the compositions during the class period as soon as I had left, and then one of the students was assigned to gather the papers and bring them straight to me. Their teacher agreed to stay out of the way. The results were pretty revealing.

Trying again to get a discussion going in my classes, I selected passages from the junior and senior papers, typed them onto six pages of Dittos, and ran them off for use in my room. My students read them, and they were off and running. Here are a few samples from those Dittos:

•If a teacher can just keep the kids interested in what they are doing, then I believe he has them. As long as a kid is interested in something, he will study to learn. But if he's not interested, then that's it. I know. I'm a student.

•What gripes me most is teachers picking out one or two students to have as "pets." It is not only unfair to the other students, and really childish for adults to do; but it really doesn't help the child you are being nice to. Did you ever stop to think what it does to a kid to get too much attention? Well, I'll tell you. They at first are envied by their friends. But pretty soon the awe wears thin and resentment sets in. The poor kid that was at first popular and friendly soon loses friends.

•Not many good things have happened to me in school. One good thing is when I get classes with a girl that goes here now. I wanted so much to go with her, but for two and a half years she has put me off.

•I have quite a few pet peeves about teachers, but there are also many things I like. It wasn't until this year that I discovered that teachers *are* human, and they themselves are just a bunch of grown-up students.

•My teachers never found time to help me as soon as I started failing. If they had, I probably would be a senior instead of a junior. If someone is doing well, he gets all the attention and usually is the teacher's pet. He gets the grade and you don't, and you get hurt.

I think teachers should spend time with each and every student in or out of class. What if they had? What if they had?

•Seventh grade: If you fell asleep in physical science, which was a typical, droning after-lunch class, the teacher made you touch some kind of big metal ball that shocked you. In gym, we had to run around to the showers in the nude, and the gym teacher checked to see if we'd taken showers. She enjoyed it.

All through my years of education, there've been classrooms with perfect order, antiseptic smell, droning teachers and frustrated kids. School has sometimes been fun, but it wasn't the teachers that made it that way.

•One thing that really used to gripe me about some teachers was that when they didn't feel like teaching, they'd give us what seemed like five million words to look up so they could kill time.

•In my school day, I find that I am happy as long as the teacher is happy. If the teacher is in a bad mood, then I get in a bad mood. Then I can't wait for the class to end. I have found that when I get anxious for the class to end, my work in that particular class is poor.

Teachers that take time to realize that a student is an individual and *not* just one out of a group are the best teachers. I had one particular teacher I will never forget. Once when I received one of my essays back, I found that she had complimented my essay, the topic, and me. She paid special attention to all of her students.

•I wish someone would help me to grow up and open my mind. If not, then I lose out my whole life. I guess I don't know how to think, or I just don't use what I've got. I want to change, but I need help.

•I remember in the first grade how much I had to stand in the corner, and how I hated that. I always had to stand and watch the kids play. I never got to go out and play too. I was miserable. By the time I was in the second grade, I didn't want to go out and play with the other kids. I stayed in and worked on my writing. I was the best writer, but up until the third grade I only had two friends.

•We have had teachers who praised the whole class when we deserved it. We need praise. It helps to keep us from getting discouraged at times. I had a teacher one time who took her free period off to talk to me because I was having trouble concentrating in class. Teachers need to be friends as well as teachers.

•Last year, every time we had a test the teacher would always stand in one certain place right behind me. He would make me so nervous I could hardly take the test. I felt he was always watching what I put down for the answers.

Another teacher would always get mad if we didn't agree with her on something. Last year there was a special on TV this teacher was pushing us hard to watch. Not many of the kids did, and this kind of made her mad. I had watched it, and I didn't like it at all. She was asking for opinions and she asked me, and I told her I didn't like it, and I told her why. She got real mad and launched into this big deal about how the kids today didn't have any knowledge of good movies. This kind of burned me up. I mean, she asked for my opinion and I gave it to her and she didn't like it.

But one teacher in the seventh grade stands out. She would always get all the sides to every story, and she would not let any of the other teachers say anything against the kids in her class. She would always take up for us. I never heard her say anything to a student in bad taste. So all the kids did their best to make hers a good class.

•Most of you are alike. A teacher doesn't need to put on an iron mask each morning before coming to school. I know your job is to teach us, and I also know that a lot of kids are almost impossible to get through to. It does take a strict and powerful approach—but pounding our heads is not how to get through. To me a teacher who is understanding and can see my problems and wants to help is the kind of person who does help. The other kind of teacher— the one who will teach by not getting involved but by standing in the front of the room (apart from students and student problems) repeating over and over again his facts is nothing. In too many classes the world is only what's there in the classroom. There is no such thing as war, love, religion, or individualism. The teacher is master. The students do what the teacher says.

•In eighth grade I had a math teacher who would call on you to go to the board to do a problem. You could tell him twenty times that you didn't know how, but he'd make you stay there until you "remembered" how. It is teachers like him who are disliked so much because they make fools out of you in front of the whole class.

•In one English class, our teacher would get into a different subject as we were discussing a book. For example, if we mentioned a place where she had been, she would tell the class what she did in that place, and the subject would be about her. All we learned in her class was about her.

•I had one teacher who was always willing to stay after class and talk to you. He would always help straighten things out. If I did something wrong, he'd tell me. I really appreciated the fact that he cared that much.

•Kids are so cramped nowadays. It's like a toy the parents wind up. Get up in the morning, dress, go to school, sit in nice rows and never express any dislike. We are not toys made for parents and teachers. We are to be the leaders of tomorrow, but in many cases we never learn about the world until we are forced to live in it.

•Teachers that treat a senior class as maturing young adults may expect to have mature attitudes and ideas returned to them in class. Those who treat seniors as fourth-graders may be expected to have the progress in education that normal fourth-graders achieve.

•Often when students' work was put up for display, only the best was shown. In my opinion this is wrong because the student who didn't do so well always gets left out—and sometimes has the feeling that he can't succeed at anything.

•"We can't go back over it again. We have to read so many pages by the end of the year and we have to *move on!*" I had a school teacher who repeated that daily.

•I really love teachers who will roll up their sleeves and pitch right in with the kids.

•When I was in the tenth grade, I had an English teacher that always said she didn't need a lot of teenage friends.

•If you come in with the attitude: "Ugh—I've got to teach this stupid class," don't think we students don't know it. We do. And when we say "Hello," don't look like a business man on special assignment rushing to the next appointment. How about giving us a friendly "Hi" back? It can really make or break a day for us.

Some of the negative comments could easily have been written about me, but that was impossible as none of the students who wrote them had ever had me as a teacher. My own ninth- and tenth-graders were warming to the task, though, and they confirmed much of what the older ones had said.

Chagrined, I began to look back over my own elementary and secondary school experiences. Like my peers—and probably like you—I had had my share of embarrassment and frustration. Having to repeat the ninth grade factored heavily.

But what things of an academic or a classroom nature had been positive? Leaving aside friendships with peers, dates, school holidays, football games, Halloween carnivals, and the like, what experiences had been memorable? Which had I carried with me into adulthood like talismans? What events had given me self-confidence? At what times had I been made to feel by a teacher that I had real abilities and might even someday make a contribution to society of some worth or substance? In what ways had my schooling eased my way into responsible adulthood? In what courses I had taken had the content remained with me, either as an adult passion or as an ongoing way of dealing with and understanding a world that now, in the mid-sixties, was a bizarre place indeed?

It would be an understatement to say that I was absolutely amazed at how difficult it was to answer those questions. Thirteen *years* of my life, and what did I have to show for it? Granted, I could read and write and do enough math to balance my checkbook. I had managed to get into—and finish—college, so someone out there must have done something right. But who? How? And why was I having such a hard time remembering teachers' names? Or positive moments—moments when suddenly I had understood things in a new way? Moments when I was awed and speechless? Moments when I was touched, or moved?

I began to make a list of memorable, positive experiences. (If you haven't tried this, by the way, I recommend it to you as a sobering—and enlightening—exercise.) I found that then experiences could be grouped fairly easily (with allowances for some inevitable overlap) into broad categories:

Times when there were visitors to our class from the world outside the classroom. Although it happened in elementary school, I have carried with me to this day, intact, the morning of the day when our Chase Street School class-room was visited by E. B. Mell, a retired, white-haired high school principal. He brought part of his collection of Indian artifacts with him, and as he spread it out before us and talked about what each piece had been used for and how it had been made, there was an electricity in the room that I hadn't remembered feeling before. He talked about how tragic it was that these bits of pottery and soapstone and flint were all we had left, by and large, to tell us how the people who made them had lived, and how vital the sleuthing work done by professionals called archaeologists was to the historical record, and how important it was for us to treat such items as we might find in surrounding cornfields with respect and not simply toss them aside into a drawer filled with socks and underwear. (I began to collect arrowheads after that day, and in college I actively considered archaeology as a career, taking several courses.)

Another of our elementary school teachers encouraged us to invite our parents to come to school and talk to our class about their work. Several parents did; my father was one of them. A landscape architect, he showed slides that illustrated what the people in his profession did. I'm not sure that I had even known before that day, but afterward I looked upon both my father and that particular career in a different way.

Whenever such events happened, the real world was allowed to invade our four-walled cell and bring an extra dimension of reality to what was happening inside that room. How many times had I made the same thing happen in my classroom now that I was a teacher? None. I just hadn't thought of it.

Times when, as students, we left the classroom on assignments or field trips. I still remember with perfect clarity our elementary school class leaving the building, paired up, in line with a teacher in front and an aide behind, and striding down Prince Avenue to the local fire station, where we were allowed to touch the engine and the hoses, and where the firemen turned out to give us a tour of the entire building. At the end, assembled in front of the call system, the chief talked to us about the necessity impressed on all his men for speed. He pulled an alarm, and from the bedrooms about a dozen men came sliding down the brass pole to jump into position. Then he reminded us soberly of the dangers—and the frustrations—inherent for them in screaming through busy intersections to answer false alarms. (I'd be willing to bet my pension on the fact that none of us was ever the cause of those men turning out unnecessarily.)

Of the few compositions I *remember* writing, the vast majority were written outdoors. Most were called "free themes," for which we were told to sit alone and write about whatever came to mind. They were always the hardest to do, as we groped helplessly through our adolescent thoughts for something worth writing about.

And I've never forgotten the time when, at the Hill School, the private boarding school I attended for four years, a group of us was taken to Philadelphia to hear Eugene Ormandy and the Philadelphia Orchestra. For the first time in my life, a symphony became something more than the theme music from a motion picture.

And now that I was a teacher, how many times had I gotten my classes out of that room into the surrounding world? Once, to write a composition. At the end of that day I was asked not to do it again. Students in some of the other classes had watched us going past their windows, had begged their teachers to let them go out too, and the resulting teachers' complaints had caused a problem for our long-suffering principal (who later let me do it again anyway).

Times when things we did, as students, had an audience beyond the teacher. In elementary school our class choir was told by the principal that if we worked up a program of Christmas music, the local radio station had agreed to come to the school and tape it for later broadcast. We worked like demons. The day before the taping, the principal appeared in the doorway of our classroom and called on six or eight of us in turn to tell her what carols we had chosen to perform. That done, she huddled with our teacher, then called me into the hall to ask me to announce each number for the radio audience. The next day the radio technician arrived, I announced each song we performed ("The next number will be 'Silent Night' "), and I don't think I had ever tried harder in my young life to get anything right. Several days later, my father and I were sitting on the living room floor together wrapping Christmas presents for our relatives and listening to the radio when that concert aired. My voice sounded unnatural, but it was there, and I was filled with a strange glow.

When I was a mediocre eleventh-grade student in the private school I mentioned, Jack Tyrer, an English teacher whom I've never forgotten, was enthusiastic about a composition I had written for his class. He helped me polish it for submission to our school's literary magazine, and it was accepted and published. I think I watched every day for that magazine to appear, and when it finally did, I can still remember taking a copy to my room and sitting there alone, holding it, for what must have been an hour. And when I sent copies to members of my family and gave copies to my friends, I waited as anxiously for their responses as I had waited for the magazine.

That single event—more than any other—changed my school career and had an indelible imprint on my life. I hated school. My grades had been so terrible that year that the scholarship I had had was taken away, plunging my father into gloom. As he wrote shortly before then, in a letter I have kept:

". . . I want you to read this in the quiet of your room in a time of leisure, because it is high time for you to begin to think out a few important decisions for yourself . . . I have received a letter from Mr. Richard of the Scholarship Committee urging me to discuss your grades with you because they cannot usually give financial assistance to students in the lower half of the class—and you have dropped well down this year. At one time you were hoping for a larger scholarship, but I am sure you realize that these things depend upon achievement and that it now seems quite likely that you will lose what you have . . . You tell me that you spend the maximum amount of time on work, work, work. I incline, of course, to believe you . . . Still, if you are working at the peak of your ability, then I think we must consider a second very important matter, your future career, in perhaps a somewhat different light than we have heretofore. No decisions to be made on this yet, but we may have to limit our plans somewhat in recognition of what I am beginning to accept as a fact proven by your three years' record at the Hill. This is that you have only average or a little below average ability as compared with a selected group of students, even when you work as hard as you possibly can, and there is no field of study which you have undertaken thus far in which you are Number 1 man. This may be hard for you to accept. It is for me, but I see no other answer and there is nothing gained in living in a world of make believe . . . I doubt if your record would get you into any good college where you had no connections and you certainly could not get a scholarship of any kind."

And then I was published. I wasn't an idiot after all. I was an author. Wanting to be published again, I labored over compositions that until that time had simply been hollow exercises without meaning or reason. Some of them were printed. Grammar suddenly had utility, and it began to make sense. The labor of other authors and poets and journalists came to life and took on new meaning. I studied their styles. My grades underwent a slow but steady change as I saw myself as someone with potential. Near the end of the year, the headmaster saw me walking across the quadrangle, came over, and said, "I wanted you to know that I just finished calling your father to tell him that your scholarship has been reinstated intact. You've earned it."

In what ways, as a new teacher, had I created opportunities for my students to have that affirmation that could bring to them a new and serious sense that the work we were doing together could have utility and function and worth and purpose and the potential for reward far beyond an entry in my grade book?

None.

Times where we, as students, were given responsibility of an adult nature, and were trusted to fulfill it.

In every grade, teachers had given certain students a taste of what it felt like to be trusted. Every elementary school class I was ever in had fire marshals, students who took attendance reports to the principal's office, students who were allowed to raise and lower blinds, students who recorded grades in the teacher's grade book (we always hated those kids, because they knew what everyone made), and students who erased the boards.

In the seventh grade, however, this sort of activity took on a new dimension for me when I was made a member of the school safety patrol. My station was the most active intersection in school range—the corner of Chase and Prince. Since there was a stoplight there and a female traffic officer, the amount of responsibility I actually had, looking back, was somewhat diminished. But I thought it was the most important thing I had ever done, and I entered into the obligation with a seriousness of purpose that wasn't matched until the eleventh grade, when, because of the success I had had with writing, I was made an editor of the school literary magazine. At the same time, I tried out for our school newspaper —a no-nonsense, professional affair published on a weekly basis, the editorship of which earned genuine (and genuinely deserved) prestige. In fact, I have rarely seen a better high school paper. I was never the editor-in-chief, but I did work my way up through the ranks to become news editor, and I'm *still* proud of that. More to the point, however, is the fact that the faculty adviser—in what I like to believe now was by enlightened design—basically kept his hands off. The articles that were written were proofread a final time and, if necessary, censored by him before being sent to the typesetter in town, but beyond that, it was our product, completely. Headlines (painstakingly written and rewritten to fit the space allotted). Photos. Captions. Articles. Editorials. Makeup and design. Everything, weekly. No nonsense. No bailing out. And as a sign that the administration regarded the project as important and trusted us, we were allowed to stay up without supervision after lights out whenever we needed to, unlike the members of many other campus groups. We were on the line in front of an audience in much the same sense that members of the high school football or basketball or soccer team are during a game. The coach can shout all he wants from the sidelines, but he can't touch the ball. Is it any wonder, then, that many high school ball players regard sports and their team with more seriousness—and give them more energy and dedication—than their academic work?

How many times had I created opportunities for my students, in a classroom context, to feel the thrill of assuming responsibility and trust (putting academic skills they were to master in my class to work with competence) in the same way they would be asked to perform as adults? To have the chance to practice, as it were, in a situation where mistakes would be treated as learning opportunities rather than more fatal, career-damaging errors?

Not once.

Times when we, as students, took on major independent research projects that went far beyond simply copying something out of an encyclopedia, or involved ourselves in periods of intense personal creativity and action.

In this category, the most vivid memory I have is of taking on, in my senior year at Hill, a completely optional project called a tutorial. Seniors who wanted to explore some subject of real interest to themselves could propose the idea to a faculty member of their choice. If he was willing to work with the student as an adviser to the project, he would present the idea to a faculty committee that would, in turn, evaluate not only the idea but the senior's ability to carry it through to completion. If the project was approved, the senior would begin work. The catch: he would be required to conduct the research and complete the writing on his own time, and he would receive no academic credit whatsoever for his labors. Seniors who completed projects would be recognized during graduation ceremonies, and copies of their papers would be held in the school library; but beyond that, their only reward would be what they themselves learned from their efforts.

I was one of about a dozen in my class who accepted the challenge, and I spent much of that year researching a rather obscure design principle called dynamic symmetry—a principle that had been discovered and taught at Yale by Jay Hambidge, the late husband of my Rabun County friend. I had never understood it before, and I wanted to, and the tutorial gave me the opportunity to do exactly that. In its final typed and bound form, the paper was several hundred pages long, complete with diagrams and photographs, and though it wasn't all I had hoped it would be, I was very proud of it.

Had I given my own students the opportunity to do anything similar? Not yet. I had simply presented to them materials I expected them to master, and had scratched my head in bewilderment over the fact that when I gave them quizzes, many of the papers didn't deserve a passing grade.

And in sum, that was about it for my thirteen years. A few lines from Shakespeare, a poem here and there, a snatch of Latin and Spanish, a biology dissection—and enough really memorable events to count off on the fingers of a hand and a half.

What does your list look like?

4

Twenty-one Project Ideas—A Magazine Begins

In late October of 1966, in the midst of struggling to figure out what had gone wrong with my classes and what remedies to employ, and too embarrassed to admit to any of the other teachers that I was stuck and needed help, I began to make a list of those ideas students were able to come up with during the brainstorming sessions we continued to hold together. Retelling some of the high school experiences I had had that had made a difference to me seemed to help somewhat, and we talked a good bit about responsibility, field trips, and the like.

One idea I threw out for discussion was the thought that it might make sense to elect a team of class officers each grading period in each class who would actually help plan and run activities. As they responded with ideas for jobs such a team might have, I wrote them on the board.

In another session, we talked about our wall-long bulletin board and how it might be utilized in some more interesting, creative ways. I proposed turning it over to the classes, letting all five English sections vote on a theme on which they wanted to focus each month, and then letting all the students bring in and tack up materials they could find related to that theme. Then, with their help, I made a list of possible subjects on the board.

In yet another session, I gathered ideas for future units, and as we brainstormed together, wrote them down, too.

When I thought they had been pushed about as far as they could go, the classes each elected officers. Then I consolidated all the ideas from the class discussions into groupings and typed them up in rough note form on three Ditto masters, ran them off, and handed them out in class with the hope that we could choose several and put them into effect immediately.

Here's what the document looked like:

* * * * * *

PROPOSED DUTIES OF CLASSROOM OFFICERS

Help keep room clean.

Put marks beside the names of those who answer questions in class, participate in discussions, and also those who interrupt the teacher.

Has authority to suggest discipline, and bring disciplinary measures before the class for the class vote.

Organize the bulletin board committee, which can receive suggestions for the bulletin board from the class and bring them up for a vote.

Has the authority to call the class to order and begin it if teacher is busy.

See that papers are returned and Dittos handed out. Also collect homework.

See that attendance is checked.

Choose the students who will teach the class each Friday (these should be chosen on Mondays), check and approve their ideas giving aid where needed, and make sure the Friday class is ready to go by Friday.

Plan activities with the class, develop ideas, present them to the teacher for final approval and polishing.

Act as a go-between. They can receive gripes or suggestions from any class member and present them to the teacher.

It is understood that these class officers can choose from the students, at any time, students who are willing to help them carry out their duties. If *you* want to help guide the course this class will take in the future, let them know.

* * * * * *

IDEAS FOR BULLETIN BOARDS

The modern world today—things that are happening around us in sports, world affairs, fashions, music, art, cars, space, cities, transportation, nature, seasons, etc. The board could be devoted to one of these, or all of them as you choose. There should be a theme of some sort, however, that binds the materials together and makes it relevant for us as a class.

People (any age you choose)—how they act, what they do with their time, what makes them tick, what influences their thinking—also how they *should* act.

Papers done by the class.

Summary of class activities for a week.

Old versus new—any theme.

Rabun County—any county or city for that matter.

Advertisements gathered with a theme in mind, such as humor, appeal to status, artistic emphasis, poetry, etc.

Satire—pictures with added captions, *Mad,* picture juxtaposition, etc.

Poems or themes with pictures to illustrate them.

Bestseller lists of books, records, etc. (top ten).

The life of a painter or author living today.

Note: Almost anything you care to do is fine as long as it does not directly insult any philosophies of this school. You must also remember that for the bulletin board to be of any value, it should have relevance to what we are doing in class, or relevance to our lives. It should be constructed with care so that it has a reason for being there—a justification—and a theme.

* * * * * *

SUGGESTIONS FOR FUTURE CLASSES AND UNITS

Students run the class on Fridays. This can be in the form of a panel discussion on any issue that interests you, an "exchange ideas" day, a day in which several students present hobbies or books they have just read—anything, in fact, that has captured their interest and that they feel may interest the class. It could even be a discussion analyzing the class for the week and presenting suggestions for vote. Again, remember that the classes you present should be well organized, should have a theme that has relevance for us—i.e., a good reason for being presented. It is a good idea to have backup material in case the thing you planned to do doesn't go over. You can also present plays, give quizzes, and read stories, etc. If you want to have Dittos run off, let me know in advance.

Read a book together in class—preferably a new book in which we can make the author come alive, too. Write a letter to the author.

More films, records, articles from *Mad.* (write our own *Mad?)*

A play. Could be for assembly program. Satire (about school, about dropout problem). Let class write it. Let teacher write it. Read one written by someone else and study it to see how it is put together. Act parts of it in class.

Literary magazine written by us. Solicit contributions from other schools. Publish.

Collect money so we can have a party at the end of the year.

A class on the reasons for discipline, rules—why we should do things we sometimes don't like to do.

How movies or records are made and directed. How books are made into movies.

Field trips.

Journals.

Grammar—quick lessons broken up by other activities.

A unit on the supernatural.

Study emotions—examples of each—how they work—how to describe them or put them in writing. What causes each.

Unit on short stories.

Unit on college—what we can expect, what we will need in preparation.

Unit on magazines. Take one and break it down completely into all its various parts.

Bring interesting things to class to share with others.

Have a news report each day.

Panel discussions, debates.

Do a musical and read the story as we go along. Study how it's put together and presented on the stage.

Have students write stories and poems—Ditto the best ones for the class to keep.

Every once in a while have in-class compositions on interesting or odd things. Topics that will make the imagination work.

* * * * * *

TEACHER NOTE

I was prouder of you all as a class after you gave me your ideas than I have been of you in a long time. You have shown me that you can come up with fascinating plans for the future of the course, and that you can choose topics which have value both for you and your classmates. You have also shown me that you care about this course, and want to help plan it in a responsible fashion; you care what happens, and this is more than any teacher could hope for.

Now show me that you can act as responsibly as you can plan. I will abide by your decisions and suggestions (no matter what the area—be it discipline or future classes) as long as these decisions are made democratically and are for the good of all of us as a class. As you take increasing control of this course, you must remember that your decisions must not be frivolous, harmful, or made without careful thought. It is pointless to have a class that has no relevance to us or what we are studying. It is pointless to have a class that is merely "play" and therefore has no reason for being presented.

Your suggestions should be reasonable and able to be carried out. A suggestion that we all take a trip to Atlanta, for example, is probably a suggestion that is wasting precious time. Your ideas should be things we *can* do, and you should have ideas for carrying them out, and be willing to help out when your help is needed. Your officers have been chosen carefully. Now help them when they need it. Respect them. And remember that they have the same authority as I do when they are in charge of this class.

It looks to me like you are ready to move under your own steam. Now prove it. I'll help whenever I can.

Mr. Wigginton

For several weeks, we experimented. Seasoned teachers, had any been watching us, would say we floundered, but I prefer the sound of *experimented*. In most of the classes, the classroom-officer idea quickly paled and became something of a joke. I just wasn't experienced enough to make it work.

The first bulletin board we tried was one in which all students were to bring in photographs and headlines from magazines and newspapers that, when put up in collage form, would make a statement about the tone and mood of the country—its obsessions and its paranoias. That worked somewhat better, and soon hundreds of photographs of war scenes and dead children juxtaposed against shampoos and automobiles and kitchen gadgets festooned the back wall and stimulated some lively conversation. One student brought in the inside front cover of *Time* magazine which, that week, formed part of a double-page ad for some chemical company. The full-page color photograph that faced the ad copy showed a side view of a beautiful female nude, seated on the floor, her arms wrapped around, and her head resting on, her knees. That precipitated some animated speculation as to whether or not I'd allow it to be put on the board; but since it could hardly be construed as pornographic photography, and since it fit the theme of the bulletin board perfectly, and since it *was* the inside cover of *Time*, and since I believed that getting past the tittering that usually accompanied such scenes was an important part of natural, healthy growth, and since the class unanimously voted to put it up, I told the boy to go ahead.

Enthusiasm for the bulletin board idea, which had built steadily for days as it grew and developed and took on its own uncanny existence, withered the next week with a note I found in my mailbox from a member of the administration that read, "I'm eager, when showing folks about the school, to show them [the classrooms]. Often I go into the room to show what's going on. I did this Saturday, but was unhappy with the picture of the near nude on the bulletin board. I wonder if such is pleasing to the Lord, complimentary to the school, or a good evaluation of the teacher? Frankly, I doubt it."

Well, slowly but surely, I was learning. I had not been aware that the Lord was displeased with the appearance of the human form, and I had regarded the photographs the students had found of blown-up Vietnamese children as far more obscene, but I obviously had a good bit more to learn about this job. Onward and upward.

During our class discussions, I had related some of my own school magazine experiences to the group, and as we continued to grope about, some interest in that idea began to grow. And so I began to look at that option more closely. There were some real problems. There was no money, for one thing—not a dime except what I would contribute myself. There was no equipment except for a somewhat battered single-lens-reflex camera my uncle had bought abroad during World War II and had passed on to me. There was no precedent for such a publication at our little school (there was not even a student newspaper), and so there was no reservoir of experience to draw on in the faculty or administration. And there wasn't an abundance of time with my load of six classes a day plus a boys' dormitory to help run. Worse, I hadn't even proposed the idea to the principal, and I had no clue as to what his reaction would be.

But then the students decided they wanted to try it. So did I. I hadn't been afraid to try crazy things before. In fact, in college, many of us had almost made a cult of being daring and bucking the conventional wisdom. In one of the journals I had kept throughout college, for example, I found:

I sincerely feel that this cautiousness stifles all individuality even more than the machinery of society. People are no longer willing to live dangerously, try things that may hurt them or possibly knock them flat. We think too damn much, and don't rely on impulse anymore. In a way, that's too bad, I think. Millions of little aspects enter every decision, and we see all the aspects and it scares us off from making any decision at all except to forget the whole thing. —April 5, 1963

The next day I went into my first-period class and said, "Okay, what are we going to have in this magazine?" It wasn't a sure thing yet by any means, but I had to have at least a working description to take to the principal. We began to put ideas on the board, and each successive class added to the list. The next day we broke the list down into categories:

1. Creative work by high school students at Rabun Gap (poems, short stories, essays, editorials, and artwork).

2. Creative work by high school students at other schools.

3. Creative work by professional writers and artists. [I encouraged the students to add this one, believing that it would be a real source of inspiration to them in their writing—and a genuinely challenging educational experience—for them to sift through manuscripts from adult poets and writers, choose those pieces that moved or inspired them, and be able to back up their choices with sound reasoning, which they would then communicate to the authors themselves through letters they would write explaining their decisions. (There was a certain perverse pleasure associated with this, also, as I envisioned adults sweating over whether or not their work would pass high school scrutiny.)]

4. Feature articles from the surrounding community. [The genesis of this idea came out of discussions in class that always began, "Yeah, but who's going to *buy* it? My folks aren't going to shell out money for a *poetry*

magazine. Neither are my friends." And so we began to list ideas for items that community students could easily collect as homework exercises (superstitions, home remedies, expressions, weather signs) that could form feature articles that local people might be more interested in reading than poetry. At this point, some of the dorm students began to grumble about the fact that they couldn't leave campus and had no way to collect such information. I told them I'd figure something out—taking them in groups myself after school to visit community contacts if necessary.]

5. Photographs taken in the surrounding community.

With this rough outline, and the students shouting encouragement, I went to the principal, Morris Brown. That meeting is a blur, now. I know it was followed by several others involving different members of the administration; I also remember that basically, the principal was encouraging. I'm not sure why, except that during the eleven years I worked with him and the thousands of situations in which I saw him with students and teachers, I never found him to be anything other than positive and supportive if there was any way possible. Above all, he was fair, willing to take a chance. He was an extraordinary man to work for.

During these meetings, I made it clear that I was not out to rock any boats, but it seemed to me that if my job was to teach students how to write grammatically correct, forceful prose and poetry, then there was a certain logic to having them produce a publication. Many other schools had magazines. Ours didn't. I thought it should. And if I was willing to give it the time it would require. . . .

In addition, I outlined the kinds of benefits I had derived from working on my high school's magazine, and though I hadn't worked on a publication since, I thought I could pull it off. And, as a final bit of encouragement, I asked them to draw up a list of stipulations and promised we would stick to them.

That list, though never formalized in written, signed, and dated form, laid out a set of operational guidelines that all of us understood:

• The school could provide no financial help. The money simply wasn't there. It would have to be my responsibility, and if the project went broke, or owed bills to printers and local businessmen, I would have to deal with that personally. My students and I would be allowed by the school to solicit donations in the community and to sell copies of the magazine; and the school bookkeeper would set up a separate account for us on the school's books, but that was about as far as the school could go.

• Our regular classroom work would have to continue according to the state curriculum guidelines. Students could work on the magazine in class only if their regular work was not shoved aside and ignored. Collection projects could be assigned as homework, but students could not leave class during the school day for any reason.

• The students would print nothing of a profane or antireligious nature that could be embarrassing to the school, the community, or individuals within the school or community.

•Legal obligations and liabilities would rest on my shoulders.

I returned to the classes and laid out the terms. Now that there were stipulations attached, the project began to take on an air of seriousness that sobered us all. We still wanted to try it, though. Not being able to set aside any parts of the assigned curriculum loomed as a real problem in terms of time, so we decided to try one issue only, doing it as an eight-week project, and then we'd see what happened. I polled each of my classes, took a final cumulative vote, and it was done.

At this point, hoping to ease the logistics of getting things accomplished, I decided to make the two classes of tenth-graders the primary editorial staff, with the ninth-graders being a junior, contributing staff. If we decided to do a second magazine the following year, the current ninth-graders would be in charge. Wanting even more official status, the older students decided to vote among themselves to elect two students to head each of five editorial divisions (literary, regional, exchange, makeup, and business), and two as editors in chief. An election was held—a very serious affair, as I remember—and twelve students were chosen, seven from the community and five from the dorms. Things began to look official.

Looking through my lesson plans from late November, I found the following note to myself: "Literary magazine: Get students to write formal letters to schools soliciting contributions; get addresses from library. Teach kids how to write letters.

"Students do edit, makeup, etc.

"Get titles from students."

Keeping the curriculum requirements in mind, I initiated a unit in formal letter writing. If I could just figure out ways of this sort to make the curriculum work *for* the magazine instead of against it, I could kill two birds with one stone. I could fulfill the state requirements and at the same time give those requirements an added dimension of reality for the students that would make their internalization and mastery far more likely. It all made sense.

Each student wrote a formal letter to the head of the English department of a high school in their hometown, if they were dorm students, or a Georgia high school selected from a handbook the principal had that listed them all by county, inviting submissions of poetry and stories from their English classes. As each student completed a first draft of a letter on notebook paper, I checked it for style and grammar and helped make any necessary corrections. As more and more students finished, to speed things up, I grabbed students who already had good letter writing skills and were proficient in grammar to help me check the others.

The next morning I went to Mr. Brown and explained what we were doing. I agreed to buy the stamps if the school would supply the stationery. He agreed, so I had some students count out the 150 sheets and envelopes we needed, and I and another student went across the street to the post office and bought the stamps.

This time, under pain of mutilation, the students copied their corrected letters onto real stationery, put them in envelopes, addressed them, affixed stamps, and several of the editors took them to the post office and mailed them—a unit on writing formal letters completed.

"You know, we really ought to have our own stationery," several said as they left that day.

"Yeah, well," I said with a laugh, "you've got to pick a name first. What's this crazy thing going to be called?"

For the next few days, my blackboard was out of commission for normal work as students added to a growing list of possible names for their magazine. We went on with classroom exercises while the naming effort stewed. From time to time, a student would jump up and add another possibility as the class clapped—or groaned—when it had read the new entry. When they were squeezed dry, I typed up a Ditto that contained all the names, and we began the process of elimination. The list included Parchment and Pine, Rabun Gap Literary Magazine, Red Hills Reader, and Soul Plus. Students could vote for as many names as they liked. Every name that got five votes or more in any given class was retained. If a name didn't get five votes or more from a single class, it was dropped from the list. It was a noisy, chaotic, laborious process, but finally the list was winnowed to a handful of favorites—and majority rule. The name finally selected was *Foxfire*—an organism that grows on decaying organic matter in damp, dark coves in the mountains and glows in the dark. Many of the students had seen it before, and those who hadn't were either fascinated by the idea that such a thing existed, or liked the sound of the word. In any case, they cheered their approval. Everyone had had an equal say. No one had been slighted or left out. To varying degrees, each had been caught up in the unfolding drama despite himself, and the classes had come together as one. Teaching was beginning to make sense.

5

The Luther Rickman
Tale: *Foxfire*'s
Inaugural Interview

A unit on poetry followed the formal letter exercise. I sent students outdoors to write haiku. We had done some work with rhyme and meter previously, working from the songs of Simon and Garfunkel and the Beatles. Now I had them write their own pieces. As I sensed they were coming to some understanding of form and discipline and economy, we tackled free verse. As each exercise ended, the favorite works were selected by class vote for inclusion in the magazine.

Meanwhile, a few of the letters the students had sent out were bearing fruit. Work had come in from students at the Montverde Academy in Montverde, Florida; the Shenandoah Junior High School in Miami, Florida; the Sequoyah High School in Doraville, Georgia; and the Rabun County High School in Clayton, and the labors of these students gave mine a yardstick against which to measure their own efforts and stimulated some of the liveliest discussions of the year. Again, the best pieces were selected by class vote, and more student-written letters went out informing peers of the acceptance of a poem or of the return of works we couldn't use.

At the same time, I had written or spoken with friends of mine who were published poets or authors, soliciting manuscripts and help. A letter I sent to Howard, for example, read:

For the past weeks I have devoted all my creative energy to putting together a framework for a literary magazine, the first issue of which I hope to be able to put out in February. I am very excited about it, as are all my students. Not only are we going to have high school work in it (we have written schools all over the country soliciting contributions) but I also hope to have the work of some older people included. Marguerite Steedman was here not long ago, and I talked to her about it at some length. She was able to give a stack of suggestions and ideas—products of her own experience in such endeavors—and she also agreed to send several of her own poems and essays for inclusion if we wished. That was a boost I needed, and I accepted with excitement. I also hope to get something out of Ammons and McConkey, and maybe even James Wright if I can woo him in the right way—what this is I haven't the vaguest idea. I have gotten the green light as far as selling copies goes, and so I think there will be enough money around to be able to have it printed professionally. Now I'm going to hit you—have you got anything, or do you have any ideas for me? Part of the magazine is devoted to certain facets of the personality and history of this section of the country, part of it is for the work of high school students, and the rest is devoted to persons of my age and up. We are looking for short essays, poems, stories, editorials, etc. Only you can imagine what hopes I have for this thing. Send us something. An essay from one of your colleagues? (or two?) An essay and poem from you? Or either? And listen—a must is a paragraph from you—a part of one of your letters—which we can use as one of the introductory messages in this first issue. You know how they read—"I am happy to see that students are trying to do this sort of thing—it's what keeps us strong as a country"—you know. Something that will make them feel good and swell their battered egos. I'm counting on you for this. Don't get angry. It's just that I count on many people I am writing to. Besides, I think this is going to be something you will be proud to be associated with.

A. R. Ammons, a former professor of mine at Cornell, sent a poem for the students to consider, as did former classmate Geof Hewitt, and Alfred Starr Hamilton. Free verse we were studying in class from published texts took on another dimension when the Ammons envelope arrived with an encouraging note, and the students simultaneously found a poem by Ammons in a book of modern poets we were using in class.

Marguerite Steedman, a novelist and journalist, also contributed a poem. The section of the magazine she was most enthusiastic about, however, was the part that focused on local history and lore. Sitting around Mary Hambidge's kitchen table one evening, she reminded me that authors like Faulkner and Twain wrote their best works out of an intimate knowledge of their surroundings and their roots, and that such investigation could only serve my students well. "Besides," she said, "the beauty into which you were born is often the beauty you never see. Go dig the gemstones out of your own hill." We began to get more serious about that section.

A unit in my classes about superstitions, and a resulting homework assignment, began to pay off. Community students asked members of their families for help, while dorm students bedeviled community adults who worked on the campus farm or in the school's kitchen. Each time a new superstition was brought in, it was posted with the others on the bulletin board, signed by the student who had collected it, creating a master list that included, "If you kill a toad, your cow will go dry," or, "If you bury your hair when you cut it, you will never have a headache, but if you burn it, a headache will follow," or, "To keep witches away, put a broom under your doorstep."

The list of superstitions became so impressive that we decided to try the same tactic with home remedies. Scores of them were brought in, and a second master list began to grow beside the first: "Carry a raw potato in your pocket to prevent rheumatism," and, "Tie a dirty sock around your neck for the sore throat," and, "For sweaty feet, boil dried chestnut leaves until you have an ooze and apply this to your feet," and, "Pour black walnut juice in your ear for the earache." We'd struck the mother lode.

At the same time, word came that Sara Rickman, a housewife in Clayton, was an amateur artist and might be willing to contribute a drawing or two. I went to visit her one evening when I was free from the dorm, described our project, and was delighted when she agreed to do two pen-and-ink drawings for us. While I was there, she also told me about her father-in-law, Luther Rickman, who was retired now but had once been the high sheriff and had a terrific story about the time the Bank of Clayton had been robbed in 1936, while he was in office. It sounded good, so that same evening I went to visit him. He and his wife were sitting near the stove in the one heated room of the house. Almost no prompting was needed to get him started, and it was obvious that it was one of his favorite stories. As he told me part of it, his eyes lit up, and he pounded the arm of his chair. And it was a story indeed, with Zade Sprinkle and the outlaw gang riding into town in a T-model and first robbing Reeves' Hardware of the guns and ammunition they needed to take next door to rob the bank. There was no way I could write it down, though, the way he was telling it. Any version I might write would sound pale and flat beside his own. Though I had never tape-recorded anyone before, I knew that the only way to do the tale justice was to tape it. Likewise, he had never been tape-recorded, but he was enough of a showman to be intrigued by the project. We set a date two weeks hence, shook hands, and I stepped out into a clear winter night, my head buzzing.

When I got back to the dorm, three of my favorite students were still up. I really wanted someone to talk to, so I corralled them and unloaded the story of my evening. They got as excited as I was and immediately became part of the project. "But what are we going to do about a tape recorder?" We all resolved to start looking for one, and went to bed.

Several days later I was in Clayton at the Kodak store buying some film. I had gotten to know Bob Edwards, the owner, pretty well as the magazine idea had gained more momentum, and he had agreed to print our black-and-white photographs for us since we had no darkroom. It wouldn't have done us much good if we had, since none of us knew how to print. When I told him about the Luther Rickman tale and our need for a tape recorder, he grinned, remembering the robbery, walked into the back storeroom, and returned with an old reel-to-reel recorder that was used but still functional. With the promise that if we decided to keep the recorder, we could pay for it whenever we had the money, *Foxfire* had its first piece of equipment.

The evening of *Foxfire*'s inaugural interview was bitter cold. I had managed to get the three students excused from their required study hall and loaded into my unheated Volkswagen bus, and we headed for Clayton, shivering all the way. Luther met us at the door and brought us into the living room, where the oil heater was cranking away at full blast. The students and I set up the recorder, turned it on, and with an "Are you ready now?" Luther began. It was obvious that in the two weeks since my last visit, he'd been practicing. Since the story was going to be put in print, he wanted it exactly right. Slowly choosing each word, he went through every step of the robbery and the resulting chase. From time to time, he would falter, and his wife, with whom he had apparently been practicing and who had been silently mouthing nearly every word with him, would get him back on track until at one point, he finally rebelled and exclaimed, "Aw, now, I'm a' tellin' it just like it was!" and she retreated into complete silence—but still mouthing the words of the tale in anxious moral support.

It was an extraordinary experience. When he finished, he told us to turn off our machine, and he relaxed for the first time that night. When one of the students suggested we play the tape back to make sure it had recorded, we did, and as it played back clear and clean, Luther, who had never heard himself before, and his wife sat nearly motionless except for their mouths, which silently told the story yet again. At the point where Luther scolded his wife, he looked at her and smiled and shook his finger, and at every pause he nodded his head and murmured, "That's right, that's right," as if listening to some third party on a witness stand relate the story for him.

That night the friendship of six disparate people was cemented for all time. The next day I played the tape for every one of my classes.

6

"Christ Our Lord Was Borned Then"

Christmas already. Everyone seemed to enjoy the Luther Rickman tape.

Yes, true, but the next day Charles broke off the blade of his Barlow knife in one of the floorboards at the back of the classroom.

Students brought in pages of remedies and superstitions. The bulletin board was full of them.

Yes, true, but half the students didn't bring in anything.

Well, at least half *did*. And anyway, Mr. Brown told me several weeks ago that Tommy had come up to him and stated that I was the best teacher he had ever had. Mr. Brown had said he thought that was a real accomplishment and that anyone who could reach Tommy was some fine teacher.

Yes, but a week later I had to move Tommy up to the front of the room to keep him out of trouble, and he tried to set fire to my lectern with his cigarette lighter and I had to kick him out of class for three days.

Well, that's mostly coming out of that sixth period, ninth-grade class. No one can teach them.

But remember that Elmer, that kid I took out into the hall to paddle the other day, was a tenth-grader. And didn't Ronnie and Kenneth and about five others follow me out there and grab me and swear they'd turn me upside down in front of everybody and paddle me instead?

Yes, well, but it turned out to be all in fun. They were all laughing, and finally I was laughing, too. And I haven't had a bit of trouble out of them since. They've all laid off.

Doesn't say much, though, for the amount of respect they have for me as a teacher. Looks like the only teaching I'm going to be able to do is just what they'll *allow* me to do. They can tear my room apart in six seconds, and they know it.

Well, maybe, but at least they *are* writing poems and bringing in ideas for the magazine. Gayle wrote up a hog-hunting story Grover Bradley told her, and she brought that in. Charlie wrote a long profile of Barnard Dillard, the druggist. We really are getting some good material. That's more than was happening a month ago.

Christmas.

December 11, 1966

Dear Senzel,

This is a letter of odds and ends. Every so often, things that I have been saving to send to you pile up on my desk (which is hardly big enough to hold my typewriter) and I have to send them on or perish in the debris—smothered by an avalanche of trivia. All these things are bits and pieces of Rabun Gap lore, you might call it, which you can file in your curiosities drawer preparatory to tossing them.

I went tonight to a performance by the glee club of a Christmas cantata entitled "A Song Unending" by John W. Peterson. It was, of course, the Christmas story in song, and it was not sung with the finesse of a professional choir, but it was very moving and I was much impressed. I got this crazy feeling after the whole thing was over of being left out in the cold. I felt very much alone. Those who had created and had sung and made us bittersweetly happy were moving on to a party, and the members of the audience were moving on to their homes, and the lights were being turned out and the floors swept clean of the remainder, and it was very cold—the feeling of time sliding away was so distinct and so pronounced that I could not possibly hope to describe it to you, but there it was. I found that I had not done many of the things I swore I would have done by this time, and many of the things I had sworn to stop doing I had not—I had stood still in one place as others moved on. Crazy. It must have been the spell of the moment, but there was a black curtain pulled across a stage somewhere inside me, and I could feel it shut. Hell yes, I'm teaching, but there's nothing concrete there. There's nothing to pick up and hold and take along with me to show what I have done. Sometimes it all seems so stupid.

Today I took some boys out to do some more work at Mrs. Hambidge's, and she told me that the word was out in the community (and it really has to be out for her to hear it) that I had told all the kids that they should experiment with drinking starting now. I thought back and remembered where it had all come from—on Fridays I let students take the class, and often they have panel discussions on what is going on nowadays. During these activities, I take the part of a student or an outsider, and I express opinions that I have heard before and know they will hear too, and I want them to have answers to these arguments and not get caught by surprise. I want them to think, to examine themselves and their beliefs and their attitudes and change those they cannot defend. I have told them that I think there should be a Negro President in 1968, that this school should be half Negro, that it is impossible for teenagers to be Christians, that parents should teach their kids how to drink, etc., etc. I made it clear to them that I did not necessarily believe the things I said when acting as a student but only wanted to get them aroused and thinking and participating. Evidently someone was not listening. I should have known.

After returning from Mrs. Hambidge's place, I was reprimanded by a member of the administration for allowing students to work on Sunday. I have been told never to do this again, as Sunday is to be a day of rest, and so the activity we have enjoyed together has ended.

Notes taken during a recent geography class where one of my community students was giving an oral report about Norway:

Tommy: It be less than 12,000 miles long, including fiords. It be 26 persons to the square mile. Chief products is barley, hay, oats, potatoes, rye, wheat, aluminum, canned fish, cement, furniture, lumber, machinery, metals, paper and ships.

Class: What? Paper ships?

T: Cellulose.

C: How do you spell that? Hey, I'm lost. You go too fast.

T: Over there they fish a lot: salmons, cod, mackerel.

C: I can't hear! I believe we better do the United States. [T. makes an obscene gesture at the class.] Hoo hee. Hey, you're shootin' birds out of season.

T: Land regions: coastal, mountains, and plateaus.

C: What are they again?

T: Plateaus. By God, you're gonna haf to get it the first time. I ain't gonna say 'em no more.

C: Well, we can't understand you! My mind don't work that fast!

T: Well, get 'cha a computer! And shut your damn mouth, Debbie. I'm the one givin' this report!

Debbie: Could'a fooled me!

T: Well, if you can do it better, you just get your ass up here!

Something tells me this system of giving oral reports just isn't working.

I sent out sixteen bottles of sorghum made at the school for Christmas presents to relatives, and discovered after the whole thing was over and done that the school puts a circular entitled *Questions and Answers* in every package when they mail them out, and so I had unwittingly sent each of my relatives an appeal for money from this place.

Following are selected phrases from a one-paragraph composition I had my kids write at the request of Dr. Anderson, who wanted me to have them tell honestly what they looked forward to most at Christmas, and what it meant to them. I enclose a potpourri of the results, just as I received them. Sometimes it's sort of fun to read a list like this which contains the meat of 150 themes from 150 different people. Gives a good idea of the variety of responses which a season like this calls up.

And, well, he asked for honesty.

I think it means that I will get to go home with my parrents. And it is a very holey time.

The day our lord and saver was born.

Christmas means a time of worship, and give thanks into the lord for dieing on the cros for our sins.

I like to get lots of gifts, like guns, sleeping bag, tent, sklitt and pans.

I like the hollidays we get out of school and that gives me plenty of time to deer hunt.

On Christmas I like to go hunting about 3:00 come in open up all my presents. Mess around awhile, go in and smell all the meats and fruits cooking. Then go to a shooting match and mess around the rest of the day. Then go Coon hunting that night. Catch two or three and and come in and skin them.

To see my little brother open all of his gifts. And going to church at my own church. And being with all of my friends.

Seeing people laughing and enjoying the day.

All the fun and fire cracker shooting and seeing the childrens faces Christmas morning.

I look for new cloes.

Christmas means to me deer, hunting in the cold squirrell hunting and getting new guns to kill animals. I am the *deer slayer*. Getting out and hunting.

I look forward to getting drunk at Christmas!!!

I think of Xmass as joyful day, a big day because everyone is gay and happy because of one reason. They received gifts. At Christmas I always never think that much about the Lords birthday. I just think of recieving and giving.

Eating Christmas dinner with your boyfriend.

To give and receive takes a person who has the heart to give something or take something big. My giving is my heart and my receiving is Christ.

Get out of school for a while and you get to do a lot of things at home that you normally wouldn't.

Prettiest time of the year because of the many lights and trees.

Christ our Lord was borned then.

Firecrackers, clothes, gifts, a christmas tree, girls, and beer!

I use to love to go to church on this day but not anymore because the people who claim to be brother in Christ aren't and to me this is a bigger sin than not beliving.

Get miles between me and Rabun Gap so I don't feel like people look at you like a low-rent brat. Or a J.D.

Go home and get to see your little brother play with the guns and cowboy suit, little cars, train, wagon and your little sister plays with her dolls and the play house, and the tea set she got.

Relatives sit me down and ask me a million and one questions about school.

I know Christmas is a time to celebrate for Christ's birth but to me, it has no meaning. I have been raised to celebrate Christmas as a time of giving and receiving not remembering. My parents tell me about God but they don't seem very inthoused about it at all.

Warmth of a warm fire place

Holly and songs

Complete rearrangement of my mind, to get a rest.

Walk around in my yard and think. Think and think and think.

Tony's Pizza!

See the new Priest and the rest of the Priest hood holders.

We should if he hadn't been born on the day we may not even be hear and if we was hear what a terrible place it would be.

I have always associated dull songs that have been sung for about a billion years with the couple of weeks before Christmas. Even though I hate this part the core of Christmas is Christ and I always get watery about it.

Pop can get off work and we get to stay at the house. We stay together like a family and play records and read.

That big christmas dinner that you get sick on because you ate so much.

It doesn't mean anything except spending money and eating to much. Most of the presents people give they do it because they have to. This Xmas might be different because I have someone to spend my money on that I love.

tidings of comfort and joy . . .

bew

7

The First 600 Copies

Shortly after Christmas, we began to raise money for the magazine; after school hours, local students from the classes approached nearly every merchant in the surrounding towns. Since the largest town in the county had less than two thousand inhabitants, there weren't a lot of them to see, but they responded, as only people in small towns do, to their children, giving one, five, ten dollars—whatever they could spare. The students also begged from the administration (every member of which contributed), their families—even their friends—promising every one they approached that a donation of whatever size would bring them a gift copy of the first issue with their names listed in the back in a donors' section, and the inside covers autographed by the students who put the magazine together.

Several times I loaded dormitory students into my van to knock on doors that had been missed, and slowly our bank account began to grow.

Another loose end was tied up with the arrival of Howard's introduction. It read:

A Letter to FOXFIRE:

When I walk in the woods, the trees that I notice most are the great strong trees. Some of their trunks are two feet thick, and I have to turn my head to see all the branches. Looking at the great trees, I wonder how the smaller trees live. How do they get enough sunlight and rainwater to grow? How do they survive this competition with the giants?

The answer must be that the little tree simply doesn't bother about them. It just does what it must do. It just grows. It just makes itself. And that act of creation is more magnificent than all the giant trees in any forest. Look what fools we are, I say to myself. It's not the giants that *make things;* it's the little trees. Foolish people all dream about being great instead of producing. We think about being grown when the important thing is growing.

Wisdom is not in the wise question, but in the asking. The poet understands this because he creates. He is a poet because he understands that this act of bringing into being has all the beauty and the value. The giants? Yes, they're very nice, thank you, but the doing has all the importance.

A little magazine does not seem like a very important thing when it's finished, and I guess it isn't. But making things—making poems, making stories, reading things and making them alive—creating whatever it is that we must, is most important. And the unimportant people who make this little magazine, whoever they are, are doing the most important thing in the world.

Howard T. Senzel

I wrote Howard on January 25, 1967, shortly after its arrival, as follows:

[We just completed an interview] which made me definitely decide to go ahead. Last week I mobilized my forces, and we descended on the town like a biblical plague. It worked. In seven hours we came away with $199.71 to help cover our printing bill. I am shooting for fifty-six pages, and a first run of five hundred copies. At the moment, we have about twenty pages of *good* material and we really *have* got some beautiful stuff. I can hardly wait for you to see it. Right now I am working on one of my students to get him to write a story for me on the perils of running moonshine. He has already given me a picture of a still in operation, and everyone knows that he knows personally every bootlegger that there is to be known in these parts. Unfortunately, he is not extremely bright, but if I can just get the details out of him, I can do it as one of those "As told to" jobs. He is quite childlike, and so the task requires infinite patience.

And you should see the home remedies that we have amassed. Good stuff like pouring walnut oil in your ear for earaches, etc., etc.

I have nothing but the highest hopes for the project.

As to the material which you sent. I am forever in your debt—you responded in admirable form, and I hope I have not yet seen the last of your creations. (Deadline for material in this issue is the end of Feb., but I am *hoping* to put out another issue at the end of the year.) First—the "Tree-creation" statement. Great sentiment. I really like it and definitely plan to use it. The last statement is beautiful; the kids went nuts.

At the end of February, 1967, the first issue neared completion. There had been some criticism over the fact that I was teaching *Lord of the Flies* and *To Kill A Mockingbird* to my tenth-graders. One group of parents who represented a local religious sect were agitated because, in the former, the boys trapped on the island wind up in a state of seminudity near the book's end. (These same parents would also not allow their sons to remove their shirts when playing basketball during PE.) A second group objected to *Mockingbird* for the obvious reasons. I had known in advance that there might be some trouble from that one, but aside from the fact that it's a wonderful, powerful story, I wanted to use it to lead into a unit on prejudice that I had spent a good bit of time and energy preparing and about which I was very excited.

One of the parent groups contacted the governor and the state department of education in protest. Our principal, who by this time must have been feeling rather like Job, took me aside to warn me of this latest development. When I asked if I should stop teaching the books and move on to something else, he replied that he thought that would only make matters worse, and that those students who were enjoying the books (which was the vast majority, if the daily notebooks and chapter summaries and lively class discussions were any indication) would turn on the others whose parents were involved and precipitate an ugly affair. When an official from the department of education turned up and began listening to my classes from the hallway, I continued to teach as before, and several days later he went back to Atlanta telling our principal that as far as he could determine, the classes were all in order and well taught, the books were on the state-approved reading list anyway, and the state would back the school.

This whole affair, though nerve-racking and unpleasant, did more to create interest in the two books than anything I could have done (in fact, I'm sure they were the only major pieces of prose I taught that year that every tenth-grader read) and led beautifully into a unit on editorial writing that produced a number of fine student editorials defending the use of the books in tenth-grade classes. Two of them were added to the growing pile of material for *Foxfire*.

A few more additions and the contents were complete. A local artist, Stanton Forbes, gave us permission to reproduce a linoleum block print from his book *Bear Hunt* as our cover. The distinctive alphabet he had created for the book's title was used to make the magazine's title as well (a logo we still employ today). Melba Huggins, the typing teacher, let her classes type the contents on an IBM Selectric typewriter they had, and, after some free lessons from the local printer on the preparation of camera-ready copy, the pasteups were completed during after-school hours and delivered. The final product was seventy-two pages long. By that time we had $440 in our account—enough to pay for six hundred copies with some left over for film and tape.

The response was immediate. The first printing disappeared in a week, and, flushed with success, we ordered a second—also for six hundred copies—never allowing ourselves to be deterred by the fact that through my own ignorance, the whole project was a financial disaster.

Howard wrote on April 6, 1967, to say, in part:

"*Foxfire.* I was overwhelmed. I think that you have turned some people on in a magnificent way. The bank robbery thing and the Manous interview were great (and how many interesting articles have you read in magazines lately?). I guess I was most impressed by the tone, i.e., the remedies, the superstitions. Nothing about the magazine was "quaint" and folksy the way an annual old ladies' local preservation meeting is. It was straight and honest. (Let me retreat to Dewey.) You don't know how something is beautiful. You just have the experience and then you examine your guts and by that examination you know.

I am not sure what to do with it. I have given copies to two people who I care about very much. They are both Southerners and they both loved it. One was a girl from Savannah, Tennessee. She can appreciate what it is like in Rabun Gap. The other is the warmest human being alive. I guess they will both send you some money, but nothing big.

I don't know what to do about money. I guess that I could get it shown around to fancy people, but I'm not sure that that is what you want. *Foxfire* is too delicate as an infant to mess around with. How much more beautiful to have it the darling of Clayton, Georgia, than to have it the darling of a clique of rich New York intellectuals. On the other hand, if you need the money, you should not be too awfully concerned.

What I will do today, or the next day is to show it to the fanciest people I know and see what they think. I think that the magazine is good enough to go around and rap many people for a fifty-dollar donation, etc. But I can't tear myself from the romance of thinking how great it would be for this country and yourself and the world, if it grew and prospered, and all that time stayed a Rabun Gap thing."

I answered on April 8:

Dear Howard,

I much appreciate your kind comments on *Foxfire*. Apparently we have rather taken the publishing world by storm. I am getting orders from such odd places as Boise, Idaho, and Cincinnati, and all from people of whom I have never heard. Adjectives like *superb* are flowing around like water. I keep myself on the level by reminding myself that the thing is full of mistakes, and that we haven't even started getting the meat out of this area yet. Also the photos, though good, are arranged badly, etc. There is much to be done, but when we are through, I think the magazine will definitely be something to be proud of. I think your piece was one of the highlights, and I hope you will let us have others. You may be interested to know that I gave permission to the president of this school to use your article in a speech he gave in Atlanta recently. He read it right from the magazine and then went on to draw a parallel between it, and what the school is trying to do with the sorts of students they accept—small trees that might otherwise be ignored.

People keep stopping him on the street and telling him how much they liked the magazine, and so he has changed his position considerably toward it.

And someone told me in town yesterday that at the shirt factory in Clayton, almost every machine has a copy beside it. When the machines are running well, the operators just sit there reading *Foxfire*. Gives one a good feeling inside. At least they aren't buying it just out of charity.

The *Georgia Magazine* is doing an article on us with pictures.

About money for the magazine—you are right about it being a beautiful thing to have it supported entirely by the Clayton area—nice thought, but I am afraid and I am trying to build insurance against the day when they lose interest. This day, I feel, will surely come. We are losing, at present, 15 cents on every issue we *sell* (they cost 65 cents to print), and 20 cents on every issue we mail out. Plus I gave away a lot. This is not a paying proposition if I want to keep the price at 50 cents (and I do). If we had not had the "Friends," we would really have been in the hole. As it is, our profit is only $65. That's not enough to go a second issue on, much less a second printing which I have already ordered, to handle the summer trade. Clayton can sell lots on the newsstands, but from a business standpoint, that can't make up our losses. We must depend at present on donations to do this. The printer must be paid. If we hadn't begged for money, there would have been no magazine *at all*. This is why I invented the little gadget known as the "Patron Subscription." Find it listed on the back page of the magazine. If we sell seventy-five of these at $10 apiece, we will be set for the whole year next year. I don't want to sound mercenary, but someone's got to foot the bill—I can't as I only take home a little over $200 a month and I'm still paying off my National Defense student loan at Cornell. I'm just being practical. Come and meet our printer and you'll get the whole picture.

So if you really want to help us, sell as many patron subscriptions as you can.

And if you can come down for a visit before you go to London, great. Just let me know. Better not try to call me—I am impossible to get due to the antiquated nature of the phones around here. Send me a card a few days before you leave. I'll be here. We might even take in a revival meeting. It's the season for it. They have a dope addict out at one church now. . . .

Eliot

Had I really stopped to look at what was happening to *Foxfire* financially, and had I been a hard-nosed businessman, I would have called it quits then. Believing that few people would pay more than fifty cents for such a magazine, I insisted on that being the price despite the fact that it was costing us sixty-five cents a copy to print. At least half of those first issues were given away to students, parents, donors, friends, and potential supporters. The sixty-five dollars we had in the bank, combined with sales of a second printing (if we sold every single copy), would about pay that printing cost but would leave us nothing with which to print a second issue; and yet I ordered the second printing anyway. This action condemned us to another round of donation-seeking if we wanted to put out a second issue, and this in the face of the fact that the several Clayton merchants we approached for money to help with the second printing— to test the temperature of the water, as it were—refused, saying, "We already helped once."

And in retrospect, though I told Howard otherwise (and allowed myself to believe it), we had not taken the publishing world by storm at all. The orders for copies that dribbled in from out of state were primarily the result of out-of-state subscribers reading the reviews of the first issue in The Clayton *Tribune* and *Georgia Magazine*—both the work of a local acquaintance who wrote a regular column and was doing me a personal favor. On the back page of our magazine, over two address blanks, was a paragraph that read:

> The purpose of this issue of *Foxfire*, quite frankly, is to test reader response. We would like very much to go ahead publishing *Foxfire*, but on a subscription basis. . . . Here's what we'd like you to do. If you liked this issue of *Foxfire* and *would buy* a subscription to the magazine if offered one, please fill in one of the blanks below and mail it to us. We will answer your card and let you know whether or not we have decided to offer subscriptions.

Less than a dozen blanks were returned.

For hard-nosed realists, the handwriting would clearly have been on the wall.

And yet . . .

And yet, the magazine, though not brilliant, *was* good. There was that Luther Rickman interview, and that list of home remedies, and those two editorials, and . . .

Parents had come to me to let me know how excited they were. The administration was positive. And my own ego, which had been pummeled to the point that I was seriously considering another career, had been bolstered. A reservoir of energy that had very nearly been drained was slowly refilling.

And I knew for a fact that several kids, in direct but unknowing imitation of me eight years before, had taken copies of that first issue to their rooms, alone, and had silently held them in their hands.

8

"Yeah, But It's Not Our Magazine"

Spring came. One of my favorite dormitory students was kicked out, and seemed delighted. A community student who had graduated several years before was sent home from Vietnam, and, as was the tradition in mountain communities, those who knew him best, including our principal, took the morning off to help dig his grave.

Life went on.

I felt I was finally beginning to make some sense of our dorm situation, but I wasn't sure. At times students were punished for offenses I was convinced warranted no punishment, but my anger only seemed to make the situation worse. Siding with those students against the administration only hurt the students, for they inevitably wound up caught in the middle between two adult factions.

When Howard wrote asking me to attend a conference in Washington sponsored by his employer, the Institute for Policy Studies, and talk to them about *Foxfire* and education, I replied, in part:

I doubt that I can make the conference, though it has always been a dream of mine to be asked to be present at such a meeting. I seriously doubt that I could contribute much of value as my attitude is so ambivalent at this point. Some days I know all the answers, and the next day a kid comes up who changes every damn one of them. . . . Sometimes I have gotten into situations so sticky that I swear that I will never take another job like this as long as I live, but then, miraculously, everything works out. The hurt goes away, and I suddenly find myself a wiser man. That's the stuff of life, I guess. The thrill of the smoke of battle. And the sobriety afterward. And the next step taken with more confidence than before. It's always an eye-opener. If the game is played correctly, it should increase the respect of all parties for each other—and respect is a cousin, if not a brother, of love.

But I'm not ready to talk about it yet to other people. There's still too much I don't know.

My classes were a mixed success. The tenth-graders had become a joy; the bulk of the ninth grade had become a curse. I tried everything I could think of. I threatened to kick the worst of them out of class permanently, thus condemning them to fail the course and repeat it next year, but they simply grinned and said they were going to drop out of school at the end of the year anyway. The combination of their newly aggressive mood, and my helplessness, and the warm weather, was infectious, and the restlessness in those two classes swelled. One day I took the sixth-period group and split it into two separate units. The classroom next door was vacant during that period, so I took the most rebellious of the students there, and started them silently reading *The Yearling*, a book I thought they'd enjoy since most of them were community students who professed to have a real love of the outdoors and wildlife. Every time I'd leave them to get the better group in my classroom working on something else, they'd tear the room apart.

One evening I prepared lessons in advance for the better group and worked with dorm students I had selected as peer teachers to help them get ready to teach all sixth period the next day so I could stay with the others.

When sixth period came, I asked my group to begin reading *The Yearling* aloud, in turn. To my amazement, they read like second-graders, one painstaking word at a time. They couldn't read! I had known they were poor students from the papers they wrote and the fact that they almost never handed in homework, but for some reason I had never made the connection. And after nine years of public school, they had mastered the skill of camouflage—of taking on protective coloration that had somehow allowed them to blend into their larger classes and escape, unnoticed, ignored, or simply passed on in frustration.

If we had ever talked about such a situation at Cornell, I had forgotten it. Now they were in my class, the last period of the day, and most of them were finally old enough to drop out of school. They had made it. They were safe. Sixth period with a new teacher was the same as recess. Since academics was no longer a factor, they could concentrate on destroying the class.

Gritting my teeth, and knowing that even if I had known how to teach reading (which I didn't), there wasn't enough time left in one year to make any progress, I decided to read the book to them and give them at least one experience with decent literature. Several days later I gave up. They thought the story was stupid.

Finally I brought the two sixth-period sections back together again. Both groups had settled down somewhat, but we were stalled, and they sat eyeing me, wondering what was going to come next.

As we had done several times before, we began to talk. "Look," I began. "We had a pretty rocky start, but we worked that out and we've had a good year up till now. We've gotten some important things accomplished. We've covered most of the material we were supposed to cover. You helped put out a great magazine. We may put out a second issue. Things are finally moving."

There was silence. Then one of the girls said, "Yeah, but that's their magazine. It's not ours."

"Whose?" I asked.

"Theirs. The tenth grade's. They get to do most of the work."

"Wait a minute. You guys helped pick the name. You wrote some of the poems. You brought in some of the remedies and superstitions we used. You wrote letters to other high schools. Come on."

"Yeah," another student said. "But that was months ago. Who got to put the final thing together? Who took it to the printer? Who takes the copies to the bookstores? Who gets to open the mail? You and the tenth-graders!"

"Well." I faltered. "That's because the editors have most of those responsibilities. You guys will be the editors next year."

"It still isn't our magazine. It's theirs. All we get to do now is these stupid lessons. Great."

"Well, that still can't take away from what you all helped to accomplish. You can be proud from now through the rest of your lives over what you've done."

"So why aren't we still doing it?"

When the bell rang, we were stalemated. What they were saying was true. The tenth-graders had taken on the bulk of the work and were getting the bulk of the glory. But I wasn't about to interfere too much with what was happening now. Students had told me that when they were treated as responsible adults, they would respond as responsible adults; that when the academic work they were asked to do was *perceived by them* as having real value, they would treat it accordingly. That was certainly happening with the majority of the tenth-graders.

The question now was how to make it happen for all.

9

The Ginseng Connection

"I'm not gonna be in class the rest of this week. Just thought I'd tell ya so you don't have to call my name and all that."

The bell had rung ending school for the day, and I looked up from some papers I was stacking at my desk into the face of one of my sixth-period losers.

"Where you going?" I asked, not really caring, but glad for a little company in an unthreatening situation.

"Gonna start a sang bed. Make some money."

"A what bed?"

"Sang. You know. Sang?"

"No, I don't know. I never heard of it before."

He looked at me in wonder. "Man, you don't know what sang is? It grows in the woods. You dig it up and sell the roots."

"How do you find it?"

"You just got to know where to look. That's all."

"And you know."

"That's right," he said, grinning for the first time in our conversation.

Suddenly I was interested. I had been fascinated by things of this sort that went on in the mountains for as long as I could remember. It was one reason I had come back here to teach. I'd been so jammed up with responsibilities, though, that I hadn't had nearly as many opportunities as I'd wanted to satisfy those fascinations. *Foxfire*, if good for nothing else, was at least getting me off campus and back into contact with a world I had loved. Maybe there was an article here for the next issue.

"Is it legal?" I asked.

He laughed out loud. "Sure!"

"Look," I said. "I don't even know what you're talking about, but I'd like to. Obviously I can't leave school, but if I could get away one of these days, would you show me how to find this stuff?"

He stopped smiling.

"I just want to see what it looks like, see how you find it."

"Well, I could meet you Saturday. You off work?"

I was, or could arrange to be. We set a time and place, walked out to the parking lot together, and said good-bye.

That night I tried to find out if anyone in the dorm had heard of this stuff. Nobody had. I tried again in classes the next day, with more success. Of sixty ninth-graders in school, sixteen had heard of it, all of them community students. Its more proper name was *ginseng*, and normally it was dug in the fall. The roots were then dried and taken to dealers in the area for sale. When people dug it in the spring, they were usually transplanting it to a central bed for easy harvesting later.

What began to interest me even more than the ginseng itself, however, was the fact that of the sixteen who had heard of it, only ten knew what it looked like, only six had actually hunted for it, and not a single one had actually been to a dealer personally or knew where to find one. My one student who did was absent that day.

When I commented on my poll to one of the teachers who was born and raised in our county, he told me his father, who was still living, had a big ginseng patch, as did many of the older people. Sang digging, though, like most of the customs in the region, was vanishing. There just wasn't enough money in it to make it of interest to most young people, and so they hadn't bothered to learn the skill. It just wasn't worth it. Neither was chair making, shoemaking, blacksmithing, coopering—any of hundreds of things people used to do when they had to be self-sufficient. But what point was there now in learning how to make soap in a black kettle over an open fire, for example, from wood ashes and hog lard—a process that took at least a day—when you could buy it so inexpensively at a local store? "And so," he said, "you won't find a single community student at this school who has the faintest idea how to make soap, even though every one of their parents and grandparents has done it. There's just no reason for them to learn."

On Saturday I met my ninth-grader, and we headed for the woods. We started out on a steep mountain slope that faced northeast at the end of a long, broad valley. It was heavily forested in large hardwoods—poplar, oak, maple—that shaded the black soil completely. Save for ferns and other ground cover, there was almost no undergrowth, so we could look straight up the mountain into the granite rock cliffs and ledges above, covered with moss and lichens.

He started walking, moving slowly, searching a wide area in front of him as he went. I followed behind, carrying a camera. After about half an hour, he found a plant, called me over, dropped to his knees, and, taking a short stick, gently scratched away the loam from a small tuberous root that forked in several places. He must have gone ten or twelve inches into the ground, and he took his time separating the earth from it, making sure no pieces broke away.

"There," he said with a smile. "That's the way you dig it." Breaking off the top, with its cluster of leaves, he handed it to me and said, "Now, you take this top out through yonder and match it up with every plant you see. When you find one that matches, yell, and I'll come help you. I won't be far." He dropped the root into a sack and went off up the mountain slope, leaving me to myself.

I searched for what must have been an hour, feeling pretty foolish most of that time, walking along trying to match my leaves with others. Many plants looked similar but none matched until finally, beside a waist-high chunk of granite, I had it. I called, and within a moment, he was there. "I told you I wouldn't be far. I've been watching you. You've been looking good. Yep, this is it all right. Now you dig it up—see if you've learned anything. I'll stop you if you get into trouble."

Carefully I eased the plant out without breaking the roots, and we saved it, top and all, for replanting. He slapped me on the back—"See, that wasn't so tough was it?"—and he laughed. "Now let's find some more."

We hunted most of the day, finding another dozen plants to add to our collection. As we walked, he told me stories he'd heard of people who had found plants that were waist-high and had roots as big as a fist. He told me how to plant it, when to dig it, and where to take the roots to sell them.

Toward the end of the day, we had worked our way nearly to the top of a long ridge. We stopped then and walked through a meadow on top to a couple of beaver dams he knew about and wanted to share with me. I took a few pictures, after which we went back to his modest, unpainted wooden house, where I met his family, sat on the porch and had a soda with them, and then drove back to school.

I've thought about that day many times since. Its most immediate effect, aside from the ache in my legs, was that I never again had a disciplinary problem in class with that boy (or his friends, whom he apparently talked to behind the scenes). The change was instantaneous. Whereas before our friendly encounters—our arm-wrestling matches and such—had tended to make things worse, this event had had the opposite effect. Instead of being a "pal," someone with whom it was safe to clown around, I had stumbled into a different kind of relationship of a much deeper quality. For one thing, our roles had been reversed and suddenly I was the pupil, he the teacher. I was amazed at the depth and quality of his knowledge about the woods. He knew far more on that score than I, and I could not help but respect him. He had his areas of knowledge and ignorance, and I had mine, and in that respect we were equal, each potentially able to share something with the other, to the enrichment of both.

And there was absolutely no arrogance about his manner. Just an easy self-confidence and assurance and a resulting gentleness. He was a far better teacher with me than I had been with him.

Oh—and I have a ginseng bed behind my cabin that I add to every year.

10

"Here's What I'd Like to Do Next Year"

Response to the first issue continued to trickle in as the last of the second printing disappeared from the stores in town and from the boxes in our classroom. One day a student would come in with a crumpled dollar bill and say, "My mom wants two more of them magazines. She's putting one away in the trunk and sending the other one to my aunt in Detroit." The next day a letter would come in from someone in a neighboring town that read, "I heard about your magazine today from a friend and I'd like to see a copy. Please send me one and let me know how much it costs and I'll return payment immediately." Or the phone would ring in the school office and Mrs. Cook, the school secretary, would grab me in the hall during a break with, "Clayton Drugs just called and said they needed ten more issues." It was like that for weeks.

We lost our shirts. Although on paper we should have come out with enough money to pay the bill from the second printing, we didn't. Many stores, realizing our situation and simply wanting to help out, did not insist on a percentage, but some did, which cut into the profit. Some issues simply disappeared from stores and couldn't be accounted for. Some copies were sold on credit and never paid for. People kept appearing who warranted free copies ("If you send a copy to so and so at the Athens paper I bet she'll write a review," or "My grandfather had some stuff in that magazine and Mom took his so he needs another copy," or "Don't you think we should send a copy to the former teacher of such and such as a courtesy?" and so forth). And of those we sold, at fifty cents we weren't recouping our per-copy cost anyway.

But it was a valuable math lesson for myself and the tenth-graders. They were getting a real charge out of dealing with the minitempest they had created, and the response was instructive. By far and away it centered most enthusiastically on the section of local lore. John Dyson, a close friend of mine from our fraternity house days at Cornell (currently Chairman of the Board of the New York State Power Authority), wrote, in part, "I read all of *Foxfire* with great interest. It's great! . . . The Rabun County section is priceless. Such a colorful area surely merits the attention and preservation which *Foxfire* will give it. I hope more stories and sayings can be included in future editions." That feeling was typical.

If we were going to print a second issue, then, if for no other reason than its marketability, it made sense to feature the area.

But it made sense for a number of other reasons that were equally persuasive. The ginseng experience had taught me, for example, that most of my community students were almost as ignorant about the past customs of the region as my dormitory students were. I wasn't in much better shape on that score than any of them, but at least I knew that at one time their grandparents had survived the incredible task of nearly total self-sufficiency and had thus exhibited a strength, ingenuity, and tenacity of will that we could only be well served by understanding in this dawning age of almost complete dependence on plumbers and supermarkets and bowling alleys and fast-food places and television sets.

Besides, the raw material was easily accessible. The living grandparents of most of my community students had been young people themselves when the first airplane left the ground, and the particular and unique perspective they had on what we had gone through as a nation, spanning as it did the frontier to the technological age, was one we were not likely to see again in our country, at least. And the information was there, firsthand and free for the asking.

In addition, the array of subject areas to research was so broad and so vast that any student, no matter what his or her particular interest, could be easily accommodated. "You're interested in hunting? Fine. Find out how your grandfather hunted as a boy your age using a flintlock rifle, and write it down and bring it in as your composition for this week. Trapping? Fine. How did the old people build the snares and traps they used before those items were available in hardware stores? Cooking? Fine. How did your grandparents cook when all they had was a fireplace? Medicine? Ask that neighbor of yours what she used to do for colds and flu and pneumonia. Woodworking? Talk to your grandfather about how he hewed logs and cut the notches to build his first log house. Ask him. Better still, get him to *show* you, and try it yourself."

Harder work, granted, but vastly more engaging than writing (or grading) compositions on topics like, "What Christmas means to me" or
"What I did last summer."

And one by-product—the collected material itself—above and beyond
the educational value in (and the pride and self-esteem that came from)
preparing it for publication, could be of tremendous benefit to the community itself. The *reasons* for preserving such information were less easily
definable once one got beyond the pure academic value of the collecting
and publishing exercise itself. It was doubtful, for example, that we would
ever be called on to revert to an age of outdoor toilets and pulling teeth
with rusty pliers and praying that our crops would make and save us from
winter starvation.

But it was likewise a fact that the community had virtually no written,
photographic (or tape-recorded oral) record of its past; that at some
point someone would find such a record useful (if in no other way than
that a future child who had never met a particular grandmother might be
able to ask that a tape of her be played so she could hear what she
sounded like); and that if such a record were ever to be made, it wouldn't
hurt a bit to start now. Already people were stopping me and my students
on the street to say, "I wish you could have met old John. Now *he* could
have told you some *real* stories." But old John was dead. And he had taken
his stories with him, not because he had wanted to but because no one
had cared.

Additionally, the collection of the material made sense for deeper,
more subtle reasons. Few of my students seemed to have a genuine
appreciation for roots and heritage and family—the kind of appreciation
that goes far deeper than simply being amazed at finding out that
Grandpa can cut down a tree and make a chair or a banjo out of it or that
Mom used to be a midwife and knows how to deliver babies. I'm talking
about the peculiar, almost mystic kind of resonance that comes—and
vibrates in one's soul like a guitar string—with an understanding of *family*
—who I am and where I'm from and the fact that I'm part of a long
continuum of hope and prayer and celebration of life that I must carry
forward. That kind of thing. Couldn't they possibly get some deepened
sense of all this through the kind of work our tiny magazine was pointing
us toward, together? Perhaps.

In addition, many of my students were already prejudiced against other
cultures for reasons that not even they could articulate, a fact that dis-
turbed me tremendously. If they could be brought to a genuine understanding of their own culture and race and background, would they then
be in a position to be more curious about—and understanding and sympathetic toward—other races and cultures and backgrounds? The jury
would obviously be out overnight on the answer to that one, but there was
a certain mad logic in operation that seemed to make sense.

And in the end, even if none of the above made sense, there was still tremendous value in giving young people a chance to exercise parts of their personality that didn't often get much exercise at that age. I was just beginning to understand how multifaceted my students were—an understanding I might never have come to had I not gotten to know them on anything beyond a classroom level.

Living in the dormitory was obviously a factor. I would have had to have been blind, deaf, and dumb *not* to have gotten to know them better. The situation gave me no choice. When a student wakes you up at two o'clock in the morning because he has to talk to someone, then there you are. Only the kind of person who should never be allowed to work with young people would say, "Can't it wait?"

A remarkable thing I had observed, however, was how different my students often were in situations that changed the signals. For example, dorm students who, on campus, were regarded by nearly all who had to work with them as rude, lazy, slovenly, devious, or rebellious (and who were often kicked out for a combination of minor offenses that usually added up to a charge of "bad attitude"), when they were off campus in small groups doing work with me to help Mrs. Hambidge, were precisely the opposite. They were unfailingly courteous and enthusiastic and cooperative; and as we raked leaves, or hauled rocks, or gathered firewood, and laughed and joked together, with Mrs. Hambidge calling encouragement and thanks from the relative safety of her porch, they worked until sweat rolled from their faces.

Students who would have been predicted to be impolite and bored by those who "knew them better" were, instead, transfixed and eager to be as polite as they knew how to be in an interview situation.

It was in large part due to these experiences that I was hesitant to agree with some of my more skeptical adult peers who doubted that my students would ever be willing or able to sustain the kind of energy that would be required to make a success of *Foxfire.*

With the printer paid, but no money in the bank, we decided to go ahead with a second issue. The tenth-graders, understanding the problem I was facing with my younger students, not only voted to include them in the decision as to whether or not to continue but also began work on several schemes to give them a more active role. One thing they began to hammer together was a system whereby younger students who were genuinely interested could, after proving their interest, be elected to a junior board of editors and begin actively preparing to assume leadership. After much discussion, it was decided to choose one local custom to highlight or feature in the issue. A list of possible topics filled the blackboard, and the subject chosen, by vote, was planting by the signs of the zodiac and the moon phases—a subject broad enough that any student who wanted to could make a substantive contribution. The more planting rules that could be found and written down, the richer the article would be. In addition, since many people had varying opinions on the practice and its utility or futility, there was plenty of room for a number of taped interviews on the same subject, each of which could be done by a different student research team, ninth or tenth grade or a combination of students from both, and prepared for publication. Dorm students, as usual, could interview local people on campus or could go with me off campus after school. And for those students not interested in the feature topic, other smaller articles on different subjects would be acceptable; and there would be another poetry section that those not otherwise engaged could design and put together. It felt good.

Since the second issue could not be finished by the end of the school year, we decided to complete as much of it as possible before June, allow student teams to do additional interviewing during the summer, and put it all together in the fall.

To pay for the second issue, we decided to sell subscriptions and solicit donations. One of the students suggested that if we had to forfeit on the promise we would be making to subscribers to give them four issues, we could send each of the subscribers a letter explaining the problem and request that each of them who wanted a refund let us know, and we'd pay each back the balance owed by holding car washes, bake sales, and the like. The feeling was that since most would only be owed a dollar or so, most would be generous enough to let the matter drop. Those who wanted their money back, however, would get it, since we had entered into a contract of sorts with them and we had an undeniable obligation.

Continuing to believe that most people simply would not pay more than 50¢ an issue, we voted to sell the subscriptions at $2 each, be far more careful about the number of copies given away, and pray that enough good people would subscribe at Patron rates of $10 per year or Sustaining rates of $25 per year to make up the difference.

It was foolhardy business, but there were indications that we might not be entirely misguided. The letter that had come from John Dyson, for example, had enclosed a donation, and we hadn't even asked for one. John said in that letter, "I only wish that I had sufficient talent to contribute to the section [of poetry and prose by adults. But since I don't, at least] allow those without talent to contribute what we can to *Foxfire*. Those little trees don't grow by themselves. Squirrels plant acorns; nature provides light and water; an occasional cow adds some fertilizer. We just want to be that occasional cow!"

The students laughed and clapped, and happily took John's check to Mrs. Cook for deposit in our account.

Almost unconsciously, I had decided to stay and teach the next year. One moment it had been a very real question mark; the next moment students and I had already made plans. It was done without my quite knowing how it had happened.

In a moment of sobriety, however, I realized that it could not happen without some changes. With the exception of holidays, I needed only the fingers of one hand to total the number of full days I had had off from work. There had not been a night spent in the dorm when I had gotten to bed before midnight. Sometimes the job had taken on surreal, bizarre qualities that seemed humorous weeks later but carried damn little humor at the time. Several weeks earlier, for example, on the night before April Fools' Day, the houseparent whose assistant I was, remembering with a shudder the previous year, had told me that we would have to stay up all night to prevent mischief and vandalism. He suggested that I stay up and watch over things until three A.M., and then come and wake him to take my place so I could get a few hours' sleep before teaching the next day. Word of this plan somehow got into the elaborate student communications system, and that night every student went promptly to bed. Nothing stirred all night.

The next day was not one of my high points as a teacher. That night, when I did get to bed, I slept as I had only slept before at Cornell after staying up for days preparing for final exams. At about one A.M., when both myself and the houseparent were sound asleep, the students got up and quietly made a shambles of the entire dorm.

I could not teach full-time, work with students out in the community on articles in the afternoons, keep a dormitory at night, and run weekend recreation programs and expect to get anything of consequence accomplished next year. There just weren't enough hours in the day.

The first step was to unload the dormitory obligation for the next year, which I did.

The second step, which I hoped would be approved, was to request a reduced teaching load (and a reduced salary) that would give me the freedom to try a number of solid things with students that I suspected they would respond to but hadn't had the opportunity to test. I drew up a formal proposal to the administration, which read:

A PROPOSAL FOR MY JOB FOR THE YEAR 1967–68

I believe that there are many students here capable of doing far more than they are doing. They must have the opportunity and the stimulus to do so if they are to get all from high school they should.

I believe the amount of factual material students carry with them from high school is negligible. Here they should learn responsibility, discipline, budgeting of time, enthusiasm, appreciation—traits that will carry over into all they do, and assure them success both in studies and in college and their chosen fields.

I believe students should be given a multitude of opportunities to express themselves, to find their talents, and to be recognized, praised, and encouraged.

I also believe that it is a cold fact that only the most excellent and skilled of teachers can provide deserving students with the above while called on to complete the mass of routine which must be dealt with first.

I suspected, when I talked with you last November, that *Foxfire* was one way to provide much of what I felt was lacking. What I saw when the magazine came out confirmed this belief. Ask any tenth-grader. They are excited and proud. The Clayton High School for the last two days has even been teaching the magazine in class. Students have already gotten in touch with me from this school offering their various talents. Look at the faces of the students whose names appear between its covers. They are glowing, and that's what we want.

I believe that I have done a good job this year. But I haven't even gotten up a good head of steam. I couldn't, because when I went home with a new idea, I also went home with a hundred papers, three lesson preparations, and two tired feet. And when I needed to get away for three days to recharge, I couldn't, because I had to face a geography class the next day at nine A.M. or a dormitory obligation that night. I did the job you gave me, but I never got a chance to show you what I could do.

Here's what I'd like to do next year (and I would very much like to be here next year):

1. Put out *Foxfire* on a quarterly basis. I have a stack of leads—enough material for twenty issues—and a group of students itching to get started. This could all be accomplished both through a literary club made up of the editors and through regular class work in all the English classes. Teachers could select their students' best compositions and submit them to us, for example. I would be more free to work with students on interviews.

2. Put on plays—at least one with each class (all grades). This does not include working with the senior play, which I am doing now and would like to continue doing.

3. Conduct a creative and expository writing class which could be of variable length depending on demand, need, etc. The class could be drawn from many grade levels, even to the extent of having eighth-graders working together with seniors. It could be duplicated each day with several groups.

4. I could supplement instruction in the art class. There are many skills in art with which I am familiar enough to teach. And why not add photography?

5. Lectures given to any grade level in an area of special interest to the class during my free periods, at the request of the teacher in charge. I could even take one class for a week or more, giving the teacher (who would sit in on the classes, of course, so she could follow up effectively) a break, and providing students with much-needed variety and excitement.

6. Field trips. Writing classes or art classes outdoors, for example. These could be taken to any spot of interest, be it an old building, a waterfall, or a mountainside.

7. Get special permission from various teachers to work with a gifted (and voluntary) group from one of her classes for six weeks, and a slow group the next, on various special projects which would be tailored to the groups' needs and abilities. Each activity would be planned carefully in advance with the teacher to avoid conflict in her lessons and help relieve her of the burdens of class size and variety.

The whole effect of all this would, I believe, be to remove some of the burden from all of the teachers of English, and provide students with numerous avenues for creative expression and good learning experiences that will stand by them the rest of their lives.

I would also be available for special projects such as hikes on various Sundays, recreation (I have several ideas for the rec center), etc.

I would be spending very nearly as much time at the school as I do now, but I would be accomplishing more than I am now, would be more excited myself as I would be working often with students who *want* to get down to work, and I could get away when I needed to without causing such an uproar. I would also be freed to do some of my own writing, as I would be freed from much of the routine that now encumbers me.

You ask about salary. Considering what I believe I would be accomplishing, and considering that I would be at the school very nearly as much as I am now, and considering that my salary as a regular teacher next year would be $5500, I should think that what I have offered would be worth at least $3500. It would be hard to do with less, as I can hardly expect much income from my own creative projects my first year on the market.

Respectfully submitted,

B. Eliot Wigginton

I also believed that I could begin a student newspaper and a student tutorial program, both based on previous experiences at Hill, but I wanted to adopt a wait-and-see attitude on those projects.

The third step was to move off campus and find housing elsewhere. The constant, inevitable contact with students while living on campus was good in many ways, but I suspected that some distance was going to be vital as I got more and more deeply involved with teaching and writing.

I was thankful when my request to the administration was approved, and shortly thereafter Mrs. Hambidge offered me a half-finished two-room cabin on her land. If I spent one summer finishing the construction of the cabin, building the cabinets and furniture and landscaping the grounds, she was willing to let me stay there rent-free.

With summer, I threw myself into physical work with the relief of a wanderer at an oasis. I traded in the Volkswagen van for a jeep and spent hours loading it with rocks from a nearby creek and hauling them to Mrs. Hambidge's cabin for the rock walls I built. I bought tools and hammered and sawed away into the nights on cupboards, cabinets, closets, and crude furniture. I varnished the walls, then sanded and varnished the floors; hooked up plumbing; bought a used oil heater and a storage tank and hooked it all up, and I finished the outside construction and stained the whole cabin forest green. I was the happiest I had been in months. I didn't really know what I was doing, but I banged away and blackened a couple of fingers and got stain all over my face and arms and laughed a lot as it got steadily closer to being livable.

A constant stream of students came by to watch all the commotion, and if they had time to stay around, I put them to work and worked them shamelessly without pay. Sometimes I'd go on campus, and dorm students who were there either for summer school or to work off tuition money they owed would crowd around the jeep and ask to be allowed to come and help. I'd go through the red tape necessary to get several of them signed off campus on a Saturday, and we'd pile into the jeep, work part of the day, and then go climb a mountain like Pickens' Nose and sit on the granite outcroppings on the very top, our legs hanging over the edges, and watch hawks drift past below us and watch the clouds color up toward dusk. That evening, as thanks for their work, I'd haul them to The Villager, Kate Cathey's little restaurant, and she'd exclaim over all the dirt and torn shirts and tired faces and fill them up with hamburgers and French fries and make jokes about how I was going to kill them all and ought to be locked up; but as often as not, we'd part reluctantly at the dorm.

Several times that summer dorm students I had worked with wrote me letters and asked permission to come up for a few days to help out, and I'd get to the cabin and find one of them sitting there on the porch, waiting.

And by the end of the summer, I had a rent-free home.

11

A Coffeehouse,
Two New Issues,
and a 501 (c)(3)

My second year as a teacher began with my determination to single-handedly salvage the careers of those students who were unhappy. It was mad, of course, but I was too young to know that. I was still naive enough to believe that school should be a place where every student thought that he or she was being stretched to capacity and where every student was actively engaged in useful, productive, positive, rewarding, exciting work. In fact, I still believe that, but I have become more realistic, with age, about the possibilities of that ever happening.

I focused primarily on two groups of students:

•Those dormitory students who were resentful, rebellious, restless, angered—justifiably or not—by their perception that they were imprisoned in an unfair institution where every aspect of their lives was monitored. Most of them chafed under the relentless scrutiny and the fact that every hour of every day was programmed, a fact that was simply reinforced by the endless succession of bells from morning to night, and many were prime candidates for dismissal. The fact that some of these had been sent to the school because they needed to be away from an unfortunate home situation made dismissal a rather unsavory option as far as I could tell.

•Those community students who were simply bored and who felt that no school was capable of serving their needs.

Naturally other students who fit neither of these categories found themselves caught up in some of the projects I initiated—which was fine —but in all cases, the projects presupposed that what the students really needed was to become involved in productive, responsible activities that would consume their energies, teach them something in the process, and dissolve their bile.

Some ideas worked; others were stillborn and never flew. But the net effect was one of action and forward momentum, of energy expended usefully. And when something failed we simply laughed, learned what we could from that failure, and walked away from it to try something else. At the very least, there was electricity in the air.

Two ideas that I had high hopes for were doomed. One was the tutorial program. Approved by the administration, I got as far as engaging the interest of several seniors through presentations in their English classes, but with no tradition of this sort of intense independent research at our school, the inordinate amount of hand-holding and cajoling and scheduling necessary to make it go sapped all the pleasure out of what should have been enjoyable work.

Another was the formation of a singing group modeled after the Peter, Paul and Marys of the day. Twenty students showed up for the initial meeting, and the enthusiasm was there, but it was a doomed venture because I had not the slightest notion of how to make such an activity work, and I couldn't find anyone who *did* know who would help. They seemed like good ideas at the time, but both died natural deaths as we found more fruitful avenues for our energy.

One of these was the creation of a monthly student newspaper. The principal and the president agreed to split the cost of stencils and mimeograph paper between their two accounts; I recruited some students and circulated Dittoed sign-up sheets among the others; and we stumbled into business with representatives from nearly every grade. With virtually no expenses, and thus no need either to sell the paper or to solicit advertising, we could concentrate on making the contents go well beyond the normal high school fare. Articles during the first year, for example, featured subjects such as what last year's seniors were doing; now, analyses of the national sports scene, including profiles of sports figures such as Johnny Unitas, Joe Namath, and Lew Alcindor; how the school itself had changed over the last twenty years; and a behind-the-scenes look at preparations for an upcoming student play. In among the more traditional news items and calendars and the apparently mandatory who-

would-be-paired-up-with-whom humor appeared reasonably logical editorials on topics like "What Makes a Great Teacher?" or "The Negro
Boycott of the Olympics." Each issue contained a letter to the students
from one of the faculty members concerning his or her particular subject
area and its relevance and utility, as well as a "Letters to the Editor"
section that was sometimes provocative.

And in an attempt to get a more reasoned dialogue initiated concerning some of the rules against which the students rebelled (and hopefully
to begin to build some understanding on both sides), I trained the students in the mechanics of poll taking. Selecting an issue that was hot at
the moment, the editors would create and Ditto off enough copies of a
questionnaire to distribute in home rooms to every student. The students, who remained anonymous, would fill them out, and as some editors tallied the results, others interviewed representatives of various view-
points (including members of the administration and teachers) and
prepared those interviews for publication. Issues of the paper that featured such special-interest sections invariably created a stir. Whether they
really uplifted the tone of the dialogue is a matter of some conjecture, but
I like to think they did. They were certainly fun to put together.

On one such occasion, we pushed the limits too far. We had worked on
assembling and stapling the papers well into the night and had left them
bundled in an office for distribution the next day. One of the more
conservative adults who worked at the school opened the office the next
morning to get it ready for the school day, read the paper, found something that set him off, and took all the papers to the basement and burned
them in the coal stoker that heated the building.

This action threw the editors into a predictable frenzy when they arrived to proudly distribute the labors of the previous month. Luckily we
had saved the stencils, and with Mr. Brown's patient and more reasoned
intervention, we replaced the offending section with some hastily created
filler and ran the papers off again.

On another occasion, I confiscated the papers myself and refused to
allow their distribution because the stencils had been so poorly typed and
proofread that the finished product was an embarrassment. I told the
editors that if they wanted the paper to go out, they'd just have to report
back to the building that night and do it over. It was a gamble, but they
talked the matter over among themselves, agreed, and that night we all
worked together to type new stencils and run it again.

Gradually we learned together, and the paper began to take on an
identity of its own. Several years later, it was being printed professionally,
in tabloid size, complete with photographs, and had matured into a
product of which I and the students were justifiably proud.

A sore spot of increasing dimensions for me during this time was the
recreation center, a drab two-story brick affair that had once been the
school's gymnasium. It was open two nights a week for the hour between

supper and study hall, and was chaperoned by pairs of teachers and staff members who endured their tour of duty on a rotating basis. Downstairs, against one wall, were jammed two bowling lanes with hand-loaded pin setters. A couple of Ping-Pong tables in an enclosed windowed area on the other side of the room, and a tiny adjoining room from which students could buy soft drinks and candy and rent bowling shoes, completed the offerings, except for a few wooden benches that defined the outer edge of the bowling lanes. Here students would sit and visit above the racket of crashing balls and pins. With its cement floor, army surplus barracks paint, and harsh fluorescent lighting, this virtually indestructible little area was about as inviting as a heart attack.

Upstairs, the remains of a basketball court were available for that game, and the noise downstairs was complemented nicely by the sound of bouncing balls and thumping feet from above. The whole effect reminded one a little of being inside a drum at a rock concert.

To this center, groups of community and dorm students would come to relax, visit dispiritedly together, and perhaps even hold hands, depending on which adults were in charge that evening. It was virtually the only recreational option available on a weeknight unless there was a school basketball game. There was no music—only an unvarying routine of activity—but if you didn't take advantage of what was there, you pretty much just had to do without.

Several of the students and I were talking about all this one evening. A couple of the students, as usual, were griping about the situation, and one thing led to another, as such conversations have a way of doing, when someone said, "Well, why don't we try to have the place fixed up?"

"Naw, they'd never do it. They don't care. In fact, I don't think they *want* us to have a good time down there."

"Well, maybe they'd let us fix it up if *we* did the work."

"Yeah? Well, they won't give you any money to do it with."

"They won't have to. Let's just vote to take the profits from the boys' dorm Coke machine and do it with that!"

The Coke machine. Each year, in the spring, the dean allowed the elected dorm council to decide how it wanted to spend the profits. The previous year they had voted to have a steak dinner for the whole dorm, and although it was fun, the money was gone in a twenty-minute orgy and that was that. Another year to wait for the next event.

At this point, I interrupted and said, "Well, if you guys want to vote to do something useful with that cash, something that'll last awhile that people can enjoy far longer than a stupid supper, I'll do whatever you want me to do to help pull it off." Since I knew the administration wouldn't let the students work in the building unsupervised, I had a pretty good idea what the bulk of my help was going to have to boil down to, but there was no question about the fact that the job needed doing and that just about anything we accomplished would be time well spent.

Besides, I had developed an abiding interest in watching the process by which negative energy could be put to positive use, and I had become fascinated, through activities like the newspaper, by how much could be accomplished for a very tiny bit of cash when that cash was multiplied by lots of heads and hands. It still fascinates me, and I've become convinced that one of the greatest adult cop-outs in any school, and the world outside, is the statement, "We might as well not even try to do that because we don't have the money." When someone says that to me, that person and I are about to enter a difficult time in our relationship.

From all appearances, the dean was delighted with the proposal we hit him with the next day, as long as the work was done during times the boys weren't supposed to be somewhere else. He gave us a key to the rec center, and we went there to begin some figuring. By the end of the session, the boys had decided that about the only area we could work in with any real profit was the enclosed downstairs room and its tiny annex. Their main concern was that they had no place to which they could take their dates and talk quietly in something resembling an attractive atmosphere. At that period of time, coffeehouses were popular, and since having a place where they could take a girl and dance was out of the question, creating a coffeehouse seemed the next best alternative. Since we had no tools, no paint, no materials, it was obvious the shop teacher was going to have to be tapped. Luckily he was a decent character named Mr. Wild, who genuinely liked young people and had a touch of solid craziness about him that had led to his affectionate nickname, Wild Man. An inveterate scrounger, he took us into the back storage room of the school shop and grinned as he snapped on the lights to reveal a secret hoard of gallons and gallons of paint, bought for virtually nothing at a local hardware store when the suppliers had discontinued a line of colors that weren't moving. Some of the pinks and lime greens were pretty awful, but here and there a can of harvest gold and some good browns looked promising.

"If you're going to build a coffeehouse, you're going to need tables, aren't you?"

"Yeah. And we don't have any."

"Well, spend some of that money on cheap plywood and one-by-fours and four-by-fours and we'll make them. How many you want? Eight? Ten? No sweat. I'll show you how to make them in one evening."

Over the months that followed, a gang of students became involved. The girls volunteered to make curtains for all the windows, including the long row of windows on the inside walls that separated the bowling area from the former Ping-Pong room. Since we knew we could scavenge wagon wheels and plow points and lanterns and metal gears and all manner of interesting junk free from surrounding farms, we had decided on a rustic, country decor; and so part of the money went for the burlap the girls and the home ec teacher whipped into plain but serviceable and attractive curtains. Community students, alerted to the project, began to bring boxes of junk from home, and what they couldn't bring on the bus, the boys and I went to their farms in my jeep and picked up. Four free wagon wheels were turned into chandeliers in the school shop. Sheets of D-grade plywood were painted yellow, and the junk was cleaned up, arranged in interesting collages on the plywood, wired into place, and then the panels were hung on the freshly painted walls. Floor tiles were purchased, and I got permission from the dorm parents for a group of us to stay up late one night and lay a new floor. When the dean dropped in to check on us near midnight, work was in full swing, a portable radio blasting away from one corner, and he seemed satisfied with what he saw and let the boys stay until they finished. Another group completed the tables, painted them brown, and hauled them to the room. Someone came up with a used hot plate and a milkshake machine, and what had previously been the soft drink and candy room became a kitchen from which students could make and sell hamburgers, sandwiches, and shakes. A pile of classroom chairs no longer in use was discovered, and they were instantly appropriated. And when it was all done, to an outside observer it might not have seemed like much, but it was an oasis to which students could retreat and have something resembling a nice evening, candles and all.

In the tradition of all great high school events, the professional student hams took over and plotted an elaborate opening ceremony complete with refreshments prepared by the dining hall crew, prepared speeches from a jerry-rigged stage, and a ribbon cutting. And it didn't damage the festive mood a bit when it was proudly noted by one of the boys that the whole thing had "come in under budget." Subsequent evenings saw the room used constantly.

There were snags. One of the more conservative faculty members insisted, during her tour of chaperon duty, that the curtains on the windows be tied back so she could "see what was going on in there." It would have been difficult to have had a respectable den of iniquity with milkshakes, hamburgers, and forty or fifty kids at seven P.M., but the students were too proud and happy to let her suspicions dampen their spirits. To their eternal credit, they cooperated without complaint, letting the fluorescent lighting from the adjacent room flood in and pretty much destroy the ambience they had worked hard to create.

By midyear, we were rolling. When Mr. Brown asked me for an interim report on my experiment, I typed and handed him the following:

February 26, 1968

Mr. Brown:

As per your recent request, I have listed many of the accomplishments which have been made this year under the status I have held with the school.

Some of the projects listed have not as yet been completed, but they are so near to being finished that I have included them.

1. Initiation of a Quill and Scroll chapter in this school. The first members of this national journalism honorary society will be installed in March.

2. Continued publication of *Foxfire.* Two issues have already appeared this year, and a third is ready for the printer. A fourth will appear in May. Student editors have participated fully in all phases of the magazine, and the number of students who have already been published (including the March issue) is more than fifty. Subscriptions, newspaper articles, etc. have appeared from across the country. The Smithsonian Institution and the University of Georgia have requested copies of our tape recordings. This Sunday I received an invitation to attend a Conference of Small Magazine Editors in Chapel Hill on April 10–13, and serve on a panel. My job will be to tell the other editors of our experiment here, how it was started, and how it works.

3. A newspaper has been started which now appears monthly. Nearly twenty students are involved in its publication. The fifth issue of this paper is now being assembled.

4. I have conducted supplementary classes in many fields, as promised:
English: 11th and 12th Grades—units in footnoting, bibliographies, outlining, newspapers, and journalism have been held.

9th and 10th Grades—units on haiku poetry and writing, Greek mythology, debating, and reading have been held. Split-class units have been taught on *Call of the Wild* (two-week unit with slow readers), *The Pearl,* and *Huckleberry Finn* (one-month units with average and above students—Miss Jones worked with the slower ones during this time).

8th Grade—unit on reading and short stories (one week).

Reading—unit on reading and its importance.

Social Studies: Units on Machiavelli's *The Prince,* and debating were held. Mr. Heffington and I also held a debate on the Supreme Court before his classes. A unit on the stock market is in the works now.

French: Unit on the Bayeux Tapestries.

Business practice: Unit on speech and personal appearance.

5. By next weekend, the room which we have been refinishing in the Recreation Center will be completed. Many community students have been responsible for bringing in the decorations for the walls; the girls in the home economics classes made the curtains, and the boys in the boys' dorm provided the labor (and most of the funds). They laid the tile, painted the walls, built the tables, hung the decorations, etc.

This center will be open to all students, community and dorm alike, and will serve as a coffee house where students may display various talents such as folk singing, musical combos, one-act plays, poetry readings, etc. Two acts have already been scheduled as of this date.

6. This year I was responsible for five pages in the annual. These pages contain photographs, and literary work by more than twenty of our students.

7. I have, in addition, tried my best to involve myself with the after-school hours of the school. This has included teaching Sunday school each Sunday with the dean, helping dorm students during study halls, personal counseling, and involving them as much as possible in activities around the school. I have also opened the gym on many occasions for basketball, driven student groups to away games and other entertainments (such as the New Folk concert in Dayton, Tennessee), etc., etc.

That's about all I can think of at this point, although I am sure there is more. Suffice it to say that more than half of the above listed activities could not have been carried on with a normal teaching load—at least not along with my particular style of teaching. I can only hope that you feel you have gotten your money's worth—and I hope you will be receptive to an even more expanded program which I have in mind for next year, barring some unforeseen consequence.

Respectfully submitted,

Eliot Wigginton

Several teachers had taken advantage of my availability and had let me prepare whole units of instruction for their classes, thus freeing them to concentrate on the needs of special students, to develop in more detail units of their own, to make good use of specialized activities that require two adults working simultaneously in a class, or to just simply take a break and have a cup of coffee. Through the rest of the year, this continued. In addition, I pitched in every afternoon in the spring to help direct the annual senior play, helped with weekend recreation, and inaugurated a Monday-evening lecture series in the coffeehouse to help fill an otherwise empty evening. One of the few occasions that year when I got genuinely angry with students was during the first Monday program, initiated by one of the faculty members, who presented a slide show. Several of our students, despite the announcement I made at supper the night of the program explaining its seriousness, the absolute necessity of good behavior, and the fact that only students who were genuinely interested were to attend, came determined to disrupt an event I had worked weeks to set up. During refreshments at the end of the program, I let my temper get the best of me and banned the offending students from the Monday evening programs for the rest of the year.

I should have handled the situation differently, but at least my action had a sobering effect on the remainder of the students, and those who weren't interested simply stayed away. Meanwhile, the sixty or so who came each week, knowing that I would not tolerate rudeness, were models of good behavior; and with increasing confidence, I brought a series of community people to campus for supper and presentations, which ranged from ghost stories told by two older mountain women to a faculty member who made knives as a hobby to two married friends of mine who were building their own house in the woods, to a retired moonshiner who held everyone in the room spellbound.

And, of course, there was *Foxfire*. During the summer, subscription requests had come in either as a result of a sales job by a student or one of several articles written about the project in state newspapers and magazines. Some of the students and I had met regularly to keep up with the business. The second issue, featuring planting by the signs (see *The Foxfire Book*, pp. 212–27), was published and mailed to people who had subscribed. In an introductory letter to the issue, I wrote:

NOTES

The first six hundred copies of *Foxfire* disappeared within the first week of publication. A second printing of six hundred of the same issue is now exhausted also. Letters and subscription requests came in to our office from across the country—literally from coast to coast. Some of the letters are reprinted in the response column.

One letter that we especially value was cautionary as well as complimentary. It warned us that it is terribly hard to produce a second issue that is as good as the first, for so much effort goes into the first issue that one's energies are often exhausted in the process. We hope you do not think that is true of the issue we give you now.

For this issue, we have interviewed nearly fifty people. Most of these interviews revolved around the feature article whose subject is the signs of the Zodiac, and how they govern the daily affairs of many of the families in this region. To these people, this is not superstition or fantasy. It is fact, passed down to them through generations of ancestors whose whole life was the land and the forests that surrounded it. The Zodiac is, to these people, a religion based on years of proof. We hope you will find the article interesting.

"Anatomy of a Revival" does something we believe to be rare in magazine publishing. It reproduces for you, word for word, a message delivered recently by a young evangelist at the Joy Baptist Church. After listening to the tape recording we made of this particular revival, we felt that the message we have reproduced here would make fascinating reading.

Our outside writers add, as usual, a new, and we think an essential dimension to *Foxfire*. Some of them have been published hundreds of times in hundreds of magazines across the country. They help us keep our balance. They allow us to feel the pulse of what is happening NOW in writing. They keep us from being too regional, too limited in scope, too small-minded and too small. We believe that we have something to tell them, and that they, in turn, have something to tell us. We exchange ideas. We exchange beauty. Thus we exchange things of great worth.

The same is true of our younger writers who are students in high school whose writing shows great promise. They are students with something to say. Students who have hit on an idea or a thought, and made it sing.

And there is much more. New remedies, superstitions—we have even added two new columns. One is devoted to the stories behind many of the fascinating place names of this area. The other contains recipes that we think are unusual. The latter is edited and compiled by Mrs. Margaret Norton of Betty's Creek. The survival of these columns will depend largely on you—the reader. Do you know something that we haven't mentioned yet? Do you *want* to know the story behind something we haven't printed yet? Tell us. You may find yourself a contributor or the cause of a whole new column or article.

We intend to create and preserve enjoyable and significant work of literary and historical value. We want to bring you days of exciting, informative reading. A huge task, but one worthy of the effort. Tell us how we're doing. Then pass the word. *Foxfire* is still here, and growing.

                                                                    BEW

As we waited for reactions to the issue, I wrote to Howard, who was in London, on October 8, 1967:

I don't know when you'll get *Foxfire*. I just found out that the lady who runs the post office here sent the magazines by surface mail instead of air mail to save me two bucks, so they are probably lost on a ship somewhere between here and there. This is a funny period—this time right now. The last issue has just gone out to those who care, and most of them haven't gotten around to writing yet, so I don't know whether they liked it or not. One is never sure what the response will be. All we have to have is one real dog of an issue and we're dead. The printer would go unpaid, refuse to do the next issue, and that would be that. That curious and mystical ritual that dictates the transference of the green stuff from one person to another is a diabolical invention. Anyway, the mag is broke and I am broke—and so I always wait out this silence in a cold sweat—rather like the moment when communication was lost with John Glenn on his way down—no one knew whether he would emerge from the static cloud victorious, or just another cinder.

And yet one goes on preparing for the next issue and the next, trying not to think about it at all. The next issue is half done.

Your father's check, and a hundred others like it, will keep the tape record-ers rolling. And that's important, I think. Many of these people speak poetry and don't even know it. Harley Carpenter, while taking us to see his ginseng patch, talked in a steady monologue about the trees around him. Stopping in front of one, he said, "When that tree's old, it looks dead, but it's as white as a snowball when y'throw a notch inta it. It'd make mebbe about a 35 B pole. Bet my watch against a dollar it's sound above that cat face. Pump it with th' axe and see."

Yeah.

                                                                    Eliot

Response to the second issue was louder and more positive than reac-tions to the first. John Dyson's letter was typical:

. . . It is superb. In particular, the idea of inserting a larger number of pictures is very attractive for those of us who are not able to see the Rabun Gap area first hand. I found the articles on planting by the signs and the revival meeting to be of exceptional merit. For those of us who fancy ourselves scientific farmers, the method of planting by the signs seems a bit quaint. But while it is fashionable to deplore these methods of agriculture, I believe it is important that they be understood because they have worked so well for so many people for so long. Your article goes a long way to expand our knowledge of this important style of agriculture in America.

Heartened, as the twelve hundred issues disappeared and more subscriptions came in, we paid the printer and went to press again, this time with an issue devoted to the Cherokee Indian, because, as I said in part in the introductory letter:

It all started with a story about some Indians from one of the families we interviewed. . . . I suddenly realized that this section of the country was once the center of one of the finest Indian tribes in America. Not only did they at one time call almost the entire Appalachian region their domain, but their first capital, Tugaloo, was nearly within walking distance of us. The same tribe that produced the first Indian alphabet and the first Indian newspaper also named most of the mountains and streams I see every day as I go to work. The same tribe that signed more treaties with the English than any other Indian group once had several villages (Sticoe, for example) in Rabun County, and a village of about 12,000 inhabitants at the headwaters of the Little Tennessee —all a stone's throw from here. A census report of 1835 shows that more than half of all Cherokees lived in Georgia at that time. DeSoto and Bartram came through Rabun County—a county itself created from lands acquired from the Cherokees in the treaty of 1812. Many inhabitants here lay claim to Cherokee blood in their ancestry.

It's all a story that needs to be told; and so, three months ago, we started getting it ready.

And as I wrote Howard on November 14:

Anyway, we are getting there. This next issue is a good one, I think. But we may have made another mistake by putting all our eggs in one basket—i.e., by making the whole thing a collection of articles on various aspects of the Cherokee Indian culture. If we did make a mistake, so be it. Too late now. And I have a hunch we didn't. We said something that needed to be said—and I am also in hopes that the center poetry section (printed on colored stock) can be removed, and the whole thing reprinted as a pamphlet for sale this summer —a handbook on the Cherokee, as it were. And perhaps the first of a series of pamphlets that will be published by us and sell for $1 apiece and provide a steady income for our other issues. But this is all in the hope stage at the moment. I am sort of counting on the belief that there is a market for this sort of pamphlet, and I can see possibilities for many others. There has to be some way to get this steady income thing down pat. This area will not support us much longer, I am afraid, so I am pushing harder and harder to get our circulation outside our area. I am still fighting, also, to keep ads out of our pages. The *Reader's Digest* would doubtless give a hollow laugh at that. And a year from now I will probably look back on the thing as hopeless high school idealism. I already look back on the first issue as horribly amateurish. But we keep experimenting, and getting closer and closer to a good thing, I hope.

Thanks to the fact that I was not carrying a full teaching load, I was also able to explore actively other options for the students and the magazine that I simply had not had time to get to until now.

Through the first issues, for example, because the only camera we had was a pretty tricky, delicate twenty-year-old affair that even I was not entirely competent—or comfortable—with, I had taken most of the photographs. Since I didn't know how to print, I had let Bob Edwards do all our printing. Both facts were clearly inconsistent with the philosophy that was gradually enveloping our whole project.

With Bob's help, I found a good single-lens-reflex camera that was sturdy, serviceable and reasonably inexpensive—one that I could pay him for over time. Through trial and error, using several rolls of black-and-white film, the students and I learned how to use it together.

Marie Mellinger, a local naturalist, and her husband, Mel, had become interested in our work. When students brought in home remedies that called for plants that we couldn't identify, Marie was the person to whom we often went for help. Mel was an amateur photographer who had his own darkroom set up in a small basement closet, and he offered to teach me how to print and let the students and me use his darkroom as soon as I knew what I was doing. Watching my first print materialize in the developing solution was magic, and I printed pictures most of that day. From then on, until we finally got our own darkroom built on campus, whenever we needed prints for an upcoming issue, students and I would drive the gravel road up Boggs Mountain to the Mellingers' house. Mel didn't have a print dryer, so we'd take a bucket along, fill it with water there, and bring our wet prints back down to Bob's Kodak shop, where he'd let us run them through his drum dryer and then go over them with us and offer suggestions for improving either print quality or composition. It was a rather cumbersome process, and at times, I'm sure, inconvenient for those community people involved, but they hung in there with us. We are still good friends today, and as I gained confidence myself, I could share the techniques to the point that students were finally taking and printing all the photographs.

A comparable situation existed with major interviews. Never having done interviews of this sort before, I was too nervous about the whole process personally—and too ignorant about its finer points—to be able to teach it well. Consequently, though I always took students on major interviews, either out of my own insecurity and fear of "empty" spaces in the conversation, or out of being caught up in fascination about the subject, or both, I often dominated the process. Students were never sure whether or not I was about to ask a question, and I wasn't sure about them, so I'd go ahead and ask one, they'd slip into the background, watching me, and I'd wind up stealing what should have been their interview.

With a reduced work load, I was able to take them out on more and more interviews after school hours and on weekends, and we grew together in skill and confidence and understanding to the point that I was willing and able to remain in the background myself. At the end of the interview, I would usually ask a few questions to pick up on points the students had missed or clarify things I just didn't understand (knowing from past experience that they probably didn't understand them either but had been too nervous or too polite to push harder into the topic), and on the way home we'd "debrief," and I'd comment on their questions and the responses they had triggered, and they on mine. We simply learned together.

Over time, I became more concerned about and skillful at identifying those areas in any project involving students where I was taking too heavy a hand, and as I sublimated my own ego and relinquished an increasing amount of control, the involvement and cooperation of the students increased proportionately and problems with discipline virtually vanished. Some of the lessons learned on a ginseng hunt had begun to bear real fruit.

At Christmas, again thanks to my flexible teaching schedule, I was able to extend my vacation a week to follow up on some possibilities for *Foxfire* that had emerged in Washington and New York. I drove to both cities in January, 1968.

John Dyson, from New York, had written several times, "I trust you will not hesitate to let me know should the financial situation of *Foxfire* become precarious," and, "I hope you will be able to come up north sometime in the near future so that we might be able to discuss *Foxfire* at greater length." I took him at his word.

Having just been in the midst of the process of setting up a nonprofit tax-exempt corporation to carry out some projects of his own related primarily to historic preservation in the Hudson River Valley, John was particularly interested in seeing me pursue a similar course with *Foxfire*. With 501 (c)(3) status, individuals could donate to our cause to their own tax benefit, and we would also become eligible for grants from various groups that could only contribute to such organizations. Until that conversation, I hadn't even known what *incorporation* meant, much less that we might be eligible for such status. John offered to have his lawyers look into the matter for us, however; I agreed, and over the next month, with their help, a set of by-laws was drawn up for a corporation to be called

The Southern Highlands Literary Fund, Inc. Its main purpose would be educational—specifically the preservation of folklore in the Appalachians and the encouragement of literary endeavors, through publishing. John and Howard and I would be its initial directors.

In the same conversation, John offered us a gift of $1,000 but suggested that rather than taking the money now, it might be wiser for me to contact several other potential donors and see if his offer could be used as a lever to get them to match with at least a partial amount. This strategy of saying "Group A says they'll give us something *if* we can find a Group B to match it" was another one of which I was ignorant, but it made perfect sense.

I was a little confused by all this—it was a huge amount of information to assimilate at one sitting—but vastly encouraged at the same time, because it was the first occasion on which someone was not only genuinely enthusiastic about the project but also willing and able to make some major commitments unselfishly in our behalf. Of course, John was prejudiced toward us by our prior friendship, but that didn't diminish the fact that someone outside our region had confirmed our experiment in some very positive and practical ways.

From John's, I drove to Washington. Luckily, one of my sisters was living in the city, so I could stay with her, avoid a lot of expense, and deal with some errands that I felt were important. Embarrassingly enough, for example, I knew nothing about copyrighting procedures, and so the first issues of the magazine had not been copyrighted. I hadn't even thought about it. Neither had I thought about checking to see if anyone else was copyrighting a magazine with the same name as ours. What if there was another *Foxfire?* A visit to the Library of Congress was obviously a high priority.

I had also heard of a group called the Coordinating Council of Literary Magazines (CCLM), headquartered in Washington, which, unbelievably, gave money to small magazines. I didn't know whether we'd qualify or not, but certainly we would pass the criterion of size with flying colors.

With John's offer in the back of my mind, I went first to see David Bournes at CCLM. They had never given money to a high school publication before, but since we were building a subscription list that was national in scope, and since we were printing poets of beyond-high-school caliber, and since there was a matching offer from the Dyson Foundation to lend credibility to our cause, there was some negotiating room. Our request, like all the requests they received, would have to go through a meeting of their board, after which they'd let us know.

At the Library of Congress, I was introduced not only to the mysteries of copyrighting but also to Joe Hickerson and Rae Korson at the Archive of Folk Song, both of whom presided over a collection of tape recordings, some of which had been made in the Appalachians by collectors like Alan Lomax, of whom I had known almost nothing. In addition, I stumbled across the spectacular files of Farm Securities Administration (FSA) photographs, some of which I had seen before in James Agee's *Let Us Now Praise Famous Men* but had never realized could be reprinted by magazines like ours since they were in the public domain. I also went to meet the library's Poet-in-Residence for that year, James Dickey, who immediately became interested in our story because his father's people had come from our area, and who agreed to call several people he knew in the CCLM organization on our behalf.

I also found out about the vital work Ralph Rinzler was doing with folk life and material culture at the Smithsonian's Department of Performing Arts. I got an appointment with Ralph, and he, like the others, became excited about *Foxfire* and the fact that high school students were involved, and he expressed an interest in having copies of our tapes and photographs for their files. He also asked for our help in purchasing some of the crafts of our area for their collection to supplement works he had bought on previous visits.

Those few days in Washington were a complete revelation. For starters, I had just been initiated into the fact that much collecting of music, folklore, and crafts had been done in the southern Appalachians but very little in the north Georgia section where we were working. As such, we were part of a long tradition with a definite role to play and a huge contribution to make—a contribution made even more significant by the fact that virtually none of the previous collecting had been done by people actually from the region, and absolutely none had been done by its teenagers. Most had been done by trained academic professionals from the outside. In profound ignorance, we had begun to plow in new ground.

The visit was also a revelation in that for the first time, I realized that institutional monoliths like the Smithsonian and the Library of Congress are actually staffed, behind the stern architectural facades and the impressive letterheads, by very approachable human beings. I had the distinct feeling of suddenly having worked up the nerve to snatch the curtain from around the Wizard of Oz. The days of "Oh, they would never have the time to talk to us" came permanently, blessedly to an end. None of the people I visited in Washington had heard of us before, and I had no reason to expect a single one of them to spend any time with a stranger like myself who virtually walked in off the street. But every one of them saw me, every one of them was helpful, and every one of them affirmed that what we were doing in Georgia was genuinely important work.

Not long after I returned to Rabun County, filled with tales for my students, a letter arrived to them from Ralph that read in part, "I am deeply impressed with the breadth of scope and concern for detail in your articles on folklife subjects. They bring a fresh approach to this type of documentation by coupling the accurate presentation of a body of fact with a warm rendering of the spirit of a people. Let's hope that *Foxfire* will make its way into enough libraries to influence the scholars' approach to the same subject matter."

And several weeks later, a CCLM grant for $500 having been approved, I and the students sat looking at $1,500.

12

"I'll Be Back to See You Graduate"

The spring of 1968, by and large, was a good time, but the degree to which I was involved with students, morning to night, despite the fact that I was out of the dorm and living off campus, was steadily escalating. A new issue featuring faith healers (*The Foxfire Book*, pp. 346–68) was published, and with it we celebrated our first birthday. To Howard, still in London, I wrote:

. . . And you should see what's coming up. Articles on stills and moonshining (some concerted and shady efforts during the past four days have turned up *six* stills, all of which were photographed completely), the extraordinary uses of the ordinary farm mule, wild plant foods, beekeeping, craftsmen (one in the area is making me two stools by hand—cane woven bottoms and all—and another is making me a quilt for next winter), mines of the area, the making of sorghum, and onandonandonand . . . It's all a beautiful thing—like, it's *working*. And that's nice. I've climbed so many mountains in the last few days that my legs are shaking, but it feels damn good. And I never want it to end.

Through Ralph Rinzler, the Newport Folk Foundation learned of us, and its director, Bruce Jackson, sent us $500 on behalf of the foundation with a note. "I think it is a splendid publication and I hope you will be able to continue. After watching professors and commercial performers and professional publisher types hack up the folk culture materials, I find it marvelous that a publication as refreshing as yours can get itself going. There is an important role for a publication such as *Foxfire,* as I'm sure you're aware, that not only includes helping people appreciate their own heritage, but also letting outsiders make themselves aware that that heritage exists. I like your format, I like the photos, I like the mix in content."

But almost invariably, just as things were going their best, the outside world would intrude in some bizarre form, or something terrible would happen on campus, and the pitch at which I was operating was such that I was invariably plunged into gloom. It was a manic-depressive existence.

From all external appearances, for example, the outside world was coming apart. The war in Vietnam was a constant, sinister companion, and the country we had been raised to believe was invincible seemed like a giant knocked to its knees by pygmies. Dr. Martin Luther King, Jr., was assassinated on a motel balcony, and we were reminded once again that the country we had been raised to believe was justifiably the very symbol of freedom and justice and equality allowed hundreds of cities to exist within its borders where blacks could not even purchase a cup of coffee at a public lunch counter or swim in a public pool or vote in a free election. The young, idealized by many exactly as portrayed by Norman Rockwell —skinny-dipping at the old swimming hole, getting regular haircuts at the friendly neighborhood barbershop, and strolling through sunny green-gold pastures with the loyal family dog—suddenly were taking LSD and staring at strange posters and letting their hair grow to their waists and listening to music that absolutely mystified many of their parents and standing in lines face to face with National Guard troops their own age, placing daisies in the barrels of the arms drawn against them: our own against our own.

In Rabun County, some still plowed with mules while their children dropped napalm from F104s. In a debating unit I conducted with my classes, the son of one of the most religious families in the county, armed with sheafs of literature distributed by his church, argued forcefully and passionately against integration. The first debates concluded, I then instructed all my students to keep the same debate topics but argue the opposite point of view. He refused. I insisted. He told his parents, and they withdrew him from our school. Permanently. Rumors began to circulate again in the community.

Some students found themselves living in the dorms of our school because their parents wanted them to be as far away from drugs and alcohol as they could be sent. Those were the days when a small group of those students discovered that jimson weed grew wild in our pastures, ate some berries, and almost went slap out of their heads in one of our local hospitals.

Some found themselves at the school because their parents simply didn't want them around. Because phone calls between parent and child in such situations sometimes turn into harangues, use of phones—wisely —was severely restricted. Phone conversations had been known to make a shambles of a kid's life for weeks. So one parent, unable to reach her son by phone, showed up drunk in the dorm parking lot to announce to the bewildered boy that she was about to marry a man he had never met, and then she drove off, leaving him standing there alone and crying. He was one of those students who, through a number of projects, I had gotten to know pretty well, and I cared about him. I redoubled my efforts to involve him in still more activities as I saw him slipping away, and when he was finally kicked out of school and taken from our campus without even being allowed to say good-bye, I almost gave it all up. To keep from unloading on a student, I unloaded on Howard:

Strange days are upon us all. The air seems fouled, and people draw their cloaks more tightly around their faces in fear and confusion. I have never been so perplexed or so involved with the things I see going on around me. Johnson has just eliminated draft deferments for graduate students and all teachers. More men leave for Vietnam this week. Newsreels show the old capital city leveled save for the central portion, which contains the most historic buildings in that godforsaken country, and our guns are trained on that portion at this moment. Cities are being totally destroyed daily to save them from being taken over by Vietcong. Hundreds and hundreds of civilians die by our hand. It is impossible to believe what anyone says anymore. Johnson is completely discredited. At any given moment I can pull out three different magazines which give three completely different "factual" reports on a situation. Kids ask me questions which I cannot answer with any faith. One fourteen-year-old cries out for help, and I cannot, not knowing how. He is shipped, sent home to an aunt and uncle who cannot stand to have him around, and two days later disappears. Not knowing this, I write him a letter, the uncle opens it, reads it over the phone to the dean, and asks if I (whoever I am) know where he is. Yeah, I know. He's in some crash pad in Atlanta on Fourteenth Street with about thirteen other runaways of the same age, getting laid every night and smoking everything he can get his hands on. And I can't find him. Garbage men in New York strike for (and get) a salary of a little over $8,300 a year—more than twice what I am making. And I do not understand. One cannot run, and yet, failing to know how to fight, cannot do anything but run . . . There is no such thing as unchallenged authority because there is no authority worthy of enough respect to make it unchallengeable. No one is right—and everyone is right. No one is wrong, and everyone is wrong. Our country needs a hero, and failing to find one in our President and our government, it turns to those without responsibility or fear—those who live without regard for others—and our country worships them with a deep, silent, and often jealous admiration, then tries to mimic. Eighty-year-old women wear miniskirts. Twelve-year-old girls turn into whores. Childhood is dead, and yet there is no one who is not a child yet. We squabble like chickens and wait for someone to throw us more corn, and complain bitterly when they do not. Sometimes I can't help but think that if there *is* a God, now is the time for him to show. I can think of no surer cure for all this than a vision of a Hell so terrifying and so awe-inspiring that it grips us by the throats and does not let go.

I know this is confusing—but I am confused. I can never remember a time when I have been more discouraged by the direction which I see us taking as a country—and I can never remember a time when I have had so little faith in the judgment of the young. At times like these I see them not as a hope for tomorrow, but only as a damnation upon their parents and those who have guided them into the position where they believe that the world is theirs for the taking, no strings attached. There is no right and wrong. There is only mindless response to every whim and every impulse. Theirs is an age without restraint and without judgment, and without responsibility—and I don't be-lieve that I say this unthinkingly. There are certain responsibilities that must be faced, no matter how unpleasant, just to keep us going. The world cannot be a twenty-four-hour-a-day Dionysian festival. It just doesn't work that way.

Hell. It's all too confusing to figure out now. I can't help it. I just rebel when I see *Esquire*'s presentation of twelve-year-old microboppers (so-called) who smoke, drink, and tell their parents where to hop off. I rebel when I see nineteen-year-old kids leveling a society in Vietnam. I rebel when I see thousands of teachers walk away from their jobs in Florida. And I rebel when I see people all around me giving up, and yet I want to do the same, not knowing anymore the difference between what is good and what is bad—what is right and what is wrong—what is clean and what is foul. Strange days, indeed. At least for me.

Unarguably, good things were happening. Sometimes everything would click and I would be in a state of euphoria for days. Then the shadow of the mad preacher in Davis Grubbs's *Night of the Hunter*—the preacher with the word *Love* tattooed on the fingers of one hand and *Hate* on the other—would fall across the campus, and it would seem as though we were all adrift in a tiny boat on a river with the ominous silhouette of the preacher and his horse riding along beside us against the darkening sky.

One night (well after dusk so that hopefully my jeep would not be noticed) I was sitting in a local roadhouse with a couple of friends having a beer, and as friends who are drinking beer are wont to do, we began to talk about what we wanted out of life—where we were headed, and how. And as we talked, I began to realize that with every move I made, my options were narrowing. *Foxfire* was in the process of being set up as a corporation, the presumption being that it would continue. Students that I was close to were, now that it was spring, beginning to talk about what we were going to do during the summer and the following school year, the presumption being that I would be around. And for the first time, I became extremely uneasy. With all the things there were to do in the world, and all the causes there were to which one could become productively committed ("Ask not what your country can do for you . . ."), *was* Rabun County, in fact, where I wanted to stay? Was teaching at the high school level for the rest of my life the best use of whatever talents I had? Was *this*—this sitting here hiding after dark drinking beer—was this *it?*

With serendipitous timing that couldn't have been choreographed more carefully, Geof Hewitt, a friend of mine from Cornell days, wrote to tell me about a graduate program he was just completing in the writing seminars at Johns Hopkins, a program that led to a master's in English, which gave the students plenty of time to write, and the tuition and expenses for which could be paid, if one wished, by teaching a section of freshman English. He further said that if I had any interest in applying for the program, he'd put in a good word for me with Elliott Coleman, the director. Within a few days, I had made up my mind to apply, and did apply, and was accepted. I was going to Hopkins.

At that point in my life, I knew I needed nothing so much as some distance—distance between myself and my students and Rabun County; distance that perhaps would give me some perspective on all that was happening; distance that would allow me to sample some other career possibilities.

I had a long meeting with my principal in which I explained the situation. The object of most concern, of course, was *Foxfire* and the obligations we had to a number of subscribers. I explained that next year the students I had started the magazine with would be seniors. Many of them had had major responsibilities with *Foxfire* for nearly two years. This group included his daughter, Jan. If I had done my job reasonably well over those two years, and if he would give the students an opportunity to meet on a regular basis during the school day, without faculty supervision, they should be able to run the operation themselves. I would stay in weekly contact with them through letters and by phone, and we would see. If the students let the magazine slide, and it had to be folded, I would come down to assist in that process and help clean up any loose ends. On the other hand, if they proved they had learned enough and cared enough to keep it going, and I decided not to return, it should be a relatively easy matter for another faculty member to take it on.

Would I be coming back? That depended on many things. But if I did come back, I'd probably be back to stay for as long as they could put up with me.

With his agreement to allow a group of students to try their hand at running the magazine alone, I met with the senior editorial staff. In many ways, it was the hardest meeting of all. I loved that motley bunch of characters, and I loved the feelings I had for much of what we had accomplished together against pretty substantial odds. It was difficult to explain that my feelings for them and for our work together were among the main reasons that, if I was ever going to leave at all and try anything else, it had better be now, for they almost had me tied down, and I just had to think about whether or not I wanted that to happen.

Besides, it was a perfect opportunity for them to prove to themselves and to the world outside that they were ready to leave high school behind and enter into adult responsibilities and obligations. It was a chance for them to put themselves on the line.

They understood, they accepted the challenge, and they vowed that *Foxfire* would continue.

Over the last weeks of school and into the summer, we collected raw material for another issue and we polished the working relationship we would have the following year. All business affairs, collecting of information and photographs, article preparation, publicity, and recruitment and training of new editors would be in their hands. As material for a new issue was finished, they would send it to me, and, to keep any other faculty members from having to be involved, I would do the final typing and page preparation from Baltimore, since the typing of camera-ready copy for these sixteen- and seventeen-year-olds, though possible, was an endlessly frustrating experience, and it was the one obstacle in the way of my being able to turn the entire operation over to them alone.

Through a series of meetings, we also made some hard decisions about aspects of the business that had been troublesome or confusing, and we created an operations manual, or editors' handbook, that laid down operating procedures and gave clear directions for handling every situation we could think of. During the summer I typed one manual on Dittoes for duplication, one copy to each editor, and included an introductory letter, part of which read:

INTRODUCTION

This is going to be short and sweet—my real message to you is on the last two pages of this manual,* so this introduction is going to be just that . . .

[This] contains our workings at this point in time, a portion of our history as

* Looking back, I see that those last two pages of the manual turned out to be frighteningly prescient. Entitled "Our Goals for the Future," the goals included:

1. A subscription base that would cover the costs of production. [That has been accomplished.]

2. A scholarship fund for students. [To date, over $200,000 has been awarded in scholarships to our students.]

3. A fund for helping to start similar magazines in other parts of the country. [Initiated by IDEAS and the Ford Foundation, there are now hundreds of such magazines.]

4. Publication of a series of books about Appalachian customs. [The Doubleday series and our own Foxfire Press have made that a reality.]

5. Promotion of area crafts. [Partially realized through the publicity that area craftspeople have received, that goal continues with plans for a retail outlet and mail-order operation being finalized.]

a magazine, our purposes, and our future goals. It contains article ideas, the names of useful contacts—even where to get paper clips and index cards when you run out. This manual *is* Foxfire, and thus it should be of special concern to you.

It is very hard for me to believe that now, after two years—and now that those of you who started this whole thing with me are moving into your senior year—that now, of all times, I should leave you alone. But my reasons are good ones, and, in fact, it is *because* those of you who started *Foxfire* with me are seniors that I *can* leave this year. Who else could I better trust our magazine to than those who started it? When *else* could I leave with confidence—and what better hands could I trust *Foxfire* to?

Many people I have talked to don't think you can do it. I don't think you can either—I *know* you can. And I know, despite the difficulties you are going to run into this year, that you will. If you can't do the job, then no one can.

Good luck. And, God willing, I'll be back to see you graduate and move on to make this world a better place for all of us to live in.

In August, I loaded my jeep with belongings and drove to Baltimore.

---

6. Jobs with *Foxfire* for former students. [Now an established part of our program, three of the students who ran *Foxfire* while I was gone have served on our adult staff. A summer job program also employs twenty to thirty a year. A priority remains hiring former students to fill new job openings as they occur.]

13

"We're Working Hard!
. . . When Are You
Coming Back?"

The first letter from Judy Brown, the editor in chief (granddaughter of
Harry and Marinda Brown, both of whom are familiar to readers of the
Foxfire books), arrived almost immediately after the school year began. It
was followed by a stream of correspondence and phone calls from nearly
all the students. On rereading those letters, most of which I saved, I was
struck by the way they shifted in tone from "I" to "We," and from "What
do we do about . . ." to "We have decided to . . ."; and by the way
school officials were obviously willing to extend a hand when it was
needed, but otherwise kept hands off and trusted those students to operate with responsible autonomy. On several occasions, the president of the
school, Dr. Anderson, took magazine editors with him to speak to various
Rabun Gap–Nacoochee Guild groups, who normally raised money for the
school but who were encouraged on these occasions to donate money
directly to *Foxfire*. It all amounted to the best kind of cooperation one
could expect from any school administration, and it made a tremendous
difference in the quality of the experience those students had.

But the best way to tell the story of that year is through these letters themselves. It is unnecessary to include them all here, but the excerpts I have chosen tell the story better than I could:

September 24, 1968

Things are running smoothly and everyone is pitching in.

David has reminded me for several days to include an inquiry. Do you have that [poem he wants to include in the new issue]. He said that if you would tell him if any changes need to be made, he would write the author and get his permission. He would like to get it ready for the next issue.

Mickey gave me two recipes from [his grandmother] Margaret Norton. Lorraine has some that I will probably send up next week.

Chuck is writing some speeches. Dr. Anderson has asked some of us to go to one of the Guild meetings. Chuck, David and I will do the agony! This will be October 31.

Jan, Mike Cook, Gail and I went to see Mrs. Harley Carpenter. In order to get the article [on making baskets out of honeysuckle] we are going to help her by getting the [honeysuckle vines] and helping her with the dirty work. By the time we get through with this article, you may get billions of baskets from us in the mail.

Jan and I have been getting the files straightened out. Next Thursday we'll probably mail out subscription renewal propaganda.

I have tried not to forget anything!

Judy

P.S. I have made definite plans to go to Reinhart College. I'm getting a job working on publications there. It's in the bag!

October 5, 1968

Now is really a time that I wish that you could be here! Monday afternoon we were in Mountain City. We got pictures of a bubby [sweet shrub] bush and a remedy to go along with it. But that's nothing to compare with what Mrs. Adams at the Rogers House gave us! An old woman, before she died, gave Mrs. Adams two old journals. On the pages she has pasted recipes over the figuring on the pages. This goes back to about 1903! This one really caught my eye: "Cure for pneumonia. Take six to ten onions according to size and chop fine put in a large *spider* then add about the same quantity of rye meal and vinegar enough to form a thick paste, in the meanwhile stir it thoroughly letting it simmer five or ten minutes then put in a cotton bag large enough to cover the lungs and apply to the chest as hot as the patient can bear." This was written in pencil in one sentence!

I'll copy some of the recipes and send them up to you. I'll give them back to Mrs. Adams as soon as possible. When you come back, that's one of the first things that you must see!

Enclosed are two poems by Chuck.

Today at our meeting, we fixed the renewal stuff to send out. Mike and Kathy are working on a subscription pitch. It should be ready to go out next week.

Mike and Joey are having trouble getting the guys to talk to them about sorghum.

I did get one churning article for #8. Linda has brought in some stuff for it. Mickey is also working on it.

Will have some tapes featuring Mrs. Lula Thomas by next week. Hair-raising tales!

Judy

October, 1968

[In answer to questions you had on the churning article I sent,] a standard size churn has a capacity of four to five gallons. Use from 1/4 to 1/2 teaspoon [salt] per pint of butter. It usually depends on the person adding it. They didn't use measuring spoons. They poured it into the palm of their hand to measure it or measured in pinches (thumb and forefinger).

We got two patron subscriptions this week.

April 5, I'm to represent Rabun Mills in the Miss Mountaineer Festival Contest. I thought I'd go through with it. Of course it's good experience, I hope!

Judy

October 10, 1968

I've been getting along pretty well with the subscriptions. I've had a few minor problems, but I think I've gotten them straightened out all right. At least I hope so!

At our meeting last week we all addressed envelopes to the people whose subscriptions have expired and not yet been renewed. I've run off on a stencil a note of thanks to new subscribers. Also some copies of the bill.

Do you remember that list of other things you gave me to run off right before you left? Well—guess what? I lost it. So would you mind sending me another list so I could get that done?

We got a subscription request from a Dr. Claude M. Ivie who is head of curriculum for the State Department of Education. He also asked for back issues of the magazine. Daddy told me he was a pretty important man and for me to send him the back issues with our compliments. He said he would pay us back out of the school fund. Then I went ahead and billed him for his subscription. I hope that's all right.

Things are going pretty well at school. We got report cards today and I'm not doing as well as I'd like, but at least I'm passing. Hope you're having a good time. Don't work too hard!

Jan

October 25, 1968

Chuck, David and I will be talking to the Senior Nacoochee Ladies Guild next Thursday. Chuck has been writing the speeches. He is using a modified version of last year's with the exception of the one I had, which was some-how lost.

Loraine has found a great source of information to get recipes and reme-dies. Mickey gave me some stuff about churning. Should we start getting information about log cabins?

In the new manuscripts, in one letter, the poet says, "I'm not a spring chicken." That really brought down the house! We liked that better than his poems.

There weren't too many manuscripts that anyone liked.

Judy

November 6, 1968

We have $600 or more in the bank. This is counting $112 that the Junior Nacoochee Guild has promised us! They put on a small project of which we get the proceeds.

We raked in $120 Thursday at the Senior Guild. We had a good time and the speeches went over great. We speak again on February 11 in Athens. Right now I don't know who to.

Judy

November 11, 1968

We beat you to the punch! Jan typed out a thank-you message on *Foxfire* stationery [to the Junior Nacoochee Guild] and everyone signed it. We will give them a complimentary subscription.

The lady from UPI called today. She will send us copies when she gets the article about us finished. It sounds like it will be great!

How's the weather there? We've actually had snow in November! It's going to be a long hard winter. Sigh.

Judy

P.S. Happy Birthday!

November 13, 1968

Enclosed are manuscripts [with the editors' comments and votes].

Everyone on the staff has been assigned, and is working on, articles. Each Thursday they are to report their findings of that week. This way they'll do a thorough job instead of a quicky that's not so hot.

Working hard!

Judy

December 20, 1968

Over the holidays we're going to wear out the tape recorder and learn how to take notes. We hope to get the log cabin article in the bag.

This may be a bad time to do it, but most of the kids are going to try to sell some subscriptions over Christmas.

Merry Christmas!
Judy

January 5, 1969

The new bill from Cross Printing is for the sum of $3,386.18. Shocking? Jan and I are wading through the mail. We took in $199.95.

Your article in *Media and Methods* was great! Have you seen copies of it?

Celestine Sibley [Atlanta *Constitution*] ran another article about us. We have already had some response from it.

Comments about the last issue have been coming in. I will send a few of them up.

I hope your new year goes well!

Judy

January 21, 1969

Last week was kind of rushed for me. This one also promised to be. My grandfather died last Thursday night. A few weeks before, I had talked to him about building log cabins. He was in a traffic accident on Wednesday.

This week is the Ragana Pageant. I'm doing a dramatization of Scarlett O'Hara. "As God is my witness . . ." My nerves are just about shot!

David has just about completed his article. [Another] churning article should be finished soon. We interviewed Andy Cope about log cabins. He and my grandfather are the only sources we have been able to find. All the others are long since gone.

The *Media and Methods* [article response] just won't quit! It has brought the most response. That is especially good since it has been mostly from school libraries.

I might end up sending two packages this week.

We sent Cross Printing $1,200.00.

Judy

January 27, 1969

Judy told me to write you and ask for your ideas for [additional requirements for new editors and how and when to pick them]. I'm to [be in charge of] that for her.

We are in English now. I made a 341 on the Verbal part of the SAT. If you can, find a workbook that I can understand that will help me get through English 101 and 102 in college next year. I will be going to Young Harris. Any ideas as to how I can pass college English, please send them to me. I have trouble with it as you well know.

We're getting a lot of newspaper clippings in the publicity book. I'm trying to keep up with all of them. I have to go study now. Sorry this is so short.

George

February 19, 1969

I have enclosed Chuck Perdue's article on churning, and David W. and

David M.'s articles on music. As soon as Loraine gives me several more local chants, I'll send what we have on churning. You might have to edit it more.

On February 11, Chuck, George and I spoke to the RGNS Guild in Athens. We raked in forty dollars. Some wanted to send subscriptions in the mail. One of the women went to Sunday School with you. I think some of the women remarked what a darling child you were then!

Next time I write, I'll try to send a copy of the page ad we took out in the Holiday on Ice program [this year in Atlanta]. We haven't had any response from it yet, but maybe it will be a mindsticker next time they see it.

We like the new plan for membership requirements tremendously. It works! George was the right person [to put it into effect].

Judy

March 1, 1969

Things are going pretty well here. We are still getting a lot of orders, some of them still from the *Media and Methods* article.

I sent those twenty-five copies off to Senator Talmadge the Monday after you called. I sure hope something comes out of that.

I just have about three or four questions this time. First, when people send the back issue order form wanting those issues we have marked "sold out," what do I do? Today I got an order from a woman who wanted issue #3 and the sold out issues and she said, "If you can get me these two copies (even used) I would appreciate it." She sent $3.00. I wrote her back and told her that unfortunately, we were unable to obtain either of these copies for her but if we reprinted them anytime soon we would notify her. I sent back $2.00 and sent her issue #3. Right?

Number two: we are beginning to get a few orders asking for five or more copies. I'm having trouble trying to find boxes the right size to fit them in. Like we've had two requests for twenty-five copies and one for eighteen and two or three for five. It seems kind of funny to send twenty-five copies in an Aero Wax box. Do you have any suggestions as to what I should do?

We have been getting some orders from bookstores [out of the area]. What should I do about discounts for them? When I sent eighteen to the Georgia State College Bookstore I gave them a 20% one which would make $36.00 less 20% = $28.80 coming back to us. But I thought I'd better write and ask you about it before we get any more orders of that type.

This time we've gotten about the same number of renewals as we did last time. Not a lot, but I guess percentage-wise it's okay.

Daddy said he paid Mr. Cross another $500 the other day. $200 of it was *Foxfire* money and I think he said he got the rest out of the activity fees and we'll have to pay that back.

George has been handling that stuff about how to get on the staff. David W. seems to be doing a lot of work as I guess you can already tell. I know I need to get a junior member started on my job—I mean showing them and letting them help me do stuff—but I can't find anybody much interested. Do you think a dorm student would have enough time to do it? I know I should get started because it isn't very long until graduation.

I hope everything is going all right for you and you are still planning to come back next year. When you have time, let me know about these things.

Jan

March 12, 1969

I have the English workbooks you sent me. I have looked them over and like what I see.

We lost in the state tournaments Saturday night, so with no ball practice, I will be doing two lessons [in the workbooks] a night. That way I will be through with them by the time you get here in the summer. I've given the answer sheets to my mother and she will be checking them for me. I am also taking the chapter tests which means I'll know if I need more work in that area.

The staff requirements you [suggested] for *Foxfire* I think will work. We put them into effect as soon as we could. Mr. Brown said the Junior Staff candidates cannot meet with us so we are setting up special meetings for them. We also changed the requirements so that the dorm people have a better chance to get in. We have about ten working for Junior Staff and six that are Senior Staff.

I believe David W. will be the editor in chief the next two years. Man he works! He also knows what he's doing. In his service record, he has as much as all the others [combined].

Write back when you have time. I'll write and tell you how it's going.

George

March 22, 1969

We're getting piled under with mail here again. Those magazine articles really help out a lot. In the last two days, we've gotten $147.00. Almost all of them were three-dollar subscriptions. Today alone, we got thirty-eight letters. Pretty good, huh?

Well, here come the problems again. Some woman wrote and said, "Please, where can I get a piece of foxfire wood? Very interested. RSVP." Well, Judy and I sure don't know. Even if we did, does she want us to *send* it to her? What should I do?

Hope things are working out about the grants—although if money keeps flowing in here like today ($107.50!) we won't need it!

Jan

March 25, 1969

Mail has been pouring in like mad! We are having a meeting at Jan's house tonight and getting some other kids to help us. At the present rate it's practically a matter of hours until every penny will be paid on the last issue!

Judy

March 25, 1969

The workbooks are helping. In English we are going over some grammar now.

Some of the people on the Junior Staff are not doing any work and I'm going to start giving them the word in about a week.

If you have any ideas of how to get these people to work, tell me. Also if you have any ideas what a person can do to beat the drag from day to day living tell me. I get up and go to bed and that's all life means any more. It's my problem. Not yours.

Do you think you'll be down for our graduation on June 1?

George

April 10, 1969

We can count on about 1100 subscribers to mail the next issue out to. Jan estimated that 200 to 300 subscriptions came in so far as a result of the article in the [National Geographic] School Bulletin.

We have decided to address the envelopes in the library at night because of the problem of getting the dorm kids out. The editors have sold quite a few subscriptions. When their relatives see Foxfire, they become a ready source of information. Great, huh?

We meet tomorrow during assembly period. I'll see if I can get a little more action out of the juniors.

Manuscripts and comments are enclosed. Write!

Judy

April 20, 1969

The supply of back issues is running low so I'm not putting an ad for back issues in with the new issue.

We may be just a little late in getting the issue out. We have all the envelopes addressed but still lack doing all the other stuff. The letters have about flooded us under. I think we have about $1,200 in the bank now, though. There hasn't been much time at all because of senior play practice, tennis matches, banquets and all the extra stuff—but after this play is over we should have more time. We are planning to work Sunday.

Bell rang. Got to go.

Jan

April 22, 1969

Bad news. David W. told me yesterday that he may go to a prep school at Rome, Georgia, next year. I forget the name of it. He is the only one who can take over the editor in chief next year. What I thought was we (the senior editors) would offer him the job anyway on the promise that if going would help him to improve himself that he go and leave Foxfire. I am going to ask the others to go along with this.

I work as much as possible on the workbooks. I don't do all the assignments but read and study what they are and work as many as I have time for.

I went to Clayton this morning. Mr. Cross said the plates for the new issue would be ready by the end of the week. I'll send a copy as soon as possible.

I'll be looking forward to seeing you June 1 for the big day. Write.

George

P.S. Parents all say hello!

14

Homecoming

All teachers have had the experience of seeing a ragtag collection of seemingly undisciplined, hopelessly varied young people come together as a working unit for a common cause. It may be anything from a sports event, a school band concert, or a dramatic production to a choral presentation (complete with dungarees and dirty tennis shoes poking out from beneath too-short choir robes). For those adults who did not assist in the birth of this new creation and see it whole for the first time, it is usually a revelation, and comments like "I had no idea Susan could do that" are the order of the day.

Those teachers who worked for months to help make it happen, however, know that there is a moment in time when this creation—be it a football team or a debating club—takes on a life of its own and becomes, almost miraculously, a sum greater than any of its individual parts; a moment when students stop thinking about personal glory and strive for the success of the whole.

Sometimes this happens in front of an audience, and at magical times like this, the best teachers recede into the background, allowing the students to savor the moment and drink in the applause. At other times, it happens with only the teacher as an audience, and the best of those teachers say *not,* "Look at what I've created" but, to the students, "Do you understand what you've just done—what you've just become?"

This backseat role is vital to the whole educative process. Nevertheless, teachers have egos, too, and they can be forgiven for allowing something inside to swell with awe and pride and gratitude as this thing they midwifed justifies the faith and confidence and energy they invested in it. It is among their finest creations, and, paradoxically, its end product—be it a play, a game, a magazine, or whatever—can be seen for what it really is: not an end in itself but merely a vehicle used to achieve an end of far greater import—a collection of reasonably whole human beings working and sharing and learning together. Together.

If you'll take a moment to look back at the letters I received in Baltimore from the senior editors of *Foxfire,* given what I've just said, you'll know one of the reasons I went back to Georgia. Note, for example, the number of times *we* and *us* are used when talking about magazine business, instead of *I.* Note the number of times students mentioned working at nights and on weekends. Note the concern over the fact that the junior editors being added to the group weren't working as hard as they should have been (read: hadn't yet become an integral part of what was very much a working whole).

By comparison, the year at Hopkins was a disappointment. That is not to say the school itself is bad; far from it. It is only to say that no experiences I had there that year came close to matching the pleasure and pride that welled inside me whenever a letter arrived on *Foxfire* stationery. I got little satisfaction from my own writing, even though some of it was published. The excitement I had once derived from seeing my name in print had largely vanished, and writing emerged as a far too solitary and introspective choice as a career (one of the reasons I've had such a difficult time with this book, and why it took seven years to write).

And so, halfway through the year, I knew where I was going to be in the fall. And I knew I'd be there for a long time.

That decision made, I began to use my free time to drive to Washington on a regular basis in search of help for *Foxfire.* Using my sister's apartment as my Washington base of operations, and using my knowledge that most of those buildings were filled with decent folks, I covered a pretty good chunk of that city.

John had been sent to Vietnam, but his lawyers were proceeding with the paperwork necessary to create The Southern Highlands Literary Fund, and it was up to me to create an advisory board that would work in tandem with the board of directors of that corporation for its benefit. I wanted advisers who could be of real help to us—not famous names and window dressing—and I set out to find them.

Many young people, after the dreams of being firefighters and police officers and train engineers have been dealt with, turn their thoughts to being photographers for *National Geographic.* That seemed like a logical place to start, and so one day I walked into their headquarters in northwest Washington, stepped up to the receptionist's desk in the lobby, and said, "I don't know a single person in this building, so I don't have an appointment with anyone. But I'm a high school teacher from Georgia, and my students and I publish a magazine, and I want to talk to somebody in here about it. I'm not even sure exactly what I want. I just know there's information inside this building that we can use."

If the woman behind the desk was surprised, I couldn't detect it. It was as though this kind of thing happened to her every day. She simply picked up the phone, dialed someone's number, and asked the person on the other end if she had time to talk to me. And it was in exactly that way that I found myself in Ethel Starbird's office.

After she'd heard my story and looked at some of the magazines I'd brought along, she picked up her phone and called Ralph Gray, the chief of the *Geographic*'s School Service Division, which published the *School Bulletin* (now *World*) as a classroom supplement to—or substitute for—the parent magazine. He was a perfect choice, agreed to become one of our first advisers, and, as one of his first acts, published an article about *Foxfire* in the March 24, 1969, issue of *School Bulletin* that brought in, at final count, over five hundred new subscriptions and, as Jan said in her letter to me of April 20, 1969, "about flooded us under."*

Revisiting Joe Hickerson and Ralph Rinzler, both of whom had expertise in the kind of work we were doing, numerous contacts that they could share with us, and the ability to nudge and guide us in some extremely productive directions, I added them to the advisory board too.

From each, I collected new names, and quickly the list of people who knew about our work and could help in various ways grew. Before long I had a notebook full of names of folklorists, anthropologists, and men and women deeply involved in the study of cultures. In fact, there were more names than I could deal with—names not only of people I should contact but also names of professional folklorists it was felt I should avoid, as their orientation was so academic that they would probably attack us for urging untrained high school amateurs to attempt the kind of collecting that "only trained professionals should be allowed to undertake."

In addition, there were names of journalists who might be persuaded to write articles about *Foxfire*, and foundation officials who might be able to help with additional funding. There were names everywhere. I'd come into town after having made appointments with as many as I could contact ("Joe Hickerson said I ought to visit with you and tell you about our project. He thought you'd be interested"), and my calendar would look

---

* Ralph's sister, Ellen Massey, a high school teacher in Lebanon, Missouri, later started a magazine like *Foxfire* with her Ozark students. Named *Bittersweet*, it ran for ten years, and a compilation of the best articles, entitled *Bittersweet Country*, was published by Doubleday in 1978.

like the catalyst for a coronary: "9 A.M., Sam Stanley, Museum of Natural History, 12th and Constitution, Room 323, get pass from guard by elephant in Rotunda/10:30, Laura Olson and Nan Robertson, *N.Y. Times* Bureau, 1920 L St. N.W., take mags/Lunch, Ralph Gray and associates, *National Geographic*, 17th and M, call from lobby on arrival/1:30 P.M., Barbara Bode, Charles Daly, John Kleinbard, Children's Foundation, 1026 17th maybe $? take mags/2:45, meet Dr. Granger in lobby of Statler Hilton to talk about Adv. Bd./4 P.M. Topper Carew, Ernestine Potter, "New Thing," see brochure, black culture pres., inner city/before 5, call Jack Conway, Center for Comm. Change, Conf. mtg. tom. w/he and Ed Kahn . . ."

On one of these typically mad sprints through the nation's capital, right at the end of the school year, I was shown into Junius Eddy's cubicle at the U.S. Office of Education. We still needed money; time had run out in terms of my living so close to Washington that I could run into town at the convenience of those people I wanted to see; and I was close to being completely frustrated by the amount of legwork involved in finding support. Well, I was a public high school teacher, and over there was the Office of Education, and I had every right in the world to be inside that building, and someone in there, by damn, was able—and ought to be willing—to help.

Junius heard me out, looked at the magazines I had brought, and became visibly excited. Though his office itself could not help us directly, he knew people who might. There was the newly formed National Endowment for the Humanities, for example (an institution of which I had never heard). Junius picked up his phone and dialed a number. "Herb? Listen. There's a young man in my office that I think you need to meet. He's got a remarkable story to tell and you ought to hear it. When can you two get together?"

Though Herb couldn't see me that day, he was more than willing to meet. It was I who had to postpone our appointment until later that summer. First I had to get down to Georgia for a little ceremony my seniors were about to go through. A call from the President of the United States could not have kept me from that graduation.

15

1969–70: Watershed

The job that I returned to was teaching all four sections of junior and senior English and one section of a newly created journalism course that would house *Foxfire* and *Talon*, the student newspaper.

Most of the summer was spent finishing an issue of *Foxfire* completely devoted to the building of log cabins (*The Foxfire Book*, pp. 53–107) that the seniors had initiated while I was in Baltimore. With students like Jan volunteering their time to keep up with circulation and correspondence until they had to leave for college, I was free to help some of the new editors like Paul Gillespie and Mike Cook and David Wilson, who had been added in my absence by the senior staff, gather the log cabin material. It was a memorable time, with men like Bill Lamb and Harley Carpenter and Hillard Green showing us how to hew logs and cut notches and split huge sections of white oak into shingles. The photographs and diagrams eventually numbered in the hundreds, and rather than trying to get into the classroom building, we assembled the final issue in my cabin at Mrs. Hambidge's, sometimes staying up until well past midnight, with material strewn across the floor, typing and gluing and cutting and pasting. Toward the end, convinced that these new students were ready to be left alone, I headed again to Washington to meet with Herb McArthur at the National Endowment for the Humanities, leaving them with instructions to finish laying out the issue and deliver it to the printer themselves. They took all the material to Paul's house in Paul's father's jeep, deciding it would be easier to work from there. Long after, they told me that when they got to Paul's, upon going over the issue page by page, they discovered that one of the photographs was missing. A search of the piles of cut-up papers and notes in my house failed to turn it up. By now it was dark. It would take days to round up the negative, get to a darkroom, and reprint it, and, panicked, they began to retrace their route, one driving slowly on the shoulder of the road, the other two hanging out the side with flashlights searching the roadside. Amazingly enough, they found it, still lying where it had blown out of the back of the jeep. Paul and Mike still laugh when they tell that story today. The issue got completed and delivered to the printer. With that experience, the core of the new editorial staff was forged.

If there was a watershed period in *Foxfire*'s history, it was the 1969–70 school year. With my English classes, I continued to explore ways to integrate the production of *Foxfire* and *Talon* into the normal curriculum. The journalism class shouldered the publications' production burden, working largely from a card table set up in the back of my classroom. After school hours, students of any age who were not in my classes were welcome to accompany editors on interviews, help us hand-address and sort subscriber envelopes in the library for a new issue, or participate fully in whatever work there was to be done. And there were scores of them who did, giving me my first opportunity to explore the rich possibilities inherent in having a wide variety of age groups and ability levels working together.

We were rocked by the loss of our first contacts—three of them almost simultaneously. In the introductory letter to Volume III, Number 3, I wrote:

I have just returned from Luther Rickman's funeral, and that fact makes me genuinely sad on a day when I should feel elated because we are going to press again. Those of you who have been with us from the beginning will remember that the first tape recording we ever made was retired Sheriff Rickman telling us about the time the Clayton Bank was robbed. A transcription of that tape appeared in our first issue.

Later he became a primary source of information for our moonshining article—a man through whom we got most of our material for that issue, and with whom we checked much of the rest. I recall in particular an evening when he took us to visit one old moonshiner whom he had arrested several times, and then set up an interview at his house for us with another. The stories they swapped on those occasions made that article one of our very best.

As if that were not enough for one issue, I must also add the recent deaths of both Andy Webb and Marvin Watts. Mr. Webb and his wife were featured in our faith healing issue and Mr. Watts in our Cherokee Indian issue. In both cases, they made major contributions to those topics.

There are several reasons for noting all this. One is as a symbol of the tremendous gratitude all of us feel for the time these three spent so unselfishly with us. They were far more instrumental than they ever knew in whatever success we can claim as a magazine.

A second reason is that I personally feel a very real sense of loss. I am not originally from these mountains, but I regarded all three of these men as friends, and I hope their families will not mind my sharing their sadness.

A third reason is that the loss of these contacts simply points up once more the urgency of our task. Through them, we have all rededicated ourselves to the job at hand and redoubled our efforts to tape and photograph those people who still know the answers to our questions. The fact that these men have reforged our determination may, in the end, prove to be their greatest contribution to us.

For all of the above reasons, the students involved in the production of Foxfire voted immediately and unanimously to give this issue to the memories of Marvin Watts, Andy Webb, and Luther Rickman.

We will miss them all.

BEW

New publicity appeared, this time in publications such as Saturday Review and the Christian Science Monitor. The Georgia Writers Association, urged on by Marguerite Steedman, awarded us their Magazine of the Year honor, and I and the three students who produced the log cabin issue went to Atlanta to receive it. This gave those students their first opportunity to spend the night in a hotel in their own room and experience things for the first time that most of us take for granted—leaving wakeup calls, for example, or ordering from a restaurant menu, or riding in an elevator. They seemed so impressed with the situation, and with their ability to handle it, that from that moment on it became part of my policy to accept invitations to speak only if the sponsoring group would pay complete expenses for several students to come along—a policy I still follow today.

The Internal Revenue Service approved our tax-exempt status, and the administration allowed us to take over our own financial affairs for the first time and keep our own books. The bank agreed to allow student editors to sign checks for the corporation as long as my signature also appeared.

At John's urging, John Viener, the lawyer he had contracted to draw up and file our incorporation papers, was added to the board of directors. A first run of new stationery was designed and quickly replaced by a new version as other individuals I had met were voted onto the advisory board by the students.

To help with printing costs, the Coordinating Council of Literary Magazines came through a second time, awarding us $750 if we could match it with $1500 raised ourselves. In two months, subscribers and friends sent in over $1700. Still wrestling to find a break-even point that would allow us to pay for each issue due our subscribers out of money already in the bank, rather than constantly selling new subscriptions to bring in fresh cash with which to pay the printer, we raised the subscription rate to $4 a year (for four issues), increased the press run from 3,000 to 4,000 copies to meet the new demand, and still the orders came in.

Meanwhile, during my spare time, I put together a proposal for the National Endowment for the Humanities (NEH). It seemed audacious. The vast majority of the endowment's funds were awarded to scholars and institutions of higher learning. There was intense competition from the academic humanists for what, at that time, amounted to a minuscule annual congressional appropriation. The idea that some of that money might actually be awarded to a small rural high school in Georgia was laughable. Herb McArthur had warned me of all the obstacles during our meeting the previous summer; and yet, with Junius doubtless cheering from the sidelines, he encouraged me to submit a proposal, telling me that the decision would not be his but would rest in the collective lap of a panel of independent scholars who would gather in Washington to evaluate all the requests and then vote. I was thankful that, in part because Herb is a naturally affirmative man, and in part because he felt our work had implications beyond rural Georgia, and in part because he responded sympathetically to the fact that I had never written a formal proposal before, he walked me through the application form, noting that it was imperative that we have our tax-exempt status, a complete and accurate budget requesting support only for those things NEH could fund, and a clear and concise statement of our project's rationale and potential value to the field. I spent months drafting it, a piece at a time, in spare evenings, and I suppose that what kept me going, aside from our need for support, was the growing realization that even if the application were unsuccessful, the process of putting it together was forcing me to analyze our work and its implications in a different way. Where *were* we going? What, if anything, made us more than just a high school magazine? So what? Who cared? Why should they?

The NEH deadline upon me, I typed the final draft. Ten copies were required for distribution in advance of the meeting to the members of the review panel. Having no access to a copier, I called Herb and asked if there was any way he could make the copies for me on their machine. I wince when I think of that now, but he laughed and agreed. And in the first issue of Volume IV—our fourth birthday—I was able to tell our subscribers:

[There is a tremendous amount to tell you this time.] First, and most exciting of all, is the fact that the National Endowment for the Humanities has just given us $10,000 to carry the cost of the research we plan during this next year. The grant is to be used, not for printing costs, but for expenses incurred in the way of tapes, film, salaries [for students during the summer], travel, new equipment, and so on. The full implications of recognition of this sort will not be known for months, but I think it is safe to say that this grant will usher in a new phase of our growth that will be truly significant and truly exciting. Now, at last, for the first time, we have some real breathing room.

Minutes after Herb phoned with the news, the students were virtually running around in circles cheering and clapping and knocking over desks. There wasn't anything we couldn't do. The administration didn't believe what was happening. I didn't believe it. Nobody believed it.

In the midst of all the noise, a letter arrived from a fraternity brother, Mike Kinney, who had become an editor at Anchor Books, Doubleday's quality trade paperback division. I had sent out a Christmas letter in which I mentioned a scheme I and the students had hatched to meet the demand for back issues that had long since been sold out. It was vague and not well thought out, but it had to do with taking existing plates from past issues and reprinting especially interesting sections of those issues either in pamphlet form or in a series of handbooks. Articles about log cabin building, chimney building, and the like, for example, or hunting, or foodways, could be clustered together easily for readers who particularly wanted that kind of information. Since the plates were already paid for and in storage at the printer's, the expenses would be somewhat reduced, and it just might make sense.

On December 19, 1969, Mike responded:

Dear Wiggs:
Many thanks for your entertaining and enthusiastic Christmas letter. I can only stand up here in New York and watch you with amazement and admiration as you develop your magazine, spread your ideas, and in general do your thing better than almost anyone else I know. I could say I knew it all along—as indeed I knew you would be a success in whatever you attempted to do—but I never suspected it would be something as interesting and as unique as you have made *Foxfire.* I hope you haven't interpreted my long silences as an indication that I am not interested in what you're up to. As an indication of renewed interest I've enclosed $10 for a subscription to *Foxfire;* if you'll send it to me here at the office, I'll be able to share it with the other editors as well.

And now to business. You mentioned that you are in the process of publishing a handbook on survival and that another is in the works. Have you already signed a contract for the first book? If not, I'd sure like a crack at it for Anchor books. From what you had to say about the book, and knowing the kind of material that *Foxfire* has been producing over the last two years, I'm convinced—as I'm sure you have been—that this could be one helluva big-selling book. I don't know who you've been talking to so far about publication, but Doubleday, with the largest national sales staff of any publishing company in the country, could do a great distribution job for you. Anchor books, which used to deal almost exclusively with college course types of books, is now branching out—and very successfully at that—and the kind of material that you're working with is just the sort of thing I'd like to see us doing. Seems like more than half of my friends have already split for the woods and as Nixon tightens his grip, more and more are leaving every day. The growing popularity of the *Whole Earth Catalogue,* the whole environmentalist thing, is very encouraging. A book of survival done in the *Foxfire* manner—or for that matter just the Wigginton manner—really excites me. Let me know where matters stand, what your specific publishing plans are, and what I might be able to do to help you out. We might even be able to make a pile of money for you. As I think you know, Anchor has just published a book of poetry anthologized by Geof Hewitt. And I think he'll testify that we're pretty reasonable people to work for.

Listen, have a really good Christmas and let me know about your book.

When I read that one to the students, the roof fell in. The whole idea of not having to pay for printing costs ourselves, and of someone else handling distribution of this past material, thus allowing us to go on to new things, sounded perfect. I sent Mike an initial response, along with the log cabin issue which he had not yet seen, and he responded on January 5, 1970, in part:

In particular, thanks for the copy of your issue on log cabins. I sat in my apartment, completely walled off from the rest of the world by what seems to be several thousand acres of asphalt, concrete, and steel, and read the issue with the same interest a starving man would read a cookbook. The explanations were clear, the photographs illuminating—a really good job.

In putting together a book on survival in the woods, do you intend to gather articles like this one on the log cabin from the various issues of *Foxfire* alone, or will you have other sources as well? It strikes me that, given the flavor of *Foxfire* from the beginning, you could make a richer book if you did not concentrate on survival altogether, but gave it some of the same folklorish and literary flavor that the magazine itself has. (It's more than likely that you've already gone through all of this before; these are just the thoughts that cross my mind after seeing the log cabin issue.)

Since I don't really know what work you've done towards doing a book yet, or what your plans are, I can't say much more other than to repeat my interest. Given the unique folkish, outdoors flavor of *Foxfire,* your own organizational abilities, and Doubleday's sometimes frightening but generally efficient printing and sales capabilities, it would be far out to do a book with you.

During spring vacation, I went to New York to see Mike personally and talk out the proposed venture in detail. I knew almost nothing about book publishing, couldn't answer any of the students' questions, and quite frankly was stumped. Pamphlets were one thing—we could print them tomorrow. But a book? We were undoubtedly shy of the amount of material that would be required. Some of the past articles would have to be added to in light of new information that had surfaced as issues had brought in reactions and questions ("Are you sure that's five spoonfuls and not three?"). It sounded like a pretty big job.

Mike and I sat in his cubicle at Anchor much of one afternoon brainstorming, I returned to the classes with what I'd found, and the students and I continued to wonder whether or not we could pull it off. We were pretty busy.

On May 20, 1970, Mike wrote again, saying, in part:

Listen, I really want to do a book with you, and I'd like to get it under contract before long, even if you don't plan to do it for a while yet. Along the lines we talked about—wood lore, survival, poetry, recipes, folklore, all put together in *Foxfire*'s rambling, easy manner. As far as the mix of these elements go, the order, and actual specific content, you'd have complete freedom to do it as you see fit. If you think you can dig this, and really get something serious going, then send me copies of as many of the different *Foxfires* as you can round up, and maybe a one-page summary of the kind of things you'd like to include, and from that I'll whip up a proposal to persuade our publishing committee to let me offer you a contract. What do you think of doing it as a paperback original, maybe 8" by 5½" (that's one of our standard sizes), offset with a goodly number of photographs, priced at about three bucks? The price might sound high, but that's what it costs to do anything other than the regular little-size paperbacks these days. (Christ, a loaf of bread and a half-gallon of milk cost more than a buck in the city now.)

I guess what it is is I'm doing my pushy editorial thing; and you may not be ready for this kind of thing, may want to go elsewhere—if so, don't hesitate to tell me. I just really dig what you're doing, and would love to be able to be involved in getting it out to the widest audience possible.

This time I told the students that we'd better make up our minds one way or the other. We needed to get this behind us. Some discussion, agreement to work extra hours, a vote, and it was done. On July 28, 1970, Mike wrote again, not only with news that he was about to leave Doubleday, but also as follows:

Success! I'm fresh back from a publishing committee meeting where I've been authorized to offer you a contract for the *Foxfire* book—far out!

Terms are as follows: We propose to publish your book simultaneously in hard and soft cover, the hardback at about $6.95, the paperback at $2.95, to be done offset (which gives you the freedom to use all the graphics and photographs you want, wherever you want them) in our "B" size—larger than Anchor, 8¼" × 5¼". We would be able to publish approximately one year after you submit the manuscript. We'd like to offer you an advance of $3,000, ½ on signing the contract, the second half payable on acceptance of the satisfactory manuscript, against royalties of 6% on the Anchor edition, and our standard royalty scale on the hardcover—10% on the first 5000 sold, then 12¹/2% on the next 5000, and 15% on all copies sold thereafter.

I hope this is OK with you—I think it's a pretty good offer. A $3000 advance is unusually high for a first book coming through Anchor, and reflects the incredibly high enthusiasm your project has generated around here—I simply can't keep track of all the copies of *Foxfire* here at the office, with people coming in all day to "borrow" them and rap with me about what you're going to do. The offset arrangement is going to give you a good deal of freedom, and the low $2.95 price for what should be a pretty sizable paperback (we estimate about 250 pages) is really a coup.

So listen: if the offer's to your liking, let me know as soon as possible. I'll need to know whether you want the contract to be in your name or in the name of the Southern Highlands Literary Fund, or whoever it is you want to be receiving the money for this. And I'd like you to give some thought to a title— it would be good to include the name *Foxfire,* and ought to suggest that its contents are both practical and romantic, craft and folklore together. I came up with the very pedestrian "The *Foxfire* Book of Country Crafts" and have been shot down by everyone who's read the proposal.

You ought to understand, also, that in undertaking to put this thing together, it's going to be pretty much up to you to say what goes in and what doesn't, where graphics should go, what photographs you want to include and where —though Paul (the editor who will take my place on this project) will be working on this with you and will explain to you when the time comes how we make up our dummies for offset books, what form you have to submit the stuff in, etc. Oh, and yes, the type will be reset, and anything you want to correct, rewrite, or add can be handled. When do you think you can have it done by?

I'm off in two weeks—getting your book through was my last major project. Now that that's done, I aim to sit back a bit. Please get in touch, call if you like, if there are any questions, anything you have qualms about, even if you just want to say hello. Collect.

I'm real glad about all this.

Love,
Mike

16

Aunt Arie, Suzy, and New Friends in Washington

An intriguing aspect of this whole period of time is that in quieter moments, try as I would, I *still* could not figure out what all the noise was about. Students in schools all over this country had been publishing small magazines for years. Granted, the majority of them were literary in nature, but there still was nothing unusual about a school having a magazine, and though I hadn't known it at the time we started *Foxfire*, it had become increasingly obvious that the collecting of folklore and oral history had been going on for centuries. The only new wrinkle I had added to that process was to have such collecting done by the grandchildren—not by professionals—and to add those findings to the contents of our own literary magazine. Was it that unusual to ask high school students to talk to their elders and write down what they had learned?

Apparently. If any others were doing it, they hadn't made themselves known to us. And that amazed me. Certainly we hadn't started *Foxfire* because nobody was doing anything similar. And we hadn't started it with the intention of making an inordinate amount of noise. We started it because it seemed like a good idea at the time and because it seemed like a perfectly logical way to make an otherwise ordinary English course more palatable and more instructive; and we kept it going because, as a teaching tool, it worked. And because it felt good. Period.

Through that watershed school year, 1969–70, despite all the racket going on about *Foxfire* outside our valley, it was largely business as usual. In my English classes, in addition to reading manuscripts for the magazine, we read from Shakespeare and Thoreau and Emerson and Sandburg and Frost. Over student howls of protest, I urged parents, through a mimeographed letter, to send each of my students to school with enough money to buy a personal copy of the grammar workbook used in the freshman English sections at the University of Georgia, and I made all the students—whether college-bound or not—work every page.

But a deep and subtle shift was taking place in our priorities. In part, it had to do with the confirming experiences caused by outside attention and the hundreds of voices saying, "Nothing you all could be doing together is more important at this moment in time than the collection and publication of your grandparents' accumulated wisdom." In part, it had to do with the deaths of Luther Rickman, Marvin Watts, and Andy Webb, people for whom we still had pages of questions but to whom we could never talk again. In part, it had to do with those letters that came to me from former students, now in college, who said that the most significant thing they had done in high school was collect material for *Foxfire*—and who asked to be involved again in the coming summer, as unpaid volunteers.

And, in part, it had to do with the day Patsy Cabe came to one of my classes. Patsy was a student at the Macon County High School in Franklin, North Carolina, the next high school up the road from ours. For fun and out of curiosity, she was going through one of our school days with her friend, Andrea Burrell, one of my community students. At the end of the class, Patsy came up to my desk and said, "I've got a relative you all might like to interview. She still lives the old way and knows how to do all the stuff you all are talking about. I'll introduce you to her if you want."

One thing you learn in this business is never to pass up an introduction. I asked Mike Cook, Paul Gillespie, and Andrea, all eleventh-graders, to go with Patsy and check the situation out. Several days later, they had done it, and Mike came up to me and said, "You're not going to believe this one."

That was our introduction to Aunt Arie.

That weekend, at the students' insistence, I got the tape recorder, and Paul and I drove up into Macon County, over several miles of gravel roads and finally up a deeply rutted dirt and mud driveway that ended on the side of a mountain in the yard of an unchinked log house with stone chimneys and a tin roof. Getting no answer at the front door, we walked around to the kitchen and found Aunt Arie, in her eighties, all alone, working with a paring knife, to scrape the hair and bristles from the severed head of a huge hog. With *Lord of the Flies* still fresh in my mind, and Paul making strange sounds behind me, I was hypnotized for a moment, not sure what to do. She still hadn't heard us, so we stood and watched, transfixed. Finally I looked at Paul, who was busy turning green, shrugged, and walked up and touched her on the shoulder. She jumped as though she'd been shot, whirled to look at us, and then, in relief, treated us to the most beautiful smile I had ever seen on the face of a woman.

If Mike had never been right a time in his life, he had certainly called this one in aces. Though neighbors looked in on her every day (it was one of them, in fact, who had brought her the hog's head from a butchering the previous day), she was so grateful for company and for help that Paul and I were instantly part of her family. With her permission, we hooked up the tape recorder, and as she worked on, recorded the conversation. At one point, confronted with the task of prying the eyeballs from the head without splitting them open, she was helpless, her fingers simply too weak to do the job. It would not do, however, to cook the head with the eyeballs left in. Paul wasn't about to help, and since I still remembered something of dissection from my days in pre-med, I was elected. I gulped a couple of times, took the knife, and went at it. As Aunt Arie laughed and talked and patted me on the back, and Paul stood, head turned away, holding the microphone in our general vicinity, we recorded an interview that became the focal point of *The Foxfire Book* (pp. 17–30). And for some reason, no matter where I go, people whose only connection with Aunt Arie was that printed interview ask me how she is.

We formed a friendship that lasted until her death, years later. Over those years, I took hundreds of students to her house, and to her hospital room when she was sick. We chopped wood, hauled groceries, threw Christmas parties, had Thanksgiving celebrations, cooked countless dinners on her fireplace and wood stove, helped her plant and harvest her garden. And today ask any of those students who met her—even if only once—about Aunt Arie, and chances are each will look down at the ground, pause a moment, and say something like, "I loved her."

The work of *Foxfire* began to take over my life and the lives of some of the students around me. When we were together, which was constantly, we talked about little else. That same year, with the help of some graduate students in graphic arts at the University of Georgia, we redesigned the magazine, greatly improving its appearance, and students finally began to acquire an eye for good, clean design. We also changed printers—a move we had debated for months. Though it was a distinct advantage in a number of ways to have the magazine printed locally—not the least among them being the fact that students could monitor the whole printing process—the increased size of our press run made it virtually impossible for our printer to continue to serve us. The largest offset press he had

I went to the Southern Appalachian Mountains to teach, partly because I had always been attracted by their special visual appeal—sometimes warm and human in scale, and sometimes vast and foreboding. The columned classroom building of the school where I began teaching gives it the appearance of a small junior college —which, in fact, it once was. The community students the school served often went from school to afternoon chores at home such as picking beans or baling hay. Some of them dug ginseng, the roots of which they sold to herb dealers in the area.

JOHN DAUGHTRY, THE CHARLOTTE OBSERVER

RABUN GAP-NACOOCHEE
SCHOOL
FOUNDED IN 1903

FOXFIRE

✵ *The Day Star fell like a little bird*

The cover for the first issue of *Fox-fire* Magazine was contributed b[y] Stanton Forbes, who created th[e] print originally for a book he ha[d] written entitled *Bear Hunt*. Whe[n] the first issue was published i[n] 1967, the tenth-grade editors and [I] gathered behind my desk for ou[r] first "official" portrait. The news[-] letter the school sent to paren[ts] and supporters featured a photo[-] graph of Tommy Wilson, one o[f] the editors, and myself with our lo[-] cal printers, R. E. Cross an[d] Duncan Taylor. By the time th[e] second issue appeared later tha[t] year, we had a few subscribers t[o] whom students mailed copies i[n] hand-addressed envelopes, an[d] several local outlets that the stu[-] dents stocked.

Series 29 No. 3 — **Rabun Gap NEWS** — May 1967

RABUN GAP-NACOOCHEE SCHOOL...

Literary Magazine Published

The ninth and tenth grade English classes, under the direction of their teacher, Mr. Eliot Wigginton, have recently published a literary magazine, Foxfire. It contains, along with poems and short stories all across the country, contributions from at least five widely-published authors including Marguerite Steedman.

One section of the magazine is devoted to folklore, superstitions, and remedies of this locale.

The magazine may be ordered through Mr. Wigginton at Rabun Gap at 50¢ per copy or $2.00 for a one-year subscription.

Foxfire Coming Off Press

Reader response to the articles that featured community people and their traditions was so strong that student interviews off campus after school began to dominate our work. Chuck Childs, for example, interviewed and tape recorded Margaret Norton (a lady who had once baby-sat me) as she churned; Lynda Gray recorded Dean Beasley as she wove handspun wool into cloth; Beulah Perry showed a group of us how to make a cotton hamper; and Harley Carpenter taught us how to find and use yellowroot, an herbal medicine. The results of such interviews were passed on to readers, whose interest seemed to intensify with each issue.

FOXFIRE

Thanksgiving '68

RABUN GAP, GEORGIA 30568

Dear Wig,

A package came from The Theatre Recording Society. Should I send it on up?

This is only a hurried note, in a few days I'll send you a million details.

The kids thought the idea of renting the Pennington's Place was great! They have recently put a new roof on it. Maybe a bunch of us can get together over the holidays and see what could be done.

We have all the envelopes addressed, we have yet to put postal stamps on them.

Well have a happy Thanksgiving!

Love,
Judy

r two years in Rabun County, I
a year off to do some graduate
k. My original tenth-grade edi-
were now seniors, and they
tinued to produce the maga-
alone while I was gone, corre-
nding with me constantly on
new stationery. While I was
y, I was also able to make the
nections that led me to the Na-
al Endowment for the Humani-
and a grant with which we
chased our first videotape
ipment and hired Suzy Angier
own in the photo making taffy
Lawton Brooks, one of our fate community contacts).

FOXFIRE

HOW TO BUILD YOUR OWN LOG CABIN

1969 SUMMER $1.00

One of our most ambitious efforts was devoted entirely to complete directions for building a log cabin. The primary editors were students who had been recruited to the magazine staff during the year I was away. Their efforts helped lead to our first award, a scroll from the Georgia Writers' Association; Paul Gillespie and Mike Cook, on my left, later returned after college to work with me as instructors in the school.

nd then we found Aunt Arie, living alone in a log house on a moun- inside. She instantly became a rmanent part of our lives, often siting my classroom, and even ore often being visited by us. e'd sometimes take her to urch, where the students would ther protectively around her, id we'd help her cook or string ans for the winter or gather pota- es from her garden. Each time we ft, she'd stand on the steps and atch until we were completely out sight.

When we outgrew our local printer, we transferred the production of *Foxfire* to Williams Printing in Atlanta, where Jimmy Fitzpatrick willingly gave every new group of students a tour of the plant. Soon we had outgrown my classroom, too, and when the new administration building was built at Rabun Gap, we were given offices, complete with our first darkroom. Even so, subscribers' envelopes were still hand-addressed and hand-sorted by zip code, and whenever a new issue arrived from the printer, our primitive mailing operation flowed out into hallways and the new building's front lawn.

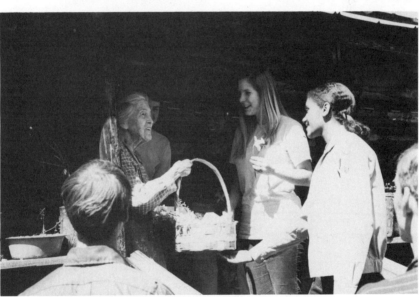

Our first attempt at a student exchange took place between *Foxfire*'s editors and the editors of the *Fourth Street i,* a magazine published out of New York's Lower East Side. Ours returned with the requisite photo of the Empire State Building (albeit from a slightly different vantage point than that employed by the average tourist) and scores of other images that caught their rural eyes. The urban students who visited us had their first encounters with such things as wells, and individuals like Aunt Arie, to whom they presented an Easter basket.

When I bought my first piece of land and built my log home, groups of students helped me every weekend felling trees, notching and lifting the logs into place, cutting out the holes for windows and doors, nailing up rafters, and mixing cement and setting rocks into the chimney. Too impatient to wait, I moved in before the ceiling was finished, as the photo by John Daughtry shows. Behind me in the photo are some of my Rabun Gap colleagues.

After the publication of *The Foxfire Book*, a portion of the royalties went into the purchase of a piece of property and a number of traditional log buildings from the immediate area which were moved and reconstructed on the site to serve as offices, staff homes, and for storage of artifacts. In winter, with the leaves off the trees and snow on the ground, I can see many of the buildings from my front porch.

Foxfire 7

ministers, church members, revivals, baptisms, shaped-note and gospel singing, faith healing, camp meetings, footwashing, snake handling, and other traditions of mountain religious heritage

Foxfire Books 10th Anniversary
Doubleday/Anchor Press, 245 Park Ave., N.Y., N.Y. 10167 · Over 6,000,000 copies sold

Dear Friends,

We want you to come to Foxfire's annual Mother's Day picnic and get-together on Saturday, May 8, 1982, 11:00 a.m. - 3:00 p.m. at Foxfire (in Mountain City). Even though we missed having it last year, we really want to make this and annual event because we are honoring you, the people of our community, who have made possible the Foxfire magazines and books, records, and video programs.

Foxfire students and staff will provide barbecued chicken and all the trimmings. We want you to bring yourself and your family and share in the celebration.

If you need a ride to come to the picnic, please call us at 746-5318 (during the weekdays between 9:00 a.m. - 5:00 p.m.) or write (Foxfire, Rabun Gap, GA 30568). We will be glad to come get you, and we will take you home when you are ready to leave.

CELEBRATE: FOXFIRE BOOKS 10th ANNIVERSARY

The Foxfire Book · Foxfire 2 · Foxfire 3 · Foxfire 4 · Foxfire 5 · Foxfire 6 · Foxfire 7

Ten years after the publication of *The Foxfire Book, Foxfire 7* was released. The invitation that year to the annual Mother's Day picnic we hold in honor of our community contacts highlighted that birthday. In addition to the annual picnic, and the unselfish and unselfconscious friendship that exists between the students and the people they interview, students are also available to help when needed in such ways as applying a coat of stain to Kenny Runion's house.

HUGH GRANNUM

Today, publication of the magazine and books continues as a daily part of the curriculum at the public high school. Students are still involved in every aspect of the work, from running our archive of tapes and photographs to speaking at conferences around the country to assisting in the creation of the script for the Broadway hit *Foxfire*, which starred Hume Cronyn and Jessica Tandy.

KIM NIELSEN

ZOE DOMI

The videotape and television division of our organization, headed by Mike Cook, has grown into a local cable channel that features shows put together by his students. Operating out of a small studio they designed themselves, the students edit tapes they've made that highlight traditional customs, issues confronting our local residents, and plays and concerts held at the school.

The Foxfire String Band

SIDE ONE
Girl That I Love
Tennessee Blues
Wicked Path of Sin
Grandfather's Clock
Redwood Hill
Lord I'm Depending
  On You

SIDE TWO
Foggy Mountain Special
Green Pastures
Slewfoot/Fox On The Run
Blackberry Blossom
How Mountain Girls
  Can Love
Daniel Prayed

℗ Foxfire Records 1982

Dean English–Banjo; lead & tenor vocals
Wayne Gipson–Lead & tenor vocals

Steve McCall–Guitar; lead & bass vocals
Tom Nixon–Mandolin; baritone vocals

The Foxfire String Band

The concerts are sponsored by our music division, headed by George Reynolds. By-products of this division include student-produced record albums and cassette tapes that are marketed nationally, an instrument-building class, and the Foxfire String Band, which has played at the Knoxville World's Fair and the Grand Ole Opry.

Bob Bennett, who conducts our environmental and outdoor classes, takes his students on field trips that vary from locations deep in the mountains to the Georgia coast. He and his students have also built a ropes course and a log classroom building on the school property. For our annual Christmas card one year, many of the students who were taking Foxfire-sponsored classes gathered in front of the half-completed structure—now finished and in daily use.

Our organization has also started its own publishing company, Foxfire Press, the products from which are distributed by E. P. Dutton. Housed in a new passive solar structure, the operation is headed by Linda Page, shown in one photograph as a student editor of *Foxfire* in 1967, and in a second with Joan Mondale and student Chet Welch. They are looking at the first offering from the Press: *Aunt Arie: A Foxfire Portrait.*

could only print two pages at a time, and then the pages had to be hand-collated and stapled in a process that took an assembly line of women weeks. At the same time as our magazine was being assembled, the weekly newspaper also had to be typeset and laid out and printed, and the numerous other small jobs that consume a printer's time—wedding invitations, church bulletins, football programs, calendars, and the like—had to continue to come out on schedule. As the pages of a new issue of *Foxfire* filled every working surface of the small shop, tempers got short and employees were inconvenienced.

And so students sent copies of the latest issue to every printing company in the area, along with letters asking what they would have charged us for four thousand copies of that same magazine and how long it would have taken them to produce it. Then students and I visited those companies that sent us the best figures to try to determine whether or not we'd be able to work well together. In the end, the students voted to give the job to Williams Printing Company in Atlanta, the same company we use today. Because of the large size of their offset presses and their automated page folders, collators, and saddle stitchers, they could print our magazine in a fraction of the time it had taken the local printer, and at a reduced per-copy cost. In addition, the company promised to provide us with free layout boards printed to indicate our page margins, tours of the plant at any time for student editors (we now regularly take students through the plant when a new *Foxfire* is coming off the presses), and free assistance in cover design and art on request.

As all that was being squared away, construction on an administration building on the school's campus was nearing completion. Several rooms in that building were offered to us as a publications area. We immediately accepted, and, with NEH money, purchased enough equipment and supplies to outfit our first darkroom. With the help of the school's carpenter, we put in work counters and shelves in the office spaces, had a telephone installed, and moved the circulation and editorial functions out of my classroom into separate adjoining rooms of their own. It was a nearly ideal setup—quickly outgrown, but perfect at the time.

Also with NEH money, we had purchased new cameras and tape recorders as well as our first videotape equipment. With the latter, we were able to capture skills such as carding and spinning and weaving in a way that was impossible with still photography; to say nothing of the tapes we could make of people like Aunt Arie, whose personality was so powerful that she seemed to explode off the television screen. For students like Mike, videotape was, if anything, a more magical, compelling medium than still photography, and he quickly became one of the students I relied on to run that equipment and teach the other students how to use it.

By spring, I was beginning to feel some pressure. I was working, to varying degrees of involvement, with close to two hundred students. More and more of them were clamoring to get out in the field on interviews, and many of them were dormitory students who could not leave campus without an adult. The interviews still had to be done after school hours and on weekends, and the sign-out procedure for the dorm students thus involved a number of other adults to whom they were responsible: work supervisors, dorm houseparents, the dean, the head of the dining hall. At any point along the elaborate checkout system, something could go wrong. A student might not be allowed to miss work on the afternoon involved, or might be kept on campus for some minor disciplinary infraction or for a failing grade. Often adults wanted to know when the students would be back, and often it was hard to tell. How long does it take to put a white oak split bottom in a chair? On more occasions than I care to count, I'd have an interview set up for three dorm students who wanted to work together as a team, only to find out, after going through the chain of command, that only one could go. In most cases, the interview couldn't be canceled, so I'd take the one, leaving the other two behind—two more waiting to get into the field. On other occasions, in the middle of a terrific interview, I'd have to leave to drive a dorm student who was in scholastic trouble back to campus in time for study hall, picking up some supper on the way since we had missed the dining hall's serving time; then turn around and go back to pick up the ones I had left behind to finish the interview, take them to supper, and push to get them back by bedtime so they wouldn't get the majors or minors that would lock them on campus for the following week. Such complicated comings and goings took time and energy, often compounded by having community students along who were either too young to drive or had no access to a car and thus had to be driven home, often to locations that were miles apart. Fortunately, in those days, gasoline was nearly free, but having to be present on most interviews, as well as the requirement that I be present whenever one of the school buildings was open after hours for *Foxfire* work, as well as having at least three lesson preparations a day (with over 100 compositions a week to grade), was beginning to take its toll. I'd be the first to admit that there were times when I wasn't very pleasant to be around. That's to say nothing of the time when I went to sleep at my desk one day in class, didn't hear the bell, and the students conspired to keep the morning classes so quiet that I slept through half the school day undisturbed.

And now, on top of everything else, we were going to produce a book for Doubleday? Right.

Salvation—and I don't use that word lightly—arrived in the form of Suzanne Angier. Suzy was a graduate of Boston University who had come to Georgia from her home in Woodbridge, Connecticut, as part of a team of VISTA volunteers assigned to Rabun County. Her team had accomplished some impressive things, not the least among them the creation of a locally owned crafts cooperative based in Tallulah Falls that is currently about to open its third shop.

We had met and visited on a number of occasions, she had visited my classes several times, and when her term with VISTA was about to end, I hired her. Our financial situation made no provision for a paid associate, but I really wanted Suzy's help. Luckily, she was willing to work on the promise that I'd find what I could in terms of money, but there might be (and subsequently were) periods of time when she'd go unpaid. I talked it over with the students and with the administration, and after a series of interviews between Suzy and the latter to make sure she understood school policies and regulations, she received her seal of approval and I was allowed to hire her—as long as she was paid by The Southern Highlands Literary Fund.

Exactly how I paid her is vague now. I remember that part of her intermittent salary came from my paycheck, and part of it came from the $1,500 advance we received from Doubleday on signing the book contract. And I have a letter from John Dyson written during that period from Vietnam that says, "Enclosed is $500.00 as a contribution from me to the SHLF . . . I hope it will tide Suzy over for now. More should be on the way soon." But that's about all I can resurrect out of my notes and my memory. I'd be willing to bet that she didn't make more than $2,000 that first year, though. (Suzy claims it was closer to $3,000, but I'm not sure I believe her.)

What is *not* vague in recollection is the way she meshed into all we were doing, bringing to our work a vibrancy and energy and patience and good cheer that won every student to her instantly. That's to say nothing of the community contacts who adopted her like a daughter. The years that followed were some of the happiest our organization has ever had.

Meanwhile, a parallel and very exciting development was underway. Over the past several years, a number of people, myself included, had speculated about the possibility and the mechanics of starting similar projects in other schools.

We started close to home. As part of our NEH grant, I had asked for funds to cover the cost of travel to area high schools to locate teachers who would be interested in creating satellite *Foxfire* editorial staffs. As conceived, the staffs would meet together to plan each issue, each of which would be focused on one theme—faith healing, for example. Once the theme was identified, each staff would radiate from its own school into its surrounding community to collect information, thus greatly enlarging the information base and enriching the treatment of the subject matter. In addition, each satellite staff would be encouraged to select and send in literary material, as well as articles done independent of the magazine's theme but of special interest to that staff.

It never got off the ground. I located teachers in several area schools, but in one case, the teacher talked with her students and told me the students weren't interested in the idea; in a second case, the teacher actually found some students who wanted to participate, and with some training and help from our group, they conducted a few interviews. The interest didn't last, however, and the project lost momentum and died. In a third school, a teacher rounded up a small class for me and several of my students to talk to. We arrived, however, to find that the teacher had turned the event into an assembly program of sorts, and we were shown into the gymnasium, where a number of classes had been dumped for the "program" and their teachers had vanished into the teachers' lounge to take a break. Completely unprepared to entertain a group of several hundred restless youngsters, we blew the presentation, and even if there had been several who were interested in working with us, there were no teachers present to grab them and put that willingness to work in some supportive way.

It's not fun to fail so completely, but it is instructive. I know now that one of the reasons for our failure was that rather than allowing the idea to grow and mature and take shape in a natural, evolutionary way inside each school, we simply presented a package that was already thought out and invited participation, not realizing that those students would have real difficulty becoming committed to an idea into which they had had no input. *Foxfire* was doomed to be regarded as "your magazine, not ours," and essentially all we were offering those students was a chance to be published—sufficient motivation for a few, but only a few.

A second reason for the failure was that I was cast in the role of a man trying to talk some already overburdened teachers into taking on yet more work and thus was regarded more as an enemy than a friend. They had already decided they didn't want to listen.

From that point on, I resolved to work only with teachers who came to me having already made their minds up *not* that they absolutely wanted to produce a magazine like *Foxfire* with their students, but that they wanted to take a careful, considered look at how it worked to see if there might be some elements worth attempting in their own classes. And I resolved to work, in the initial stages, only with teachers, having found that it does absolutely no good to get some young people excited about doing similar work only to discover that they can find no teachers willing to help. That simply adds to the burden of frustration many of them are already carrying, and it is counterproductive.

So it was with a rising sense of excitement that I listened to Diane Churchill, a Georgia native, describe to me her work with high school age students in New York City's predominantly Puerto Rican Lower East Side. Diane, who operated out of one of the Catholic churches there, was primarily involved in community work, and she had already decided that involving the young people with whom she worked in the production of a magazine about and for their community could be a valuable endeavor. In fact, she and her group, completely independent of us, had already started working toward a first issue. Over several conversations during which we talked about such things as finding money, building circulation, getting publicity, and so forth, the idea emerged of an editor exchange. Diane would send several of her group to Georgia for a week, and we would then reciprocate with several of ours. We parted, resolved to pursue that option with our students to see what would happen.

At the same time, a parallel development was taking shape that would plunge us into the work of assisting the development of new projects with an intensity we could never have generated alone. During one of my previous summer trips to Washington, as a result of almost inexorable pressure to find out somehow whether or not a project like ours would make sense in another location, I had started looking for guidance. Having never worked with distinctive cultural groups other than Appalachian people, I was lost. Through contacts, I was steered to the office of Dr. Sam Stanley, program coordinator for the Smithsonian Institution's Center for the Study of Man. Sam is an anthropologist who had done his fieldwork among native groups in Alaska. I explained our work to him, described my mounting frustrations, and urged him to become a member of our advisory board to steer us in appropriate directions and prevent us from making any serious blunders. I knew little about other cultures, but I knew enough to know that my middle-class white perspective on the world could cause me to be completely blind to cultural nuances and values that would absolutely determine how a project like ours would be perceived and implemented. Sam agreed to help.

Shortly after I left his office in the basement of the Museum of Natural History, in one of those serendipitous occurrences that seemed to happen more and more frequently to us as our network of contacts grew, Sam was visited by Brian Beun, the president of a Washington-based organization called IDEAS, and his associate, Ann Vick. The primary work of their group—Institutional Development and Economic Affairs Service—was to find responsible ways to be of assistance to minority cultures, primarily through encouraging self-help economic and educational ventures. Sam showed them some copies of our magazine that I had left behind, they saw it immediately as a potential model, and Ann called me to ask if we could get together.

Our first meeting several months later almost didn't happen. It was scheduled for late one afternoon in their office near Dupont Circle, an area of Washington I did not know well at all. Trying to drive, watch street signs, and coordinate them with an inadequate mental map, I ran a stop sign in northwest Washington and was made to follow a policeman to his precinct station. I didn't have enough cash to pay the fine. The officer behind the counter refused to accept either a personal check or traveler's checks; neither would he let me leave the station to cash one elsewhere, despite the fact that he had the car impounded as a guarantee that I would return. I tried to call my sister at work, but she had left for the day. I was already late for my appointment, and we had reached an impasse.

To fully appreciate what I felt at that moment, you must also know that the car I was driving was not my own but a station wagon belonging to the school. I had borrowed it because I had been promised a large piece of used videotape equipment as a gift to our organization from a group that liked our work, and the equipment wouldn't fit in my jeep. On the afternoon I reached my sister's apartment building in southwest Washington, I had to park in a supermarket lot next door and go upstairs to her apartment to get the key to the building's locked parking area. Minutes later, I returned to find that the car had been broken into and my camera and a number of other items stolen. The next day I went to pick up the piece of equipment, only to find that there had been some policy misunderstanding among the organization's board members and it could not be released to us at all. That same afternoon I had an appointment with IDEAS at an address in a strange part of town.

False leads and dead ends and mishaps and efforts that seemed to have been wasted at the time were—and continue to be—so much a part of the work with a project like ours that one is forced to make a critical decision early on between two simple options: give it all up as a bad idea or shut up and shove on through. That's it. A precinct station in Washington is not the proper atmosphere in which to make such decisions, and so in desperation I called Brian and Ann, explained the situation, and said, "It looks like if you want this meeting to happen, you're going to have to come down here and bail me out."

A few minutes later they arrived, laughing, and we headed for their offices. The result of that meeting was our agreement to begin tentatively identifying other locations to which *Foxfire* might be transplanted. IDEAS would bear primary responsibility for finding locations and startup funding, and our students would provide such consulting and training as was requested by the pilot sites.

Things were beginning to move in some new directions.

17

"It Works in Georgia, but Will It Work Anyplace Else?"

During the summer of 1970, three former editors (Jan Brown, Tommy Wilson, and Mary Garth), then in college, returned to work with us. With the permission of NEH, I was able to offer each of them a $500 stipend, paid out of our grant, which hopefully would help with their college expenses. They were the first students we had ever paid, but the summer went so well that it established a paid summer job component that we have continued to this day.

The three, along with Mike Cook, formed the core of a group of constantly shifting size and composition that spent the summer keeping the business affairs of *Foxfire* in order, gathering new material, and documenting a number of skills with our videotape equipment. Splitting shingles; making barrels, froes, turkey calls, white oak splits, and chairs; and cutting dovetail notches for log cabins became part of a growing video archive.

And by the time the new school year began, Suzy and I and several of those students were well into the selection of material for *The Foxfire Book*.

In most cases, the magazine articles were full and rich enough that they were able to be used intact, and so the bulk of the work became reprinting photographs, retyping material in manuscript form, and long discussions about chapter sequence. In those cases in which magazine material we wanted to use was not quite what we thought it should be, new interviews helped add additional material to bring it up to strength.

Shortly after Christmas, the manuscript was delivered, and Doubleday paid us the second half of the advance.

In the meantime, the idea for an exchange with Diane Churchill's group in New York had grown and taken root. I was fascinated by—but apprehensive about—the idea of sending high school students long distances, alone, and catapulting them into totally different environments from those they were used to, and giving them the opportunity to try their hand at acting as responsible, contributing adults among strangers. I suspected that if they could handle such a situation successfully, they would be well on their way toward making an easy, graceful transition from adolescence into competent adulthood. I hadn't had the nerve to test it, though.

Diane became the catalyst, initiating the exchange by sending Freddy Gonzales and Ramón Rojas to stay with us, in student homes, for five days. Three days after they returned to New York, Suzy accompanied Mike Cook, Paul Gillespie, and David Wilson (who had never flown before) on a plane to La Guardia, where Diane and Freddy and Ramón met them and took them into the Lower East Side.

For both groups, it was a powerful experience. Freddy and Ramón confronted "White Appalachian hicks" for the first time, and Paul and David and Mike came face to face with dreaded "knife-wielding Puerto Ricans" for the first time—and in both cases, the stereotypes and prejudices largely vanished in the glow of friendship and face-to-face communication. Freddy and Ramón had their first dealings with mountains, cows, wells, and outdoor toilets; Paul, Mike, and David had their first dealings with tenements and the unique pressures of urban existence—and in all cases, they coped. They made it. And in the process, they all grew. An article Mike wrote for our local newspaper summarized the feelings of the students:

> We began an exchange program for one big reason. That reason was to allow two different cultures to see each other face to face, not through a wall of hearsay.
>
> It began with two Puerto Rican kids coming down from the city expecting panthers behind the trees and a large population of fat white racists. Instead they found beautiful mountains and streams . . . and friendship, not racism.
>
> Some of us went to New York expecting to get mugged or maybe knifed by some freak on the street. Like those who came here, we found friendship and a second home.

There seem to be people who think that the problems the poverty areas have are the fault of the people living there. There is a feeling (which I shared to some extent) that those people are lazy and won't work. Now I know differently, and when people tell me that these people could help themselves if they wanted to, I can say it isn't so. . . . and I will know because I've been there.

This is what I saw: I saw people in tenement buildings which were so badly run down that people here wouldn't use them as barns. I saw no business capable of hiring enough people to provide employment for slum dwellers. I saw schools so crowded that the officials actually encouraged drop-outs. I saw kids so down and without hope that they saw no escape but drugs, even as young as nine years old.

I no longer see the problems of city slums as far off and unimportant. I see these things as problems that affect close friends.

Those of us who took part in this first phase of the exchange programs would like to see it continue. The more people that can have the experience of meeting another culture on its home ground, the more understanding there will be between them, and understanding is the key to it all I think!

Perhaps it is best summed up as David Wilson put it when writing about the way we all got along: "either hillbilly became Rican, or Rican became hillbilly; or both merged as a rare breed of human called Brother . . . which is what it was all about anyway."

Perhaps in some small way a program such as this can help make that breed of human a little less rare. If such a program can change just a small number of people it is still worth it.

My three talked about little else for weeks, and when Diane suggested we try it again, this time with girls, we didn't hesitate. To calm the parents, Suzy again agreed to fly with Andrea Burrell and Laurie Brunson to New York and deliver them to Diane personally, after which she would go on to Woodbridge to visit her parents and return to pick the girls up and bring them home at the end of their stay. That plan was agreed to, and shortly after our girls' safe return, three of Diane's followed. Jane Stine of *Scholastic Scope* found out about the exchange, and in return for being able to interview the girls and write an article for her magazine (October 4, 1971), she helped pay the transportation costs involved. Fortunately, our NEH grant covered the balance. On either end, community residents provided meals and beds with the kind of generosity that always seems to surface on such occasions.

How much help our group was able to be to Diane's in terms of magazine work is open to question, since their situation was so different from ours, and since they were already so far along with their own plans for the bilingual community magazine they had decided to call *The Fourth Street i.* In truth, their contribution to us was probably greater than the reverse, for they taught us how a student-produced magazine of substantive content could exist in an urban location. And thanks to Diane, I have continued to send my students on such exchanges with confidence.

At the same time, making good on their promise to find a native American group that might want to start a *Foxfire* project, Brian and Ann at IDEAS located some native adults on the Oglala Sioux reservation near Pine Ridge, South Dakota, who seemed genuinely interested. Funded by IDEAS, a delegation arrived in Georgia from South Dakota for the first formal "workshop" we had ever given, in interviewing and magazine-production skills. The group returned to Pine Ridge to begin gathering material for a trial issue. From the beginning, the belief dominated that only if such magazines were totally owned and operated by their respective groups would students and adults give of the time required to make them successful. Thus whatever assistance we gave was entirely dependent on the amount of assistance asked for. Third parties like IDEAS would provide the support needed, including initial startup and printing costs, through foundation grants, to test the efficacy of the idea in diverse locations.

I mention this only because of the number of people who suggest that we treat the *Foxfire* idea like a fast-food franchise, opening new outlets and sharing in the proceeds like some hamburger empire. Such a notion is unthinkable.

During the same school year, knowing that our first NEH grant would expire one year from the date of issue, I applied for funding assistance for a second year and received it: $9,401, the amount I requested, to be used to pay Suzy's salary ($5,000), to hire four summer students at $500 apiece, to pay travel and expenses for continued exchanges ($1,000), and to purchase a year's worth of tapes, film, videotape, and supplies ($1,401.20). The people at NEH seemed pleased with the way their money was being used, and we certainly couldn't have been happier to have it. I think we could have kept the magazine alive without such help, but its existence raised us to a different level of performance, gave us some financial breathing room, and allowed us to experiment with some ideas and some new directions that we might not have had the chance to try otherwise. Their faith in us said, in effect, "Okay, you've got a good idea. You've proved you can make it work at one level of achievement. We certify the value of that, and endorse what you're accomplishing. But now let's see what you can *do* with that idea. Where else can you *go* with it? With whom can you share it? Push yourselves. Reach a little higher. Stretch. *Then* let's see what you've got. We'll take a chance on you with some risk capital. If the new things you try work, we'll all learn something in the process. If they don't, and the money is lost, well, we'll learn something from that too. Whatever the end result, chances are we'll all win in the end through what we learn together."

The idea of sending students out alone to undertake major responsibilities took another tentative step forward in the summer of 1971, when Suzy and I allowed three of the seven students we hired for that summer to go up into the mountains of North Carolina to do research. Some time earlier I had turned my old Bronco over to the Southern Highlands Literary Fund to be used for interviews and errands, and bought another for myself. With parents' approval, the three girls loaded the organization's jeep with camping gear, food, tape recorders, and cameras and drove away, believing that the area around Bryson City would prove to be rich with new contacts and new friends. Nearly a week later, they were back with satchels full of recorded tapes, exposed film, and enough stories to keep us entertained for days. They had so much material, in fact, that Suzy and I let them take the bulk of an entire issue of *Foxfire* as their own and fill it—themselves—with what they'd found. Because of the circumstances of our teaching situation during the school year, Suzy and I knew we wouldn't be able to make that same thing happen often, but this gave us a look at how a *Foxfire* would be run in the best of all possible worlds, and those girls proved to us that it was not a futile dream. It was just deferred by circumstances and rules. As a team, they had gone alone into a strange area, taken care of themselves, found and interviewed and photographed numerous new people on their own, brought that material back, transcribed the tapes and printed the photographs, selected and edited the material they wanted to go into print, typed and corrected it, designed and laid out the pages and delivered it to the printer—while Suzy and I stood around feeling basically useless but very proud.

Meanwhile, there was *The Foxfire Book* to think about. We didn't know exactly what to do to get ready for its publication, but we knew we should be giving the matter some thought. As I wrote on January 19, 1972, in a journal I was keeping at the time:

This is an interesting time because there are so many unanswered questions —so many promises and threats and dreams and possibilities—all clouds that are impossible to pierce or see through with any clarity at all. They all rise before me now—all demanding to be dealt with, but impossible to deal with simply because one has no way of knowing exactly what it is he is being demanded *to* deal with. There are merely vague shapes that cry out, "Here I am. I'm coming at you with the speed of wind. Catch me and hold me and use me." But one puts up his arms and finds nothing solid there to grasp. One can only speculate and wonder . . .

[For example, *Foxfire* has grown considerably since its beginnings in March of 1967, and I wouldn't be able to handle the load now without Suzy] but the growth has been fairly steady—almost imperceptible. A little more each day. Nothing *really* noticeable . . . And despite the fact I spend an increasing amount of time in the office, I am really happy . . . I feel as though something good is being accomplished.

And now all that is about to be shattered. Or *is* it? One of those clouds, and it's building into a real thunderstorm. I'm referring, of course, to the fact that the book is about to appear. Review copies are going out January 21 and the publication date is scheduled for March 17 . . . And the publicity rush is on.

A team from *Life* magazine has been here and that article will be coming out soon. A writer for the *National Observer* arrives the 27th of this month. *Smithsonian* did an article about us in December and promises a review, as does the Atlanta *Constitution*. *Publishers Weekly* has already announced the book three times.

. . . And so we are about to become, seemingly, famous. And then what? I truly believe that we can deal with the royalties wisely. There are so many dreams—salaries for people like Suzy, a museum/archive, our own publishing house, all the new programs for students . . . But how, if we *indeed* become famous and sought after, do we deal with success? What if we suddenly have forty thousand new subscribers? What if there are suddenly hundreds of requests for appearances by the kids at various organizations? What if we are responsible for flooding Rabun County with tourists? What then? And what of the visitors?

Perhaps all this is far too exaggerated. Perhaps the book will be promoted as a "back to the land" encyclopedia just at the moment when people are saturated by and sick of the *Whole Earth Catalogue* syndrome. Then it will doubtless fail miserably.

But what if it doesn't? Then what? And that's the problem. How can one prepare for forty thousand subscribers . . . when it is impossible, absolutely, to imagine what that would be like. Impossible to see bags of mail in the hall. Impossible to imagine two phones in our office. Impossible to imagine doing *anything* more in the space we have presently . . . I don't know what's going to happen. No idea. Just guesses. Poor stuff to build on.

We were balanced on a set of scales, in one pan the knowledge that the boost the students would get seeing their work published in a real book, and the credibility that fact would give our work, and the new opportunities it would create for us through the doors it could open and the capital it could bring us with which to work, balanced against the problems that would surely tear at us if the book was a success.

We waited in suspended animation.

18

The Foxfire Book—
"They've Even Got
Copies in Atlanta!"

The initial reaction gathered itself slowly on the horizon, heralded, like the first faint blast from the whistle of an unseen train, by the arrival in our offices of the first copy we had seen.

In my journal, on January 20, 1972, I wrote:

> Today, in my pile of mail, I spotted instantly a box from Doubleday that looked suspiciously like the book. For some reason I put it aside and went through the rest of the mail first—tantalizing myself, I guess. And half afraid that it might *not* be what I hoped.
>
> It was. The first copy of the hardback with a long letter from Ronnie [Shushan, our editor at that time] and a quotation from Pete Seeger [for promotion].
>
> Funny feeling. Almost anticlimactic. I had never seen it all together before, and yet I had seen it all in pieces a hundred times. I flipped through it almost casually, mostly with a "Well, it's finally here" feeling of relief [then I passed it on to Suzy].
>
> Later in the day, I began to come back to it more and more frequently,

reading snatches, studying photographs more closely. Now, twelve hours later, I have carried it home with me and cannot put it down. It's beautiful. As Suzy said after she had gone through it, "What I like about this book is that it's so honest. It's really solid. It's a *real* book. People are getting their money's worth." She's right. It *is* a good book. I *know* it. It's packed with meat—no flab. In a burst of elation after supper, I found myself saying, "Christ. It's going to sell a million copies. It's irresistible."

In class, the reaction was excitement also, only slightly muted by the fact that all the material in the book was contributed by students who were no longer in our school. Jan, Mike, Paul, Mary, David, Judy, George, Andrea, Laurie—all of them were gone. The challenge for this new group was to prepare for the response and to dream and figure. What if—just what if—we made, say, $25,000? How would we spend it? What if all those subscriptions came in that I had worried so about? How would we deal with them, knowing realistically that students could only work several hours a day, and knowing that if all they had time to do was wrestle with mail, working with *Foxfire* might become a curse rather than a time to look forward to.

All that would come later, though. For today, I just wanted them to celebrate and to dream out loud. As part of that same January 20 journal entry, I wrote:

Suddenly I was drawing plans for a museum on the blackboard, shouting and laughing just like a kid. "Now what would you add? What would you put here? What would it look like? Where would it be? How would students be used? Could they be in charge? What piece of it would you like to be in charge of? What would you do instead of a museum?" We all got a little carried away —but in a good, healthy way. Enthusiasm. The main point I kept coming back to, hoping to implant it in their minds forever, was that, sure, these were dreams now. But so was the magazine five years ago. People then had said again and again we couldn't do it. Mr. Brown had admitted today, as he looked at the book, that he had firmly believed we'd never find enough information to keep the magazine going more than a year.

[I said, "You can *do* it. *Believe* it. If it makes sense, and you want it badly enough, you can make it happen. The students who preceded you did."] And then I got into my belief that life just isn't worth living unless you're willing to take some big chances and go for broke. Such a man may fail, but at least he spent his life living for a great cause—a great dream—and even in defeat his life was far more worthwhile and exciting than that of the man who sat helpless and watched the show. At least the one spent his life passionately.

Classes like that one, in which the students got agitated and cranked up and started talking big talk, were always my favorites. And as often as not, some jack-leg kid would come up with an idea that rang like a bell. Everyone would fall silent for a moment, then jump on it, tear it apart, refine it, and make up their minds to do it. Those days were—and still are —ones that shine.

The first wave of publicity hit us like the engines of that train heard faintly, far away. The *Life* article appeared, saying the book was the product of "an ingenious and wildly successful education project . . . *Foxfire* is the most widely acclaimed publication of its kind." A book reviewer for *Time* wrote, "Much clear-eyed love, surprising beauty, and the straight, tough grain of authenticity." A *New York Times* correspondent said, "An authentic bit of Americana . . . all the qualities of a book that will last." Nelson Bryant, in the *New York Times Book Review*, stated, "Delightful. I will put it on my bookshelves close to Joshua Slocum and Thoreau and Henry Beston, for I know those stalwart New Englanders would have enjoyed it too." In the Atlanta *Journal* appeared, "Packed with folklore and jammed with illustrations. If you get to worrying what the younger generation is up to, take a look at *The Foxfire Book.*"

Hundreds of reviews appeared, and not one of them was negative. The Book of the Month Club picked up the book and featured it as one of the main selections. I and two students were flown to New York to be interviewed on the "Today" show.

As the first reviews began to come in, Ronnie Shushan, our editor, had called to say she was sure the book was going to make it now, and she wanted proposals for subsequent volumes as soon as possible. The continuing wave of attention caught Doubleday completely by surprise, however. Orders were in hand for the entire first printing of the book by March 17, almost before shipping to bookstores had begun, and by March 24, the second printing was also sold out and Doubleday's printing plant manager had been told to clear the presses and proceed with a third printing immediately. The paperback and the hardback had been published simultaneously, and by the time the former hit the *New York Times* Paperback Bestseller Lists—the first Anchor book in the history of Doubleday to do so—people were charging around in New York without a clue as to when the book would peak and how many more printings to order. Like a snowball rolling downhill, each new event simply added to the momentum and the critical mass to create that odd runaway monster known as a publishing phenomenon. Reviews created customer demand at the bookstores and attracted television interest; the television shows added to the demand, stimulated new reviews, and drew the attention of organizations like the Book of the Month Club; resulting sales placed the book on bestseller lists, simply creating more demand; and the fact that the supply was scarce only served to increase demand still further rather than the reverse. If the marketing managers at Doubleday had set out to orchestrate all this and create a bestseller (which, in this case, they didn't), they couldn't have done a better job. In fact, as of this writing, *The Foxfire Book* still sells several hundred copies a week, has long since passed two million in sales, and is one of the most successful books in Doubleday's publishing history.

And much of it was put together by high school students, the majority of whom had hated English.

Back in Rabun County, meanwhile, we began to learn some hard lessons fast, for right on the heels of the publicity of March and April came free-lance writers, television news crews, film producers, convention program chairpersons, tourists, and long-lost friends.

Fortunately, the very fact of our relative geographical isolation served as a vital buffer. Many people who might otherwise have camped on our doorstep were discouraged by the distance, and by the facts that the nearest airport was hours away, there was no train service, and no interstate highway came within sixty miles of us.

That same relative isolation served another vital purpose: for the most part, the people in the county remained unaware of all the media attention. Nobody here subscribed to the *New York Times* or the Washington *Post* or the Chicago *Tribune*. Few of the television shows on which our work was featured were seen. Many, in fact, didn't even have television sets and didn't want them. Aunt Arie had seen television once and didn't like it because it hurt her eyes.

And so our best friends remained unchanged, grateful for their copies of the book simply as something to pass on to their children and grandchildren—a little awed by it all, but largely unaffected. Once in a while, someone would come back to the county from a trip and stop me on the street and say, "You know they've even got copies of that book in *Atlanta?*" But that was the extent of it. The Aunt Aries continued to welcome the students because they loved them, not because they wanted to be famous. The latter just didn't compute.

And luckily, Suzy and I had learned through experience not only that we could place an enormous amount of trust and confidence in our students, but also that it was absolutely vital to their education (and to our sanity) that we do so. We still had a lot to learn about teaching, but one thing we were sure of already was that the new demands being made on our organization could be turned to the students' advantage if we were just smart about it.

Thus when journalists and free-lance writers called asking for permission to come and interview us for a story, Suzy, I, or the student who answered the phone would simply explain to the person that all such requests had to go through a meeting of the entire group, and when a decision had been made, someone would call them back. Often a copy of the publication they wrote for was requested, or copies of articles they had written about topics of a related nature. In group meetings, such requests were processed, and if the group was generally warm toward the idea, and if several students were willing to "adopt" the journalist, make all the arrangements, structure the person's itinerary, and make sure the person got what he or she came for within reason, the request was passed and a member of the student team called the person back and began to make plans.

In some cases, requests were simply denied or deferred. Sometimes the reasons were as simple as the fact that we were about to go on vacation or enter a period of final exams. Sometimes they involved students disliking the publication and not wanting their story told in its pages. Sometimes the students simply felt besieged and told the person they just couldn't handle another request at this time. On one occasion, shortly after a front-page story appeared in the *Wall Street Journal,* a writer from a well-known newspaper was refused an interview because the students were simply sick and tired of being probed and prodded and picked at. He became openly hostile and said, "What you've got to understand is that you have no *choice* now. You're news. I'm coming anyway, and if I can't talk with any of you, I'll just have to do the story without you. I'll call you when I get there."

The first reaction of the students, predictably, was to tell the guy to go straight to hell in a bucket. In a long meeting, one of the students said, "Yeah, but what if this jerk gets up here and starts banging around the county alone, harassing our contacts and making a lot of racket about the fact that we wouldn't talk to him? Then what do we do?"

Finally it was decided to let the man come into the class so that all the students could talk with him as a group, hopefully satisfy most of his needs, and then let him go around the county alone and talk with whomever he wanted, with the provision that if it was with one of our contacts, we be allowed to check with that person first to make sure his visit would be welcome.

He arrived, agreed to the conditions, came to class, apparently got what he wanted, and wrote his story. Under other circumstances, however, a team of two or three enthusiastic students would have taken him under their wing, made motel reservations for him, taken him into the community on actual *Foxfire* interviews set up in advance with contacts who didn't mind a journalist being along, introduced him to the principal, school officials, and anyone else he wanted to meet, shown him through our entire operation from top to bottom, and answered questions for as long as he felt like asking them. If he didn't like what he saw, fine, but at least he'd have seen it all.

Fortunately most of the journalists who came to us were genuinely friendly and interested, and we were generally able to make as much use of them as they had hoped to make of us. Early on, for example, Suzy and I began to ask them, as part of their visit, to come into the journalism class to be interviewed by the students about their own lives, how they had gotten into the field, and what it was like to be a professional journalist. By far the greater benefit to us, however, came as students struggled to answer questions they were asked—without our help. Questions like,

"What do you think the impact of *Foxfire* has been on this community?" or "Where does *Foxfire* go from here?" or "What are you and your fellow students *really* getting out of the experience of putting a *Foxfire* together?" or "Does anything you learn from *Foxfire*'s classes carry over into your other school work?" or "Do you think your work with *Foxfire* will affect your career choice in any way?" All these were the kinds of questions students had thought about to some extent, but when they were cornered by a sometimes skeptical journalist who really probed, they had to look at the work they were doing through a different lens. Usually they continued to think about what was happening to them long after their interrogators were gone. They'd come into class, for example, and in the middle of a discussion say, "I got asked a question the other day about where our organization is going in the future. Where *are* we going, anyway? What's *Foxfire* going to look like when I come back five years from now?" And as often as not, Suzy and I would answer, "Well, where do you *want* it to go? What *should* we be doing in five years that we aren't doing now?" The rest of the time would be spent scratching our heads and speculating and plotting—and dreaming.

In at least three instances, the experiences we had with journalists were terrible, but we learned from those, too, and in the process the students became more and more concerned about and protective of *Foxfire* and the community people involved. Nothing Suzy and I could have said would have made this happen more forcefully than the time when, for example, a professional photographer came through on assignment from a wire service. I was in Washington at the time, having been invited by NEH to sit on one of those panels that evaluates proposals, and so Suzy and the students handled the request. In the midst of my work, I got a phone call from Suzy, who said, "I think we may have a problem." The photographer's assignment had been to put together a photographic portfolio of Appalachian life, and he had requested the aid of several organizations in the mountains to take him to people and places he could photograph. The students had agreed to take him around but by the end of the first day began to rebel. Suzy helped me reconstruct the incident for this book, writing, "I remember being impressed and feeling like we should accommodate him, and going to some lengths to do so at first, [but by the end of the second day the students were] somewhat disenchanted with him. He was getting pushier and greedier every day, it seemed. He wanted to go out again the *next* day to meet even more people. He was acting as if he had struck gold, and you could see the hunger in his eyes. That made [the students] uncomfortable, and it made me *really* uncomfortable. We were bringing this stranger into people's homes for him to photograph as if they were specimens instead of people. We didn't know who this man was, and we began to have grave misgivings about what we were doing. He had no personal relationship with the people we took him to meet; *we* had a relationship with them and felt like we were betraying them, taking advantage of their trust in us. He struck me as a person who was only concerned about his photographs, *not* the people he took photographs of. So at the end of the second day . . . we decided we needed your help. On the morning of that fateful third day, I spoke with him when he and his cohort came in, and told them that I had spoken to you about it and that we had decided that we would wait until you came back before we took him out to meet any more people. That's when he blew up at me, and ranted and raved how he had been planning to do a big article about *Foxfire* which would give us a tremendous amount of publicity and set us up for life, but that now we had blown it and therefore would never amount to anything. Something like that. Then I remember [the manager of the motel where he was staying] returned several unsold magazines to the office and said, 'If *Foxfire* won't cooperate with us, we won't cooperate with *Foxfire!*' At that point, I could not believe what was happening to me, to all of us, and handed the whole mess to you when you returned."

By the time I got back and got briefed on the situation, it was the evening of the third day. The photographer was even more furious. I found him in his motel room, alternately sulking and shouting about the fact that he had won a Pulitzer prize for one of his photographs and he wasn't going to put up with such treatment from teenagers who obviously didn't know who it was they were mistreating. Earlier he had called his editor and presumably screamed at him for a while, and then he had made up his mind that he was going to destroy us. When I arrived and introduced myself, he was ready and launched into his "You don't understand how much power I have, I am going to see to it that you never sell another copy of that ———— magazine" routine.

It was the first time I'd been faced with such a situation, and I wasn't particularly comfortable, but I sat there for about half an hour and let him yell and pace and work off some of his anger. When he'd wound down somewhat, I quietly explained how our project worked, how the relationship that Suzy and I had with our students had evolved, the fact that we would back the decision they had made and that he was finished in our county as far as any cooperation from us was concerned. As I left, I said he could try to destroy our project if he wanted to, but it seemed to me to be a pretty small target for someone of his prestige and esteem to waste time attacking.

The next day he was gone, and we never heard from him again.

In another case, a television crew arrived from New York to film the students at work. Since videotape had become part of our program, we had decided to insist that any such crews we accepted be willing to show the students how they set up such things as lighting and microphones in difficult filming situations; use the students, when possible, as part of their crew; and answer any questions the students might have. I had a rather idealized vision of students and professionals working together as an interdependent team, which never fully materialized due to professional egos, time constraints, and certain union regulations, but students at least were able to get closer than they had ever been before to the mechanics of putting together those on-the-road news features most of them had seen on national television. In addition, it gave us a chance to show a different side of Appalachia to a national audience than the stereotyped, stilted version so often presented by the media.

In this case, several days earlier, we had set up an interview for the crew with Aunt Arie, who always enjoyed the attention and activity. I sent the crew up with five students, and, as I wrote in my journal later:

I'm getting more and more leery of this sort of thing, and this clinched it. . . . Today, she was sick. The crew got her out of bed and propped her up in front of the fireplace and turned on the lights and filled the house with wires and cables and moved furniture and got her to talk for an hour and a half—shot 2,000 feet of film. But by the time I got there, the kids were furious. Aunt Arie was exhausted and white, and the men still were shooting, even as she rose to throw up off the front porch. I held her head while her body heaved with the pain of dry retching, and the producer looked on sort of sympathetically, but as though discouraged that she wasn't giving them more—that she was somehow letting them down. I made them turn off the lights and pack their stuff up and got Rhonda and Barbara to put her to bed. One of the problems was that she was taking rubbing liniment (for external use only) internally, so I got David and Dickie to throw it away and go get some antacid from [her neighbor and use their phone to call one of her relatives].

When things calmed down, we got the crew off (they asked us to find a moonshiner for them and let them film him making a run, and the three boys just fixed them with a stony, silent stare). Then David remained behind, and I took the others back to school, got some medicine from Butch [a druggist], picked up Rhonda, and we went back. The preacher and Ruth [the relative] were there by then and Aunt Arie was much better. She got out of bed, got some supper down (potatoes roasted in the ashes of her fire), and when all was well, we left, and Ruth spent the night.

It was quite an experience, and a warning of sorts about what can happen with this sort of thing. It reemphasizes again our need to protect the people we have now exposed to the outside world. There's going to be some heavy reassessment made this coming month of our policy regarding more publicity.

Through such experiences, painful as they were at the time, and uncomfortable as they are to recollect, all of us learned and grew, and we found that a person's or organization's reputation is no reliable indicator of how that person or the people working for any given organization are going to behave. No one deserves to be immune from the laws of common human decency and consideration, and we got better at making that clear to others—and reminded ourselves of the same—as time went on.

During this time, students learned how to be more and more assertive, and they became fiercely protective of all they cared about. When people from outside tried to intimidate them into bowing to their wishes, they soon learned when and how to stand fast, independent of me.

Permission was given to an internationally known television production group to develop a script, but when the script was submitted for review, the students discovered that, among other things, it called for a simulated destruction of Aunt Arie's house by fire and its subsequent rebuilding by concerned community people. Since it was a fictitious event (as were many of the others in the script), the students decided that our name should not be used in the film or titles in any way. The playwright flew in from California and met with the students to plead his case, but they wouldn't budge. Finally he threatened to make the film anyway in another part of the Appalachians, and they told him to go ahead, promising that if *Foxfire*'s name appeared, implying that the events he portrayed had happened here and were truth, they'd have him sued.

The matter went as far as a meeting in New York between the corporation's executives and our lawyer, John Viener, ending when John spelled out precisely what would happen if the company used our name. Since no contracts had been signed—we had simply agreed by phone to let them work up a script with the understanding that it would have to be approved before anything was signed—the matter was dropped.

Ronnie, our editor and one of our best friends, inevitably ran afoul of this growing assertiveness. A journal entry of March 8, 1972, reads:

Ronnie called us offering a $10,000 advance on the second volume which she wants delivered by May 1. Crisis. We talked it all over in journalism, and the kids vetoed it. We need more time—more working room.

[I called her and told her of the vote] and she was somewhat worried, but that's the situation. We'll really shape it up this summer and deliver a *beautiful* book, and if it's less than beautiful, we just won't deliver it. That's all.

The kids are really proud of the magazine and what it's done, and they— and I—are determined that the second [volume] be at least as good (and hopefully better than) the first, and they aren't going to push it—even if it means losing a chunk of that advance.

I was never prouder of them.

Hard on the heels of the media pressure came the letters, and though not in the mailbags I had feared, there were thousands of them. In fact, we calculated that by the first anniversary of the book, well over thirty thousand pieces of mail had come in and been processed by the students involved. Some requested subscriptions. Some wanted to purchase crafts produced by people we had documented. Some came from teachers who wanted information about starting a similar project with their own students. Some came from university professors who informed us that they were using the book in their courses. Some were written by people in the midst of building log cabins who wanted additional information.

I had hoped from the start that the book would be seen, enjoyed, reviewed, and appreciated as far more than just a back-to-the-land survival volume, and most of the mail confirmed that the readers saw it as a much richer, more fulfilling document. Our favorite letters came from people like Mrs. Queen R. Stone of Milwaukee, who wrote:

You should be told that *The Foxfire Book* is an answer to prayer from an eighty-six-year-old grandmother with three grown grandchildren, who has tried for years to recreate in their minds a time—some of it lived through, but most of it family stories I have heard all my life. Somehow I felt instinctively that the world was moving so fast I had become a kind of link from a forgotten past to a bewildering present. . . . Some of my friends, my contemporaries for the most part, seem to regard such knowledge to be something to be hidden and lived down. I'm sure I'm thought to be a little "tetched in the head," but the young folks beg for the stories. They seem to have an unconscious need for some reassurance in this uncertain time. . . . Maybe you will realize how much *Foxfire* means to me and to all of us, and how we thank you for following your inspiration to start the marvelous project which has brought us all together.

Few things did more to make the students aware of the audience their work had beyond Rabun County than such mail, and the fact that I could say to them in all honesty, "Thousands of people are going to read the article you're working on now, so make sure it's right grammatically and factually," was, and still is, one of the most powerful motivational tools at my disposal.

Another, of equal power, was the option that now existed of going on a major trip to give a speech. Suzy and I had continued to maintain that the only invitations that should be considered were those from groups willing to pay all expenses involved in my bringing students along. Other invitations were refused automatically unless there were compelling extenuating circumstances. There rarely were. Using this system, spacing the commitments as carefully as possible to avoid complete disruption of our work at home, and taking different students nearly every time, I and they —many of whom had never flown before or given speeches before, or been farther from home than Atlanta—moved out across the country. A year after the publication of the book, in the introductory letter to Volume 6, Number 4 of *Foxfire*, I told our subscribers:

[I have now been able to take] Stan to the Oral History Association Convention at the L.B.J. Library in Austin, Texas; Gary to the Hill School in Pottstown, Pennsylvania, and a television show in Cleveland, Ohio; Barbara, Claude, and Dana to the annual National Trust for Historic Preservation meeting in Washington; Randy, Annette, and Phyllis to the annual National Association of Secondary School Principals meeting in Washington; Mary Thomas and Julia to Columbus, Ohio [through the National Humanities

Faculty], as consultants to an Appalachian elementary school there; Gary, Stan, and Claude to speak at the University of North Carolina at Charlotte; Ray and Don to Lookout Mountain, Tennessee, as consultants to the Mountain School Project there—and on and on it goes with no end in sight.

To say that it is exciting to be able to offer high school kids opportunities like these would be the understatement of the century. *Foxfire* is indeed beginning to glow—thanks to all of you out there.

19

Land—and a Six-sided Log House

In the winter of 1971, I made one of the biggest decisions of my life. I decided to buy myself a piece of land.

I had seen it coming. It wasn't a surprise. I wanted to stay in Rabun County, but I had lived on the school's campus before and I knew I couldn't make that work because the contact with the students was too close and too intense, and when I needed to get away and think things through, there was noplace to go. At the Hambidge Foundation, it was better, but Mrs. Hambidge was getting older, and philosophical problems I had with her board, which was readying itself for the inevitable takeover, made it clear that I was not going to be able to stay there much longer.

For months, in my spare time, I followed leads. My father came down to Georgia when I told him I thought I had finally found the right place, and we walked over it together in the midst of a snowstorm, picking out possible house sites and studying the lay of the land. Obviously I couldn't afford it. I was only making $500 a month. But Dad, believing in land as an investment, agreed to back a loan for me through the bank with which he did business, and I decided to take the plunge.

At the last moment, the woman who owned the land decided not to sell it after all, and that night, about as depressed as I've ever been, I went to

Henry's and started drinking beer. Had he been allowed to sell anything stronger, I would probably have been drinking that.

Henry's was the friendliest tavern in Rabun County. It was little more than a shack out on Highway 76, inside which was one small dark room with worn wooden floors dominated by a potbelly stove around which customers would sit in the winter, propping their feet up on the stove's footrail. Around that central circle, there were several battered wooden tables and chairs. The back of the room was divided from the front by a long bar/counter behind which, in plain view, Henry and Eileen Phillips, the owners, cooked hamburgers so gargantuan and awe inspiring that word of their "Henryburgers" spread far beyond the borders of our little county. Unopened cardboard cases of beer stacked unceremoniously along the walls, quiet conversation, the heater's warmth, the pop and sizzle and smell of the frying house specialty, and the uninhibited friendliness of Henry and Eileen made it a perfect place to work off a good dose of the blues.

After about an hour there, a former student of mine came in, spotted me at the bar, and sat down beside me to visit. Sensing that something was wrong, he asked me what the trouble was, and I told him. I simply let him have it for what must have been half an hour.

When I was through, he began telling me about a man he worked for who was ready to sell some land he owned outside Mountain City. He offered to show it to me, I agreed, and the next day we walked the lines of what turned out to be 110 acres, most of it too steep to do much with, but a piece of land far enough away from the main highway and with enough level plateaus to have real potential. The upper boundary shared the ridge line with a state park. There were several fine springs that could supply all the water I'd ever need. An old logging road provided access to the center of the property, and with a day's work from a good bulldozer operator, I'd have a passable driveway. I could have the upper, 59-acre, steeper portion for $600 an acre. The remainder would sell for $800 an acre. Or I could buy both pieces. I called Dad, and agreed to buy the 59-acre tract. In my journal on January 19, 1972, I wrote:

Tomorrow I am to close the deal on the land I have bought. Despite its flaws, I know I will write that check tomorrow, thus putting myself in hock forever. . . . Nevertheless, I am hungry for my own piece of land. I have a desire so great for my own place that it may force me into making a mistake—but I move headlong into this deal anyway, tired of the waiting, tired of the searching, tired of the negotiation—hungry to have it all settled and done with once and for all. Hungry to start again. My own home. My own garden. My own spot.

The next day, on January 20—the day, coincidentally, that the first copy of *The Foxfire Book* arrived in the mail—I added in the journal:

After class I went to Clayton to finish up this land thing, writing a check for $32,400—probably the biggest check I'll ever write.

A strange experience. They didn't get excited at all, but I was so awed by the whole idea that my life almost passed before my eyes. In a daze, I went with the lawyer to record the deed in the courthouse and declare it all done—finished.

It was so simple, so short, so uncomplicated, and yet I was so keyed and tensed I could only mumble the questions I had been instructed by Dad to get cleared up: title search (the lawyer was satisfied), water rights (I had them), etc. The most unbusinesslike transaction for my part that I have ever been involved in, and yet they were so businesslike—so in control—that I felt numb. I just signed away my life, relying on my previous investigations and soul searchings. Dad would have been horrified, and I guess I was too. But in fifteen minutes it was over, and I was sitting in my jeep again wondering what I had just done.

Well, that's it, and I pray it will all prove to have been a wise move. I am horrified at my lack of real emotion. I have just done it. That's all. And yet I know that, deep down, nothing will ever be the same again. I now own fifty-nine acres of land. Period.

By March, I had designed a two-story log house that I thought would fill my own needs and be large enough to accommodate a family when and if I married. I decided to make it six-sided (so the logs I would be wrestling with wouldn't have to be so long), with a central fireplace into which would be mounted the beams for the first and second floors and the rafters. By this time, noise about *The Foxfire Book* was building to a peak, and the land became a weekend refuge that more than made up for its cost. And despite the fact that I had never built a house before, I had no doubt that I could do it—especially considering the fact that so many students had volunteered to help out for free that I couldn't imagine how I could use them all.

I think I learned more about students while building that house than in any classroom in which I've ever taught. It was an experience that became simply one more massive chunk of evidence to buttress my conviction not only that young people are often hungry for opportunities to be engaged —heart, body, and mind—in positive action, but also that they can be counted on to carry their share of the load when a project truly interests them. Without those fourteen- and fifteen-year-olds, I could never have built that house. They were with me from the first day, and they never gave up. And they never expected a dime in payment. A partial record of one weekend survives in a journal entry of March 8, 1972:

Ken, David, and I spent Friday afternoon gathering rocks off the mountainside for the chimney, and Carlton and Kevin dug a huge, two-foot-deep foundation hole for it. That one act committed me, I guess, to the house location. . . . It was all strangely arbitrary—sort of a "What the heck, let's put it here." I look at that hole now and think, "Someday, there'll be a house there."

The next morning, Kevin and I took off from campus early and turned over six rows of the garden by noon. It was hard work. The ground was full of roots and rocks. But it was good work, too. We didn't have a watch, so we set a borrowed alarm clock out on the hood of the jeep and set the alarm for 11:45 [so we could get back on campus by lunch and pick up some other students who had had to work on campus that morning] and started in. We worked side by side, laughing, swearing at roots, exclaiming over the quality of that black soil, imagining rows of sweet yellow corn and fat beans. Kevin has been locked up on campus for weeks with his before-breakfast and after-school dairy obligation, and it really seemed to do him good to be off campus, working at something he enjoyed. He carried on about his father and how he used to raise a garden, and what it was like when he was young. The ground was so hard he had to place the point of the shovel and then jump up on it, landing with both feet to drive the point into the ground, and then haul the clump of earth over, but he kept jumping and hauling and laughing, and sometimes he was even ahead of me. I look at him and think what a fine little man he's going to make. He's got more spunk and spirit than kids twice his size.

Back for lunch, we picked up ten more kids—made two trips in the jeep. The first crew (Kevin, Beals, Carlton, David, and Gary)—the tree cutting crew —started in on trees while I went back for the second crew. I put the latter out in the garden finishing up what Kevin and I had started. The soil was just too good to let it go any longer. Then I joined the others. At one point, Kevin left the group and headed down to check on the garden crew to find them not doing it to his satisfaction, so he instructed them all over again and got them going right. Nobody was going to mess up *his* garden. I could just barely hear him: "Look, damnit. Do it right or get out." Nobody argued with him.

Trees began to come down . . . amid great shouts of glee and triumph when one fell exactly as they had wanted it to. We made a quick survey of the strings outlining the house place, verified that they were sixteen feet long, and decided to cut the logs into eighteen-and-a-half-foot lengths. That was our second commitment. Now the wall length is set. No turning back.

We tried to cut selectively, getting out "cull" timber to thin the woods in the process, all of which resulted in long, vociferous debates at the trunk of each poplar:

"This one."

"I don't know. Looks big."

"Yeah, but you can use the top two thirds."

"Yeah, but how do we move the bottom?"

"Besides, it's an awful nice tree."

"Yeah, but . . ." And so on.

But slowly they fell, and were cut up. After hauling three or four lengths up to the house place, uphill all the way, we got our heads together and decided to drag the rest using a chain and the jeep. Kevin thought that was great, and rode with me, hopping out to supervise the attaching of the chain, and then hopping into the jeep to ride to the top of the hill with me, sometimes hanging out the window to make sure the log was still following us, talking all the way. At the top, two would meet us, unhook the chain, roll the log out of the way to the edge of the road to be lifted up the five-foot-high embankment to the house site later, and we'd return for another log.

We had quite a system going for a while. Carlton had decided that one fine birch was not to be touched at all, and so he was taking special care to fell each poplar so that it didn't even brush against his birch. Each time one would fall (accompanied by that absolute concentration and intensity that only kids seem capable of), and fall correctly, he would rush over to me, his face full of glee and pride. "Look at that! Look at that! Perfect!" And then he'd laugh and head for the next one.

The teamwork was great. When all the logs we were going to cut for that day had been hauled up, all twelve of us muscled them up the embankment to the house place together, grunting and straining. At one point, some uncanny bit of timing lofted one huge log right into the air, over the top, and well up onto the flat ground above. Everyone just stopped dead for an instant, amazed, and then started yelling and shouting and laughing. The whole job was filled with the normal cracks about who was stronger than whom, filled with all the bravado kids have. It was almost like a great catharsis where everyone was suddenly released from the tension of school and the tension of constant scrutiny, and suddenly kids that didn't even like each other were working side by side and pounding each other on the back and shouting encouragement: "All right, now, this one's going to scare us when we try to pick it up, but we can do it. Just don't drop it!"

Or someone would yell, "One, two, three, *lift,* " and then not lift himself, breaking up while everyone strained and swore at him to grab on. Gary was absolutely tireless, steady as a rock, solid as granite. Always friendly. Always encouraging. Spectacular kid. And Kevin—we'd get a log up on our shoulders, and Kevin would barely be able to reach it, but he'd dance around underneath, pushing when he could, chattering encouragement.

Near the end of the day, I had to take the garden crew back, and when I returned, the others had built a small fire and were seated gazing at the stack of logs they had piled up for the house-to-be and listening to Carlton exclaim, "Look at those. They're perfect. Just perfect. What a house it's going to be." He's so caught up in it all that he's taken over as though it were to be his house —urging me on when I'm down. "Look, buddy. We've got to get the rest of those trees. Understand?"

That night, we went to a tourist restaurant in Clayton where you could get all you could eat for $1.50 each, and they strolled in, filthy, and grinned every time one of the diners saw them and gasped. We all looked like we had just come out of the mines, but they loved it. People kept coming up asking them what they'd been doing, and they'd turn with just a hint of disdain and superiority and tell their interrogators how they were cutting trees for *their* log house, and then savor the expressions of those who had wished all their lives that they had had the nerve to try that same thing but had passed up the chance.

They ate like hogs.

On the way back, they pleaded with me not to take them back to school. Kevin didn't care *where* we went. "Just ride around awhile. I don't care." No one wanted to turn loose of the day, so we wound up going out to my cabin and putting on some records. Paul Wolford [one of the teachers at the school] came in, and they told him what they'd been doing, and we all just sat for an hour in front of a blazing fire in the fireplace and savored the day.

When I did take them back, finally, *they* were thanking *me*. I was the one in their debt, but they couldn't see it that way. For me, it was one of those moments that one relates to people who are mystified that anyone could stay friendly with kids. How can you not? . . . I couldn't turn my back on them now for all the money in Georgia. When I get discouraged, I hope I recall moments like these.

During this same period of time, in the midst of a visit with Aunt Arie, she casually mentioned something that had happened to her "down there by the old mill." None of us knew the place she was referring to, so we pressed her. It turned out that an old building, completely covered with kudzu, that stood at the entrance of the road leading to Aunt Arie's house had once been a grist mill. We had passed within an arm's length of it scores of times by now but had never looked inside as we didn't want to trespass, and we assumed it was an empty building anyway.

As we went out that day, we stopped, entered it, and almost fell over from surprise, for inside stood the hand-carved wooden gears and works of a complete grist mill, still set up and ready for action. The outside water wheel had long since rotted away, as had part of the main shaft, but otherwise it was intact. There was no way we could allow something that rare and unique to simply rot.

Within a few days we had located the owner, talked him into selling the mill and setting a price ($2,000). The students voted unanimously to use some of the royalty money from the book to buy it, and we gave the owner a check. But now what were we going to *do* with it?

I had harbored a dream for a museum of some sort for years. We already had a respectable collection of artifacts, for often, when we asked someone to show us how to make something, the response was, "Well, I'd be glad to do it if I had the tools, but after I stopped doing that kind of work, mine got away from me. You bring me the tools and materials I need, and I'll make it for you." And so, over time, and partly with an $1,800 grant from the Georgia Council for the Arts, we had accumulated our own collection of tools and supplies, as well as the items our contacts had made for us in demonstrations. The items were stored in friends' barns around the county and in our offices.

Acquisition of the log mill building afforded a perfect opportunity to have our own display and storage area—if we could find a place to which to move it.

A local businessman and motel owner had urged me to consider building a museum on property he owned in the town adjacent to the school. He even offered to give us the property, his reasoning being that such an attraction would be good for his tourist business. I was tempted, now that we had a building, to accept his offer, but the students were dead set against it. Unpleasant encounters had convinced them that they wanted no part of a tourist attraction.

We briefly considered asking permission to use some of the school property, but there were problems with that option, too. What if, for example, the relationship with the school soured, the Foxfire operation was no longer welcome, and we had more than one building? Could we really afford to dismantle everything, pack it up, and move it all again?

The longer we talked, the more attractive the idea became for Foxfire to own its own piece of land, away from the main highway and closed to the tourist traffic. The students became more and more excited about the idea of having their own place to work off campus after school hours, on weekends, and during the summers. And the more they talked, the more sense it all made.

In a meeting held in April, 1973, the board voted to allow the organization to purchase the piece of property below and adjacent to mine. I had assumed the owner would want to develop the lower tract and sell it off in lots, and I was prepared for that eventuality, but he agreed to let us purchase it, and a fourteen-year-old student wrote out the check. He and I signed it, and Foxfire had its first piece of property.

With that, and since we couldn't afford the chance of further damage to the grist mill, we disassembled it, moved it, and reconstructed it on Foxfire's land.

Tommy Wilson, a former student, was hired full-time during the summer of '73 to do most of the work on the mill, with other students pitching in on a volunteer basis when he needed help. The experience of saving that building and researching its history was so rewarding and so relatively inexpensive that we began to look for others. And we found them. By the end of the summer of '74, eight more had been purchased, dismantled, moved, and set back up again under new roofs.

20

Do We Have to Be an Organization?

To everyone's surprise, *The Foxfire Book* continued to sell. The royalty checks that began to arrive from Doubleday every six months (some in excess of $100,000) imposed some major new burdens, albeit welcome ones, on the shoulders of Suzy, myself, and our students. There were obvious, wonderful uses to which part of the money could be put—guaranteeing Suzy a regular salary and some job security, for example; and guaranteeing students summer salaries and college scholarships, to say nothing of equipment and supply needs that could now be met without eating into magazine subscriber income. It also meant that we could hire additional staff members, with the approval of the school, to help enrich the options we could offer students.

Now that we had tangible assets, however, including property and buildings, it was time to make sure the organization was not only stable but had some clearly articulated answers to some very thorny and ominous questions. What would happen to existing and future assets, for example, if Suzy and I both decided to leave Rabun County and pursue other careers? Obviously we couldn't split up the money and equipment between us. In the first place, it simply didn't belong to us, and in the second place, under the laws of tax-exempt status, assets can only be disbursed in certain ways. Presumably, Suzy and I and the students would have some say over this process, and presumably we would try to ensure that the project continued under strong new leadership. But what if the organization collapsed nevertheless? What legal entity would take over ownership of our copyrighted products? What group would assume responsibility in case of legal problems or lawsuit? To whom would Double-day make out royalty checks if the books continued to sell for another ten years? Would the school step in and take over? Probably. Would school officials allow the students to participate in decisions as to how the money would be spent? Probably not. And so where would it go? Into Ping-Pong tables and kitchen cleanser and toilet paper? Into the kinds of teaching materials that we might oppose philosophically?

You see part of the problem with which we were faced.

And what of that portion of each royalty check not needed for daily operations? The money could be split, as it came in, among the students who had produced material included in any book that generated royalties. But would each get an equal share? Would a student who had written a two-page section get the same as one who had written a forty-page chapter? Would length be the determining factor? What if, because of the differing ability levels of the students, it had taken a student twice as long and had required twice as many rewrites and late nights to prepare the shorter section for publication? Should not time and effort expended be the determining factor? What about those students whose work appeared in the magazine but could not be included in a book? Did they get ignored? And what about the contacts who had been interviewed? Shouldn't they get a share? And how would that be determined? By the amount of time they had given us? Should a person who had given us one home remedy get the same as Aunt Arie, with whom we had spent days and who had given us information that resulted not only in a chapter that featured her alone but also in other pieces scattered throughout the book? What of people we had interviewed whose information was not included in the book at all but who had given generously of their time nevertheless? And what of the contacts who were dead? Give their shares, if they could be determined equitably, to their estates?

Perhaps the problem could be alleviated somewhat simply by paying the students and the contacts in advance for their time, and get each to sign a paper releasing any claim on future royalties, which could then be put to some other purposes. Again, the same problems rose, compounded by new ones. Pay contacts a straight fee per interview, regardless of length or the amount of information later used? What if none of it was used? And what if we were just visiting someone socially and in the context of normal conversation that person mentioned a weather sign we wanted to print? What if people decided to start releasing information in driblets so they could multiply the number of times they got paid? What would it do to our project if students decided to work with us *only* because they got paid? What of students who wanted to get into the journalism classes but couldn't because of size limitations? Who decides who gets in and who stays out? And what's the next step? Students who will play varsity basketball only if they get paid out of gate receipts? Annual contract negotiations and bidding wars between coaches for promising fourteen-year-olds? Player strikes supported by angry parents? A sixteen-year-old quarterback endorsing, in the area media, the local bank on the board of which sit several school board members, in return for a Trans Am and a year's worth of gas?

I could go on like this for pages, but at this point the potential humor of the situation, for me, is replaced by cynicism and gloom. Obviously it was past time to get our act together.

I can't remember a single discussion in which Suzy and I hadn't both felt that one of the finest things that could happen to the Foxfire organization would be for it eventually to be owned and run by local people who had gone through the program as high school students, had gone on to college and graduated in a related field, and had come back home to take it over and run it in a sane, responsible way. One of the options that certainly confronted us now was to begin to put that into effect. We had no college graduates yet, but many of our best former students were in college and two of them—Jan Brown and Mike Cook—had decided, after several years, to major in journalism at the University of Georgia. There might be some hope there.

Almost coincidentally, Pat Rogers graduated with a degree in journalism from the same school and came back home looking for work. Pat had been a senior when I began teaching at Rabun Gap and so he had not been directly involved with us, but a short story he had submitted had been published in that first issue of our magazine, and he had stayed in touch over the years. Suzy and I and the students liked him immensely, he was a favorite of our principal, had been a top student at our high school, his parents were among the most respected in our county, he wanted to work with us, and so we hired him.

Pat immediately took over responsibility for the student newspaper, *Talon,* and he and the students decided to do away with the mimeographed format we had used from the beginning and turn it into a full-size, professionally printed publication complete with photographs, full-size headlines, and a more frequent and regular publication schedule. In addition, he pitched in with Suzy and me to help get increasing numbers of students out on interviews, help those students prepare their work for publication, help me with administrative duties, and, like most teachers at Rabun Gap, help out whenever an extra pair of hands was needed (including running the time clock at school basketball games). Like all good members of any team, he allowed himself to become so completely absorbed in our work so quickly that it was soon hard for any of us to imagine how we had made it without him. And his wife, Ruth Ann, who had found a job with our local bank, lifted the bookkeeping chores off my shoulders, thus freeing me from what had become an increasingly unwelcome albatross.

Meanwhile a board of directors meeting was called for April of 1973. John Viener and John Dyson made their first trip to Rabun County. Reflecting a growing need for committed, actively involved leadership, two board members (including Howard, who was now living in England) were replaced by Roy Sinclair, one of the closest friends John Dyson and I had (and another fraternity brother of ours from college), and Pat, who had been with us for nearly nine months and had more than proved his worth. Pat was made vice president and thus my successor should I move on.

We also voted to completely revamp the advisory board, keeping people like Joe Hickerson, Ralph Rinzler, Ralph Gray, and Sam Stanley and adding people like Herb McArthur (who had by now left NEH), Carroll Hart (director of the Georgia Department of Archives and History), and Robert Gray (director of the Southern Highlands Handicraft Guild). In response to some criticism our work had drawn from professional academic folklorists like Richard Dorson, who felt the program wasn't rigorous enough and might lead students into a misguided notion of what folklore really was, we also added Sandy Ives, a folklorist at the University of Maine, the director of the Northeast Archives of Folklore and Oral History and a former student of Dr. Dorson's. A regular annual meeting was called for, and it was decided that we should offer to pay all expenses, including travel, for all board members to ensure their attendance, their firsthand familiarity with our work and our goals, and hence the quality of their input.

It was also decided to change the corporate name from the unwieldy Southern Highlands Literary Fund, Inc., to the tighter, more appropriate Foxfire Fund, Inc., and John Viener drew up the necessary papers. All copyrights, including any that had been registered in my name, were reassigned to the fund.

From this new, much firmer foundation grew our present system of a board of directors completely committed to our philosophy of education and a twelve-member advisory board, three members of which rotate off at each annual meeting (after having served four-year terms), to be replaced either by a colleague each has hand-picked to serve our needs or by a person the staff selects from a continually growing list of experts in various fields whose expertise and guidance we covet. The board members, who only rarely miss the occasion, arrive on a Thursday, spend the day Friday in school with our students, and from Friday evening through Sunday morning are immersed in a whirlwind of meetings, barbecues, picnics, and intense small-group discussions with students, staff members, community leaders, and friends.

Spearheaded by Suzy, a community advisory board was also formed. It is now made up of a dozen community adults who serve on a rotating basis and are drawn from parents of students currently in our program, former students, our school's administration, and various business and political leaders. Meeting monthly in the evening, usually over supper, and chaired by one of its members, the primary functions of the board are to monitor our work continually to make sure it serves the real needs of our community and to help us chart and guide future directions. Students involved in our classes are encouraged to attend these meetings and participate in the discussion of any and all issues. Should the time ever come to dissolve the corporation, these boards would meet to dispose of its holdings.

The thorny question of payment to staff, students, and contacts underwent steady scrutiny and intermittent classroom discussion for years. It has long since been resolved as follows:

To eliminate the possibility of any person being able to accuse a staff member of "getting rich off students and contacts," all adult staff members who teach are paid at the same salary scale as their fellow state-paid teachers. Others are paid less, but on a scale that fairly represents the "going rate" for the work they perform. Our organization began paying my salary in the mid-seventies so that a state-paid position could be freed, thus allowing the school to hire another English teacher and reduce the average number of students per English class. I am paid at the same salary scale, however, and all honoraria generated by presentations I and the students make go into a special Foxfire account to pay for unreimbursed student travel to folk festivals, selected conferences, and schools with which we are conducting student exchange programs. This travel fund is also tapped to cover expenses of staff and students who are on major overnight interviewing and collecting expeditions outside our immediate area.

During the school year, with the exception of seniors we hire through the school's early-release work/study program, students are not paid for the work they do in connection with any of our classes. They receive academic credit instead, and in the opinion of all concerned, that is as it should be. Certain fringe benefits (the opportunity to travel, for example) are awarded on the basis of merit to students who are carefully selected by the staff members during the staff meetings we hold as a group once a week. (For a time, we allowed students in the journalism classes to pick their own representatives for trips, but as the number of students involved in the growing number of Foxfire-sponsored courses approached two hundred, everyone agreed that the new system would be more satisfactory.) Such opportunities are spread through the group as equitably as possible. It would be rare, for example, for the same student to be allowed to make more than one major trip per year.

Cash rewards to students for work well done come primarily in the form of summer jobs and college scholarships. Before the publication of *The Foxfire Book*, those few students hired each summer (at $500 each) were former students already in college who intended to use the money to help defray their school expenses. Now as many as twenty-five to thirty students may be awarded summer jobs, they range in age from seventh-graders to college students, and there is no expectation as to how they will spend their salary, which can amount to as much as $1,500 for a ten-week job, depending on how many summers they have worked with us. We encourage them to save as much as they can, in some cases helping them open their first savings accounts; and if some of them want us to withhold all or part of their check weekly and pay them the balance at the end of the summer, we will do that gladly. But a confrontation with an angry parent who said, "Don't you ever try to tell my son how to spend his money. He's old enough to make his own decisions without your help" cured us of some of the zeal with which we once pushed for individual fiscal responsibility.

To assist deserving former students who are going on to college or trade school, a scholarship program was initiated. Awards are based on individual need and can be large enough to pay all tuition and expenses for all the years involved if the need is serious enough. In recognition of the work they did with Foxfire, which generated the money in the first place, the students are under no obligation to repay the organization. If they wish to make tax-deductible contributions at some future date, they may, and those contributions are placed in a special scholarship fund for future use. Now administered by the community advisory board, the members of which interview each applicant before making a final award determination, nearly $35,000 was awarded for the 1983–84 school year alone.

In addition, the option exists for the best of our students to return home after beyond-high-school training to work in some capacity with Foxfire as adults. Several have.

Payment to contacts depends on the situation, the fact being that most are delighted simply by the friendship and the attention of the students and by the reward that comes from knowing that knowledge they possess is being preserved. But beyond this, contacts and their families receive free copies of any books or magazines in which their interviews appear. Theoretically there is no limit to the number, though rarely have we been asked for more than twenty-five or thirty copies. Contacts and their families can also receive free copies of photographs and tapes upon request.

When a contact shows us how to make something (a wagon wheel, a pair of shoes, a rocking chair, etc.) and lets us document the process, we purchase the item for the Foxfire collection, taking the price the maker traditionally charges—or a price he or she deems fair—and doubling it to reflect the fact that it takes twice as long to make something when one has to stop constantly and explain what he or she is doing.

In addition, contacts who need help or assistance of any sort are encouraged to let us know so that we may try to respond. Alerts also come in to us from former students and community friends. The requests run the gamut from assistance with social security and Medicaid and Medicare regulations and forms, through help with marketing crafts (we receive orders for such craft items at the Foxfire office, pick up the items ordered from the craftspeople, give them the full purchase price, and pack and ship the items at our own expense), to taking contacts who are living away from home back to visit relatives or the old home place. One of our staff members accompanied an area wagon maker to Washington, where he was featured in the Smithsonian's Festival of American Folklife; and another staff member and a team of students replaced the roof and the porch of another contact's house, insulated and Sheetrocked the walls and ceilings, and installed a wood stove—at our expense.

Each of the contacts with whom we have developed a long-lasting relationship also receives free copies of each of our books or magazines, whether or not interviews with them are included; and their names are on a master list that is passed around at each staff meeting. Staff members who have visited any of them socially during the previous week place their initials and the date of the visit beside the appropriate names. If the list reveals people who have not been visited for several weeks, staff members volunteer to check on them before the next staff meeting.

Every Christmas each contact receives a card signed by all the staff and students, along with some small gift. One Christmas, for example, every contact received the card, a plate of cookies, and a group photograph the students had made of themselves and autographed. That, combined with a personal visit to wish them well, brightened a number of homes. More recently, in addition to any other gifts, contacts have been given our annual calendar filled on every page with the autographs of all our students. And the Christmas parties we threw every year at Aunt Arie's before she passed away rivaled any I've ever been to.

And on the Saturday of every Mother's Day weekend—that date selected because so many former students who have moved away or are attending college are home then—we sponsor a covered-dish dinner and party for our contacts to which hundreds of people come.

In these far more appropriate ways, some of the royalty money with which we have been blessed is directed back into the community. It was decided in meetings with board members and students to use the rest in two ways: to expand the program beyond simply producing a quarterly magazine and a school newspaper and actively experiment with other educational options that could be implemented at the high school level; and to invest the remainder in an endowment fund that would continue to support that experimentation long after the *Foxfire* books themselves had stopped selling. With luck, we would never have to beg for money again.

21

Moving to the Rabun County High School

Though to some, our purchase of land and the reconstruction of buildings may have seemed frivolous, its wisdom became clear when it was announced to a shocked audience at a teachers' meeting in 1974 that a bond issue had just passed that would allow construction to begin on a brand-new consolidated county public high school that would serve all community students in grades seven through twelve. Only community students whose parents could afford to pay the tuition would remain at Rabun Gap. The rest would attend the new high school.

For obvious reasons, the situation threw us into a philosophical panic. Who was Foxfire for? Community students and their families, dormitory students from out of the region, or both? Up until now, both groups had benefited and both had contributed equally to its success. In one very real sense, the dorm students had probably benefited more from the project, for the ones I had spent the most time with, for example, were often the ones who were unhappiest and had thrived on the kinds of real-world experiences and the attention my staff and I had been able to give them. For many of these, Foxfire's offices were a sanctuary.

But the fact that the *real* beneficiaries of the program *should* be community students—students who needed to know their roots and their community well if they were ever to initiate some responsible guidance over its future—was inescapable. And the fact that we could easily become divorced from a community we had long since made up our minds to serve was a disturbing—and potentially fatal—reality. Besides, if we were really serious about testing options that other schools might want to scrutinize, the public schools were where we should be. For anyone grappling with the issue of how to make education truly effective, the public schools have to be seen as the front lines. Ideas tested elsewhere by researchers who ignore the realities of the everyday lives of public school teachers often do not transfer well, and those philosophers who aren't in the trenches daily with those who are expected to implement their wisdom are simply shouting into the wind. They have no credibility.

And so, hat in hand, I approached the principal of the Rabun County High School and explained our dilemma. The biggest question, of course, was how the 760 students at his high school would regard Foxfire —a product of their "rival" institution. My credentials were no problem. The fact that the school wouldn't have to pay any of us was an attractive feature, but would the students respond to the program? To find out, the principal, Leland Dishman, along with his guidance counselor, Del Rucker, carved out an experimental English class composed of twenty-five tenth-graders who were willing to participate. During the 1976–77 school year, I would teach at Rabun Gap in the mornings, drive to Clayton for lunch and the pilot class there, and then return to Rabun Gap to finish the day. Members of the administration would monitor the course and the students, and all of us would be better able, by winter, to make some sort of decision about Foxfire's future.

Needless to say, it was a fairly confusing year, but the students at Rabun County High understood the seriousness of their role and responded. When I told them at the beginning of the year that whether or not Foxfire moved to the new school was largely up to them, I wasn't kidding.

In the introduction to the first issue of the magazine published that school year, after explaining the course to the readers, I wrote:

This issue of *Foxfire,* then, delayed on purpose to include RCHS students' material, represents genuine cooperation between the two rival institutions. Though the work of Rabun Gap kids fills most of the issue, the cover photographs as well as the articles on Clyde Runion, Amanda Turpin, and remedies are products of the new class composed entirely of students who had never before in their lives done this kind of work, and who are, I think, doing a magnificent job. In an attempt to test still further the students' willingness to work together, I had several untested Rabun Gap eighth-graders working *under* trained RCHS students on the Clyde Runion article. Hence that article has two introductions—one by a student from each school.

This move presents us with nearly unlimited new possibilities for articles. John Helms, for example, an RCHS student, introduced us to his stepfather, Clyde Runion, a man we had never met before, and then he took the cover photographs. It also presents me with some comically interesting situations: since I now work at both schools, which set of bleachers do I sit on when Rabun Gap and RCHS square off in basketball?

And the move also represents an ironic twist of fate: the school to which I applied for a job first when I was still a student at Cornell was—what else— RCHS.

By the spring of that school year, all parties concerned had made up their minds: we would move to the new school but continue through the transitional year to work with a core group of Rabun Gap dorm students we had trained already and could not, in good conscience, simply walk off and leave behind.

The decision to leave Rabun Gap also meant a loss of our office spaces and darkroom, for in the new high school, we would have only one classroom. Thus the land we had purchased took on a critical new dimension, and the summer preceding the move was one of the busiest ever. Community carpenters and students were hired to convert several of the log houses we had moved into office buildings that could be used year around. Others were converted to provide comfortable staff housing. Buildings we hadn't intended to use immediately suddenly had to be wired and plumbed. Phones had to be installed. Boxes full of tapes and transcriptions and negatives and correspondence and bookkeeping records had to be moved. Filing cabinets and office furniture had to be purchased. Almost overnight a village sprang up below my new (once peaceful) retreat.

But it was beautiful. Hundred-year-old log buildings that had stood empty for years came to life again and hummed with activity as students swarmed over them with tools and supplies. A reservoir was built and connected to a spring high on the mountain. All wiring and the water system were buried underground, and temporary power poles removed. Lights flashed on. Toilets flushed. We were in business.

When the new public high school with its nearly one thousand pupils opened south of Clayton and Rabun Gap in fall, the transition to the new environment proved to be far smoother than I had hoped for. I had made several good friends on the RCHS faculty, and all of them were there. A number of teachers from Rabun Gap were there also, because the conversion of Rabun Gap to a private school meant that their salaries would no longer be paid by the state and so to stay at Rabun Gap would take them out of the state retirement/benefits system. Most of the community students I had known from the north end of the county were there, too, so there was an abundance of familiar faces.

In addition, I found on the first day of school that every single one of the twenty-five students from the experimental pilot group at RCHS had enrolled in another Foxfire class. They were all back for more.

22

A Guided Tour—
Nine Years Later

It is September, 1984. The early morning sunlight is slanting through the yellow tulip poplar trees into my bedroom on the second floor of a six-sided log house built around a central rock chimney.

I close my eyes, and I see myself in a classroom with huge windows and a polished wooden floor facing thirty-three restless adolescents. We are choosing the name for a magazine. We need to raise four hundred dollars. We don't know how.

I get up, shower, dress, pick up the paperwork I've done over the weekend, and walk downstairs onto the porch. Below me, scattered across the mountainside among dogwoods and poplars, are twenty-four log buildings. The one I can see most distinctly is a grist mill. They are all blended so gracefully into the landscape that they look as though they have grown out of the ground as naturally as the trees around them. I close my eyes again, and I see their lights winking on for the first time, and I hear the new pipes filling with cold spring water. That was years ago. Past is past. It's gone. Today is today.

It is Monday, 8:15. I have to go to work. Come with me if you will. I don't mind.

I drive down the steep gravel road past the mill and park beside my garden at the two-story log building that is our main office. Cheryl is already at work. She's a former student who just got her degree in teaching from the University of Georgia and worked with me all summer to help me guide the five students we had hired to do the final interviews and editing for *Foxfire 9*, the last in the series begun with *The Foxfire Book*. She is maneuvering through some of the material one final time before its delivery to Doubleday, and before her leaving to take a job in Washington, D.C.

I put down the papers I am carrying and we talk for a few minutes, checking bases. Steve comes in. One of our summer students, Steve is about to enter the University of Georgia as a freshman. He's been working an extra few weeks before school starts to finish some construction that needs to be done before winter. Today he's going to begin putting up gutters on one of the staff houses, but before he starts, we're going to honor a three-week-long tradition we initiated after the summer students who are still in high school finished up: sitting on the front porch of the office and visiting for about twenty minutes while I have a cup of coffee (Cheryl and Steve don't drink the stuff) and we ease into a new day together. I put on the coffee.

Two cars are coming up the gravel road, their tires spinning in places. One contains John Puckett. A graduate student in education at the University of North Carolina at Chapel Hill, he's been in Rabun County for nine months now examining the inner workings of our organization for a case study of Foxfire, the subject of his Ph.D. thesis. John grins his hello and heads for the coffeepot. He has spent five months in our classes, a summer poring over our records concerning community economic development, and is now beginning a series of interviews with our contacts and our former students concerning their experiences with us. He has scores of names and phone numbers. Lord knows how he's ever going to make sense of all the information he's collected.

Joyce comes in right behind him, having just dropped her son, John, off at Head Start. At about the time Joyce arrives every morning, the phone begins to ring incessantly, unrelentingly. Joyce is not our secretary. She's my administrative assistant. But since we don't have enough money to hire a secretary, she deals with the phones and somehow orchestrates the flow of noise into and through our organization, along with her other responsibilities. John Viener is on the phone from New York already to talk with me about a contract we're developing with a neighborhood organization that wants to use water from our property for their homes, which adjoin our land. That completed, Joyce connects me by phone with Roy Sinclair, also in New York, so we can talk about a possible meeting in Atlanta the Friday of the upcoming board meeting to make some changes in our portfolio with one of our investment officers. Later in the day, looking at my schedule, Joyce sees I'm going to be in Lexington, Kentucky, at an oral history conference the day before, and with Roy's secretary and the airlines, she arranges it so that both Roy and I can arrive in

Atlanta Thursday at about the same time, have rooms in the same hotel, and have an evening together before the Friday meeting, which she also then sets up.

The main business this morning, however, is to go over the draft of a proposal Joyce and I are developing together to send to a foundation that has expressed some interest in supporting our educational work. I've done a rough draft of the narrative over the weekend, and she has collected the supporting material and drafted a budget.

She also has a small stack of phone messages from people who want to visit and organizations that want me to help them out in some way. The visitors Joyce will take care of. She controls the calendar for the organization and knows where all of us are going to be at any time, and so she is the logical one to schedule visits from legitimate individuals or groups (teachers, for example) who want to see certain staff members or certain programs. She'll put more complex visitation requests that involve several days and all students and divisions on hold until the students can have group meetings and discuss the requests and vote.

The requests for me will have to wait until this afternoon. It's already 9:30 and the day is heating up.

On my way down the hill, I stop in at the next office building—another converted two-story log home—to meet with Ann, our bookkeeper, accountant, and magazine circulation director for nearly ten years. She is typing the proposed budgets for the next fiscal year that the students and staff members in each division drafted, and it looks as though our proposed expenditures for the year of nearly $450,000 are going to be well above our projected income levels of $410,000. Copies of the typed draft will have to be brought to the staff meeting this afternoon to be examined and then taken back by the staff members to the students in the various departments for revision and additional planning. Before I go, Ann gets me to add my signature to *Foxfire* books that have been specially ordered that she has already had autographed by other staff members and summer students. She will mail them out this afternoon when she picks up the Foxfire mail at the Rabun Gap post office. She also has a birthday card for me to sign for one of the staff, to be delivered, along with a card she and Joyce have conspired together about, at the meeting today.

Continuing down the hill, I pass the blacksmithing and woodworking shops, two cabins that are furnished with period artifacts, and two more staff houses before I come out on the main highway and turn north to drive the half-mile to Foxfire Press. The press represents one of our attempts to establish a new business in Rabun County—a publishing operation that distributes books having a potential national audience through E. P. Dutton (a New York publishing house bought in the early 1980s by John Dyson); and distributes books and pamphlets and monographs of purely regional interest itself. The press is located on one square ten-acre city block of land that fronts the main highway that bisects our county north and south. The land is in the middle of Mountain City, a town halfway between Rabun Gap and Clayton. The press offices are in a passive solar home designed by Paul Muldawer, an architect friend of mine whose offices are in Atlanta, and it was built for us by Claude Rickman, a former student who has his own construction firm in our county. As a student, Claude is the one we sent to Kennebunkport, Maine, to help start the *Salt* project in the public high school there. The home was designed to be comparable in cost to a double-wide mobile home, so that community residents who have been led to believe that they can afford only a mobile home because of their income levels can see that there are options—options that will escalate rather than depreciate in value over time. It is located on the highway instead of up on the mountain so that at least one part of our operation will be easily accessible to tourists and community residents and commercial delivery vehicles. If the funds materialize, the rest of the block will eventually be a city park and community archive and museum complex (see the introduction to *Foxfire 8* for a complete description of the plans).

Inside the solar house are Linda, Tanya, and Hilton. Linda is one of the former students who ran *Foxfire* while I was away at Johns Hopkins. Her name is on the masthead of the first issue of the magazine. With a degree in elementary education, she now directs the new publishing venture. This morning we go over the outlines for two new books we are proposing to Dutton. If they are approved, she will coordinate the gathering of the material for those books by the students in our classes. She has been on vacation for the last week, and we need to catch up with each other. She and her husband were away celebrating because, after a long campaign, he has just been elected the sheriff of our county. In the not-too-distant future, their two young sons will perhaps be in some of our classes.

Tanya, who has been with us for two years, is in the next room updating the mailing list on our word-processing equipment. One of the summer students kept it up all summer, but now that she is back in the high school every day, Tanya is picking up the slack. She is our marketing director, and she has her business degree from the University of Georgia. During this week, with the play, *Foxfire*, about to open in Atlanta, she will be making arrangements for some students and staff members to be present on opening night. She will also be putting together the guest list of book reviewers and friends for a publicity party she has coordinated in Atlanta that will combine a luncheon and a matinee performance of *Foxfire* with the release of our new Appalachian cookbook. Several of the student authors, like Chet Welch, are now in colleges in Atlanta like Georgia Tech, and they will be the speakers at the luncheon. I give Tanya the draft of a letter she requested that will become the introduction to a Christmas catalog she is helping to assemble. The catalog will feature products from five other Appalachian organizations besides ourselves, and it represents our first effort to market products jointly (each organization having agreed to send copies to every name on its own in-house lists, thus expanding by thousands of names the number of potential customers each of us can reach). She'll go over my letter, make changes, and add it to the catalog.

Tanya, incidentally, just married Paul Gillespie. Paul is the former student who was with me on the first interview with Aunt Arie. When Paul graduated from the University of Virginia, he was hired by us to take the place of Pat Rogers, who had been hired from us by IDEAS to coordinate workshops across the country for teachers who wanted to start magazines like *Foxfire* in their own schools. As vice president, Paul ran the organization while I was on sabbatical in Athens writing this book. During that time, he and his students also edited *Foxfire 7*. His two high school students who were most heavily involved in the final editing were Keith Head (one of the warmest, most likable and talented students we ever had— recently killed in an automobile accident), and Wendy Guyaux (who majored in journalism at the University of Georgia and is now producing shows for the NBC affiliate television station in Spartanburg, South Carolina). Now Paul is in his third year of law school at Mercer University in Macon.

Hilton is the newest member of our staff. With twenty years of experience in the Atlanta public schools, his current project is to go over the two years' worth of material students have collected for a Foxfire Press book devoted to several hundred traditional Appalachian toys and games. At the moment, the material is in stacks in boxes and files, and it is Hilton's job somehow to impose some temporary order over the piles of data and then work with students on the final table of contents, the final bit of collecting to be done, and the final editing and manuscript preparation and delivery to Dutton.

It is 10:10. I am late for second period. I finish at the press and head south to the Rabun County High School, now in its eighth year in the new facility. I wave to the guard at the gate, who smiles and waves back, drive through and up the hill to the faculty parking lot in front of the complex. Gathering a bundle of papers under one arm, I enter the double glass door of the building and run up the steps to my second-floor classroom. I don't like to be late, but I know Margie will be there working with the students in my place, and so all is well. I walk in, and Margie and the group of students working with her around the back table look up and wave and go back to work. Margie has been with me for over twelve years now. She is a vice president of the board of directors, but more importantly, when Suzy left to return to Connecticut after ten years with us, Margie became the organization's sounding board and conscience, part of the glue that holds it all together. She's a constant, steadying presence over the whole. At this moment, at 10:20 A.M., she is running one of the magazine classes. Some of the students around her were working with me this summer on articles for *Foxfire 9* that they didn't finish, and it is those articles, some of which will coincidentally be used in the new issue of the magazine, that they are working on now.

Just as I finish making sense of the papers I've carried in, the bell rings. From now until 3:10, students will fill the room. Four classes to go—five total, thanks to the fact that Margie can cover for me through all those mornings that I simply cannot get here by 9:30.

Within four minutes, there are twenty-five students seated in desks arranged in a semicircle in the room. I only have twenty-four desks, and so that is the number of students I try to hold my classes to, but a new student has just entered our school, three weeks late, and the guidance counselors have added her to my third-period roll. To make room, one of the students sits at the table in the back where Margie was working when I came in.

The course is Foxfire I, a grammar and composition course within the English department. Today is the day we'll learn how to load and unload cameras, and the kids know it, and they're excited and a little apprehensive. That may not seem like an activity that's appropriate for grammar and composition, but cameras become one integral tool I use in the service of language arts skills. The students are listening, focused on me with an intensity that would be completely absent had I just asked them to open their grammar books and turn to the chapter about adverbs.

The apprehension mounts as Margie and I hand out six cameras and six boxes of film to groups of four students we arbitrarily carve out of the larger semicircle. The student at the table pulls up a chair and joins the nearest group. There is tension because only two of the students in the room have ever used a single-lens-reflex camera before, and they know these things cost over two hundred dollars apiece; and those same two are also the only ones in the class who have ever been on an interview. Brand new kids, starting from scratch. Every semester it's the same. A new crop, green as grass. Start at the beginning.

I take them through the steps involved in opening the cameras, loading them, closing them and advancing the film two frames, and then rewinding the film just far enough so that the tail doesn't get rewound completely into the film canister. At this point, the students who loaded a camera take the film out, close the camera, and pass it on to the next person in the group, who repeats the process as the others watch, squirming and/or shouting directions. I tell them not to be embarrassed if they foul up and rewind the film too far. "Just *try* not to, but let me know if you do and I'll bring you a fresh roll. No problem. It's okay." Chris, a ninth-grader and one of the two who has used cameras before, in his impatience to show the rest of the group his facility with the equipment immediately rewinds his film too far. We all laugh—"Wouldn't you know it?"—and I replace the roll. None of the other students makes the same mistake. Business as usual.

By the time the bell rings, all the students have loaded and unloaded the cameras several times apiece. They replace the cases, return the cameras and film to my desk drawer, and file out of the room laughing and talking. A few poke at Chris good-naturedly, and he grins.

There are three lunch periods. Margie and I are assigned to the first. We leave for lunch, students swirling around us shouting hello and rushing on. They're good folks, these kids. I like them. Margie and I, like the other teachers, get our food from the same cafeteria line the students use and sit down at a table populated mostly—but not entirely—by other teachers. The noise level sometimes makes it hard to visit. Lots of these faculty members are friends, though, and we shout good-naturedly among ourselves above the din.

Mike sits down with us. He's been with Foxfire almost ten years. Another former student, he and Paul were both recruited onto the magazine staff as tenth-graders by Linda et al. during that Hopkins year. He and Paul wrote the Aunt Arie chapter in *The Foxfire Book*, as well as the one about building log cabins (that's the same crew I talked about earlier that lost the photograph and had to go out late one night with flashlights to find it). As a student, Mike spent a summer with the Navajos in Ramah, New Mexico, under IDEAS sponsorship, to help them start *Tsa Aszi*, a magazine project that still exists today in the Ramah Navajo School. He went on to major in journalism at the University of Georgia after learning how to use that videotape equipment we bought with the NEH grant.

Mike is one of the first staff members who was added with instructions to create a new department within the organization, but in an academic area different from language arts. To allow new students to experience some of the best of that sense of suspense and mission and we're-all-in-this-together closeness that had been a hallmark of the earlier days of the magazine, I instructed each new staff member like Mike to begin to work toward creating an autonomous division that would build on the groundwork already laid and remain inseparably linked with the parent organization, but that would have its own classes, its own academic emphasis (an emphasis that had to remain consistent with our developing educational philosophy), its own budget, its own products, its own identity, and that would plow new ground and point us all toward future options and educational strategies. I wanted each to test, to experiment, to push the boundaries back, to take calculated risks, to gamble, and, to the extent possible, to follow the lead of *Foxfire* and work toward carrying the lion's share of its own weight financially. With the principal's enthusiastic cooperation, staff members like Mike began to draw up plans for distinctive new spinoff divisions and class offerings.

Mike took the potential that existed for television and ran away with it. Now operating out of a studio in downtown Clayton and a studio in the school, Mike's classes produce a series of programs that encompass a range of subjects from the folklore and material culture of the region through politics and community issues, and include broadcasts of school ball games, plays, and concerts. The students receive elective credit through media sciences.

Let me share the introduction Mike wrote for an issue of *Foxfire*, to inform readers about his students' new accomplishment:

In September of 1979, I and a group of students walked into a room full of junk. The room had served, at different times, as an apartment for the Charles Marchman, Sr., family, a furniture showroom and most recently as a storage area. Now, the Marchman family, owners and operators of the local cable television system, were giving us permission to build a local origination television studio in the thirty-by-forty-foot available space. Just enough room. . . .

Now, almost a year later, we're almost through. The journey from start to finish has been filled with all of the frustrations and stories any worthwhile project entails and I leave you free to imagine them. What I want to talk about here is people.

There have been the adults, like the entire Marchman family, who have bent over backwards to help us out. Or like Robert Mitchum who came downtown on several occasions to check out the student-done wiring. Or Rick Edmundson who took time to help us design the studio lighting and then find the best prices on the equipment we needed. Or Bob Mashburn and Alvin Carnes who repeatedly volunteered expert carpentry help if we ever needed it—same for Jack Pruitt and others. Then, there was the patience and support of the rest of the Foxfire staff. All the things these people added, I am thankful for.

Important as these people were, you still have to hear about the real stars. The real nose-to-the-grindstone work was done by the students. I won't call them kids. Somehow, in this case the name doesn't fit.

How can I call "kids" a group of people who have researched, designed and built a television studio *and* managed to do it for around $6,000? These people are my friends and colleagues who have worked with dedication and attention to detail which has to be seen to be believed. Technically I am the teacher but *together* we have learned. (Note that the $6,000 does not include new television equipment. The miracles only go so far.)

So, to you—Mark, Sandy, Glenn, Gary, and the others, thanks—for the work and dedication. You've really made me proud of you. But especially to Doug Young, Stephen McCall, Gary Gottschalk, and Kurt Jarrio I say thanks. These have worked, on their own, during the hottest summer on record in the windowless upstairs of a brick building, without complaint. Their professionalism has constantly amazed me. (Doug and Kurt are going to the Navy this fall and the Navy is damn lucky to have them. I'd hire them back if I had the money.)

So these are the people who have done the thing and created local origination television for Rabun County. I'm sure there are others I haven't mentioned. I'm equally sure that this stands again as proof of what high school students can do. Kids . . . ?

Hewing to the philosophy of having students involved in every aspect of any project, whether they are an inconvenience or not, Mike also insists that any television or film crews that want to come into the area to film either our work or that of our contacts include students from his classes behind the scenes in all phases of the production. If they do not agree to those terms, our organization refuses to cooperate with them. It's as straightforward as that.

Mike and Margie and I finish eating together. It is noon. Students are filing in for second lunch. By the time I get back to the classroom, it is filling with seniors—my college English class, designed to get students ready for English 101. Margie goes into the English teachers' workroom to type an article she has just written about a new lesson she and I tried with our magazine classes that seems promising. The article will be published in *Hands On*, the newsletter we sponsor that has become the communications link between our organization and other teachers nationally who are experimenting with experiential, community-based options in their schools.

I return the narratives my seniors handed in on Friday, which I graded over the weekend, along with the grammar sheets I typed up and made copies of that are composed of sentences I took from their papers that contained problems in mechanics, grammar, or style that all of us need to look at together. We go over them, and toward the end of the period, several students read their narratives aloud for the rest of the class to enjoy. The paper for this week, which we will start tomorrow, is a cause-and-effect paper.

One of the students in the class is working alone. Having been allowed to take the course as an eleventh-grader, he is now in a special 102 curriculum I have designed, and he is writing a research paper. The subject is a scientific description of the three varieties of mushrooms that are phosphorescent, one of which, in one of its life stages, is known as foxfire. The paper, along with footnotes, will appear in *Foxfire 9*.

The bell rings, and the room empties and fills again, this time with students in an Appalachian literature class George and I designed together this summer. We are teaching it for the first time. You haven't met George yet. He has his master's degree in folklore from Western Kentucky University, and he is also a professional bluegrass musician. Hired at about the same time as Mike to start a new division, he contributed a folklore course (through the social studies department) to the curriculum, and several music electives. His students founded a record company called Foxfire Records, which now produces a series of albums and cassette tapes featuring contemporary songwriters and traditional musicians. Students record, mix, design, produce, and market the albums as part of their work. When the second one was released, George informed the magazine subscribers about it in an introductory letter that read in part:

This record is not just a product. Several years ago, a student, David Green, and I went to Chicago for a convention of the National Association of Independent Record Producers. One of the most often-heard terms at that meeting was "product." We were in the midst of business people, people for whom the key word was "product"—stock of the trade—the thing that you sell to make money in order to pay the bills. This is an unavoidable reality for the record production program. We fully intend for the production of records to be a self-supporting operation. Still, I was never comfortable with the business term "product." *It Still Lives* is the tangible end result of a complex process that has involved experimenting, learning, and celebrating.

When I first came to the Foxfire staff, there was a rather heated debate in academic circles as to whether the *Foxfire* books had enough scholarly "backbone" to hold up as serious documents of Southern mountain folklife. The debate was healthy and worthwhile. While scholars began to take a serious look at our work, we began to make a serious attempt to document our publications with additional research. *It Still Lives* represents our most extensive effort in that direction. Accompanying the record is a twenty-page booklet, half of which is devoted to background reference material. Beginning in the fall of 1978, the students and I visited numerous libraries, took endless notes, photocopied countless pages of reference material, and painstakingly collated the accumulated historical and geographic information about each tune, riddle, and story included in the recording. We worked hard and long and our work will stand the scrutiny of academe. In many ways, this effort was a great experiment. Can high school students do serious documentary research? Yes. Is it something we will continue to do in every record? I'm not sure. It takes an enormous amount of time and energy to introduce teenagers to academic literature, to train them to do critical investigative research, and to teach them to write objectively and cautiously. Then again, each one of those young people is a product much more precious than the record itself.

As part of the music program, George finds and brings into the school a continuing stream of area musicians who work with the students in class, helping to make them aware of their musical heritage, and who often, during several class periods, give concerts to which other teachers may bring their classes. An instrument-building class has been added that has students designing, creating, and playing instruments made out of salvaged materials such as tin cans from the lunchroom and scraps of wood from one of the shops.

George's most spectacular achievement to date, however, has been the creation of the Foxfire String Band, a bluegrass group composed of high school students who have their own class, have extended practice sessions at George's home every Thursday night, and have become so polished that they are asked to perform all over the Southeast. Their appearances range from local benefits (which they do for free) to paid affairs such as a fleet blessing in Brunswick, Georgia, an appearance in Atlanta at the Governor's Awards in the Arts ceremony, and a Terri Gibb concert, which they opened. In 1983, they performed on Roy Acuff's show at the Grand Ole Opry in Nashville—a performance that caused Roy to exclaim on the air, "Well, I figured you boys was good or you wouldn't have got here, but I wasn't expecting *professionals.* I wouldn't mind introducing you boys on the Opry every Saturday night"; at which point the packed house cheered and whistled its approval.

Today George and I, through tape recordings of several of our contacts and stories printed in past volumes of the *Foxfire* series, are trying to help the students draw the structural parallels between traditional stories told orally and short stories written by area authors. As we discover the common traits, students construct individual drafts of a chart that will eventually become a classroom poster.

Tonight, after the staff meeting, George and the Foxfire String Band will be in a local recording studio until one in the morning, recording their second cassette tape.

During this class period, Margie is with her husband, Bob, teaching a group of thirty-three seventh-graders. You haven't met Bob either. He works through the science department, where students in his classes have designed, built, and tested solar water heaters, have studied energy conservation in depth, and have monitored and analyzed the performance of Foxfire Press's passive solar offices. Students working with him have also laid out nature trails for a neighboring elementary school's science department, developed the nature and wildlife study areas for the science and Vo-Ag departments of the high school, restored through pruning and grafting an apple orchard on Foxfire's property, and planted blueberries and done landscaping there, and have experimented with American chestnut seedlings in hopes of finding a blight-resistant strain. They have also learned to conduct microbiology and dissolved-oxygen tests on the springs, streams, and lakes around their own homes, using equipment borrowed from Bob's supply cabinet. Bob has also forged an alliance with the physical education department, and working through them, he conducts a state-approved hunter safety course each year. He also works with students in a ropes and obstacle course area laid out in the woods behind the school, with the help of a team from Project Adventure, and built using Bob's students. A runner himself, he has also organized and coaches a cross-country team so that students not interested in football will have a fall sports option; the team consistently places first in the region. He and Margie also take groups to the mountains on weekend camping trips (for which students must plan all menus and purchase all food, working within a specific minimum budget allotment), and on field trips to other environments such as the coastal wetlands of Georgia, where students as well as teachers from our school are introduced to that environment by scientists working there.

The bell rings again, and the larger of our two magazine classes fills the room. Margie is back. John Puckett is here also. He's sitting in the back of the room each day during sixth period, watching what Margie and I do with this class and taking notes. These are students we know very well. They've all been through Foxfire I, and many of them have had the magazine class previously. Some worked with me this summer. The first five minutes are always given over to visiting and laughing and general chaos. We look forward to seeing each other every day, and an uninitiated visitor might think we hadn't seen each other in weeks. Today, when we do begin to work, we spend most of the period listing what still needs to be done to finish *Foxfire 9*. The students each volunteer to complete some item on the list, and then Margie and I work with each individually so that by the end of the period, every student knows what he or she needs to accomplish this week. The class is intense, but the flow is smooth and easy. It feels good. It's one of my favorite classes, and a nice way to end the school day.

Another bell—3:10 P.M. The students race for the buses. Suddenly everything's quiet and hollow. In the distance, we can hear the buses starting up, their gears grinding as they move out in a long yellow line that takes five minutes to pass through the parking lot.

Margie and I get a soft drink from the machine in the teachers' lounge and return to the room to go over our lesson plans for the next day. By 3:30, when the bell rings that allows the teachers to leave the building, the rest of our staff is assembling for the weekly staff meeting. Bob will be late. His cross-country team is competing with Rabun Gap's this afternoon. Joyce comes in with the calendar and a stack of phone messages, some of which have been added today; Ann comes in with copies of the budget for everyone. Tanya arrives with a revision of my letter she's been working on that she and I glance at quickly before the meeting starts. Linda and Hilton are right behind her with copies of materials—a review of the new cookbook from *Publishers Weekly*, for example—that they pass out to the rest of the staff. John Puckett is getting ready to take more notes. Mike and George come in last, a fact that has given Joyce and Ann a chance to set out the cake and card they've brought and alert us to the fact that it's George's birthday. For the first fifteen minutes, we all eat and talk.

For the next hour, we wade through organizational business: the budget, division progress reports, the calendar for the week, and requests that have been made of us. Items that need students' input and/or decisions are listed on the agenda for one of the periodic group meetings for which, as each school period begins, all students taking a Foxfire course during that period gather in my classroom. Through every period of the day, each group gets caught up on organizational business, has a chance to volunteer to work with visitors who have already been scheduled for the following week, signs up for special projects, and has an opportunity to raise questions or voice criticisms concerning any organizational directions. Decisions that students need to make are presented during each period, and their votes are carried forward through the school day (each new group not knowing how previous groups voted), giving us a cumulative total and decision by the end of sixth period.

At about 5:15, we break. Joyce takes a few minutes to hand out individual messages she didn't have a chance to give out earlier. She checks with me about the requests she's been holding for my answer, and we postpone looking at them, again, until tomorrow morning. It's a familiar minuet we do. We'll get to them.

Then, as we do every week, Margie, George, Mike, Bob, and I, and any other staff members who wish, stay behind to talk specifically about our current courses, students we may be having problems with, and to trade ideas for new courses that are constantly being developed and readied for testing with a pilot group of students if approved by the administration. We have created master charts that list all the state curriculum objectives and Foxfire curriculum objectives in columns, and all our individual courses and their activities are keyed to these columns. Today nearly all of us have at least one classroom activity we have planned as a means of getting at one objective or another, and we each want input from the rest of the group as to whether the activity looks strong enough to meet the objective. Sometimes we plan, as a group, to do the same activity in every one of our classes and pre- and post-test all the students so that the following week we can compare strategies and results.

By 6:30, we are finished, physically and emotionally, and we quit for the day.

I drive home, stopping at the office on the way to pick up the mail and answer any phone calls that can be dealt with after working hours. Then, taking the mail with me, I head up the last stretch of gravel road for home. Usually I get a beer, throw a frozen dinner in the oven, and carry the mail and my beer upstairs to my desk. There I answer a few letters, eat, and do a little work. Tonight, for example, I am rewriting this final piece of Book I for the third time. I still haven't got it the way I want it.

At 11:00, I turn the television on and watch the news. Usually I also watch Johnny Carson's monologue before going to bed. Tonight, though, his guest host is Joan Rivers, so I turn off the set. There's been enough noise in my life for one day, and I'm tired.

23

The End of Innocence
—Now What?

And so, the end of Book I.

Told sequentially, in narrative form, the story of the years between 1973 and 1984 would take a document at least twice the length of this one, and it would not serve at all the purpose of this particular book, which is to talk with you about teaching. Appropriate anecdotes from those intervening years that serve the discussion have been included in the two books that follow, but from now on, what I want to talk about is things *all of us* can do in our classrooms, and for that discussion, what you know about Foxfire now is really all you need to know. It's enough. Let's move to higher ground.

In order to do so, there is one last piece of the puzzle I must drop into place.

Two kinds of teachers who look at our work make me nervous. The first is the teacher who looks at *Foxfire*, decides to start a similar magazine, and then gets disappointed and discouraged (and perhaps even thinks that he or she has "done it wrong") because the end result is not a book from Doubleday and lots of money.

Our story is fairly extraordinary, and it is a story filled with lucky breaks and serendipitous events: fraternity brothers like John Dyson and Mike

Kinney, a reading public that was primed in some weird, unpredictable way to embrace a book like our first one, things like that.

Besides, there's a definite down side to that visibility and that money. We made several million dollars. We didn't set out to make it. Suddenly it was there, and we had to react to that fact, get some control over the situation, and use the money as wisely as we could in the service of a larger goal. Despite those good intentions, part of it was wasted. I honestly believed, for example, that we could have a visible impact on the economic situation in Rabun County through assisting in the creation of numerous small businesses via catalytic efforts like Community Development Corporations and the like, and we found early on that that kind of work takes far more horses than we have in our stables. Nearly everything we tried failed, and not one of our in-house departments—the record company, for example—has made even close to the kind of income it needs to be self-supporting.

That includes the press. Publishing is a strange, unpredictable business. The first national offering from Foxfire Press was *Aunt Arie: A Foxfire Portrait*. For my money, it's the warmest, most human book we have ever published, and it was awarded a Christopher Medal for 1983, the year of its release. It is the kind of book I established the press to produce: an antidote to the diet books and workout books and cartoon books and Hollywood books and pop movie books of today. In terms of sales, the latter won hands down. No contest. It's all a crapshoot; hot dice, cold dice.

I also believed that any person we would ever hire would get completely caught up in the idea that they were part of a grand mission, and they would never cause me a moment's problem. There are now people in Rabun County who hate me and the ground I walk on because I had to fire them.

I also allowed myself to believe that the work we were doing was so positive and beneficial that no one in the community would ever see it otherwise, and though a huge percentage of community families support us completely, there are those individuals like the one quoted on the front page of the *Wall Street Journal* who, when referring to me, said, "He's just a damn Yankee who came down here and struck an ace."

It's a complicated world, and those who believe otherwise are fools.

The second kind of teacher who makes me nervous is the one who looks at our equipment and our layout and says, "I can't do *any* of the things you are doing at all. It's too big and too complicated, and I'd never be able to find the funds to do it with anyway." And then he or she returns to the texts and workbooks and tries nothing.

Both those teachers need to remember a simple point: during the early days you read about in Rabun Gap, we had one used tape recorder, one used camera, a borrowed darkroom, virtually no money, and an idea we thought made sense for some English classes. Talk to any of those early students and they'll tell you that they probably learned just as much in the days that we were broke (if not more) than my students learn today. If mine learn more today, it's only because I've become a smarter teacher, not because I now have six cameras instead of one. The goal is still the same: to bring a class to life through those projects and applications of the course material we can do together with our students, *whatever* our resources may be. Government grants and sudden wealth don't make that crucial difference in the caliber of our work with kids: it's the quality of the interaction between us that carries the day. All else is icing—nice, but nonessential.

The vast majority of the money we spend now (which we are blessed with thanks to Doubleday's marketing prowess and the income from our modest endowment) is for salaries for other adults—the ones you just read about—to test courses and projects, few of which are expensive, inside a public school that is probably not all that different from the one in which you teach. By design, the courses we continue to offer or initiate in our school are those that represent the best and brightest hopes for models of better delivery systems for skills all our schools are mandated to teach—low-cost models that may be of use to teachers and school systems elsewhere. We have been blessed. People beyond the boundaries of our county have greeted our work with enthusiasm and generosity. Now we have some additional debts to pay. If, in the future, people examine what our tiny organization tried to do, I hope they will find that we did not turn our good fortune to our own benefit alone but that, to the extent we were able, we tried at least to make a useful contribution to the world beyond.

Book II

24

As Teachers, We Can Make This System Work

I remember all those thousands of
hours that I spent in
grade school watching the clock,
waiting for recess or lunch to go
home.
Waiting: for anything but school,
My teachers could easily have
ridden with Jesse James
For all the time they stole from me.
—RICHARD BRAUTIGAN, *Rommel Drives On Deep into Egypt*

There is a row of people seated on my writing table. Having just read the first part of this book, each is now complaining bitterly.

One, an athletic young man in a green Izod shirt and khaki slacks, says, "I teach all day, go to a second job in the afternoon, and if you're implying that I should work after school either with students or on ways to change the way I teach, you're just yelling into the wind. My life is complicated enough without someone like you coming around to make me look bad."

Another, an attractive young woman in slacks, a gray sweater, and a gold add-a-bead necklace, apologizes, "I took education courses in college because that was the easiest major on campus to turn into a regular paycheck. I don't really like teaching all that well, and I'll even admit I'm not very good at it, but I'm not going to be doing it much longer. Maybe a couple more years, and then I'll be out. So I don't want to get into anything long-range or complicated. Teaching just isn't going to be my life."

Another, a slim, esthetic-looking, dark-skinned man with curly black hair and darting eyes, dressed in jeans and a T-shirt bearing a political slogan, mutters, "You're spouting a lot of sixties jargon about making the world a better place to live in and all that, but by working in the public schools you've already sold out. The public schools are merely an instrument of a capitalist society that is inherently corrupt, exploitive, and evil; and as a teacher, you're merely a tool of a conspiracy cleverly designed to perpetuate an indefensible social order. Until your students rise up and lead their parents and grandparents into the revolution that must come, you won't have anything to say that's worth my listening to. I've got work to do."

A middle-aged woman in a designer dress and stunning jewelry pouts and says, "I teach only because I have to. You have to appreciate my situation. My husband, by himself, does not make enough to support our family in the style in which he and I think we have a right to live. That extra monthly check is all that separates us from comfort and an unbearable strain on our financial resources. I don't really want to teach at all, but my work enables us to have things we could never afford otherwise. Are you trying to tell me I should take this job *seriously? That's* not why I'm teaching."

A ruddy, open-faced, wide-eyed girl in jeans, a blue work shirt, and round glasses gasps, "I really feel joyful and opened up by what you're saying so far. But you haven't gone far enough at all! *Now* you have to work as I've done to get the teachers and students open to their *attitudes* about their *sexuality* and their *personal power,* and get them involved in healthful activities that will be *impactful* experiences and more *self-empowering!* Then we can all be happy and be one glorious human family!"

A gray-haired woman in a conservative blue dress with a closed neckline and no jewelry admonishes, "Young man, I've been a teacher for twenty-eight years and I know what I'm doing, and don't you dare imply that I don't. When you've been around as long as I have, then maybe you'll have room to talk. Meanwhile, you should visit my class sometime and see what teaching's all about. I have no discipline problems, no parent problems, no problems with the administration, no problems with the school board. I know what my students need, and that's what they get, and you should be learning from me rather than implying there is something I could learn from you."

A middle-aged man with a noticeable midriff overhang, wearing a white shirt and dotted tie and dark slacks, a line of white dust across his rump revealing that he's been leaning against the blackboard's chalk tray again, complains, "Teenagers are hopeless now, and it's getting worse instead of better. I turn my back to write something on the board and they tear the room apart. They won't listen to anything I say. I just let the ones in the back carry on and talk to the few who will listen. It's gotten to the point where I dread coming to work, but I'm forty-eight years old now, and this is the only job I've got. I keep hoping things will get better, but until the young people change and get off this dope and alcohol and learn to have more respect for their elders, not much of what you talk about will work. There's no *way* you could turn my kids loose with cameras and tape recorders. They'd have them stolen and sold before you could blink twice, and they'd come in the next day as high as kites. It's crazy. Let me tell you. And it's getting worse, too, buddy."

A somewhat plain but nevertheless attractive girl in a beige pantsuit and a yellow blouse complains, "Look, I'm doing the best I can. I got into teaching because I *wanted* to teach. And I still do. But they give me one hundred and eighty-five students, four lesson preparations a day, and all kinds of other duties that aren't teaching related; and despite the fact that I really like the job and the kids, the administration has got me so loaded down that I just can't *move.* I'm swamped. I do about three hours of work at night at home trying to keep up, and I *still* can't do the job I know I should be doing. The kids and I are both trapped—them with upcoming state competency tests and me by the results of those tests. I just can't think about taking on more. I'm sorry. And on top of all that, I have to direct the senior play. There's *got* to be a better way."

A paunchy man with black hair, a mustache, and a plaid suit shouts, "I represent a powerful teachers' union, and let me tell you, anything extra you suggest teachers do above and beyond what's already been agreed on will have to be negotiated first through our membership. We've finally gotten control of a situation that's been out of control for years, with schools ripping off teachers left and right, and we intend to make sure that situation never happens again. If you think teachers ought to do more, you better spend a chunk of your time figuring out how to pay them more. I wouldn't let one of my people work the way you're talking under any circumstances unless they were making about fifty thou a year."

Another man—middle-aged, three-piece suit, short hair—points his finger, wags it, and says, "As a school principal, I can tell you that what you need to know before you come into my school and talk to my teachers is that I and my assistant have finally gotten our plant squared away. All the kids are where they're supposed to be. Visit our school and you won't see them hanging around in the halls or necking in the smoking areas. Along with basic skills and better SAT scores, discipline is what my school board and my parents want, and that's what I'm going to give them. If your game is increased student freedom and decision-making power, you

needn't come around my school. We played that game once before, and it
took us five years to get things back the way they should be."

I look at the last person in the line. She's been quiet up until now,
looking confused and apprehensive. Her long red hair falls over her
shoulders and over the dark green jacket of a green suit. She looks at me,
shrugs, and states flatly and a little apologetically, "I'm sorry, but I've
read the first part of your book, and I still don't know what you're saying.
I'm lost. Maybe you'd better start over."

Okay, let's back up. From now on, this book is not going to be about
Foxfire, except as I draw on my experiences in Georgia for illustrative
material. From now on, this book is going to be about teachers, students,
and education in general in the context of public secondary schools. Who
is it for? Well, for starters, it is not for most of those people seated in a row
on my writing table; and having never taught on the elementary school
level or in an alternative school, I would not be presumptuous enough to
say that what follows will be of value to those people who labor there. It is,
rather, for a very specific group: those who, like myself, know that the
public schools are not ideal learning environments but that they are here
to stay; that the public schools will continue to be the front lines—the
institutions to which most of our nation's young people will continue to
be sent despite any rhetoric advocating the opposite; and that despite the
fact that we've been given an almost impossible job, there are strategies
we can use to make the situation work if we can both find them and
summon enough energy from within ourselves to implement them.

I know the job is hard. George Dennison, who wrote one of my favorite
books about education, called *The Lives of Children*, was interviewed on
National Public Radio several years ago, and he said of the public schools,
"There are pretty good teachers who are trapped in a system where their
decisions are taken from them. This is absurd, you know? A teacher who
is trying to hold down a job by answering the demands of the administration, and also has to cope with thirty-five kids or something. It can't be
done. It can't be done . . . I've never taught in the public schools. I
couldn't stand it for a minute."[1]

Every time I read that, I have to laugh. I visited a school recently where
teachers have eight-period days and deal with nearly two hundred students a day. (Dennison, by contrast, taught for a couple of years in a free
school on New York's Lower East Side that had twenty-three children
total and four teachers.)

Men and women of great strength and compassion are chewed up and
spit out of the public school system every day, their confidence in themselves and the future of our schools shaken to the core. I've seen things
happen to adults and children in that system that would curl a hardened
cynic's hair, and so have you. Plainly, the job will not tolerate much wide-
eyed idealism. Teachers routinely have to teach over 140 students daily.

On top of that, we have lunch duty, bus duty, hall duty, home room duty (complete with attendance registers that make our income tax forms child's play). We go to parent meetings, teachers' meetings, in-service meetings, department meetings, school board meetings, curriculum meetings, county-wide teachers' meetings, and state teachers' conferences. We staff the ticket booths and concession stands at football and basketball games. We supervise the production of school plays, annuals, newspapers, dances, sports events, debates, chess tournaments, graduation ceremonies. We go on senior trips. We go on eighth-grade trips. We go on field trips to capital buildings, prisons, nature centers, zoos, courtroom trials. We choke down macaroni and cheese and USDA peanut butter at lunch (and have to pay for it). We endure endless announcements of staggering inanity on PA systems that invariably interrupt our most carefully planned lessons and give the kids an excuse to go berserk. We break up fights. We break up couples. We break up underground rings that dispense everything from pornographic literature and sexual aids to knives and dope. We search lockers during bomb threats. We supervise fire drills and tornado alerts. We write hall passes, notes to the principal, notes to the assistant principal, notes to parents, notes to ourselves. We counsel. We wake up every morning to the realization that the majority of our students would far rather be someplace other than in our classrooms. They are bored to death. They hate their courses. They hate their texts and workbooks. They hate the school. Sometimes they even hate us.

On top of all that, everyone's yelling at us. National SAT averages, though rising, continue to be an embarrassment. The state legislatures are demanding competency-based curricula and mandatory testing as a prerequisite for student graduation. We're being sued for everything from paddling children to the fact that Bert couldn't pass his college freshman English course. Parents are screaming bloody murder, convinced that their children are getting dumber at our hands instead of smarter. Money is being cut from school appropriations so fast we sometimes don't know whether or not we'll even have enough chalk to make it through the year, much less how long our jobs will last. To add injury to insult, colleges and universities are getting all huffed up and grumpy and indignant over the increasingly poor preparation of the students we're sending them. Well, just who in the hell do they think taught us how to teach? How much support and prestige do they accord their own schools of education? How come it's one of the least demanding majors on campus?

None of us, of course, is immune to this flood tide of criticism. After nearly twenty years in Rabun County's schools, I am still widely regarded as one of those teachers who ignores the basics and is consequently part of the problem instead of part of the solution. And that stings. Especially considering the fact that most of what I do is designed to be a better delivery system *for* the basics. But I've gotten used to it now. You will, too, if you haven't yet. And I rest secure in the knowledge that my program can largely withstand the scrutiny of anyone who takes the time to *look* instead of shoot from the hip.

Meanwhile, despite all the racket and the pressure and the odds against it, life goes on. Inside every public school in this country are good and decent people working far harder than their critics will ever know to make things right, and to prove to all of us that the job we've been given, though hellishly difficult and draining, is *not* impossible. In situations that would shrivel my soul, there are teachers who have somehow managed to figure out how to do a fine job. And in most cases, these extraordinary people are more than willing to help their flailing colleagues—when those beleaguered associates swallow their pride and ask for it. Unfortunately, many don't ask but simply grit their teeth and suffer in silence as their dreams for a productive year come apart at the seams.

Also unfortunate—and more than a little frightening—is the midnight admission each of us must make that in some measure, the criticism our profession is reeling under now is justified. It is at this point that this book becomes hard to write—not because I find acknowledging criticism distasteful, but because I don't know you personally. Consequently much of what I have planned to say may be totally irrelevant to you. Your teaching style, though perhaps completely different from mine, may well be one I should be learning from rather than the reverse. We may have nothing in common at all in terms of our specific teaching situations. When I read in *Newsweek* about teachers like Leroy Lovelace, who teaches English successfully in a situation far tougher than mine in Wendell Phillips High on Chicago's Near South Side,[2] I get the feeling that he should be writing this book instead of me.

But here I am, and somewhere out there are you, and all I can do to clear the impasse is urge you to ignore what I write if it isn't applicable. Having broached the subject, however, I must acknowledge the criticism we're receiving as teachers that seems accurate and on target to me. And I do this out of love, not anger: love for my profession, the students we work with daily, and for the world they're about to enter as adults.

Shortly after the program that my students and I began in Georgia received national attention, I began to get invitations to speak at teachers' conferences, conduct in-service sessions, and hold workshops. Some I accepted, taking students along to help out. I was not a master teacher by any means, and I'm still not. But I had the opportunity to see hundreds of high schools and meet thousands of teachers. We compared notes. Sometimes some of us sat up until all hours of the night drinking beer and talking. Policies and procedures I had disagreed with in my own school system and had become convinced over time and through experience were wrong, I found to be commonplace. Teaching practices I knew, through experience, to be counterproductive, I found everywhere I went. I began to read about education in earnest, and I found, to my alarm, that much of the methodology we teachers use contradicts decades' worth of research and experience in the subject of how and under what circumstances young people learn best. I devised a questionnaire for teachers that I thought would be revealing, and I began to take it with me on trips and give it to groups of teachers who were interested enough in the profession to show up at the workshops and who seemed willing to answer it honestly and fairly. I gave it to teachers in Georgia, Tennessee, Pennsylvania, Arkansas, Oklahoma, Florida; and everywhere the results were somewhat embarrassing and largely the same. (That questionnaire and the results are referred to in the sections that follow.)

And though I am now convinced that much of what we are doing is right, and that some of the paranoia surrounding our schools is misplaced and unjustified, I also know that we do, indeed, have some problems, and some of them are damn serious. So what do we do?

Well, with affection for that teacher who says, "I still don't know what you're saying. I'm lost. Maybe you'd better start over," and to help me sharpen my own thinking and my own approach to my school and my students, I'm going to begin with information so elementary that many of you will either laugh me out of your lives or slam this book shut in disgust. But bitter teacher workshop experiences have taught me that it's necessary. There are few new ideas in education about technique; only new applications of old truths, some of which we tend to forget in the heat of battle. So the correct place to begin usually happens to be at the beginning.

We'll never do everything right, God knows. We're human, and we're fallible. We can't give this crazy job our entire lives. We can't allow it to drain us and dispirit us so completely that we lose our enthusiasm for life itself. Every year there will be students we'll write off as lost insofar as our ability to help them goes. Every week we'll make mistakes we'll regret and say things we'll wish we could recall. But each of us, no matter what our age or experience, has the capacity for self-evaluation and for growth. Each of us can do the job better. Each of us can work within the system to create space and let in air and light. I've met thousands of you out there who *want* to. The rest of this book is for you. And I sure hope it helps.

25

The Question of Power

The first thing we must acknowledge as teachers is the extent of our power, for, in large measure, the understanding (or misunderstanding) and the application (or misapplication) of that power determines our success or failure as teachers. *Power*, obviously, is a loaded word. Some of us shy from it instinctively, saying, "I don't want power. That's not why I'm teaching. I just want to teach, not control." Others embrace it eagerly and take great satisfaction in being able to say, "You won't find me having problems with *my* kids. One thing I decided early on in this game was that no damn teenager was ever going to push *me* around." Still others approach it tentatively, almost wishfully, saying something like, "I'm not really comfortable with the word, but sometimes, when my students are in control of my class instead of me, I wish I had more of it." Funny word. And even those of us who say we wish we had more *do* have it. We just don't know how to use it.

It might help to get some perspective on the word by looking at those who have power over us. Our principals, for example. Or our department chairmen. Some know how to apply it positively. Some manipulate us with it and make us like it. Some manipulate us with it and make us hate it. Some destroy our confidence with it. Others never actively use it at all, hiding in their offices all day doing who knows what.

And to some extent, interestingly enough, the ability these people have to use power in all its various ramifications depends on how we feel about them and how much power we're willing to let them have—at least in terms of how it affects us personally.

I think of Morris Brown, for example, my principal for the eleven years I taught at Rabun Gap. He was widely respected because he deserved to be. He worked tirelessly to stay on top of the endless flow of papers and people and phone calls that flooded his office. He was even-tempered, patient, good-natured, friendly, and consummately fair and just to students and teachers alike. He was deeply involved in the life of the school, never missing, for example, a student dance, a ball game, or a senior play. Both he and his wife, who was the school's librarian (and who worked with students constantly after school hours on one student event after another), were a steadying, beneficent, positive force on all our lives. And when Morris Brown came up to a teacher in the hall, looked that teacher in the eyes, and said, "I want you to know that one of the students came into my office this morning and said you're the best teacher he ever had. I think you're doing a fine job," that really meant something. It was a simple compliment, but given the source, it counted. And when asked to take on extra duties or responsibilities, most of us responded willingly, knowing that the duties had to be performed, that they had been parceled out fairly, that he was going to work just as hard as we were, and that they were for the general good of something bigger than all of us: a school we cared about.

Given the extent of his power, and the fact that it flowed from his credibility, his wisdom, his character, and the desire we all had for his approval, he could also have destroyed us. He could easily, through slights or snide comments, have undermined our confidence in ourselves as teachers. He could easily have driven most of us out of the profession had he wanted to. He could have turned us as a staff against ourselves and created a school filled with apprehension, tension, and dread. Had he tolerated strife, he could have been the midwife of ruin.

Though I have never worked for one, I have heard stories about principals who are somewhat different. I have heard of principals, for example, who are quick to give compliments, but because they are basically devious people who are not above giving compliments to win favors or friends, or to pit one faction against another, the compliments are paid in devalued currency and accepted with scorn.

I have also heard of principals who have either actively disliked their jobs, or have accepted them with indifference, or have become tired and disheartened and frustrated. In most such cases, their ennui spreads like a mist through the halls, and we find ourselves adrift without a compass or an oar. We do our jobs as best we can, but the life is gone. We are spiritless.

In other cases, principals are too ambitious and overzealous or critical and negative. They turn into strutting, unbearable martinets, flinging orders in all directions, rushing to and fro from one end of the campus to another confronting us individually about the flaws in our programs, and haranguing us collectively at teachers' meetings about SAT scores or poor school spirit or late attendance registers or lack of discipline; and we actively rebel, or retreat in sullen silence, and our dislike for the school and its administration grows like a malignant tumor.

Obviously there are endless variations on this theme. The point is, clearly, that we must respond to these individuals in some way. They have power over us because of the situation. We may not give them all the power they may want; we may work from inside to undermine their strength, banding together to create a new "quasi-administration" among ourselves; we may actively rebel against them, ignoring their shrieks and protestations and commands; we may let them get the best of us and become sullen and dispirited; we may let them divide us from one another; or we may be fortunate enough to have one who nourishes us (and we'd better remember that such a person needs nourishment from us also) and has the power to help us grow in ways we never imagined possible. But come hell or high water, we will resonate to them in some way, despite ourselves. And we must also acknowledge that they always have artillery they can use against us that is mightier than ours: unless they have been completely discredited, they hold the keys to doors of opportunity or privilege or permission that we cannot open by ourselves; they can enhance or tarnish our reputations; they can get us fired.

And that's power.

Now reread the examples I have given, starting at the point where I begin to talk about principals. For *principal* or *department head*, substitute *teacher*. Let *teacher*, *I*, *we*, and *us* indicate students. For *fired* substitute *kicked out*. You get the idea. Now what have you got?

For you see, with only slight variations, the situations are exactly parallel except that we have even more power over our students than our superiors have over us. For one thing, we spend more time with them than our administrators spend with us—at least fifty minutes a day. Imagine spending an hour a day with your principal. Imagine your students spending an hour a day with you. . . .

For another thing, most students have yet to build up the elaborate defense systems we have built against the onslaughts of a sometimes hostile world. Most of them are, in a word, more vulnerable. Oh, I know. Some classrooms have been taken over by sixteen-year-old ringleaders so tough that it's hard to imagine them as vulnerable. But they are, despite protestations to the contrary. And far more common are those who are wide open to our slights and our ability to intimidate. Most of us have forgotten what it's like to be young. The image is burned into my mind of an eighth-grade boy, handsome, active, popular, aggressive, healthy, whole, standing beside our assistant principal, Alvin Smith, crying in great choking gasping sobs because he had just been scolded by a teacher for forgetting his textbook.

Our weapons? For starters, we're older than most of them. We have tricks we can use against them acquired through college and through experience. We have the authority that comes with our job to dictate their every move, backed up by disciplinarians we can call on if the going gets tough. We can have students suspended. We have access to their parents or guardians, many of whom will believe us over their children. And we have our grade books and the eternal threat of failure. That's pretty heavy artillery to bring into array against youngsters.

And that's power.

Many of us have the power, through a few well chosen words, to bring a young person's world crashing down. We have the power, through careful selection and manipulation, to divide students against themselves and break them up into warring factions, some basking in the glow of our pleasure, others outcast, the victims of our sometimes open hostility and scorn. We have the power, through simply ignoring certain students, to make them insecure and fearful. In fact, through numerous means, we can give any students we choose to single out reasons to doubt their abilities and their competence. We have the power to make them hate our subject matter forever because of us; to recoil in fear or hatred every time they come up against it in subsequent classes; to say, as adults, "I've always hated math because of that ninth-grade teacher I had," or, "I never could do English then and I still can't do it now."

Conversely, we have the power to do the opposite. With a word or a gesture, we can make a kid's day. We can cause students to fall so deeply in love with our subject matter that they choose it as their career and point to us, years later, as the source of that adult passion. Almost all of us can single out a teacher or two who, possibly short of affecting our career choice, at the very least awakened us somehow to our potential and our strength. You know already how all that happened in my life, through a tenth-grade English teacher who helped me get an embarrassingly over-written composition into print; and you know how it happened in yours.

And knowing that, we must acknowledge our power and the incredible opportunities we have been given to open doors for—and with—children. And acknowledging that, we must also admit that that realization—and the wise and humane and responsible use of that power—is what drives the best teachers on and constantly refuels them and keeps them young. And, acknowledging that power, we must also admit that *not* to continually strive to use it well is almost sacrilegious. It is like having the power to heal, but never healing. Or having the power to erase starvation in the world, and choosing to watch television instead. It is almost unforgivable.

Do you understand how important we are?

In an article for *Harpers*, Bartlett Giamatti, the president of Yale, wrote,

"[The teaching profession is on the verge of losing] that without which none of us can be effective as people at all, its sense of self-respect and self-esteem, its sense of dignity." But he also admonished us to remember that "those who teach have done something without which most people could not do for themselves whatever it is they do, [and although] no teacher is due more respect or affection than he or she has earned . . . the drive behind the teaching effort is a positive one."[1]

We are members of a profession driven by goals as lofty and as important as those of any person who has ever lived or of any profession that has ever existed, for our goals are no less than to assist in the creation of a better world. Why else teach?

It is for that reason that I become impatient with those teachers I meet who have accepted the job not because of a love for young people and the potential our profession has, but because they simply want another paycheck for the family, or have become bored sitting at home, or are using teaching and the educational system for personal career advancement. Likewise I become impatient with those who entered into teaching with the vaguest of motives, adopting it perhaps because it was an easy college major or an easy way to make a living; and, once in, they sit there behind their desks like toads, croaking over every imagined slight or every imposition on their time, watching the clock as eagerly as the most bored and restless of their students. And likewise I become impatient with those who are endlessly negative and complain interminably about the difficulties of accomplishing anything of substance, and spend the larger portion of their time parceling out blame for their various gripes to an impressive array of causes, and conclude, finally, "Well, I just do what I can on a day-to-day basis and hope for the best. That's all I can do."

Teaching is too vital an occupation to be left to the lazy or greedy or negative, and whenever I meet one of these, I am always tempted to say, "You could at least have the decency to find a different job and make way for someone who cares."

But I never do, believing that there have to be ways to turn all that around, and believing in the strength of the profession to cleanse itself, and believing in the strength we all have, when inspired and excited, to reach inside ourselves and find that source of energy and commitment we must find to be worthy of our jobs. We are members of one of the best professions on earth, and the better teachers savor that fact like a tonic.

26

Some Overarching Truths

So how do we make teaching work? I am going to say again (and it probably won't be the last time) that I am still trying to figure that out. Every year I try new approaches, tearing apart lessons and activities and putting them back together again, living for those moments when my classes transcend the ordinary and soar. It is a never-ending process, but it makes the job interesting and it keeps alive my sense of anticipation.

Nevertheless, characteristics common to effective teaching remain, within which all manner of experimentation is justified, desirable, and even necessary as the needs of our students change. Attendance to these principles, to the extent that it is possible given our constraints, makes the difference between effective teachers and ineffective ones.

Fine Teachers See Their Subject Matter Whole

The finest teachers I know, for example, are passionate about the material they teach, and they know it so thoroughly that they could continue to teach it well if every one of the classroom textbooks and teachers' guides vanished overnight. They are the Carl Sagans, who see their subject matter at work in every facet of their own lives and the world around them. They see the interdependence of their own discipline with all others. They see their subject whole. They are infused with it, and it is an inseparable part of their existence.

They are like the history teachers who see instantly in every major news event the precedents out of which it grew and its future implications. Their fine minds easily draw the parallels between Appalachian, Welsh, and Polish coal miners, for example: their life-styles, their needs, their gripping struggles to give birth to unions that work, and to forge the necessary alliances between management and labor. Effortlessly they then draw the connections between miners and all labor and management conflicts; they see the principles behind such conflicts—and the modifying forces—clearly, whether they be in South Africa, Australia, America, or Wales. They see economic forces whole. They see the interdependence of Saudi Arabia and South Africa and the Western world; they see McDonald's in Nigeria, Coca-Cola in Japan, Renault in Michigan. They can relate the War Between the States to upcoming, inevitable conflicts that have economic roots. They are masters at reading the minds of politicians and can recite their speeches for them before the speeches are given. They see Saudi armies being supplied and trained by South Koreans backed by America; and they see Salvadorian leftists being trained and supplied by Nigerians who were trained and supplied by Cubans who were trained and supplied by Russians. They can nearly predict America's response to any international crisis before it is made. They have perspective. They can see more than the fragments and pieces. They have a window on the world through their knowledge of the past. And with a wave of the wand all good teachers have, they can put Rabun County, Georgia—its grocery stores, its post offices, its politicians, its carpet mill, its living rooms, and its future—squarely into the middle of all that, and leave their students breathless.

They are like preachers who draw the kernels of their best sermons out of the serendipitous events they observe from behind their shopping carts, or while bowling or getting their hair cut; like photographers who walk through the world constantly framing shots and evaluating angles and the slant of light.

They are their subject matter, and for them, the inescapable linkages between that subject matter, their communities, their students, and the globe come so automatically that for them to teach otherwise—to teach a course in isolation from the world outside the school facility—would be literally impossible. The two are seen as inextricably married. Shopping lists and card games become math problems. Carpet dyes and gymnasium floor waxes and cans of beer become subjects of chemical analysis. The first spring flowers become targets of botanical scrutiny. And never in isolation, for each step inevitably leads to the next: Why do those spring flowers have color and fragrance? How do they acquire it? Of what is it made? What is the connection between flowers and bees? How do bees work? How do they communicate? How do they build? Why are the cells in their combs hexagonal? Are there relationships between their architecture and Buckminster Fuller's domes? What is the mathematics involved? What materials are strongest? Why do people write poems about flowers? What have they written? Why do they give flowers to each other? Do the colors of the flowers they give mean anything? Why? How do nurseries work? How do people create hybrids? Why? Why do some plant species become endangered? How can we stop that? Why should we? What do environmental scientists do? What do landscape architects do? Why?

And as each tiny object of scrutiny leads to the larger world, teachers and students alike are caught up despite themselves. They are three-year-olds again, alive with curiosity. They are fueled and refueled by what they find. And the best of these teachers are led thus to say, "If my course has no direct application to, or utility within, other courses being taught in this school as well as the world outside these walls, and I can find no way to help my students make those linkages and relate them to their own lives, then I can only conclude that the course should not be offered at all."

Whenever I poll groups of students as to teachers they have had so far who have made a difference to them, one recurring theme goes, "Once I had a teacher who *really* knew her subject. She loved it. She brought it alive for us. Lots of times we'd put the books away and do related things together, or just talk—really talk—and I still remember those classes today. They were something."

And what do we do about the students who, hearing that, almost mystified, respond, "Whew. I never had a teacher like that."

They Know How Learning Takes Place

The best teachers also know *how* learning takes place; they know how to apply the principles of learning, and thus they are living embodiments of a parallel principle: all young people can learn. This conviction is at the heart of the teaching profession.

The capacity for learning is enormous from the instant of birth on. Human beings constantly process data and information. It is as natural to learn as it is to breathe. Two of the most complex skills of all are learned without formal education: walking upright and talking. In his *Aims of Education* (first copyrighted in 1929), Alfred North Whitehead writes, "The first intellectual task which confronts an infant is the acquirement of spoken language. What an appalling task, the correlation of meanings with sounds! It requires an analysis of ideas and an analysis of sounds. We all know that the infant does it, and that the miracle of his achievement is explicable. But so are all miracles, and yet to the wise they remain miracles. All I ask is that with this example staring us in the face we should cease talking nonsense about postponing the harder subjects."[1]

Dr. Maria Montessori established her first school in Rome in 1907.

Graduates of her schools routinely go into the first grade reading at a fourth-grade level. Shinichi Suzuki's pupils play concert violin at ages three and four. In fact, Benjamin Bloom, an educator at the University of Chicago, suggested in 1964 that by age four, half of all human intelligence is developed (others say 60 percent). He went on to postulate that an additional 30 percent is established by age eight.

Whatever the figures, the fact remains that humans begin to internalize staggering amounts of knowledge early, and *naturally*, and they can continue to do it throughout life, and that most of what they learn is acquired not in our classrooms but in the daily confrontations with and manipulations of life itself. It is this process of natural learning without the constraints of our artificial environments that can point us in so many important directions as teachers *within* those environments. Teaching while ignoring what has been discovered over hundreds of years about how people acquire knowledge, and then to fail to apply this information, is analogous to fishing for native brown trout in a dry bathtub with an unbaited hook made from a coat hanger.

We know, for example, that no learning takes place without motive. That's easy enough. But our failure really to understand how motive works leads to endless circular discussions in teachers' lounges centering around statements like, "My students have absolutely no motivation," or questions like, "How do you motivate your students?" Our fundamental misunderstanding of the principle leads us to offer only extrinsic motivations for learning (a grade, a prize or a piece of candy, approval—"Do this for me and I'll appreciate it and I'll like you"—or even outright bribery— "Do your homework for me tonight and I won't give you any tomorrow night") instead of intrinsic motivations that take advantage of the usefulness of the material and the skills in our lives, and bolster and nourish such traits as natural curiosity and the natural desire for competence and mastery. Students in every classroom in the country are looking at us and asking (if not verbally, then with their eyes), "Why are you making us sit here and *do* this?" Too often our answers resemble the ones our mothers used to hand out when we questioned them about the wisdom of eating boiled okra: "Because I said so!" or, "Because it's good for you. Trust me," or, "Because if you don't, when your father gets home you're going to get the whipping of your young life," or, "Because if you don't eat everything on your plate, you won't get any dessert! That's why."

Such answers may serve our short-range goals, and we may even make it through the year with them, but they defeat the larger goal too many of us have forgotten: to create students who have an insatiable curiosity about life and the way the world works, and who will go on learning independently and eagerly long after they have left our classrooms behind, just as they did before they entered them. Boiled okra is still boiled okra, no matter how it's disguised, and we don't keep on eating it after the heat is off unless we have intrinsic motives for doing so. Same with algebra.

We know that the degree of motivation also depends, to a large extent, on some expectation of success. People don't enjoy doing things they're not good at, or things they are already convinced they can't do. And so they don't do them well. And so they fail again. And around and around it goes. Teachers who have failed with large numbers of their students dread Monday mornings. Consequently their job performance is affected, more students fail to measure up, and something truly dramatic has to happen to blast them out of the cycle; or else they find new jobs, or spend the rest of what could have been productive careers in padded cells with boxes of crayons and Mother Goose coloring books and animal crackers.

Students are no different, and every time we hear one say with a sigh, "But Mr. Jones, I just can't *do* this," we know we've got a problem that probably won't be fixed by handing out another failing grade.

We also know that the work of students in school is deeply affected by how much sleep they've had, when they had their last meal and of what foods it consisted, what their last class was like, how things are at home, what their relationships are with their peers in our classrooms, what their feelings are about us, whether or not they were just jumped up and down on by the assistant principal, whether or not they are in love—or wish they were, what kind of shape they're in physically (how many students failed courses for years before some enlightened soul discovered they were dyslexic or visually impaired or hearing deficient?), and all the rest of the physical and mental baggage all of us carry. Thus it becomes incumbent on us to know our students on something more than a superficial basis (more about this shortly).

Students often don't *know* what's distracting them so terribly or why they feel the way they do. I'll never forget the instant when I first discovered I was nearsighted—and some of you out there are already nodding your heads. (We're members of a special club, we nearsighted folks.) I was twelve or thirteen years old, walking down a street with my best friend, Jimmy Patrick. I think we were kicking a Dr Pepper can. He had glasses, and just for the heck of it I asked him if I could try them on to see what it was like and *holy Christmas* the world just *jumped* at me! I could read stop signs for the first time. I could see every leaf on every tree. Hell, I could see the *wind* blow. I stopped absolutely dead in my tracks, my mouth hanging open in awe and amazement. Jimmy looked at me, smiled, and said, "Yep, that's the way it was for me, too."

For months I kept my new discovery a secret, brooding about it, touching it in wonder, afraid my parents would get mad if they found out, afraid my teachers would scold me, afraid my classmates would laugh, afraid of everything—and hopelessly ill prepared to deal with it. Finally my younger sister, Hydie, forced the issue while our family was at a movie I couldn't see, and Dad, instead of getting angry, simply made an appointment with an eye doctor. I was excused from school, went through a few simple tests that any school nurse could have performed (and *had* performed when I was in about the second grade, but not since), and sat sweating as the doctor called my mother at home. "Yes, ma'am, he needs glasses all right. I doubt if he can recognize his friends across the street."

"Damn," I thought to myself. "Now how did he know that?" And was my eyesight, then, the reason I had such trouble catching fly balls, and the reason I had to endure the totally unnecessary agony of always being chosen last for every team we ever formed during PE (and why do coaches let teams get chosen up that way *anyway*)? And was my eyesight, then, the reason I could never read anything written on the blackboard (made worse by the fact that I was usually seated at the back of the room because of the first letter of my last name)? And was my eyesight thus the cause of most of the early insecurities I suffered as a youngster?

And to what extent are the students I teach now similarly affected with either physical or mental burdens they cannot deal with or identify? And to what extent do I as a teacher add to those burdens or help alleviate them? It's not my job to help? Might just as well say it's not my job to teach. Those of you who can think of no other justification for helping must at least agree with this one: we simply can't do our job if our pupils can't see, or hear, or concentrate because they are bedeviled. The extent to which we can identify and help relieve some of that pressure is the extent to which we begin to gain ground.

We know also that young people (and we) acquire enormous amounts of information from active problem solving, and that once solved, the solutions to those problems are simply absorbed into the storehouse of "What I know now" to emerge later in the solving of more complex problems.

While I was in Athens writing this book, for example, I was sitting outdoors on the deck of the duplex apartment I had rented, and I watched two young boys, perhaps second- or third-graders, walking down my street. At one point, they were distracted by a culvert that ran parallel to the street and underneath a driveway. As all children do, fascinated by holes in the ground, they got down on their knees, peered in, and spotted a bottle about halfway down its length. For the next half-hour, they were completely absorbed in an attempt to get it out. They tried reaching it, but couldn't; they tried pulling it toward them with a stick they found nearby, and couldn't. One went to the far end of the culvert and tried to bounce the bottle to within reach of the other by throwing dirt clods at it. That didn't work either. All the while they talked animatedly with each other, shouting encouragement or expressing disgust. As one would begin to give way to frustration, the other would excitedly conjure another scheme, however ridiculous. Finally they disappeared, only to reappear with their mother's broom—which also would not reach. They disappeared again, leaving the broom behind, and reappeared with a long forked stick from the nearby woods. At last the bottle came. After a brief examination, they tossed it away and continued walking down the street, talking with each other. They had no use for the bottle itself. The problem was solved. The information gained was stored away, whether they realized it or not. The bottle had simply been the vehicle through which something higher was learned. The motivation ("Let's see if we can get it out") was intrinsic and natural and unforced. No one stood over them demanding that they retrieve it. No one went over to them, gave them a solution (thus removing any element of fun and intrigue the problem held), and ordered them to implement that specific solution.

There are parallels here that are strikingly obvious, but important for us to note nevertheless.

Children don't learn the complex act of speech by sitting at a desk for hours at a time engaged in drill and imitation and listening to someone lecture about how to talk—someone who threatens to fail them if they don't learn it precisely so. George Dennison makes the point better than I can:

> No parent has ever heard an infant abstracting the separate parts of speech and practicing them. It simply does not happen. Even in those moments that we might think of as instruction—when, for example, we are bending over the baby, saying "wa-ter" to correct his saying "waddah"—our inevitable élan is that of a game; and in any event, as every parent knows, the moment this élan vanishes and mere instruction takes over, the infant will abruptly cease to cooperate. . . . A true description of an infant "talking" with its parents, then, must make clear that he is actually taking part. It is not make-believe or imitation, but true social sharing in the degree to which he is capable. We need only to reduce this complex actuality to the relative simplicity of imitation to see at once what sort of loss he would suffer. . . . His experience would be reduced to the dimensions of a chore. . . . The infant, in short, is not imitating but doing. The doing is for real. It advances him into the world. It brings its own rewards in pleasure, attention, approval, and endless practical benefits.[2]

Suddenly, and unfortunately, we have about three elements going on here at once, but let me see if I can steer us out of this developing thicket, for all these elements really revolve around the same point and are variations on a single theme.

What is taught in public schools is too often the bottle in the culvert, with little or no attention to the culvert, the neighborhood it serves, the tools with which the bottle can be extracted, the process of selection of those tools, the interaction of two boys, the function of adults in the situation, or the use of the bottle itself. We assume the students want/ need the bottle, and so we give it to them. And, like two small boys, they throw it away, which disturbs us mightily, and so we strive to make them keep it ("Save that! It might be valuable someday"), and all we wind up with is a trash can full of bottles. We are like George Santayana's definition of a fanatic as someone who redoubles his efforts when he has forgotten his objective.

We focus on bottles. We say, "Memorize the causes of the Franco-Prussian War for a quiz tomorrow." "Memorize the definition of a noun." We cannot give very good reasons as to why anyone should do this. Worse, we hand the students the bottles already cleaned and processed in the form of texts and lesson plans and lecture notes. We tell them what to do and how to do it, and we fail them if they don't. We make them sit and appear to listen.

I have often been amused by the sight of teachers in church, squirming in abject discomfort after ten minutes of sermon, glancing at their watches and staring out the windows, wishing that the ordeal were over. After fifty minutes, it is, and they explode into the sunlight outside with relief. How relieved would they be if that were just the first in a series of six or eight they had to endure that day, with only a four-minute break between each, and twenty minutes for lunch? And what if it were only Monday, and there were four more days to go? Operating on a principle espoused by a friend of mine named Lucille Thornburg, most preachers realize that "the mind can absorb only as much as the tail can endure," and so they keep their sermons short (remember the day your preacher talked for twenty-five minutes straight and everyone in the congregation got angry, or the day the principal talked for forty-five minutes and half the faculty went to sleep and the other half never forgave him?), leaving plenty of opportunity to stretch ("I'll have them stand and sing four hymns today, at four different times") and focus on things other than the preacher ("I'll have the choir sing something here, and my assistant can lead the responsive reading, and . . ."), and still there are so many of us who can't stand the ordeal that we stop putting ourselves through it entirely.

And we have the nerve to wonder why fourteen-year-olds won't stay still, and to get angry at them when they squirm. Try what we put them through yourself and see how well you do.

And how well does it work? Well, for starters, we run students through language arts activities and lessons for *twelve years,* and yet every college and university in the country still finds it necessary to have a freshman English program because even most college-level youngsters cannot yet function competently. What is going on here?

And still we focus on bottles. "Memorize the definition of a noun."

There is a fundamental question that should be carved in stone over every school entrance to remind us all, daily, of a problem we must battle on a continual basis. That question: "Who processes the information within?" At the moment, in too many classrooms, it is teachers using texts in ignorance of the fundamental educational corollary to that question:

"The extent to which the learner processes the information to be acquired is the extent to which it is acquired."

I have now become convinced that the greatest disservice to education ever to smite the public schools was the wholesale stampede to textbooks as the primary vehicle for learning. It's not that the texts themselves are bad (though many of them are), but the way in which we use them. They have spread like a cancer inside our classrooms. They have been allowed to dominate everything we do. We have willingly allowed them to rob us of the greatest educational tool of all—the active grappling with the subject matter itself for ends other than its own acquisition; the collective probing of the unknown. They have become a curse and a damnation, and the extent of their takeover—and our dependence on them—is reflected graphically in the exasperated teachers' comments at the beginning of every school year: "How can I possibly be expected to teach this course? I don't have enough texts for all my pupils."

I have in mind the image of classroom after classroom, the teacher poised at a lectern, text open upon it, students seated in rows, following along as the teacher goes over the lesson line by line, occasionally asking a question that students who can locate the answer first in the text answer, and receive their due reward. The process is stylized to almost minuet perfection. "Good" students (those who locate the answers with facility) are called on the requisite number of times to keep things moving along. Others, who haven't found the answers yet, or who are talking among themselves instead of paying attention, are called on purposely so that they may be embarrassed and thus kept under control. And there is no learning going on in such a classroom at all—unless the students already have so much personal experience with the subject matter itself that they know immediately what the text is talking about and can share intuitively their experiences with those of the authors of the text. Though this situation may be common in college, it is awfully rare in secondary schools.

And there, of course, is the crux of the problem: the relationship between printed information—the accumulated experience of decades—and the accumulated experiences of the students themselves. Quite simply, in too many instances, students just don't know what we or our texts are talking about, or they cannot make any connection between that information and their world. Thus they cannot internalize the information or make use of it, and thus it is discarded as irrelevant as soon as the tests are taken.

James Coleman continues to make the point that in today's society, unlike previous ones, young people are "information rich and experience poor," their time dominated by school and television instead of the rich fabric of experiences in the world itself that used to be commonplace, and which, if it still existed today, would give the information they're receiving some context in which it could be tested and applied.

Instead, we have botany courses taught indoors, through texts, with no relevance to or application within the out-of-doors except in imagination. "Imagine, if you can, a plant." Pretty difficult for students who spend all day inside our schools, the late afternoons inside the buildings of their employers, and the evenings in front of television sets. This perverse bastardization of education in the interest of utility and control is undermining the quality of the information our students receive as surely as the oceans undermine and collapse the sea walls constructed in an elaborate attempt to contain them.

A human does not learn how to ride a bicycle, make love, solve a problem, conduct a laboratory experiment, write a magazine article, think creatively, handle a job interview with facility, or make friends through reading books or memorizing directions. One may learn the directions and be able to parrot them back as they were given for a test, but they have no meaning without personal experience. To deny that personal experience—to present only prepackaged information and to assert that it is correct—is to deny the opportunity for the student to discover that there may be more than one way to solve any given task or approach any given problem, and thus to learn how to approach and solve those new and unfamiliar problems that will surely come.

One can memorize the parts of a bicycle and their functions in a classroom, through a text, and even pass a major test on the subject, but without a meaningful personal encounter with a bicycle, one will still not know how to ride, and the names of the parts and their functions will largely be forgotten by the time of the final exam. A midnight review gets them back, briefly, but soon, without that meaningful personal encounter, all is lost again. And one still does not know how to ride. Thus it is with the names of the parts of speech and their functions. Simply reading a chapter about them or writing a composition in which they are put to use *is* an encounter or an experience, but it is not what I mean by a "meaningful encounter" or a "meaningful experience." The widespread failure to miss the application of these two phrases is why we still have freshman English courses in college. It is also why our push to make students master the "basics" through yet more workbooks and computer software and memorization may improve test scores but will do little to improve the students' abilities to apply the information usefully. To paraphrase John Dewey; you don't learn the basics by memorizing the basics, but by doing projects (or creating products) where the basics have to be utilized—a fundamental principle of education many of us have ignored.

Learning which leads to the retention, use, and articulation of knowledge happens when we progress from meaningful experience *to* texts and/or teachers (who presumably have more experiences with and knowledge to share about the subject than we), to evaluation and analysis and reflection, and then back to "hands-on" experience again. This natural ebb and flow between experience and somewhat more passive reception of information and concepts, and back to experience again armed with new approaches and insights and questions, is the way we are stretched and grow mentally. It is the way we learn "on the job," and the best schooling simulates and exploits the pattern.

Children learn this way naturally, the emphasis being on hands-on trial and error. It is what Piaget has so lucidly elaborated in writings based on the observation of his own three children. As Piaget noted, at any given point in a child's development, the child is a knowing system, trying things and getting information back about the world that is fed back into the system of knowledge that is being constructed. Once the actions leading to a discovery have been made, those actions are internalized and stored, and the learner moves on to new and richer ideas and possibilities that have been opened up by these discoveries. Thus the two boys, the culvert, and the bottle. This process is vital, and adult interference must be so sensitive as not to impede it or squash it backward or make the child dependent on the adult for answers, growth, and direction. As Piaget says, "Every time we teach a child something, we keep him from inventing it himself. On the other hand, that which we allow him to discover for himself will remain with him."

As children grow and their questions and their ability to understand and apply what they learn becomes increasingly complex, their need for experience grows also. Without it, the material we pass to them cannot be internalized and used in the growth process. Our bits of information float in their heads like toy boats without anchors, until they are forgotten and left behind.

The same rules govern the growth of teachers. When someone in the role of a teacher of teachers speaks to us for an hour in an in-service meeting, or writes a book like this one and presents it to us, the amount of information he or she gives that we will find useful—and will be able to utilize—will be directly proportional to the number of experiences we have had as teachers that are related to the methods being advocated. No experience? No understanding. We don't know what the lecturer is getting at, we can't imagine how to do it, and we disperse in confusion.

The same with students, but threefold. Our capacity to retain is better developed than theirs, but there is still a gap there, and we still don't know how to apply some of the methods being touted, and so rather than trying, most of us continue to teach in our normal way. *Without the testing*—the experience—we become frozen in time, unable to try new ideas and thus assimilate them, change them, learn from them, and *grow*. And thus we forget even the ideas presented in that in-service meeting. We say, "But I don't know *how*," and then we walk away. For the same reason, without practice teaching experience, we forgot nearly everything encountered in the college educational psychology course that preceded that experience, and thus we could apply precious little from that course when we finally got to teach.

Thus students: "But I don't *understand.*" "I don't know how to do what you're telling me to do." "I don't see what any of this has to do with me." With those words, the role of the teacher snaps sharply into focus: not to answer the questions but to assist in the applications of the material through which the questions will answer themselves and lead to further growth.

I can sit in your in-service meetings and answer your questions about Foxfire all day, but until we move beyond dialogue and into action, you will not truly understand and internalize and know how to apply what I'm sharing with you. "I hear and I forget, I see and remember, I do and I understand." At which point a new set of questions comes. . . .

There is no need for you to apologize to me—or anyone else—for that lack of understanding. It is as natural as a young child's. Like children, we have to move to understanding through action and through play. I have no compunction about getting better at the job of teaching through trying some crazy new idea with my students (my form of play), getting feedback from them as to whether it is of any value (and how it might be changed to *be* of value), and then talking to peers (or reading articles by other teachers who have tried the same technique) and comparing notes. The spirit of active revision is good for me and my students, for it turns us all into learners together in the interest of increasingly effective education.

Likewise, when I try out ideas *with* you, as a teacher, and we work side by side, and I am smart enough to know when to get out of your way and give you your head and let you run with something, the amount of your learning and your confidence increases far more than it would if I gave you an instruction manual, said do it *this* way, and then stood over you waiting for you to stumble so I could pounce.

The same with students.

This whole matter of meaningful experience and its relation to our subject matter is a tremendously important—and widely misunderstood —point, and one that I'll return to in the curriculum section. Let me talk about these misunderstandings for a few moments, however, before we move on.

Though hands-on, meaningful experience may be the best way to learn, it is not the only way to learn, and it remains (and should remain) only one of the methods in our bag of tricks. Why? First of all because it may be virtually impossible to obtain. We cannot take our 150 students to an African village so they can study that culture firsthand. We cannot fly them to the moon so they can study the solar system from a new and powerful vantage point. Neither can we take our students backward in time to the front lines so they can observe World War I being fought. Nor can we bring a cow into our third-floor inner-city classroom so that our students can learn, hands-on, about dairy products and butterfat; and our principals may not allow field trips so that we can take the students to the cow. Obviously there are limitations on our ability to utilize what, on paper, sounds like a great way to learn.

Second, experience can backfire and do the opposite of what we intend. Like fire, it must be applied carefully. Our goal in its use must be to assist in student growth. What if an experience is so terrifying, however, that it arrests that growth and the student retreats, never to confront a certain aspect of the world again? What if a student gets shocked, for example, and is ever after destined to live in abject fear of electricity? What if a student is so embarrassed by an experience that it inhibits future growth in that area?

Third, learning by experience can be slow, cumbersome, time consuming, and frustrating in the extreme. Imagine, for example, a well-meaning science teacher who decides that the best way for his or her students to learn chemistry is to systematically rediscover all the major principles, step by step, that led the field to its present theories and beliefs. Great course, but how many years would it take, and how much money would it cost?

Obviously there has to be some middle ground between the techniques of teaching only by lecture and text and teaching only by direct experience. And it is in trying to find that middle ground that so many teachers stumble. Consider that well-meaning teacher, for example, who realizes the impossibility of taking the students back into history but is determined that they "experience" those times and so creates a curriculum that was later reflected upon ruefully by a former student as follows:

"The way we learned history was by trying to re-create its least important elements. One year, we pounded corn, made teepees, ate buffalo meat and learned two Indian words. That was early American history. Another year we made elaborate costumes, clay pots, and papier-mâché gods. That was Greek culture. Another year we were all maidens and knights in armor because it was time to learn about the Middle Ages. We drank our orange juice from tin-foil goblets but never found out what the Middle Ages were. They were just 'The Middle Ages.'

"We knew that the Huns pegged their horses and drank a quart of blood before going to war but no one ever told us who the Huns were or why we should know who they were. And one year, the year of ancient Egypt, when we were building our pyramids, I did a thirty-foot-long mural for which I laboriously copied hieroglyphics onto the sheet of brown paper. But no one ever told me what they stood for. They were just there and beautiful."[3]

Thus we have a teacher who has stumbled.

Likewise the teachers who say, "Ah, yes. I agree with the theory that students learn best through independent investigation into subjects that interest them. Thus I will send each to the library to research his or her chosen subject and write a paper about it." What they get for their efforts is a stack of papers, each laboriously copied out of an encyclopedia. What was learned? I got my first hint of how much such work is understood and internalized during my first year at Rabun Gap, when I was watching over the required evening study hall in the boys' dorm. I walked into the room of one of the most conscientious students in the school, and I found him preparing his biology notebook, a section of which was due the following day. He was copying sections of the text in order to reach the required ten-page minimum, and in curiosity, as he finished a sentence, I reached over his shoulder, closed the text and the notebook, and said, "I'm really curious about something and I don't want to embarrass you, but tell me what the sentence said that you just wrote." He couldn't tell me. Had I held a pistol to his head, he couldn't have told me. He was copying, and his mind was elsewhere. Gain in knowledge? Zero. Time wasted? All. I've tried the same thing many times since with similar results, finding nearly every time that though the student may be able to roughly paraphrase a section just written, there is almost never any accompanying *understanding*. And a week after the term papers or biology notebooks are turned in, there is virtually no recollection on the part of most students as to the essence of what they wrote. It has all vanished like mist.

And we teachers *know* this. Yet we persist. The students have been involved in an activity more experiential (less passive) than listening to a lecture, but it has not been a meaningful (thus internalized) experience.

Similarly we stumble when we say, "Okay, I agree that the way students master the basics is not through endless drill but by doing projects (creating products) where the basics have to be used," and then in direct misapplication of that philosophy, *we* devise and construct those projects and impose them on our students. It's better than lecturing. At least the students get to do something besides sitting and listening. But in the end, projects so conceived and imposed prove to be little different educationally from the exercises students work out of their texts. There is no learner input. The information has already been processed. The correct outcomes have already been predetermined.

I was conducting a teacher in-service meeting recently at which a teacher described such a "project" situation exactly, concluding that she had tried just what I had proposed but that it didn't work. The students didn't like it. No wonder. All she had done was present them with a glorified version of a text and, consequently, a bogus experience. When I explained the probable causes of the students' disinterest, she protested, "I can see how my brighter students might be able to help me, but what do I do with the slower ones? They won't be able to come up with anything."

Luckily a teacher of learning disabled children was in the room, and she gently reminded her colleague that all the planning for the day's refreshments, and all the necessary cooking, decoration, and execution of those refreshments had been done by her students, and that, in fact, such work was the *only* way they could learn, for texts were beyond them at the moment.

In another in-service meeting, a teacher described how one of her colleagues, in an effort to help her slower students understand the concept of geographical direction, had applied for a small grant of about $100 from a local CESA organization with which to purchase paints and brushes to paint a map of the county on the classroom floor, so that when students stepped from one town to another, they could tell whether they were going north, northwest, and so on. Not a bad idea, and a worthwhile project for CESA to assist. The problem? The amount of potential learning on the part of the students was only a fraction of what it could have been had the students been helped to come up with ten or fifteen possible projects, had selected one by class vote, and had then divided into groups to plan the execution (as a geography lesson); price the paints and brushes and create the budget (as a math lesson); write the proposal itself, complete with rationale (as an English lesson); send the proposal off, and then receive the money, purchase the supplies, draw out the map and paint it themselves, notify the local newspaper to come to the school and publicize the activity—and so on. Imagine the numerous opportunities for building real involvement in such a tiny project. Imagine, for example, the class electing a chairperson, the teacher making sure the CESA officials would deal with that student instead of her, the PA announcement asking that student to come to the phone, and that student being told that the group had just been awarded the hundred dollars it had requested. Imagine that student bursting into the classroom with the news, and the class cheering and clapping in amazement and delight. How much fuller and more complete an experience it could have been than that of a map simply being enlarged and painted on the floor by a teacher.

And what if the project had not been funded? A wise teacher would already have discussed such a possibility with the students in advance, and contingency plans would already have been in place. Imagine, for example, an elected group of students from the class going with the teacher to the offices of a local industry (with a promise of publicity for and credit to that industry), presenting a tightly reasoned, well-planned request for assistance in the amount of a hundred dollars. It's hard to imagine an industry refusing, given the fact that nearly all designate a certain percentage of their income for donations in the communities from which their employees come, and given the fact that many employees' children probably attend the school from which the request originates.

Failing there, the other options are so numerous they would take pages to list. The money would be found—and by the students, not the teacher. The difference in involvement and learning is obvious. And that is part of what is meant by a "meaningful experience" as opposed to an "experience."

The same bastardization of the idea of meaningful experience comes at the hands of well-meaning, concerned teachers who want to move their classes beyond texts and lectures and who believe true education is problem/project/product oriented (read: experiential), but who then jump the track deciding themselves to start a *Foxfire*-type magazine, select its name, dictate its design and contents, raise the money, handle all business affairs, and, since their own egos are so directly involved, rule it with an iron hand. I have seen more examples of this than I can shake an eraser at, and in nearly every case, such teachers (who *allow* the students to take part in something that is very much the *teacher*'s enterprise) wonder aloud why their students are not more enthusiastic and involved.

Granted, they have gone one step beyond the ordinary language arts or social studies class, but they have about ten more steps to go before real learning begins to happen. Perhaps this is the way it must be. Perhaps teachers need to learn and be rewarded and praised and gain self-confidence themselves—just like their students—before they begin to sublimate their own egos and relinquish some control. Certainly that's the way it happened in my life, as you've already seen from Book I. It's a hard lesson to learn, but it's so necessary. Until that lesson is learned, a project like *Foxfire* magazine is, like the definition of a noun, just one more type of bottle in a culvert. The teacher assumes it has worth in and of itself, and so dictates the activities and the methods and the outcomes with such zeal that it loses its potential as a *vehicle* for education. This is to focus on the bottle rather than the process of—and the resulting education inherent in —its extraction. It is product *versus* process. And just as it is appropriate that the bottle be left behind—a now relatively worthless shell not unlike the hollow carapace a cicada leaves clinging to a tree—so, too, it is appropriate that a magazine be left behind by those students who have learned what there is to learn from the process of creating it and have now moved on to broader, more comprehensive and more complex goals. For the good teacher, such a magazine has value only insofar as it can be a vehicle to serve the purpose of learning. The values *others* ascribe to it (public relations for the administration, visibility of the community for the chamber of commerce, preservation of culture and folklore for the oral historians and folklorists) provide additional motivation to do the job well, but they are absolutely secondary to that *primary* value. And the heavier a hand the teacher takes in the creation of the product, the less the students will learn and the faster they will discard it and move on to other options either physically (leaving a teacher with a magazine class for which no students have enrolled) or mentally (refusing to participate and get involved).

Skills such as knowing when to step aside or let go take years for teachers and parents to learn. I'm still learning. It's hard. After I've helped a student learn how to use a single-lens-reflex camera, I take the student into the field on that initial interview. The student takes pictures.

As I see great, once-in-a-lifetime shots revealing themselves, many of which the student is unaware, I stand on the sidelines gritting my teeth and chafing, pacing back and forth, wanting nothing more than to grab the camera out of that kid's hands and snap away myself—knowing all the while that to do so would destroy the educational value of the experience. The student, whose self-confidence is in a fragile enough state already on this first time out, would retreat in dismay, and all learning would cease.

Some gentle reassurance, a low-key suggestion here and there, genuine congratulations at a fine camera angle taken advantage of, and then teaching the student to print using his or her own negatives, and a person begins to develop who is a far cry from what would have developed otherwise.

And mistakes? Well, what's a mistake? Is a scratched negative a mistake? I suppose. But the bigger mistake would be the wrong reaction to it. Scream and yell? Fail the student? Fine. I find I don't get many photographers that way, though. Treat it patiently as an opportunity to learn, and refuse to embarrass the student at fault? Of course. That's the function of the situation, isn't it? To help students learn?

Or has the student made a mistake because his or her photographs aren't as good as ours would have been? If that's the way our minds are running, we're in the wrong profession.

That's not to say we let go of a standard of excellence and allow all manner of sloppily printed and out-of-focus photographs, grammatical errors, and factual inaccuracies to fill the magazine's pages in the interest of letting the kids learn by doing. But it is to say we work patiently behind the scenes to help the students find within themselves the best they can give us at any point in time. We add to their existing repertoire of skills some tricks we've learned, and we make sure our criticism is not punitive or random or unthinking—the kind of criticism that would break a student's enthusiasm for continuing to test and grow and learn—and then we back the resulting product without embarrassment or apology.

And we keep always in mind the fact that often, in the right atmosphere, our students will come up with ideas they want to try that prove to be better than any we might have imposed on them out of our repertoire. Each represents a moment in time when a student learned enough through me to begin to experiment alone, and thus grew beyond me and beyond my shadow into independence and sunlight. Those expressions of independence, rooted in conviction and self-confidence and thought, are successes far greater than those that result from underlings carrying out my directives. They represent growth, the vehicle for which just happens to be a magazine—but doesn't have to be.

We take such a heavy hand when we move beyond lecture to experience. Is it because we are afraid that our reputations hang in the balance? Or because we are afraid that our students will run amok? Or because we are afraid materials will be wasted, or equipment broken, or end products not up to our standards of excellence? I'm not sure. But I've been on the receiving end of both approaches, and I hope I've learned something in the process: a father, for example, who showed me how to drive nails and cut lumber, and then let me build a dog house for my dog instead of building it himself and letting me only sit by passively and watch, perhaps handing him a nail once in a while. It wasn't, perhaps, the best dog house that's ever been built, but it served the purpose well. And later I went on to design and build a house for myself.

In contrast, consider a shop teacher at my old high school, to whom I went to ask permission to make a simple 6-by-9-by-4-inch-deep maple box with dovetailed joints and a hinged lid, which my father had requested for his birthday. By the time the shop teacher got through with my plans, the box had turned into a two-layer rosewood affair with little legs and drawers lined with green felt that didn't even resemble what I or my father had in mind. Reluctantly I got as far as cutting out several of the pieces, and then abandoned the project completely and, embarrassed, never went back to that shop to build anything again. So far as I know, the pieces of rosewood for that terrible project are still tucked away somewhere in the recesses of one of those cabinets, looked at with mild curiosity by each new group of students that passes through.

And I couldn't care less.

They Know Their Students and Their Environments

Knowing the subject matter and the laws of learning, however, is no guarantee at all that a teacher will be able to apply such knowledge effectively. One of several missing ingredients is a deep-seated, unshakable interest in young people and a corresponding willingness to get to know students on a level that goes beyond the last-name-first, first-name-last basis, and a willingness to become familiar with the environments and cultures from which those students come. The extent to which this happens (and one of our frustrations is the difficulty of making it happen at all when we have 150 students) is the extent to which teachers can tailor-make their curricula to their clientele, and feel comfortable encouraging a certain amount of student input and cooperation in that process.

When I know students reasonably well, I know the extent of the demands I can make upon them; I know something about their talents and abilities and likes and dislikes, and thus I can lead them into educational activities with reasonable hope of success. I know the kind of criticism they will respond to and not be crushed or repelled by; I know their strengths and how to make those a large part of the work we do together. I know what intimidates them, what infuriates them, what excites them, and thus I can usually move them forward into a deeper understanding of my subject matter without losing them along the way. I know when to provide encouragement and support and ballast—and how and in what amounts—and I know when to get out of their way and leave them alone to work independently or even just to sit and think. I know something about their readiness to accept responsibility, and in what amounts. And they know me.

It's a tricky area, one that most teachers sidestep either because they think it's improper to get to know students or because they don't think it's necessary, or because they just simply don't want to, or . . . One result, however, is the awkwardness that invariably envelops both parties when students run into the teacher accidentally at the local fast-food spot or the supermarket. It is as though teachers have life and meaning only inside the school buildings, and they never exist or function in the real world. They are lowered from the skies each morning in chariots surrounded by sunlight and the music of harps, and at 3:10 they ascend again into the heavens to leave the real world to its own devices until their carefully timed return. Ridiculously artificial situations result.

During my semester of practice teaching, I boarded in the home of an older, veteran teacher who had some pretty firm ideas about the teacher-pupil relationship. The school was only a few blocks from her home, and being the only junior high that served her neighborhood, I and many of the students walked to school. I took her dictums seriously, being inexperienced, but since hundreds of us were on the streets simultaneously, all heading for the same place, it was pretty hard for me to completely avoid contact with the students. I would have had to go an hour early, or sneak through backyards and alleyways to do it. The students and I got along together famously, however, and many good things happened that semester—things that have led me and several former students and parents to stay in touch to this day. But I still remember the tongue-lashing that older teacher gave several of those junior high kids when they came to the house one morning to ask if I wanted to walk to school with them, and I still wince at the memory of the anger with which she delivered the same message to me after she had chased them away.

Seemingly the same set of rules governs the relationship between many teachers and the communities from which their students are drawn. Rural teachers who live in a county like the one in which I teach often know only a tiny segment of the population well. Urban teachers routinely commute an hour each way, teaching in a city but living in a suburb. Teachers on Indian reservations live in all-white isolation from their students, sometimes in compounds surrounded by fences. At a recent workshop, a teacher admitted to me that part of the difficulty she was having with her students probably stemmed from the fact that she was from the urban East, was teaching in the rural South, and just didn't know anything about her students or how to get through to them. Though the year was almost over, she still operated in isolation, and her classes were still chaotic and floundering. Our conversation reminded me of nothing so much as a memorable section of *To Kill A Mockingbird,* one of my favorite books. It concerns Scout's first day in school:

"Miss Caroline began the day by reading us a story about cats. The cats had long conversations with one another. They wore cunning little clothes and lived in a warm house beneath a kitchen stove. By the time Mrs. Cat called the drugstore for an order of chocolate malted mice, the class was wriggling like a bucketful of Catawba worms. Miss Caroline seemed unaware that the ragged, denim-shirted and flour-sack-skirted first grade, most of whom had chopped cotton and fed hogs from the time they were able to walk, were immune to imaginative literature."[4]

Miss Caroline's ignorance of her students and their community led her deeper and deeper into quicksand. When lunchtime came and she discovered Walter had not brought his lunch, she offered him a quarter, which he refused, making her impatient. Finally Scout tried to explain, saying, " 'Miss Caroline, he's a Cunningham.'

"I sat back down.

" 'What, Jean Louise?'

"I thought I had made things sufficiently clear. It was clear enough to the rest of us."[5]

By the time Miss Caroline suffered through an explosive situation with another student (who left school for the remainder of the year) and then, recovered somewhat, opened a book and "mystified the first grade with a long narrative about a toadfrog that lived in a hall,"[6] we knew she was going to need far more than her degree from college to be made into something resembling a productive teacher *in that environment.*

The community in which I began to teach, and still teach, is completely different from the one in which I was raised, and most of my students come from a home environment largely different from the home in which I was raised (with a father who was a college professor, a heavy emphasis on reading, and the foregone conclusion that someday I would go to college and then make a substantive contribution to society).

Suddenly I found myself in a situation in which very little made sense and all my acquired mannerisms and assumptions instantly and permanently identified me as an outsider. A situation where Buchanan was pronounced with a short instead of a long *u.* Where when I asked students if they would like to do something, and they replied, "We don't care to," they meant not that they didn't want to but that they wouldn't mind doing it at all. Where males used *hey* as a greeting instead of the more effeminate *hi.* Where people waved to each other from their pickup trucks and automobiles even if they didn't know each other, and spoke to each other unfailingly on the street even if they didn't know each other, and where not to conform to such social niceties identified one as being stuck-up and arrogant. (As one of my students said of someone he disliked, "He never speaks [waves] and I ain't got no use fer 'im.") Where when people ended a conversation with, "Well, go with me," the proper response was not, "Fine, I'd love to," but, "I guess I'd better stay around here." Where not to be able to take care of oneself in at least minimal fashion by raising a garden and some stock, fixing one's own car, and doing basic wiring, plumbing, and carpentry was a sign of real weakness. And so on for at least another book.

And it was—and is—a wonderful community. But it was not until I had made a real attempt to understand it that I realized the terrible traps into which I could fall by trying to impose my middle-class values on my students and their families, and by trying to impose certain types of literature and poetry that I had considered appropriate on students to whom it was alien and false and inappropriate. Such behavior is as wrong-headed as insisting that poor Southern blacks or migrant Chicano children learn to read best from Dick and Jane readers. It is like a white teacher of Indian children insisting that they all start a magazine like *Foxfire*, only to discover that the culture forbids the writing down and sharing of many cultural customs with the outside world. It is at such times we meekly say, "Oh. I didn't know," and we realize how far we have to go.

Sometimes we are so convinced of the righteousness of our beliefs, that the gulf between us and our students' communities becomes a chasm. Others of us, determined not to let that happen, take an equally disastrous tack and try to sublimate our own values and customs and merge seamlessly with those of the community. In our part of the country, such a person appears in front of the drugstore in town wearing a new pair of bib overalls, alternately sucking and chewing on a plug of chewing tobacco, and drawling on in a ludicrous imitation of mountain dialect about moonshine and "hawgs" and "taters." Such people are universally despised—especially if they're teachers. They are just as bad as the teachers who rail against such things as hunting and carrying guns when such customs are so firmly and inseparably a part of the culture of our students (who, in the fall, routinely get up at 4 A.M. in order to get in several hours of deer hunting before school) that to battle them is like trying to bail out the ocean with a colander. Each stance discredits its owner.

Without extreme sensitivity and care, we can also blunder in our well-meaning desire to know our students on a more personal basis. Young people shy away automatically (and justifiably) from adults who come on too strong, who try to smother them with affection, who "want to get to know them better," who want them to share their secrets and their fears. Such adults are just weird, period. Young people lose respect for adults who invade their territory and take on customs and mannerisms they have reserved for themselves and use as part of their personal identity kit. Those pathetic adults who, for whatever misguided reasons, talk in the jargon of their students, dress like them, sidle up to and sneer with them over dirty jokes and snide remarks, and hang out after school with them, have fallen off the edge of the world and may be irretrievable. Certainly they should not be teachers.

But, as in all things, there is firm middle ground on which to stand.

How well should one know the community in which one teaches? Well enough to know its customs and mores and values, so it is possible to be, if not in agreement with them, at least able to operate comfortably within them and not contradict them, while keeping one's own identity intact. Well enough to be able to share unselfconsciously in many aspects of its life without intruding. Well enough to know—and be able to nourish and perhaps expand—its hopes and dreams for its children. Well enough to know when one is overstepping one's bounds of authority.

Well enough, in sum, to be able to operate *appropriately* within it. And that takes practice, and a willingness to start getting to know all those people out there we normally drive past with our windows rolled up. It begins with gentle entry through appropriate channels (barber shops, community markets and shops, local restaurants, churches) and grows as a result of desire and patience and love. And if you've never done it before, you're just like the student whose book tells him how to ride a bicycle but who has never seen one except in pictures. Words can only help so much. Next comes action, and the assurance of scraped knees and bruised elbows.

And how well should we know our students?

Certainly well enough to know and adjust for those events and situations that conspire against their progress in our classes. I had a student once, for example, who never turned in homework assignments and who could rarely stay awake or alert in class. All my warnings to him about the certainty of a failing grade made no difference except to make him more defensive and withdrawn. I checked the school records (which sometimes turn out to be one of the worst sources of information available because they so often cause us to make mistaken assumptions about students) and found little more than a repeating pattern of bad grades, teachers' comments like "can't stay awake in class," and the indication that his IQ was well within normal range (and that was obvious without the test scores to confirm it). I was still stuck.

Finally I found out that after school each day, he rode the school bus to a little tavern owned by his grandparents, with whom he lived. Partly because they were afraid of his getting into trouble with friends, they required him to stay there at the tavern with them. He was there until closing time at midnight, eating a supper of hamburgers and french fries or whatever happened to come off the short order grill, and then, after closing, he and his grandfather cleaned the place up and then slept there in sleeping bags the rest of the night to prevent robberies, and they were constantly awakened by drunks at two and three in the morning banging on the doors in the hope of being able to buy beer after hours. Homework was nearly impossible in such a situation, with the jukebox blaring away, and sleep was furtive at best. His grandparents were doing as well as they could under the circumstances, and the boy was certainly getting an education of sorts, but it wasn't quite the kind the school board or the state had in mind for him when it opened our county's public schools.

Teachers who simply shrug their shoulders when confronted by such evidence and say, "Well, it's not my problem. There's nothing I can do. He either does his work or he doesn't. I can only grade what he turns in," are obviously not part of the solution. Failing the student solves nothing. Teachers who become sympathetic and pass the student on because they realize the "extenuating circumstances" aren't part of the solution either.

The approach must be to find the cause of the problem, get to know the parties involved well enough to determine whether there's some room to maneuver, then enlist the help of the guidance counselors and the other teachers involved to thrash out some possible solutions (assuming the welfare of the student is important to them, and it usually is), and then approach the student and the parents or guardians with some courses of action that seem feasible without putting anyone on the defensive, or condemning certain life-styles, or getting into any of the self-righteous postures of which so many of us are capable. Easier said than done, true. And short of that are other avenues: getting together informally with a couple of the student's other teachers to talk through the problem; enlisting the help of a school-based adult trained in working in such areas; sitting down with the student and saying, "Look, I'm really worried about this. What are we going to do?" and so on. Still too time consuming? Well, what are you going to do? Fail the kid?

I have found that short of getting personally involved ("sticking my nose in other people's business where it doesn't belong"), some simple genuine and discreet concern shared with my peers does wonders, if only because it gets two or three of us looking at the problem and puzzling over it together. Often solutions come.

Let me give another, less extreme example. A student goes to sleep in class. One teacher looks at the situation, reminds himself of the overwhelming value of the subject material that day, and becomes angry. He wakes the student, embarrassing him in front of his classmates, all the while knowing that he's not going to be able to concentrate anyway.

A different teacher looks at the same situation. He and the student are on friendly terms. Because of this fact, the student, a thirteen-year-old, has proudly confided in him the previous day that the upcoming night is going to be the biggest of his life thus far; his uncle has just told him that he's now old enough and responsible enough to accompany the uncle and several of his adult friends on an all-night coon hunt. The boy is given a new shotgun, is told he will be allowed to let his dog run with the rest of the pack, and then is sent off to school, his head swimming. The student tells the teacher how long he's been waiting for this night and tells him how he's watched his other brothers go through the same initiation process and how glad he is that his uncle finally said, "This year is your year. You're ready now." The boy shares this information with the teacher, as he would with any other friend, knowing that the teacher will not laugh at him but will congratulate him, confirm that he really has matured the last few months, and will quietly share his excitement.

The next day the boy sleeps. Rather than waking him, the teacher has the good sense to realize that there are events that happen in young people's lives that are far more important than whatever agenda he may have mapped out for any given day, and that he must take such facts into account. He explains the situation briefly to the class, the students smile in understanding, knowing the teacher would be equally patient with them, and the lesson proceeds. In fact, the teacher, rather than ignoring such moments in students' lives, is even able to enlist their active participation in building a unit of his language arts curriculum around these moments, affirming their value and helping students come to a deepening understanding of maturity, responsibility, and entry into the adult world.

To which of the two teachers will the class respond most positively? With which of the two teachers will students continue to share their excitements, their hopes and their dreams?

Just as I could have punished the boy who slept in class, so, too, I could have punished the student who took me ginseng hunting because of the several days of class he missed. Some teachers did. But in my class, rather than fueling his resentment, we laid the foundation for a relationship that still continues. We weren't "pals," cruising town and raising hell together, but we did become friends, each with something to contribute to the other. We stopped being adversaries. I found him to be smarter in many areas than I, and I learned from him unselfconsciously. As I was able to merge his knowledge and his strengths into his language arts activities, I was also able to build on those interests and bring him forward into new competencies and understandings that he had not had before. And thus he learned from me. As I became open to what he had to say, he became open to what I had to say. We shared. Had I been his only teacher, I could easily have built a complete curriculum for him around his interest in herbs—a curriculum that would have included not only forceful writing and correct grammar but also solid aspects of botany, chemistry, math, geography, biology, economics. And with his growing awareness of the applicability of those subjects to his world, with a little skill, I could have brought him far beyond ginseng. As it was, he dropped out of high school before finishing. But he made a real contribution to my teaching career and my life. I hope I contributed equally to him.

To make our education effective, we must start with the real-world reality of our students' lives, be it centered around raccoons, ginseng, a little tavern, McDonald's, or a ghetto street—accept that, build on that, and broaden that. Otherwise we demean that reality, or negate it. We imply that nothing they've learned in their lives is valid or has relevance.

We deny their past, deny their present, and proceed from the assumption that they're ignorant and deprived and that we must correct the situation or they're doomed.

To bring our education and their lives together, we must know them better. I don't think there's another way to do it. And just as we must be careful about the way in which we learn about their communities and their backgrounds, so, too, must we be careful about the way we approach them. I never say, for example, "I'd like to get to know you better." Rather, I have my classes broken down into small groups, and as I work with each of those groups on their projects, we simply get to know each other better. Likewise with the work we do on projects after school hours. We simply work together on something of interest to all of us, and rather than being focused on each other, we are focused on "it," and we learn one other's moods and likes and dislikes and limitations gradually, naturally, automatically. Their parents come to pick them up when we're finished, or I take them home, and soon I know their families. A working relationship evolves, and we see each other in a completely different light.

They Are Careful About the Assumptions They Make

The best teachers never make negative assumptions about the potential of their students. Unfortunately, the atmosphere of too many of our schools almost forces us into this counterproductive posture. We build schools on the disease model ("Your students have the following defects and deficiencies, and it is your job this year to remediate these") rather than on the more subtle but immensely more powerful strength model ("Your students have the following strengths and abilities, and it is your job to begin there, and build on those, and take advantage of them, and in the process turn areas of weakness around").

The fact is that what you see is often what you get. A customer walks into a restaurant. Because of the way he is groomed and dressed, the waitress assumes he's not going to leave a very big tip. Therefore she gives him poor service, and so he *doesn't* leave a big tip, and as he goes out the door the waitress comments to herself, "Yep. I can spot 'em every time."

And exactly the same thing is going on in too many public schools. So many studies have been conducted about this phenomenon that they would fill a bookshelf if pulled together. Tenth-grade teachers are told by their ninth-grade colleagues that the class they're about to get is so far behind grade level that fixing them is going to be nearly hopeless; and so the tenth-grade teachers, assuming this to be true, and assuming that since the class as a whole is stupid, it will also be filled with discipline problems, gear up the discipline and gear down the academic demands, and what they get are discipline problems and low academic achievement.

In the opposite direction, we have the "Pygmalion effect," first described by Harvard psychologist Robert Rosenthal in the mid-sixties. This study, since demonstrated and confirmed again and again, shows that "when teachers are told certain students are gifted or have high potential, whether the students turn out to be gifted or not the teachers look, smile, and nod at them more often. 'They also teach them more content, set higher goals for them, call on them more, and give them more time to answer.' The favored students do better."[7]

We have to be very careful here, now, that we are clear about what's going on. As a result of our negative assumptions, at least two things can happen. One is that as a result of our expecting less than star performance, and consequently demanding less, students truly do *not* advance academically. A second is that the students we assume are flawed may make great progress *anyway,* but because we believe our assumptions about them, we are unwilling to change those assumptions based on the facts in front of us. Thus we assume that when such students turn in fine papers or tests, they cheated, and we continue to give them low grades. This is especially true in courses like English, in which so many of the grades are based on subjective judgment. A "bright" student and a "poor" student each write a composition. The bright student is exhausted by the extracurricular demands being made on her time and by her work load, and so she turns in a halfhearted, mindless attempt that is far less than her best. The poor student, determined to turn things around academically, stays up half the night and turns in a far above average attempt. The bright student still gets the better grade. Result? *Then* the poor student gives up, realizing that the job is hopeless and the deck is stacked. And you know I'm not exaggerating. You've seen this happen too.

Likewise with the Pygmalion effect. The students who receive the attention, have higher goals set for them, and have more demands made of them often really *do* advance academically. But a second possibility? Even when they are not advancing at all—and in fact may be sliding—we allow ourselves to believe they are making spectacular advances under our tutelage despite all the evidence to the contrary. We are blinded by our assumptions and our hopes.

Compounding the problem, often, is our method of drawing our own assumptions and rightly ignoring those of others. Often unconsciously, we turn the classroom into a mirror of ourselves, rewarding those students who reflect our values and reflect back an image of ourselves and our likes and dislikes. We reinforce those who already shine brightest in our eyes, ignore or patronize the others, and thus create the situation in which students read us like a book and "give us what we want." Students that are best at this get the better grades, even if not deserved, and the self-fulfilling prophecy takes over again.

Compounding the problem even further is that the students we wish to reward, or the students we assume are bright, are too often given all the opportunities to go on field trips, pursue independent study options, and take on responsibility. The problem? They may have been selected for such opportunities for all the wrong reasons. Such activities can enhance academic growth. That much is clear. And yet the very students who may need that growth most get left behind and thus do not grow. Hence we have projects based on the *Foxfire* model run by classes of "gifted" students, when a strong argument can be made that the other students need and deserve such options more. Students reluctant to learn from texts may be led back to those texts through meaningful field trips and out-of-school, real-world experiences, and yet such experiences are often reserved for those who need them least, or, worse, as rewards for good behavior. In the latter situation, the potential academic value of such experiences may be replaced by the value they may have in helping to keep students under control. Discipline by the carrot-stick method. "You be nice today and we'll let you go on the trip tomorrow."

So what are we to make of all this? First, we must not allow ourselves to become blinded to what is really going on in our classrooms. I have to watch myself constantly, for example, when I take on a supposedly poor student. Sometimes I am so eager to prove to the person who so characterized the student that the opposite is true that I inflate the student's "progress" unrealistically and allow myself to believe great leaps of improvement are being made when that may not be true. I may accept poor work, convince myself that it is grand, and thus deprive the student of some much-needed, positive, helpful criticism. I have to remind myself constantly to be absolutely objective and not be blinded by what I subconsciously *want* to see in a student's work.

Second, we must not believe others' assumptions about our students, and we must constantly mistrust our own assumptions, especially if they're negative, and base our approach on fact. This is where getting to know students better plays such an important role, for too often the "facts" we base our assumptions and consequent approaches on are misleading (test scores, quality of homework, classroom performance, behavior) and are not the best indices of potential or ability. Too many of us think they are.

For example, based on his test scores and his papers and his performance in class, I had assumed the boy who took me ginseng hunting was stupid and largely incapable of real academic work. Wrong on all counts. He had plenty going on upstairs and plenty of ability. I just hadn't known how to tap it, and since I had assumed he wasn't really worth wasting much time on, I hadn't tried very hard to get behind his scrawled papers to find out just what was going on there.

Had I allowed myself to believe, based on the quality of their work and their behavior, that my students weren't ready for high school yet and ought to be in sixth grade, I would have tailored my lessons to that assumption and we never would have started *Foxfire*. Watching them run the project alone while I was at Johns Hopkins taught me a lot about how misplaced my original assumptions were about their abilities, their trust-worthiness, and their potential. The problem in the beginning had been with me and the silly lessons I had been demanding they complete, not with them.

The sister of all this is making assumptions based on real facts but drawing the wrong conclusions as to remedies.

Fact: all but two of my students flunked my last quiz on the definitions of the parts of speech.

Assumption: since some of them were talking while I was explaining, and some of them were daydreaming, I assume that that is why they flunked.

Conclusion: we have to do it over again, and this time I have to make them listen. I just have to keep doing this until they get it right.

Right fact, partly correct assumption, wrong remedy. Explain until the cows come home, and on the final exam, most of them will still foul up that section. The teacher has forgotten the rules of learning. The teacher has also forgotten the work of people like Ebbinghaus, which shows that 66.3 percent of what one learns is forgotten within twenty-four hours without constant review.[8] And review in a classroom situation with a teacher lecturing and the class silent—even if they're listening—is not remembered. Every year, therefore, the students review parts of speech, and the level of boredom and the lack of retention escalates in direct proportion to the number of times of review. It's the methodology that's the problem, not the facts themselves or the students. Allow yourself to believe that the facts are too hard for them to grasp or the skills are too difficult for their current stage of development, and these assumptions may lead you into the swamp as you scale down your expectations accord-ingly, go on teaching the old way, and miss the real culprit.

Every day we see our negative assumptions contradicted, and yet too frequently we fail to look at those contradictions closely for the lessons they may hold. And it starts as early as the first day of school.

We assume, for example, that a certain method of teaching and a certain time line must be adhered to, and so we ignore the individuals in our own classes who refute those assumptions, and we squash them into a mold that will not hold them.

Or we assume that major projects and undertakings are not appropri-ate in elementary school ("The kids aren't ready for work on that level yet"), ignoring all the while evidence to the contrary. Phillip Lopate, for example, who wrote *Being With Children* (Doubleday, 1975), recently mounted a full-scale three-act production of Chekhov's *Uncle Vanya* in a neighborhood theater in New York City. The cast? Fifth-graders from one of his public school classes. I saw the production myself with Bill Strachan, my former editor at Doubleday, and both of us can attest to its complexity and scope and the style with which those students pulled it off —onstage nearly nonstop for well over an hour.

Similarly we assume that student speeches (if they're to be made at all) should be made in public only by older students who have had some experience and who have a well-developed presentation that they have rehearsed until every shred of life and spontaneity has been strangled. I have taken students on the road for over a decade now. Nearly every time I go, I take students who have never spoken to an audience before. I show the students how to make an outline and a few reminder notes several hours before the presentation, and then I leave them alone to develop their part of the program, leaving time for them to go over it with me if they want to. I insist only that they not have their speeches written out, but instead just talk to the audience honestly and clearly about what they've been doing in our classes and how they feel about school; and I've seen more standing ovations in the last fifteen years than many professional performers see in a lifetime. I've watched grown teachers break down and cry. And I've seen students, after speaking to audiences that routinely number from four hundred to a thousand people, sign autographs until their hands are sore.

On a recent trip with two eighth-graders who made presentations to several different groups, we accepted an invitation to speak to three classes of eighth-graders at their local junior high. We were in a large room, alone, setting up our slide projector, when the bell rang and the eighth-grade audience was marched in in a tight little procession, guarded all around by adults. First the front row was filled completely, then the second, then the third. And all the while the air was filled with tension and with comments from the teachers like, "Now we have *company* today, don't we? And we want to be on our *best behavior* today, don't we?" "Now you *know* that isn't the way I *taught* you to *sit, is it?*" "Now let's give our complete attention to these *nice* people who are going to show us some *pictures* today. Wasn't it *nice* of them to come and *see* us?" All the while I could feel my lunch moving around like a live thing in my stomach as I watched the trapped expressions on the faces of sixty thirteen-year-olds. I showed the slides, and then my two eighth-graders stood and spoke, and then answered questions with an ease and maturity and natural poise and sincerity that held the room spellbound; and as they talked, I watched the faces of their peers and wished more than once that I could load every one of them into our jeep and take them home to our school, out from under adults who treated them like six-year-olds on the assumption that they were capable of nothing more.

In my early years of teaching, because my students had such a difficult time memorizing poetry and internalizing facts, I assumed their brains were somehow deficient in that skill area; that somehow the lobes that govern memory had atrophied for lack of exercise. Then I took four of the worst of these, as a team, on a weekend interviewing trip into North

Carolina. As they became more comfortable with me and realized I wasn't going to shout at them every time they opened their mouths to talk about anything other than the upcoming interviews, they relaxed. Gradually I became aware of a strange game going on in the backseat with which I was totally unfamiliar. They were throwing around names like Mack and White and Peterbilt and dates and numbers, and then they'd argue and laugh, or one would say, "See, I was right. That's ten points." Finally I couldn't stand it any longer and said, "What are you guys doing, anyway? I can't figure out how whatever you're doing works."

So they explained it to me. As soon as a tractor-trailer rig was spotted coming toward us on the interstate, the boy whose turn it was had to identify the tractor by manufacturer, model number, horsepower, and so on. When it was close enough to be seen clearly, the others would double-check his answers, award (or subtract) a certain number of points based on his accuracy, and then the next in turn would go. The game then became to teach me how to do the same, and though I got somewhat better at it (gradually beginning to pair up grille shapes with manufacturers, and so on), I never did figure out how they could tell the manufacturer when the grilles were covered with canvas, as many of them were. It went on for hours, and my brain literally ached from the exertion of trying to juggle the lists of facts and figures these boys who could not memorize had mastered. When we tired of that, they turned on the radio, and as the first notes of every song began to play, they effortlessly named the artists, the songs, other songs the same artists had made, positions of the songs in the top-40 list as of last week, cheered as various disc jockeys confirmed these facts; and they sang along with nearly every song. And when the songs weren't playing, and the boys weren't receiving "clues" as to the next verse, these boys who were unable to memorize poetry could *still* sing every word. And, as you know now I often do, I found myself saying, "What is going on here?"

Students constantly amaze me.

I remember once a student who consistently failed English and who was transferred into a special experimental class I had created exclusively for students who hated to read and write. An English teacher who had had him previously warned me, "Boy, you better watch out for that one. He can't do anything. You'll have to take him from ground zero. I didn't manage to teach him a thing. I think he's learning disabled or something. He can't read at all." I gave him a Slossen test, and he scored at the third month of the second-grade level. I started working with him through photography.

The week he was moved into my class, the English teacher who warned me about him was leaving school early one day, tried to start her car, and couldn't. The student was in my room, saw her standing beside the car in complete frustration, and asked me if he could go and give her a hand. I watched from my second-floor classroom as he walked out, said something to her, raised her hood, had her get in the car and try to start the engine as he poked around inside the car's innards, and then signaled her to stop. He walked to the automotive shop and returned with a voltage regulator and some tools, and within ten minutes, she was on her way. I later found out he could tear a motorcycle engine down into all its component parts and put it back together again in a matter of days. In fact, I once gave him a ride to a parts store in town and listened as he ordered a double handful of tiny parts the names of which I had never heard before. Later that year, in time for the appropriate birthday, this boy who could not read had devoured the state driver's manual and had passed the written exam and received his license on the first attempt.

And again I found myself asking that old question, and cautioning myself, "Boy, I better watch who I'm causing to feel dumb. One of these days the tables are going to be turned and some kid is going to take sadistic delight in making me feel as stupid as I've made him feel so often."

We make students cripples with our assumptions about what they are and are not capable of or ready for. Over the years, I have watched in amazement as students have willingly mastered the skills I and my staff members offer, knowing that those skills are going to be put to use and that they are going to have the chance to prove to themselves and the world that they are ready to accept adult tasks.

In the early 1970s, for example, I watched high school students of mine, both boys and girls, operating in environments that to them were frighteningly unique and strange, teaching teachers and students in those locations how to set up *Foxfire* projects in their own schools (and how to deal with administrators, school boards, class scheduling, copyrighting, incorporating, etc.). With the exception of their host groups, they worked alone—neither I nor any other Rabun County students or families were there—and not a *single one* of them failed. In every instance, a magazine was founded, its first issue ready for the printer by the time my students returned home.

On another occasion, while still at the Rabun Gap School and in the midst of that period when I was still experimenting with dorm student–community student alliances, I began to work with two boys who were so interested in flintlock rifles that they had each made one, using a kit, in our school's shop. Neither of the boys liked English. After a semester's worth of training in photography, article writing, and accurate documentation, I took them into Kentucky to live with Hershel House, a rifle maker, for a week and document his entire process for making a traditional rifle from beginning to end. On purpose, knowing that if I were there they'd defer to me, I stayed in a motel in Bowling Green, some twenty miles away, and spent my days with Lynwood Montell and other members of the folklore department at Western Kentucky University, studying the setup of their fine folklore archives as well as some of their collecting techniques. In the evenings, I'd drive out to check on the two boys and see how things had gone that day, and then I'd return to town for the night. Since I wasn't there to help, and since I had never made a rifle myself, the two students knew they were on the line—that if they missed photographing or documenting any part of the construction process, there'd be a hole in the article that would be hard to fill, since Hershel lived several hundred miles from our school—and they stayed with it all the way, working eight to ten hours a day every day and then helping Hershel fix dinner and clean up the kitchen afterward.

When we got back to Rabun County, the stacks of recorded tapes and exposed rolls of film and notes formed the core of their work in language arts for the remainder of the semester. It took them months to get everything transcribed and edited and worked up into publishable form, and there were periods when the masses of material nearly overwhelmed them and they'd hit a low ebb in terms of energy and enthusiasm, but they stuck with it and slogged through. In the end, the finished article was so lengthy and complex that we decided against printing it in the magazine first. Instead, it went straight into *Foxfire 5*, becoming the longest chapter in that book. You can take a look and see for yourselves how they did.

My staff members and I have placed students in just about every conceivable kind of situation, from performing at the Grand Old Opry to building the log cabin environmental classroom on our campus, and watched them perform magnificently. While reviewing proposals for the National Endowment for the Arts in Washington, D.C., I sent two of them out alone, my heart in my throat, to master Washington's subway system, get themselves out to Crystal City to obtain copies of two patents we needed for a chapter in *Foxfire 6*, and then meet me at National Airport for our flight home. Right on time, they showed up, waving the patents excitedly in the air and grinning like two possums. In a Church of God where members handle live rattlesnakes and copperheads to prove their faith, I watched as teenage girls and boys clenched their jaws and waded into masses of chanting people and poisonous snakes to photograph, tape-record, and videotape a three-day series of church services for *Foxfire 7*. While I was on leave in Athens a tenth-grader managed our audio tape archives alone, indexing and cataloging each new entry—a complex task that must be done properly in order for material to be retrieved from those tapes with ease in the future. During any summers when Ann, our bookkeeper, is on vacation, two girls she has trained run the circulation and bookkeeping departments themselves, paying all bills, writing out all paychecks, and dealing with all subscriptions and mailouts. Ann checks on them each Friday, but otherwise, it's their operation.

It takes a certain leap of faith to allow these sorts of things to happen, and even after the years I have watched students perform successfully, I still sometimes have to be nudged past assumptions into faith. For years, Doubleday insisted that the color photographs for the covers of the hardback Foxfire books be taken by a professional photographer they sent down from Connecticut, his aluminum suitcase of cameras and lenses in hand. The company was comfortable with our controlling the contents of the books, but the packaging was another matter. Finally, at Paul's insistence, I told our editor that the color photograph for the hardcover volume of *Foxfire 6* would have to be taken by one of our students, and that that student should be paid the same fee for the photograph as the professional would have been paid. He agreed, with the provision that if our students couldn't come up with anything the art director was happy with, their professional would have to be sent down. We accepted that compromise, Paul conducted a cover contest in his photography classes in which any students who wished could participate, and about twenty transparencies were selected to send to New York. The slides were coded by letter as to their photographer, since several of the students whose work was sent had met the people at Doubleday and we wanted to eliminate any chance of favoritism. Several weeks later, the word came back: the art director had found a slide he could use. The photographer turned out to be sixteen-year-old Carol Rogers, who had been taking photographs for only a few weeks under Paul's guidance and who had taken the picture with one of Foxfire's simple single-lens-reflex cameras and an ordinary unfiltered 50-millimeter lens. When the cover was completed, the publishers admitted that it was one of the handsomest in the series, and several weeks later, two of our girls—one of whom was Carol—appeared with me on the "Today Show" in New York with the cover blown up and reproduced as the backdrop behind us. Carol took her check from Doubleday, purchased her first camera, and is currently majoring in journalism at the University of Georgia. (Two girls also took the cover photograph for *Foxfire 7;* and the slide for *Foxfire 8* was taken by one of our eighth-grade boys.)

Now that's the kind of thing I really get excited by, and when teachers ask me how I keep myself excited and "up," that's the answer I give them —and it's true. Some people get their kicks from watching formula racers at Le Mans. Others get theirs from watching students literally amaze themselves as they discover talents and competencies they had perhaps never even suspected were there. The fact of the matter is we often have to have more faith in them than they have in themselves. The corollary is that *not* to put students into situations in which such things can happen to them is an almost criminal negation of the opportunity we have, because of our positions, to make positive things happen in students' lives.

It's not easy. Teachers who are new at all this sometimes get discouraged when they give their students responsibility and the students abuse it. They fail to realize that it all takes time; that sometimes abuse comes as a result of natural exuberance; sometimes it comes because students are in such early stages of a project that they can't see yet where it's taking them and how serious the work they're involved with is; sometimes it comes because they've had so little real responsibility before that they haven't gotten much exercise; sometimes it comes because the responsibility they've been given previously was perceived as fake or sham responsibility, without real consequence in the real world. It takes time. Teachers have to build up credibility like money in the bank. Each act with a student, carried through to successful completion, is like a deposit. The student's reaction, communicated to peers through that elaborate grapevine of theirs, is like interest. Unfulfilled promises and self-serving uses of student energy or goodwill are withdrawals. At the end of the month, we tally up, readjust strategies, and move on, hopefully steering clear of bankruptcy. Students believe us as we become believable. Slowly we get to know them. We find their strengths and interests. We set aside negative assumptions one by one. We build credibility to the point at which, when we say, "Look, I know how you can handle this. I trust you," and we believe it, they believe it too. Because we don't give them impossible tasks, they accomplish and soon are doing things we would have assumed impossible. We demand their best, wrestling constantly with the balance between hard line and soft touch. We watch the process like hawks. We rejoice in every accomplishment, learn from every failure, never damning, but remaining constantly optimistic. We get tired and discouraged, but, with experience, learn that things are moving forward *anyway* because we care so much. And our fatigue is eased. As I said in an issue of *Foxfire:*

There are many times when it seems as though, with certain kids, very little is going on. They have their moods, just like the adults that surround them, and there are times when they are listless, bored, unmotivated. And as a teacher, you tend to focus on the kids who are in the grip of that ennui because you believe *all* the kids should be busy and active and involved. And as soon as you get one kid through that listless stage and involved, along comes another that needs a spark, and so you spend lots of hours wrestling with uninvolved kids. The end result of that focus is that sometimes you come to feel that little is happening and that therefore you are failing as a teacher—losing your grip on things.

Then, suddenly, there comes the day when another magazine is finished, and with a sigh of relief you realize that there was a lot more going on than you had noticed.

The best teachers accept personal responsibility for each student's success or failure. They do not lay the blame elsewhere. They do not allow failures to fuel negative assumptions. They build on success, and expect it of all.

A student I had years ago came to see me recently. She wanted to tell me she had named her son after me. We talked for a long time. At the end of our conversation, she said, "You are one of the few who treated me as if I were an adult, and that made all the difference."

What you see is what you get.

They Understand the Role of Self-esteem

A concept tightly intertwined with much of what I have been saying, and one I have skirted around so far in order to give it the full focus it deserves, is that of self-esteem or self-concept. It is so fundamental to human health that its implications permeate all we do with young people, peers, families, and society at large. It is so fundamental because self-definition predetermines how we perceive, react to, and act within the world around us.

Self-esteem is what the motion picture *Rocky* was about. "If that bell rings and I'm still standing, then I'm gonna know for the first time in my life, see, that I weren't just another bum from the neighborhood." We are caught up in the story, and we stand and cheer like idiots at the end of the film, because it is—or we wish it were—our story too. (It is interesting to note, by the way, that Sylvester Stallone was kicked out of a succession of high schools as a teenager.)

On January 21, 1981, on the "Today Show," Yul Brynner's son, Rock, was interviewed, and he admitted that the problems he had had in adolescence that had propelled him into drugs and alcohol had been related to his self-identity and the fact that he was constantly identified not as himself (on the basis of his own accomplishments and value) but as somebody else's son. His salvation came at the hands of people who befriended him based on his own merits, not on the fact of his connections. At the end of his interview, he said, "Self-respect cannot be inherited. It has to be earned."

An article by psychiatrist Seymour Fisher says, in part, "The psychiatric patient is often one who, in his own eyes, has failed or suffered major rejection by the culture. He feels lowly and unwanted and [has a] downgraded view of himself."[9] The same is apparently true of many criminals.

Harvard psychiatrist Robert Coles, when asking young black children to draw pictures of themselves and then pictures of their white counterparts, found a consistent pattern: the self-portraits of blacks were nearly always poorly rendered, ill-defined, and smaller in comparison to those they drew of whites.

Teachers are not exempt. Most of us wrestle constantly with our own feelings of worth and esteem. One alarming thing to me is the fact that so many teachers, given the power they have to affect young peoples' feeling about themselves, are often among the more fragile and insecure adults I meet. They may appear tough and together outwardly, but probe a little and underneath one finds a teeming mass of emotions: they can be threatened by their students, threatened by their superiors, unsure of their abilities as teachers, unsure of the value of their subject matter (and hence their own worth), frightened by the thought of someday slipping and letting down their guard and allowing students a glimpse of the real person behind the mask, and on and on it goes. That insecurity, of course, lies at the heart of much of the blind acceptance of texts and prepared kits and learning games, and much of the adherence (with relief) to rigid schedules and rules, and much of the fear of coming out from behind the desk or lectern and doing a little experimentation. It is one of the reasons teachers constantly ask me "exactly how to do it" (whatever "it" happens to be) rather than working in tandem with their own students to find out.

Some teachers are so insecure that they depend on their students—the very people whom they should be helping—for their sense of self-definition and self-worth and ego massage. Getting their students to like them becomes the main agenda of the day, sometimes to the exclusion of all else. They routinely inflate grades. They bow to student requests to "take the day off." You see them at student basketball games, nestled pathetically in among a group of teenagers who inwardly are laughing at them for their weakness. They are soft, like little marshmallows, making no demands and asking only to be loved. They are trapped in ineffectiveness by their own behavior, believing that if they decide to crack down and get tough and get something accomplished, their students may turn on them with unexpected fury and resentment.

And students get trapped in exactly the same way, through their insecurities and fears; trapped in postures they may not even like—academically excellent, macho and tough, sexually available, class clown, soft touch, jerk, biggest drinker, fearless, cocky, wide-eyed and innocent, cute—trapped in roles like a ten-year-old held underwater.

And who's *really* behind that mask?

That's one of the reasons I take students with me on trips. It gives them a chance, in a different situation, among strangers, to try on different hats. Shy and speechless suddenly becomes articulate. Brash and bold and uncaring suddenly becomes polite and gentle, even deferential. Academic pariah breaks out of mold, sneaks into closed motel pool at one A.M. with student roommate long after I've gone to bed in my room, and then watches late-late show and only gets three hours' sleep. . . .

Self-concept depends on so many factors. It depends, in part, on how one perceives one's body. In the same article referred to earlier, Fisher says, "A person who regards his body as weak and fragile will behave less boldly than one who perceives his body as a well-defended place. Similarly, a person who turns away from his body because he experiences it as bad and ugly may turn to intellectual activities as compensation."[10] (The implications for the PE department may snap into focus at this point.)

It depends, in part, on the extent to which the universal adolescent needs of affection, esteem, security, recognition, and belonging are met. (When they are unmet in adolescence, we find ourselves with adults who are frozen in time as children and constantly and loudly draw attention to themselves, or beg through their actions for acceptance and belonging. Those of us who have not met these adult children have lived a sheltered life indeed.)

It depends, in part, on us and how we make our students feel about themselves and their abilities. It depends, in part, on the assumptions we make about them that form our modus operandi. It depends, in part, on our classroom environment and the extent to which it is sensitively monitored by us. If, for example, most of our students do not want to be seen by their peers striving to excel academically, what can we do to create an environment in which everyone excels so that that striving is no longer unacceptable behavior? If students are afraid to express their opinions because they don't respect their own feelings and instincts, or because they are afraid of opening themselves up to ridicule and embarrassment, have we changed the climate to ensure that all opinions will be considered equally and ridicule simply is not allowed—ever?

During that critical age when, as a necessary part of independence, many of our students have decided their parents are idiots, the only adult feedback they get about themselves may be from us. Scarier still, they may *trust* it. What happens if we confirm, even unconsciously, the dark fears some have that they'll never amount to anything? What happens when one tells us of hopes to go to college, and we laugh? What happens when one says he wants to be a photographer for *National Geographic* and we tell him that's impossible? What happens when we get angry and state, "This is the worst class I've ever had." And what happens when we do the opposite?

We need to know the answers to such questions, taking into account, always, the fact that simple, pat answers usually get derailed by variables that always enter in—that's one of the things that makes our job so hard—but there are some fairly universal rules that can stand us in good stead.

One is a keystone: the one sin that is unforgivable is to diminish a student's sense of dignity and worth.

The corollary is that it is equally wrong not to work to enhance that sense of dignity and worth. And many students, having turned from their parents temporarily, want it from us (unless we've been discredited too). That fact should render our own needs less important while we are in a teaching situation with young people. Several years ago, for example, I took two girls to Atlanta to give an evening speech before a group of nearly six hundred people. We had put in a full day already with the drive down there, two errands, and finding and checking into the hotel, and so we were bushed and a little apprehensive before the talk.

It went very well. We received a standing ovation, and both the girls and I were pinned down by autograph seekers and hand shakers afterward. I was feeling pretty good about the whole thing, and when the crowd subsided and we were picking up our stuff, one of the girls asked, "Well, how did we do?"

I said, "You *know* you did well. The number of folks that mobbed you proves that. I heard them telling you how much they liked what you said."

"Yeah," she said, "but I wanted to hear it from you."

We drove back to the hotel in silence, and on the way she sort of hugged herself and grinned. "It really makes me happy that you think we were good. That we did okay. That really makes me glad."

Variations on that same theme have happened nearly every time I've had students on the road.

One of the most readable and believable books I've found on adolescence takes the discussion even further, and you might want to get a copy. It's called *The Adolescent Predicament* (by J. J. Mitchell; Holt, Rinehart and Winston; Toronto, 1975). Mitchell confirms the adolescent needs for affection, esteem, security, recognition, and belonging, but then further argues that, in fact, there are two distinct phases of adolescence, and that those needs just stated are more urgent in the early phase, when the child is forming his or her sense of identity and is largely dependent during this time on the assessments and reactions of others. This helps explain the tremendous amount of attention paid to fads, styles, and the judgment and evaluation of peers.

But then a second phase, late adolescence, begins to emerge, and even though the early needs are never completely outgrown by any of us, the extent to which the needs of the second phase can emerge and be satisfied depends largely on the extent to which those of the first have been dealt with. The need that bridges both phases is that of self-importance. Met in the first phase (and either satisfied or not) by the reactions of others, it continues on into the second, ideally to be satisfied by allowing the adolescent to *do things of importance*—to do real work of real consequence in the real world. When this happens, the adolescent begins to become very adultlike in the best sense: he or she acquires the confidence that can allow independent investigation and exploration of the environment; the reserve of psychological strength that enables the person to deal with tension, anxiety, and frustration; the strength that allows the person not to be intimidated by new people and novel situations but to welcome them; and the independence that makes the reactions of others less important than it was before. In other words, the individual can stand on his or her own feet and not be a prisoner of conformism. The individual having filled the need to know "I am" can get on about answering the question, "To what end?"

In the best of all worlds, this transition from "child-adolescence" to "adult-adolescence," as Mitchell calls it, would be a graceful, natural progression. The student does, receives input, does something else, receives additional input, and gradually becomes able to act or to do with-

out the need for constant external assessment. The student achieves
independence.

The major problem is that our schools, which could be ideally suited to
serve this transition, provide so few avenues for it to happen. Through
our rules and regulations and imposed curricula and near-complete dom-
inance of their lives, we hold students in a state of enforced early adolescence through all of high school, ignoring the tremendous hunger all
young people have to do important, significant work; to make a difference
in the community; to begin to feel that the future really does consist of
opportunity rather than denial. As students make contributions that they
perceive as important and real, their self-esteem increases dramatically.
Conversely, trapped in enforced childishness, self-esteem of an adult
nature declines and they remain dependent on their peers, with all the
fads and styles and postures, for those scraps of self-esteem they are
allowed.

As Mitchell says, "All healthy humans, universally and without fail,
abhor not making a difference. It is the closest thing to nonexistence man
can experience." The abundant evidence shows not only that adolescents
are hungry to—and *can*—make such a difference, but also that to deny
them the opportunity cripples them, or forces them to strive to make that
difference illegally or in ways we cannot accept. And so we make more
rules. . . .

It's complicated, isn't it? The magic of our situation, though, is that we
can provide such opportunities easily for young people when they are
ready (and most are ready earlier than too many teachers assume), and
without crushing them with responsibility or setting them up for failure
and then turning away; and that we can also make such opportunities
serve not only their personal needs but also their academic ones. We can
kill at least two birds with one stone. The students who create *Foxfire*
magazine *know* for a fact that they are doing something perceived by their
peers, their parents, the community at large, and the outside world as
important, valuable work. They get letters all the time that tell them so.
People ask them for autographs. Friends ask them to pull strings and get
them into Foxfire classes. Parents encourage them to take the classes.
And at the same time, they learn how to deal with quotation marks and
comma splices and parts of speech. It is this point that I will return to
frequently in the curriculum section, for it is about this that I have the
most questions from teachers. Constantly I get asked, "But how can you
let students run around doing interviews and taking pictures and still get
them the facts they have to have to be able to handle SATs and competency tests?" The hardest thing for me to help teachers understand is that
the two are not mutually exclusive. Rather, they must be inextricably
wedded. Those basic skills everyone is so paranoid about will be only
superficially mastered if the sole motivations we can offer students are

extrinsic. Okra is still okra. And we will not serve their personal needs at all.

Recognition of this need for self-esteem and confidence is one reason I take different students along on nearly every trip rather than having elected Foxfire spokespersons. It is one reason I and my staff members are constantly looking for opportunities like the taking of the cover photograph for *Foxfire 6* and placing students into those opportunities. When Carol realized that her work could stand adult standards of scrutiny, I suspect she became a somewhat different person, far more ready than before to enter the adult world. It's the reason I insist that I and my staff members keep our hands off cameras and equipment during interviews. It's one reason the magazine has no photographer or editor—all students handle every phase of their articles from beginning to end and gain some control over every skill required, from interviewing to transcribing to photographing and printing to editing to layout and design. It's one reason we have a staff rule that goes, "Before you start to do anything associated with this organization, be it as simple as a long distance phone call, ask yourself first why a student isn't doing it instead; and if you don't have an awfully good reason, then go find a student—preferably one who's never done it before." It's one reason, as likely as not, when I am asked to speak at the local Rotary Club, I'll bring along a student—and not necessarily a student perceived by the administration and other teachers as "gifted" or "a fine representative of the student body," but often one who is in the midst of a crisis of some sort and greatly needs a boost to turn all that around.

I constantly try to turn the tables on those assumptions I talked about earlier. On one occasion, for example, I took a student with me to speak at a luncheon that I knew the principal would be attending. The student I picked was one in the midst of some serious disciplinary problems, and his academic work was suffering accordingly. He was regarded by most of the teachers as a hopeless troublemaker and an almost certain dropout, and those attitudes simply increased the size of the dark cloud he was under at the time. I worked with the boy briefly before the speech, gave him a little pep talk, and turned him loose. At the end of his talk, the audience crowded around him to pat him on the back and shook hands with the principal, making comments like, "You're really lucky to have such fine young people like this in your school. He's a credit to your good work." The result? One student with a different perception of himself; and one principal willing now to sit down with that student and say, "You proved something to me today. I saw a side of you I hadn't known was there. Let's talk." How many other schools would have chosen a student who had already proved himself or herself and whose self-concept, accordingly, was already squared away?

On another occasion, I had a group of students at a journalism conference at the University of Georgia. During the proceedings, many student publications, including *Foxfire*, received awards. One of the students I had along was a dorm boy who had been kicked out of another high school, and by complete coincidence, one of the teachers who had disliked him intensely was in the audience with her journalism class. My student recognized her, told me about her, and when our award was announced, I sent him to the stage to receive it. On the way back to his seat, I saw him smile and wave at her specifically, one unhappy chapter of his life now closed forever.

As another aspect of all this, I like my classes to be composed of students who represent all age groups. In my larger classes, for example, I'll have four or five students from each of the grades, eight through twelve. With this mix, the kinds of interactions I can create are sometimes wonderful, with eighth-graders who are cowed by seniors occasionally put in the position of teaching seniors how to print photographs, or older students who have, or are in the process of acquiring, real self-confidence put in positions of adopting younger students who are floundering, adding them to their teams and giving them genuine roles to play that make a substantive contribution to the work of the whole.

We have to watch constantly for such opportunities and take advantage of them, knowing that we're making a difference, and knowing that we're turning around completely negative, defeatist attitudes about self and potential.

Sometimes it's so simple and easy. I chose one student who was tremendously insecure for an interview at the Museum of Appalachia in Norris, Tennessee. The reason was that I knew the family in charge of the museum, and I knew the man was a former school superintendent and would be sympathetic to the student's plight. When we got there, John Rice Irwin took the student under his wing and gave him a fantastic afternoon. He remembered his name, addressed him as an equal, let him take objects from the display cases out of doors to be photographed, and generally made sure the student knew he was trusted, respected, and welcome. All the way back home the student kept saying, "That's the nicest man I ever met," and from that time on, he pestered me to take him to John Rice's museum again. In fact, they even exchanged letters; and when I did take him again, John Rice remembered him, called him by name, and it was all I could do to get the kid home. I took the same student to see Stanley Hicks, a banjo and dulcimer maker, a toy maker, and one of our favorite North Carolina contacts. He interviewed Stanley, they got along famously together, and as we were leaving, Stanley gave him a little hug and told him to come back soon. On the way home, the student said, "Did you see that? He hugged me. He must really like me a lot." And I said something like, "That's because you're worth liking. You're a good man." And I watched that student turn himself around. I could introduce you to that student today and he'd tell you all about it.

When *Foxfire 6* came out with some of his work in it, I gave him several copies. The next day he was back for more. Kiddingly, I asked him what had happened to the others. Turned out his mother locked them in a trunk for safekeeping. Later that day, I saw him showing another teacher his picture in one of those I had given him to replace the ones his mother put away.

Doors can open on tiny hinges.

As always, we have to be careful. Overpraise or false praise is quickly spotted and devalued. When I see a well-meaning teacher say to a fifteen-year-old, "Oh, *my*. Look what we've *done*. Isn't that *nice?*" my instinct is to backpedal as fast as I can. Students know when they've given something an honest shot and when they deserve praise—and when they don't and are being patronized or bought off.

The standards we set are important, for if we do away with standards and simply hand out praise and thanksgiving indiscriminately, we not only diminish the possibility of students developing self-respect but very nearly render the concept meaningless. We simply must know the students well enough to know what kind of encouragement and help they need to be able to live up to those standards—and then make sure they don't fail.

And as they grow and become more whole and self-confident, we must realize that our job is only starting, for at that point, we must fight against inadvertently creating a room full of self-indulgent egomaniacs and get about the business of helping them continue to grow past their own needs into a consciousness of the needs of others. But first things first. The plain truth is that students cannot enter into unselfish, caring relationships with others and with the community when they feel they have nothing to offer.

And we must watch their eyes. Through their eyes, we can tell if they're alive or dead. When they're dead, we struggle to bring them back. When they're alive, we celebrate that fact and say to ourselves, "I will not willingly contribute to the death of a soul. I will do all in my power to nourish that spirit and keep alive the spark of life."

They Are Not Afraid to Be Seen as Fallible and Human

Many of the teachers I have met are reluctant to get to know their students a little better because of a subconscious fear of scrutiny by those students. They are afraid, in short, of being known—afraid their fallibility will be revealed, afraid they will be seen as less powerful and more human, afraid the well-developed mask of their invincibility will crack and reveal the flesh-and-blood mortal hiding behind.

This notion of teacher fallibility is a fascinating one. Fear of admitting it leads us to adopt all sorts of awkward postures. It is part of our insistence on control over every aspect of our classes' activities, assignments, seating arrangements, disciplinary measures, and so on. It is part of our determination to maintain a "united front" before our students, backing every move our superiors and peers make even when we personally disagree. Principals will insist on this stance on the theory that if students sense the teachers are divided on a school rule, for example, or a disciplinary action of some sort, or an administrative decision concerning a student activity, they will take advantage of that split and topple us, reducing us to a flock of chickens squabbling over half a grain of feed. It is very much part of the statement I have heard so many times that goes, "I can't teach students how to use a camera (or tape recorder or enlarger or printing press or whatever) because I don't know how myself." Or, "It would be hard for me to find visitors to bring into class because I don't know anyone in the community. How do you find people to interview and talk to anyway?" Or, "I can't do any of the things you've suggested so far. I've never tried them before. What if they didn't work and the kids went wild? I think I'd better stick to what I already know best." It is also part of our determination to mumble out some sort of answer to a student's question, even when we know we are mumbling a half-truth or perhaps an outright lie. Most of us have a hard time bringing ourselves to say, head on, "I don't know." Worse, we usually don't take advantage of that ignorance and *use* it in a positive way to stimulate some of the best learning activities of the year.

Such stances do not enhance our credibility. They undermine it, make us look foolish, and add fuel to the students-versus-teachers, us-against-them adversary relationship that so often exists.

We are not infallible, and the students know that, whether we care to admit it or not. The fact that we are salaried adults does not make us right. We can do things with elementary school students that high school students see right through. They know all about postures and stances and half-truths, and rather than being intimidated by this, we should take advantage of their growing ability to see things objectively, for this characteristic should be nourished, not stomped. It is part of the examination they must be about in deciding what kinds of adults they themselves will be. If they decide the adult world is all about making excuses and stammering and refusing to admit to ignorance and adopting silly postures and being generally untruthful for dubious ends, what kinds of adults will they themselves become?

Sometimes we look so silly. Let me give you an example. I've been embarrassed to tell this story in print until now, but this seems an appropriate time, and I don't think the people involved will mind my telling it so many years later. Especially considering the fact that the adults who were involved are now dead or have moved on to other jobs.

When I was a high school student in the early sixties, the head of our humanities department was a well-meaning, rather gentle but somewhat pompous man who took great pride in the depth and breadth of his learning. He was continually engaged in some sort of esoteric discussion about this or that, citing books and authors and studies to support his point of view, and nodding wisely and stroking his chin over any contributions made to the discussion by students or faculty members eager to appear equally learned and worldly.

My roommate, who is now an environmental lawyer and was heavily involved in the snail darter controversy in Tennessee, had a student job in the school's library where this Polonius-like figure reigned, and one day he came back to the room greatly excited because a rented exhibit had just arrived from New York that was composed of valuable and historic papers—letters from Abraham Lincoln and such. The man in question was nearly beside himself as he fondled the exhibit and made plans for its mounting, and it seemed a priceless opportunity to give him a little tweak and perhaps deflate that ego a tad. We didn't really want to embarrass him greatly or bring him down off his pedestal—just give him a little jolt to help put things back in perspective.

We enlisted the help of a classmate and sat up late into the night plotting some way to accomplish this goal, something clever and ingenious that everyone could have a good laugh over later and then go on about the business at hand.

Finally we decided to draw up a document of our own that my roommate could slip in with the others just before the exhibit was to go up. It should be something outrageous—obviously a fake—so that when our victim came across it, he would be startled at first, confused, and then would dissolve into laughter, appreciating the prank in the spirit that it was intended.

I was taking Spanish at the time and off the top of my head suggested that we draw up a letter from Queen Isabella of Spain to the Bank of Madrid (not even knowing whether such a bank existed at that time in history). In the letter, Queen Isabella would introduce Christopher Columbus to the bank officials, explain that she had given Columbus some pearls and rubies and such, and direct them to give him their cash value so he could go out and buy three ships and the supplies he'd need to find out whether the world was flat or round.

That was it. Our partner in crime ran to his room to get a bottle of India ink, a calligraphy pen, and a book he had that had been published in the 1800s. I got my Spanish text out and began to draft the letter. I was a pretty poor language student. My grades in Spanish were terrible, and I hated those times when we had to write exercises in Spanish, but I muddled through, finally coming up with a message in the most elementary terminology imaginable—about the best I could do, given the lateness of the hour and my academic inadequacy. Our friend, meanwhile, had torn a yellowed flyleaf out of his old book and sanded all four edges to make it equally worn all around, and as I dictated the letter ("*Mi caro muchachos, Mi nombre esta Queen Isabella . . .*" etc.), he carefully scribed it in black ink onto the sheet of faded paper. That done, my roommate put it in his notebook, took it to the library the next day, and slipped it in among the other documents.

Several days later, he came running into our room out of breath and wild-eyed and cried, "My God, we've really done it now! We're in big trouble!" He grabbed me, dragged me over to the library, and there, in the most important display case of all—the one introducing the exhibit itself—beside the printed title card and above two other samples of the wonders that lay ahead, was our letter, complete with a typed translation by the head of our Spanish department. For several long moments, we stood looking at it, then retreated to the dorm to huddle anxiously with our co-conspirator and figure out the next move.

For days, we deliberated as the whole school filed past our creation and the head of the humanities department strutted and preened among the treasures. Finally, desperate and embarrassed, the three of us made an appointment with the headmaster, filed in and sat down in his office, waited for him to light a cigar and lean back in his desk chair, and, fully expecting to be kicked out of school, confessed. For several minutes, he studied our faces. "You know, this is a very serious thing you have done." Mentally I composed the letter to Dad telling him to come and pick me up. After an endless pause, he blew a cloud of smoke into the air and said, "Your punishment is that you must never tell anyone about this incident for as long as you remain in this school and for as long as the man you have embarrassed is alive. Is that clear?" We nodded, and filed out.

The next day the offending letter and its translation were gone. The exhibit remained for several weeks. I never found out what happened to the letter or who got it out of the case or how. Polonius greeted us as always. I continued to make terrible grades in Spanish. Life went on without a ripple. I've always wondered what the head of the Spanish department must have thought, though, of a nearly illiterate Queen Isabella begging the officials of a probably nonexistent bank to hock her jewels.

Meanwhile, I had learned something about arrogance.

Some of the best classes I've had have been those in which I knew no more about how to accomplish a given goal than my students did, and we just had to learn together, stumbling together, admitting our mistakes, laughing, regrouping, and pushing on. That's not to say that I'm advocating that all teachers go into their classes, sit down, and say, "Okay. Here I am. I don't know anything about my subject matter or how to teach it, so let's just relax for the rest of the year and have fun and maybe someone will come up with an idea or two. If not, well, at least we enjoyed each other's company." Not at all. I *knew* my subject matter. I knew about adjectives and Shakespeare and themes and why English was important, all that. I just didn't know how to teach it, and at the moment of despair, rather than saying, "All right, damn you. Open your books. You're going to get this stuff or I'm going to fail every bloody one of you," or saying,

"All right. Go ahead and talk. I don't care whether you get any of this stuff or not," I said, "Okay. You've got me. I'm stuck. How can I help you see how useful this information is?"

When we decided to spend six weeks putting out one issue of a magazine just to see whether that was a promising solution to our problem, I didn't know how to take and print good photographs. But it didn't take long to find someone who could show me and the students the fundamentals and then let us experiment and learn together. I didn't know how to find new people in the community to talk to, but it didn't take the students long to introduce me to some folks I hadn't met before. I didn't know how to price and sell a magazine, but the students and I decided on a price that seemed fair, and when we went broke, we were able to sit down, scratch our heads, and figure out why collectively. And when I made a mistake, I had no compunction about standing in front of the class, explaining the mistake, apologizing, and asking for some help in fixing it. And neither did the students. And when a student raised a question none of us could answer honestly, I had no reservations about saying, "Look, I really don't know the answer to that. I want some volunteers to help me find out. That's an important question and we *ought* to know the answer." If that meant having one of the students call an expert long distance, and having another get the librarian to help order a book or some materials, and having another go to see someone locally who might have some clues, that's what we did. That's what we still do. The subject matter wasn't shirked. It's just that the students began to take an active role in the planning, methodology, and execution. And in that atmosphere of active groping and trial and error, things happened that all of us still remember with affection and surprise. I was enjoying the excitement of learning again—the thrill of the chase, if you will—and that excitement communicated itself to the students, who became caught up in the whole process also. We became learners together; not equals, just equally curious and confused on some occasions, and equally frustrated and upset on others, and equally triumphant and happy on others. As an adult, I would help point all of us toward the sources of answers when we were confused, help temper responses that were clearly inappropriate ("Let's kill him!" or "Let's burn his house down!") when we were angry, and clear the decks and authorize celebrations when we were happy. Thus they learned something more about how an adult functions, I learned something more about how a student functions, and we met somewhere in the middle over common goals.

As we began to respect each other and discover that we were all equally concerned about those goals—be they putting out a magazine or drawing up a successful ad campaign or producing radio spots or raising money—it was relatively easy for me to make the transition from one who makes all the decisions to one who participates in discussions leading to decisions but has only one vote. Thus when Hume Cronyn and Jessica Tandy

wanted to purchase the dramatic rights to the *Foxfire* material and create a
play in association with co-author Susan Cooper, Hume and Susan had to
come to Georgia to present their case before the students and staff. The
article Susan wrote for the playbill when the show opened at the Guthrie,
entitled "The Making of the Play," recalled the event:

> Hume applied to Eliot Wigginton to acquire the dramatic rights of *Foxfire*,
> and we both went to Georgia to explain to a group of stern-eyed youngsters
> that we were not out to frame their cherished old people in another version
> of *L'il Abner*. They gave us the only two chairs in Wig's office and sat round
> us on the floor; we felt singularly nervous and about a hundred years old.
> When our pitch was made, we went out and paced the green cricket-shirring
> hill while they deliberated; then a lad in jeans and boots came and whistled.
> "Y'all can come back in now," he said, sphinxlike; then grinned, relenting.
> "I guess we think you're okay."
>
> That was one milestone: a rush of relief that told us how much we now
> wanted to translate the spirit of *Foxfire* into theater.

The play, with regular student and staff input during creation of the
script to prevent any slander or bad taste, premiered in Stratford, On-
tario, during the summer of 1980, then at the Guthrie in Minneapolis in
the fall of 1981, and then Baltimore, Boston, and Broadway in the fall of
1982.

When the JFG Coffee Company wanted to make a series of coffee and
tea commercials showing our community contacts demonstrating various
traditional crafts (the theme being, "Just as these people take pride and
care in their work, so too does JFG"), I was against the idea, but the
students wanted to pursue it. Writers from the ad agency flew up from
New Orleans, presented their story boards, and then the students fanned
out across the county to poll contacts and community advisory board
members as to their thoughts. The final decision, the result of heated
class debates, was to allow the company to proceed provided that:

•Teams of students would actually participate in the filming process.

•Students would locate all contacts and set filming dates in advance to
minimize strain on the participating community people and make sure all
went smoothly and no one was inconvenienced or put in an awkward
position.

•All contacts would be paid on the spot at the completion of filming
their segment.

•No contacts would be asked to comment on JFG products at all, or
"taste" them for reaction, etc. Thus a contact would be shown making
butter or bottoming a chair, for example, and would talk briefly about
that process, and then at the end the JFG message would be added.

The company agreed, a dozen people were filmed, each was paid on the
spot, and all concerned were pleased. The company admitted it was their

most successful series of commercials ever; and one of the contacts told the students involved, "That's the most money I ever made at one time in my life. That will pay for my seeds and fertilizer this year and pull me out of the hole, and I want to thank you for that." And in our part of the country—which is JFG territory anyway—the commercials were watched eagerly by families and friends and were very popular. I would have vetoed the project if the decision had been left to me, but the students wanted to do it, they proved to me that people in the community wanted to try it, and they convinced me that it would be a worthwhile project. Had I voted no, they would have outvoted me, and they stood ready to take the consequences had the whole thing proved to have been a mistake. And so I backed them, and I'm glad now that I did.

As people who come to us with ideas have found, they get put through some of the toughest questioning they've ever faced, and as likely as not, if their ideas are flawed or they aren't willing to let the students participate fully and have some control, they'll be sent packing.

They Understand the Nature of Discipline and Control

The best teachers I know have no discipline problems. This is true not because they are retired Green Berets who know how to break skulls (although, granted, such teachers do tend to be "in control"), but because everyone in their classes is too busy to give much thought to getting into trouble. And I'm not talking about being busy doing the appropriately named "busy work," but work that is perceived by the doers as being useful and important.

Now we are about to come full circle. Just as all the previous sections resonate to each other and are artificially and rather awkwardly broken apart because of a perhaps mistaken notion of mine that we could look at them more closely that way, so, too, do all those sections on such things as linking the subject matter to the students' reality and knowing the students personally and allowing them to know you, and the value of experience in learning and the dangers of being ruled by negative assumptions, and the need for attention to self-esteem—have everything to do with discipline. For just as the best motivation for learning is intrinsic, so, too, is the best solution to all potential and real discipline problems. Students who value what is going on inside a classroom will not tear it apart.

Because there is such an overweening emphasis on classroom management and discipline, however, it deserves some mention in a section alone. Experience tells me, though, that teachers who attend to the previous sections don't have to worry about this one. Discipline (and its Siamese twin, motivation) takes care of itself. I'm not being glib; I know this for fact. I've seen the principle at work successfully too many times to hedge on this conviction.

During my first year of teaching, I was often preoccupied with the chore of keeping students quiet, in their seats, and on task. I felt that my reputation among my peers and the administration depended greatly on my ability to do this. I spent more time fretting over eruptions than on the job at hand. Some projects I proposed were simply tricks to keep them quiet, and at times that strategy worked, but never for very long. Soon they would become bored, and I could feel the fever rising again.

When there were real outbreaks that I couldn't deal with, I'd kick offending students out of my class for three days, during which time they'd have to report to the library for a study hall at the time they'd ordinarily have been in my class. They usually came back to class even worse than before, grinning from ear to ear as though they had just won some mysterious victory that only their classmates could understand. Putting checks in the grade book that would lower their grade point average only increased the resentment. It wasn't fair, and all of us knew it. It would only have been fair had I been hired to baby-sit and monitor and grade behavior. It was a cheap trick based on the flawed logic that since the amount of school work accomplished depended on behavior, the two could legitimately be graded together. But what, then, was the column on the report card for that was headed "Conduct"?

The harder I pushed, the harder they pushed back. Had I known more about the philosophy behind the martial arts, I might have been able to figure out ways to take their physical aggression and use it against them in subtle ways rather than meeting force with force, but I was ignorant of that option.

I tried embarrassment and guilt, using all the snide, surefire lines in my arsenal: "Where were you when I went over this *before?*" "Why did you volunteer for this project if you knew you weren't going to be able to handle it?" "After you prove you can be good, I might consider that request." "If you guys can't do any better than that, you ought to go back to grade school. You're more like children than high school students." "If you all wouldn't stay up so late at night hanging out and getting drunk, you might be able to concentrate." "I asked all of you to bring pencils today, and so naturally only half of you did. I knew that would happen." "Why don't you use the bathroom before the bell rings? I'm going to outfit all of you with diapers." "Now this quiz isn't tough. Naturally those of you who haven't been listening are going to have a tough time with it, but that's your problem now, not mine." "This story was written for sixth-graders, so you shouldn't have any trouble with it. Most of you, anyway. Unfortunately there are exceptions to every rule." And so forth.

After *Foxfire* began to roll and take on a life of its own, much of the problem disappeared. After the ginseng hunt, and after getting to know several of the other problem students more personally and finding activities they could relate to, more of the problem vanished. We were getting tired of being at one another's throats, and the harder I tried to involve them in actively planning more appropriate lessons and activities, and the more honest I became about my own frustrations, the more willing they were to hold off, give me the benefit of the doubt, and at least try a couple of the things we had planned together. With that spirit, my classroom came under control.

There were still problems. The fact that I kicked several students permanently out of the recreation center lecture series solved the problem of behavior there for good, partly because most of the students who came that first night, having helped give birth to and carry out the idea, wanted it to work as much as I did and wanted the troublemakers out themselves, and partly because that was an optional activity anyway. It was one time when being tough and decisive made a real difference—but it didn't do much to help the students I had banned. For them, it was still adults versus kids, Act III, Scene 4.

At other times, I literally agonized over what my approach should be to dorm students, for example, who were fine when working with *Foxfire* but who broke other rules of the school and were thus prevented from going off campus on interviews or working with us after school hours. The problem intensified as *Foxfire* grew and began to draw on the talents of students who weren't even in my classes but needed, I felt, the boost our project could give them. As late as February 4, 1972, I wrote in my journal:

Yesterday, [two students], taking advantage of the fact that we had no school, hitched to Sky Valley, breaking restriction, and getting ahold of some booze on the way. They got caught, of course, and are now restricted to the dorm.

My anger was immediate, selfish, and probably irrational. Someday I'll look back on that all and think about how foolish and immature I was—but I got terribly upset. I think that part of it was that I set *Foxfire* up [in my own mind] as some sort of inviolable virgin, and hence was upset and angered when [one of the students], who has so many responsibilities for this new issue (Maude Shope, the log cabin and mill chart, the burials article photos, etc.) threw everything to the winds and got himself restricted to the dorm. I know I felt that *Foxfire* should have been so important to him that he would not have jeopardized his freedom to work with us for a brief fling at Sky Valley. But he did, thus proving again my idiocy at believing that this [project] is so powerful a force that it transforms and hypnotizes and captures all that youthful energy and channels it into creative, fine directions.

Anyway, in the face of being proved wrong again, I erupted with anger and frustration and hurt and restricted him from our office for two weeks. Someone else will have to carry out his contributions to this issue—and that ego boost I had carefully set up for him thus evaporates like smoke. I told him I didn't even want to see him for two weeks, and during that time he could decide whether he wanted to go the carefree, vagabond, no-ties, fun-loving, no responsibility to anything or anyone route, or come our way and be someone we could count on and use.

I honestly don't know at this point what will happen, but I am filled with remorse at the thought of losing someone so talented and bright. And yet there has to be a point at which one draws a line of some sort. He is good, and I need him, and yet he's no good to me if I can't *get* him when I need him. He needs to make a commitment of some sort—to adopt some course of action passionately. If it means I lose him, I guess that's the price I pay. Hell, I lose him *anyway* if he's continually restricted to the dorms.

Many of you will be able to spot the mistakes I made in that incident. Luckily, the boy in question did come back with us and developed into one of the finest students I ever worked with, and we're still friends today.

I overreacted, of course. In part, that was because *Foxfire* was still a very risky venture, and despite the fact that it was now attracting media attention and a book was about to appear from Doubleday, there was no guarantee of success. Its future so preoccupied *me* that I couldn't understand anyone involved not being as completely devoted to it as I was. And yet this boy and his classmates had not been in on the conception and founding of the project, and so naturally they could not have been as caught up in it as I. My anger *was* selfish. In addition, I had ascribed a power to *Foxfire* that it could not—and should not—have had for students. No course or project should be so powerful that it commands every ounce of devotion students have to give. Such a situation (be it football, chemistry, drama, math, or *Foxfire*) simply creates one-sided students who are strong in one area but helpless in many others. The key is balance and strong, compelling offerings in all the disciplines.

Part of my overreaction was due to the fact that several students I had worked with closely in the past had been kicked out of school at just the time when some real potential was beginning to be tapped, and I was genuinely worried that the same thing might happen to this boy. But I had draped around my own shoulders the cloak of salvation—*I* was the one who would save him—and thus took it as a personal slap in the face when he got into trouble. The fact, of course, was that he was not trying to hurt me personally. He was simply reacting, as all healthy students must, to a situation in which too many adults had too much control over his existence. I happened to be one of them, but I wasn't the only one. In fact, most of his waking and sleeping hours were monitored by a succession of adults, and his rebellion—if one can use that word for such a minor incident—was perfectly appropriate and not calculated to hurt anyone specifically. And who among us has not done exactly the same thing? His timing was unfortunate from my point of view, and I had—and have—a right to expect students to live up to a certain amount of responsibility when they take it on willingly and of their own accord, but I did not—and do not—have any right to expect them to give up the bulk of their adolescent lives for me. The egos of adults are frequently the source of a misunderstanding of discipline problems and, thus, application of wrong solutions. ("These kids are out to get me." "They're trying to hurt me." "No teenagers are going to push *me* around.") And we fight back.

Let me back up and come at this another way. One of the most fascinating books I've come across is Erving Goffman's *Asylums* (Aldine Publishing Company, Chicago, 1961), in which he vividly describes life within "total institutions" such as mental hospitals. Some observations from *Asylums:*

Asylums, like prisons, exhibit "encompassing tendencies," designed to control the lives of the people within them. Physically, for example, ingress and egress are carefully prescribed; and the interiors are designed for maximum crowd control and surveillance (halls are clear and open, potential hiding places are eliminated whenever possible, bathrooms are set up to make observation possible).

Asylums are relatively impermeable to entrance by the outside world. Aside from them being physically intimidating, visitors to them are usually made to feel unwelcome or intrusive except during carefully set up times, such as visitors' days.

In addition, internally, control is enforced by rigid time-space scheduling. Every movement is predetermined, authorized, scheduled—or simply not allowed. Inmates move through the day in lockstep routine.

Asylums also gain control over inmates by stripping them of their outside customs (their "house culture") and reassembling them, through such methods as "will-breaking," "divestiture of identity kit," and "ritual humiliation," into new and often unnatural norms of behavior that are compatible with enforced crowding, enforced silence, enforced control of emotional states. There is loss of privacy, the requirement to display submission through accepted methods of addressing superiors, and an attempt toward complete mind control in which individual feelings, thoughts, and concerns are largely irrelevant.

Reinforcement of accepted behavior is accomplished partly through an elaborate reward and privilege system inside the walls, where even the most trivial benefits are noted by the inmates and reacted to. In addition, there are numerous punishments for those who do not conform, one of the most effective, since time hangs so heavy, being the threat of having to do *additional* time within.

The job of the staff is surveillance. The staff generally regards the inmate population as bitter, secretive, and untrustworthy, while regarding itself as superior and righteous. Inmates view staff as condescending, high-handed, and mean, and see themselves generally as inferior, weak, and guilty. This is not completely consistent, however, as there is sometimes a split between staff and superiors, or even among staff itself, as to emphasis on curing versus discipline and order. Some staff members see themselves in terms of the curing/humanitarian ideal, but observation shows the bulk of their time to be spent in control and surveillance anyway.

For me, the most fascinating aspect of the study is the reactions of the inmates to such a situation. Some display "conversion" and internalize the institutional norms as their own, becoming "model" clients. (A parallel here can be found in Elizabeth Janeway's *Powers of the Weak* (Knopf), where, when talking about blacks and women, she says such pressures lead them "to do what one is being forced into as if one actively chose to do it [which] advances the illusion that one had choice.") Others display "intransigence" and not only rebel but openly or secretly seek to disrupt the institution's functioning. Others slip into "situational withdrawal" and become withdrawn, passive, apathetic, disinterested. Others display what Goffman calls "colonization," in which the inmate redefines the outside world in terms of the inside norms and thus experiences no deprivation and says the institution is "not so bad."

In all cases, however, the reaction, whether pure or a combination of several forms, is designed to minimize physical and psychological damage. Each develops a personal approach to playing the system for survival.

In the face of such control, nearly all inmates display some form of "underlife" behavior that—unlike attacks on the institution itself—are simply violations of minor or hard-to-enforce rules, the main goal being a reassertion of personal independence and self-worth. Violators admit they did it "just because I felt like it," and they usually know specifically what rules they violated. The more rules the institution has, the more such rules focus and elicit the behaviors they prohibit and the more opportunity they afford inmates for an elaborate, rich, varied, and detailed expression of individuality through underlife behavior. The staff nearly always misses the point, sees such violations as the result of inmate weakness, contrariness, or lack of personal control, and terms such behavior persistently as "messing" or "fucking up." Their solution? To focus on the individual inmates and their lack of personal control, and their personal flaws so in need of remediation, instead of the environment where the source of most of the trouble lies lurking.

Other aspects of underlife behavior include illicit transmission systems for information and objects, clandestine economic activities, even over-zealous participation in some prescribed activity to confound and frighten the staff.

The parallels between Goffman's asylums and prisons (and his explanations of the behaviors within) and schools are so obvious that I'm not even going to attempt to draw them all, but to ignore the reasons for the persistence of underlife behavior (which is the form most of our disciplinary "problems" take) would be irresponsible, particularly since so many of us are so preoccupied with it.

Obviously, in a school, some form of control is essential. One cannot crowd several thousand adolescents into a building together, demand that they stay inside for six hours, and then simply sit back and allow whatever happens to happen. Like it or not, there must be rules. All of us are governed by codes of behavior, expectations of superiors and society, demands made on us by the government, and so forth. It's a fact of life.

With schools, however, I am convinced that it is safe to say that the amount of underlife behavior is directly proportional to the "totality" of the institution. It depends on its size (the more students, both in classes and in the building, the more rules and the more control and surveillance required); it depends on the extent to which the real world and the school world are separated; it depends on the extent to which the teachers are vindictive and punitive (one of the most revealing and most famous experiments in this area was conducted in a well-known university where the guards in an experimental population of "guards" and "prisoners" got into their roles with such vicious enthusiasm that the two-week experiment was ended by the frightened social psychologists after only six days); it depends on the extent to which the incentive for buckling down (the diploma, for instance) is valued; it depends on the extent of "mind control" (read: curriculum control) by the adults in charge, and the extent to which the curriculum is perceived as important or useful; it depends on the extent to which individualism and identity are enhanced or squashed; and it depends on the extent to which students see themselves as being bought off to achieve control, or legitimately rewarded and valued. It depends on all that and more.

But it depends, in summary, on the student reaction to the institution as a whole, and on the perception of the amount of unfairness, stupidity, or genuine good and valued activity within it.

And we must remember that no matter how fine and sensitive and responsible the school, there will be a certain amount of underlife behavior within it *anyway* (negotiating for free space; loud, flamboyant activity during breaks; attempts to manipulate kind teachers into bending rules and taking the day off and going outdoors), *just* because it is an institution and every individual, unless completely cowed or blindly accepting of his or her fate and circumstance, is going to feel a need to assert his or her independence from such a place. With adults, it is no different, but it is especially true with adolescents, whose identity is in the process of being formed, and who also (along with many of us) idolize the trickster heroes of mythology and today and celebrate them and give them power because of their willingness to take risks—the opposite of the weaker and more prevalent stance that allows the more powerful control by default.

And thus two boys take off to Sky Valley and do a little drinking on the way.

The best education I ever got related to discipline and behavior (aside from my own high school career in both a public and then a private school) came while I was teaching at Rabun Gap, which was a combination of both types of institutions. During the school day, as a public school, there was the usual garden-variety underlife behavior (students smoking in the student parking lot, laying out of school, and getting the best of new or vulnerable teachers), but because the school was small, generally humane, headed by a fine principal, staffed by some pretty fine teachers, and filled with students who were basically clean cut, cooperative, and polite, discipline, overall, wasn't that big a problem. Classrooms like mine, in the beginning, got out of control because of my own stupidity, but school-wide, the situation was one most teachers would envy.

After the school day, when the community students went home and the 130 or so boarding students returned to their dormitories to change clothes for work, the amount of underlife behavior escalated so dramatically that it was staggering. Students who had been a joy in school turned into demons. It was the craziest thing I have ever observed.

It could be explained in part by the fact that private boarding schools are, by definition, more "total" institutions than public schools and hence are more preoccupied with control. That's obvious. But in the boarding school I attended (which required coats and ties for classes and meals, and classes six days a week, and all the rest), the underlife behavior, though rich and delicious in retrospect, was of a different type. There it tended toward getting the best of the system, but not in a malicious sense. It was simply a natural assertion of independence. And most of us believed that there were good reasons for our being there—and that the diploma was something to be valued. They worked us hard, and with good reason: we were all going to college. We were reasonably inspired. We saw much of what we were put through in a positive light. There were abundant opportunities for individual excellence and exploration (the newspaper, magazine, tutorial program, etc.), and punishments we received, since the rules were fair overall, were generally deserved and accepted as such. We earned them, just as we earned grades. We were frequently treated as responsible and adult, and so there was balance there that carried us through to graduation. The atmosphere was positive. There was momentum into the future.

At Rabun Gap, there had been a subtle shift in a different direction. In all fairness, and from all I hear today, the situation is dramatically different at the school now. There's a new headmaster, scores of new programs, enrollment is up, and there's a waiting list for admission. At that time, however, the atmosphere was often negative. The boarding students, many of whom came from disrupted family backgrounds, frequently did not want to be there. Most of them were not college-bound, they did not see a Rabun Gap education as being particularly advantageous or helpful (even though for many of them it later proved to be), and they perceived most of the rules as being punitive and petty. Added to this was the religious emphasis, which dictated behavior even more alien to most of their backgrounds (no dancing, no smoking, no unsupervised dating), and they absolutely chafed. Thus the underlife behavior proliferated like algae. Students pulled out all the stops to get the best of a system they saw as being out to get them, and rather than focusing on the *environment* that bred the underlife behavior, houseparents focused on individuals. New rules proliferated as fast as new offenses were found; the student handbook got thicker and thicker; and all this served to accomplish was to increase the hostility and provide even more opportunities for underlife behavior by focusing on and eliciting the prohibited behaviors. Students were punished continually for the euphemism "bad attitude"—simply a phrase to describe this underlife behavior, or "messing," in the words of Goffman's asylum staff. Scores of students were "shipped," or sent home. The resentment of houseparents was further escalated as they saw students "breaking rules on purpose just to make us mad," and they clamped down even tighter, just making things all the worse.

In the *Tao Te Ching*, Lao Tzu says, "The more laws you make, the more thieves there will be." That was certainly true at Rabun Gap, but the amount of misbehavior on the part of the student body fueled the negative attitudes of the staff to such a great extent that it was almost impossible to turn the whole thing around. Underlife behavior took on an ugly, purposeful dimension that fed more negativism, more scrutiny of student behavior with the express purpose of "catching them in the act"; and the situation escalated again. Houseparents, separated from the real world by their jobs, lost all perspective. The war consumed them. I remember especially a directive one of the girls brought me from the dormitory bulletin board. Posted on January 14, 1974, it reflected the demented state of a housemother obviously out of control: "You have had a week to be stopping the use of 'baby' and 'man.' Today minors will be given for their use on this floor. Example: 'Judy-man,' 'Nan-baby.'

"Also a minor will be given to *anyone* using 'darn' and 'dern' on this floor. This does not refer to darn as a darning thread, but darn as a byword.

"When [the upstairs houseparent] is off, this will apply to both floors."

The note was signed by the houseparent, who flew into a rage when she discovered that her directive had been taken from the board. The girl who brought it to me, in fear of serious punishment, slipped it back onto the board that afternoon.

In another dormitory, near-rebellion broke out when a public address system was installed in an upstairs recreation room. Put there so that students could be paged by houseparents, student suspicions that the houseparents were eavesdropping on their conversations were confirmed almost at once, as the houseparents began to confront them with things they had overheard that had been stated by the students, on purpose and only upstairs, in their attempt to find out if they were being monitored. Under howls of protest, and despite administrative denials that the system was being misused, its existence generated so much dissension that it was finally disconnected.

That refueled the long-standing assumption that student mail was being opened. Accusations grew so loud and prolonged that the administration, in a letter to parents dated October 3, 1973, said in part: "From time to time we hear that young people have told parents that letters are not put in the mail, or that they are opened by school officials before they are given to the students. This interference with the government mail would be foolish on the part of anyone. We do not hold back posting mail, nor do we open students' mail." The letter went on to explain that occasionally incoming packages that appeared suspicious were, however, opened in the presence of school officials, as "we imagine you would want that kind of vigilance so that illegal drugs might be stopped before they got onto the campus."

Several days later, a student brought me a letter he had written to his mother the night before. He had left the sealed, stamped letter on his desk to be picked up by the houseparents for the outgoing mail. The letter, which contained some profanity, had obviously been opened and read, for clipped to it was a note from the housemother that read, "You may give me an explanation of this filth! Also! Clean this messy desk!" Underlined by the houseparents were some lines the student had written concerning the housemother's refusal to allow the students to cook some popcorn in the dorm kitchen because it smelled up her apartment.

In such an atmosphere, with adults increasingly discredited, negativism breeds as a result of increasing control to quell rebellion. Instead of watching for things to praise, adults watch like hawks for imagined infractions or slights. Things get more and more absurd. I remember, for example, the time a student of mine had spent days doing shadowgrams in the darkroom to enliven the poetry section of Volume V Number 4 of *Foxfire*. One of the pages was to be a collage, and he was sitting on the floor, prints in a ten-foot circle all around him, cutting and piecing together images and singing to himself. It had taken him a while to learn how to use the darkroom, but once he became confident, he had taken to it like a duck to water, and he was truly proud of the creation he was pasting together. Some of the most effective images had come as a result of shining the enlarger light through various soft-drink bottles. The scalloped Coke bottles were especially good, as they refracted light in fascinating ways. So were Dr Pepper bottles, as the labels showed up with a mysterious halo around them.

In the midst of all this, an administration official walked up behind him, and rather than being curious and supportive, ordered him to remove the Dr Pepper shadowgrams with a scolding reminder that the building he was working in had been paid for by a member of the Coca-Cola family and that images of no other soft drinks would be tolerated. The student's day and mood were ruined, his feeling that the adults around him were petty and narrow-minded was reinforced, and he still remembers the incident vividly today and will for the rest of his life.

What would his reaction have been if the accuser had been openly curious about the images that had been made, had gotten the student to show him how, and let him try a couple for himself, and had concluded by saying, "There's one thing here that might give us a problem, and that's this label. There's a lot of money that comes into the school through a Coca-Cola foundation, and some of those folks may ask me about this. But I'm really impressed with what you've done here, and I like what I see, and if you want to leave it in there, do it, and I'll back you up. Frankly, I don't think any of those people would be narrow-minded enough to object, anyway. They know there are other soft drinks on the market besides theirs. And you do have Coke represented here too. But if any of them does say anything, I'll let you know, and maybe we can draft an answer together. I'll stick with you in any case."

The whole incident was so petty it wasn't worth comment anyway, but if something had to be said at all concerning anything other than the overall quality of the collage itself, at least it could have been stated in such a way that the student would remember, years later, "Remember that thing about the Dr Pepper label? You respected my judgment and stood behind me, and I never forgot that."

On another occasion, it was decided not to purchase awards for a team because they had cost thirty dollars the year before, and that price just couldn't be afforded anymore. How much better to have said, "You deserve them, and you're *going* to get them."

It's so easy to be negative and put students down. They're such easy targets. I remember that the times it hurt me the most were those times I'd done everything I could to get a student over the effects of a bad week and get that student into a positive frame of reference again, only to have all that work blasted to smithereens by a few unthinking comments or actions:

• A student works with me all afternoon on a special project in the office. We lose track of time, get to the dining hall late, but the kid is excited and proud until he finds out he's been given a major for missing supper and is restricted to the dorm for the weekend.

• A group of students have a fine afternoon working with me on my log house, and, full of accomplishment and pride (and hamburgers from Kate's), they return to the dorm for study hall, where they are greeted by a houseparent who, rather than sharing their success and congratulating them and laughing with them, yells at them for coming into the dorm dirty and tells them they have four minutes to get cleaned up and quiet before study hall starts.

• A student is wrestling to complete a double exposure print for the cover of the magazine, printing it over and over to get it perfect. Suzy and

I can hear him in the darkroom, talking to himself and urging himself on, every gear in his brain engaged and turning. Finally he bursts out of the darkroom in triumph, waving the print, takes it to someone to show it off, is late for English, and is greeted by a teacher who, rather than checking for extenuating circumstances, simply sees lateness and makes him write three hundred times, "I will not be late to English class again."

• A student accompanies me to Berkeley, California, to work with a group of teachers there. He is respected, listened to, appreciated for his obvious talents, and treated as an equal. He grows before my eyes. Back at school, in the dining hall, he asks, "Would you pass the sugar?" The adult at the table glances up sharply, wags her finger, and croons as if to a two-year-old, "Ah, ah, ah! You forgot to say the *magic word!*" He sits there, stunned, the contrast between the two worlds almost unimaginable.

• A student playing tennis for the school team finally wins a lengthy match, runs to the dining hall for supper, is sent back to the dorm to change clothes, and thus misses supper completely—after a victory for the school team.

That's the kind of thing I mean by a negative atmosphere, dominated by surveillance and rules, all of which only serves to foster underlife behavior with a nasty edge.

At times, it was almost funny. I remember a houseparent, convinced there was contraband of some sort in a student's trunk, ordering him to open it so he could examine the contents. The student refused. The houseparent, now assured he was hot on the trail of a budding criminal, ordered the trunk opened at once. The student still refused. The disagreement escalated, becoming louder and more hostile, and a crowd began to gather. His imagined honor at stake, the houseparent began to make threats that everyone present knew he had the power to carry out. Rather than dispersing the crowd, he allowed it to swell, wanting all present to see him win a battle he knew was inevitably his. At the climactic moment, he played his trump card, the student relented and opened the trunk, and as the lid was raised, all present strained forward to have a look at the cause of all the commotion. But the trunk was completely, absolutely empty. Not even a pair of dirty socks lay hidden within, and the houseparent retreated, having shown the majority of the dorm his backside.

Another effective way of confounding the authorities took the form of entering into a sanctioned or imposed activity with such gusto and enthusiasm that it thoroughly rattled those in charge. I remember, for example, times when students in a religious service would suddenly begin to sing with such volume and intensity that the adults around them would begin to glance at each other nervously, watching for some indication from a superior as to what they should do. When punished for such conduct, the conversation would take on absurd nuances.

"What were we doing wrong?"

"You *know* what you were doing!"

"We were just singing the hymn."

"You were singing too loud. You were showing disrespect."

"But we just *liked* the song."

"You know what I mean. Don't get smart with me."

"You told us to sing, so we did. Don't you want us to sing anymore?"

And so on.

In every institution with which I have been associated, including the public school where I now teach, I see evidence of such conflict. So do you. Even in the very best of them, students engage in completely normal, healthy, and usually harmless underlife behavior in an attempt to remind themselves of their individuality in the face of an institution that would control them—however gently and humanely. There are rules all of us must live by, though, and students understand this. They constantly establish rules themselves to govern their own behavior, especially in the games they play. Our organization has rules for student behavior that I enforce unflinchingly. I will not allow students to be rude or discourteous to visitors to our classroom, for example. Neither will I allow students to be unkind to each other. I will not tolerate ridicule, for instance. Nor will I allow students to throw $250 cameras out the classroom window at passing delivery trucks. Such rules are natural and unforced, however. They are so obviously right that students buy into them from the first day on, and I simply never have to enforce them. We work together in an atmosphere of unfailing mutual respect and trust, and rather than being authoritarian and punitive and petty, the rules that govern our behavior are seen as just, and students know they are free at almost any time to bring them up for discussion, reevaluation, and, if warranted, alteration. Normally, however, they are seen as being so logical that they aren't even perceived as "rules" in the sense of restricting freedom or behavior— despite the fact they do just that. They're just accepted as fair, and class goes on.

So does underlife behavior. But in a situation of relative equality and give-and-take, it is so minor and generally good-natured (a student hides my chalk, or writes a kidding message to me on the blackboard) that *not* to accept it as such and laugh along would be crazy.

It is on this point, of course, that so many adults go astray and allow innocuous events to build to absurd heights and consequences. I visited a boarding school one evening, for example, where I was to show some slides to the student body. I arrived while the students were finishing supper, and a young woman teacher was reading some announcements, including the time and place of my talk that night. When she finished announcing my talk, she wondered to herself, but out loud, whether she should require them to return to the dorms first and dress formally (coats and ties for the boys and skirts or dresses for the girls), and as the students pleaded with her good-naturedly ("Ah, come on, Miss Jones. You're not really going to make us change, are you?"), she flared up and sent them all to the dorms to change clothes. It was a ridiculous display of adult insensitivity, lack of humor, and pettiness, and since I was the cause of it, in part, it embarrassed me deeply. By the time the students got to the auditorium, they were so resentful of the event itself that all the cards were stacked against me. I was simply one more in a long line of silly impositions to be endured, and if someone had told me that that teacher had discipline problems, I would not have wondered at all. She ruined the evening for all of us, not because of the "rule" but because of her punitive, mysteriously nasty attitude. On that evening, she was, to put it bluntly, a bitch.

Sometimes such behavior has serious consequences. A student I knew well got trapped in a situation in our public school that changed his life. Caught in class for doing something silly and harmless, he was sent by his teacher to the assistant principal, who paddled him, despite his protests that he had done nothing wrong. He was returned to the class and, upon entering, the teacher said something like, "Now, since you insist on being a child, I'm going to have to treat you like one. Bring your chair up here by my desk and sit facing the class, where all of us can watch you and have the benefit of any little entertainments you may want to put on for us." As a ninth-grader, big for his age, he resisted, embarrassed at being made a fool of, and the teacher sent him back to the assistant principal, who suspended him for three days for insubordination.

Upon his return, the teacher made a remark like, "Well! Here's our little third-grader back again. Let's all welcome him. Shall we?" And the student walked out of school never to return. The last I heard of him, he was working for a construction firm in New Jersey.

A similar event with another student escalated to the point at which the student's parents threatened to burn down the teacher's house, preferably with her inside. She is no longer teaching school.

Far-fetched? Yes, but I saw it happen. Those who laugh at such seemingly ridiculous examples of adults versus young people might be counseled to watch a rerun of the "60 Minutes" show of December 13, 1980, in which an adult becomes so overwrought and intimidated by the youthful pranks of some neighborhood teenagers that rather than coming to peace with them and entering good-naturedly into a truce, he comes out shooting and kills one of them for hitting his house with a snowball.

By and large, students treat us the way we deserve to be treated, and I have found it more productive to focus on this fact rather than to espouse the more typical adult statement, "I'll treat my students the way they deserve to be treated. When they can learn how to act like adults, I'll treat them like adults." The fact is, they all know how to act maturely and responsibly, but our condescending attitudes toward them often mitigate against this behavior. When we're having discipline problems, the fault is usually ours, not theirs. We provoke the behavior we get, good or bad. Some adults will lay the blame for their problems on the "chemistry" in the classroom—the volatile, hopeless mix of a certain group of young people who set each other off—but this sidesteps the real issue: the adult and what he or she is doing with or to those students. How else explain the fact that the same group of students will hound one poor teacher mercilessly in second period, will be cowed and apprehensive in third, and be cooperative and helpful and enthusiastic in fourth?

This Jekyll-Hyde syndrome is one of the more fascinating aspects of school life. Students I have been able to do little with shine under some other teacher's direction or influence, and vice versa. Students who are model citizens in one class become demons in another and go to sleep in a third. I'll never forget the day that one of the best students I ever had—a girl who was unfailingly polite, cooperative, enthusiastic, and basically generous and kind—came into my class bragging and laughing about the fact that she and her classmates had finally gotten the teacher down the hall. In fact, they had reduced him to tears in class, and he left the school shortly thereafter and never taught again. I was amazed that she could derive any satisfaction at all from that accomplishment, but on looking into it further, it didn't take long to find that though he was basically a good, well-meaning, gentle man, he had been weak, ineffectual, boring, and had never enlisted the help of his students or his peers in making things work in his classroom. Underlife behavior proliferated, and in panic, he lashed out wildly, trying to get things under control. Discipline became the main agenda rather than the subject matter, and the more obvious it became to all that he didn't know what he was doing, the more distraught he became. As he thrashed about helplessly, shouting one ineffectual threat after another, the students, like sharks in a circle, watched him dispassionately and then closed in for the kill. I felt sorry for him, especially since I had gone through roughly the same experience as a first-year teacher; and had I realized the extent of his distress and/or been asked by him for help, I certainly would have pulled out all the stops to give it to him. But the hard facts are that the fault lay not with his students, most of whom I was also teaching at the time and knew well, but with himself. He was the cause of his own downfall. The students just adminis-tered the coup de grace.

Discipline is essential in schools. The students themselves will admit that. Teenagers who obviously do not belong in that setting because they are determined to be antisocial and destructive, and are beyond self-discipline and the capacity to reason, must be swiftly and surgically re-moved to another type of educational environment, not coddled or fret-ted over. Removed. Period. None of us can afford to have our attention and our energy completely dominated by some sixteen-year-old jerk with the IQ of a cantaloupe whose only reasons for attending school revolve around clandestine pursuits. That's a tragedy of a different sort, and with 150 students to serve, none of us is equipped to deal with that one.

But with individuals like that removed and a reasonably normal population within our schools, discipline carried to excess and wrongly administered by adults who should know better, and the removal of all privileges and freedom in the service of "control," is a fuse on a ticking bomb. Soon the word is out in the community, and the parents are involved. "We want a school with order, but we don't want a prison." And the following year, as often as not, we find ourselves being introduced to a new school principal.

John Dewey was right: the best form of discipline and control is that exerted gracefully and appropriately by the nature of the activities taking place—and the resulting atmosphere—within the school and the classroom. Discipline is not a problem in a class where our magazine is being produced. There's just too much of importance to get done, and too little time, and the rare students who try to create problems are dealt with by their peers.

They Help Students Analyze and React
Appropriately to the Actions of Other Adults

There is a related area that has to do with student perceptions of adults. I touched on it briefly in talking about allowing students to see us as individually fallible and turning that fact to advantage rather than artificial defensiveness and embarrassment. I'm sure you realized, however, that the topic is much broader than the piece of it I mulled over briefly. The subject of discipline and adult control is an appropriate one for continuing the discussion initiated previously.

In an institution like a public school, students will inevitably see some adults as unfair and petty. They will perceive some of the demands made upon them as stupid and unjust. Administrators realize this. It is one of the reasons they insist on our maintaining a united front in the face of the unhappiness these student perceptions may cause, for once the faculty itself becomes confused and divided over rules and customs and demands seen by the students as unjust, the whole institution comes apart at the seams and breaks up into warring factions and enemy camps. Or so the general paranoia would lead us to believe.

Whether or not the latter actually happens depends on numerous variables and is much too complicated a condition to blame entirely on the faculty's failure to maintain a united front in the face of the enemy forces, but that's another discussion entirely.

In the face of imagined or real injustice, students react in a number of ways, depending on the offense. Sometimes they try to find sympathetic adults to unload on or to enlist as allies. Failing this (upon meeting the indivisible adult front lines), they may fall back on adults outside the school for support or a sympathetic ear. Since adults outside the school *normally* side with the teachers and the administration, students find themselves unloading on and banding together with their peers against the school itself. Discontent usually takes the form of grumbling and some increase in underlife behavior, but may erupt into more serious forms of action.

Principals know this. It's one of the reasons they abhor dissent. It's the main reason they have assistant principals. It's also a reason most of them stress school spirit, value fine coaches and winning teams, and give students such things as extra "breaks" for good behavior, all of which has to do with putting a sugar coating on a bitter pill and, in most cases, is not a malicious or devious act but simply a completely justified attempt to keep things running smoothly. And who can blame them? No one can work effectively in an institution dominated by discord.

Thus teachers who continually and vocally side with students against the other teachers and the administration get fired. Usually they deserve it.

But—and here's the clincher—what happens when a student approaches you, wants to talk, and it turns out the student has a genuine and legitimate grievance against an adult? To wave it aside in the interest of keeping peace and a united front (making some innocuous comment like "Oh, I'm sure he didn't mean that," or "Oh, I think you must have misunderstood the situation. Surely she didn't . . . ," or "Well, you'll understand as you grow older that that's just the way the world works, and all of us get caught on the receiving end once in a while") is to denigrate the student's perception of right and wrong and to add fuel to the fire of the student's suspicion that the adult world in general is a very unfair and hypocritical place. Is that what we want our young people to believe?

What do we do, knowing that if we're not extremely careful, we may only make the problem worse? What happens if we approach the adult, and he or she gets so defensive and angry that our ability to work together productively is destroyed? What happens if the adult takes out his or her anger on the student who approached us? What happens if the student gets caught in the middle between two warring adults, each of whom is yanking the student back and forth between opposing points of view? What happens if the student, encouraged by our defense and support of his or her position, decides to get even with the offending adult and gets kicked out of school? Have we really helped matters? Is anyone better off for our having entered the fray? Would it have died a natural death had we sidestepped the whole thing and left it alone?

My first reaction to such questions (and I've made most of the mistakes that can be made) is to say that teachers who are approached by students who are genuinely troubled are, because of the opportunities presented to nurture growth and provide support or solace, in an enviable position, not a cursed one—provided they are being approached because students view them as strong and fair and honest, and not weak and indiscriminately supportive of student gripes. Teachers who are being supportive just because they want students to like them (and I have made this mistake) really do tend to cause more problems than they solve, and I don't want one of them working for me.

Conversely, those teachers who are never approached because students know in advance they'll simply adopt the party line, no matter what the problem, or won't take the time to listen, are also of little help. They float serenely above the fray, refusing to get involved and leaving students to fend for themselves and draw whatever conclusions they will from their experiences.

If we are really concerned about education, we must be concerned about student development in all its aspects. That means going beyond the freeze-dried content of many of our courses and helping students as they struggle to decide what kinds of adults they will eventually be. And that means not only scrutinizing the example we ourselves set as individuals, but also helping them interpret accurately and react appropriately to the behavior of others.

My formal initiation into this nest of stinging nettles came during my first year of teaching. During the second week of school, I loaded eight dormitory students (four couples) into my Volkswagen bus and took them to a horse show in South Carolina to which we had been invited by the parents of one of the students I had along. When we got to the show ring, I turned the students loose so that they could roam the field, visit the horse barns and the concession stands, and allow me to visit with the student's parents. Those who wanted to stay with me were welcome to, but since they were seniors, I felt no reason to make them stay with me, an unnecessary restriction that probably would have come close to ruining the afternoon for all of us. All I asked was that they stay in the horse show area and not wander off the property, and that they be back at the van at the prearranged departure time. They agreed, we split up, and through the remainder of the afternoon, I caught sight of them intermittently here and there around the arena, drinking soft drinks, eating hot dogs, and laughing and chatting with each other. From time to time, they'd check in with me and then wander off again to resurface on the other side of the ring.

All of us had a fine time, and that evening we drove back to school and I returned them to their dorms.

Shortly before Thanksgiving, one of the boys was caught by a houseparent smelling of cigarette smoke. His name was turned in to the administration, along with a pack of cigarettes the suspecting houseparent had found upon searching the student's room the next day while he was in class. One of the administration officials went to the dorm, searched the room again, found a locked diary, took it to his office, read it, copied portions of it, and returned it to the boy's room. Shortly thereafter, I was summoned and asked to read those portions of the diary that had been copied. The offending passages began by saying what a tremendous guy I was and all that sort of thing. They then went on to talk about the horse show, the fact that I had allowed them to roam freely within the park confines, the fact that some of them had smoked cigarettes, and the fact that on the way home that night, they had held hands with their dates. I had guessed that they would do the latter, but having only been a teacher for two weeks, I had not yet been completely initiated into all the school's customs, and I could see no reason seventeen-year-old boys should not be allowed to hold hands with girls of the same age. My fault . . .

And so, when pressed, I admitted that all that was revealed in the passages of the diary I had been asked to read could well have happened, though I had not observed any of it directly—which was true. I had, however, given them their heads and let them run free for a few hours. My fault again . . .

Meanwhile, the boy who wrote the diary had returned to his room, found it in a location different from the one in which it had been left, guessed that it had been read, and began to warn those friends whose names he had mentioned. Most of them panicked. As they were called to the main office one by one to affirm or deny passages they were shown, the situation worsened. And when the boy whose diary it was was kicked out of school (despite the fact that he had spent four years there and was part of a family that had had at least one boy in the school for eleven straight years), the hysteria spread like a brushfire through sage grass. I had never seen anything like it before in my life. Two more students followed, both kicked out for good. Both had been on the horse show excursion. Both were accused of smoking and "bad attitude."

For obvious reasons, a number of students came to talk with me, fearing both for their own necks and for mine, since it was now common knowledge that I had been featured prominently in the offending document. Additional punishments followed, including several students being kept on campus during Thanksgiving vacation to dig a ditch for a new gas line. Finally the furor died, but the atmosphere of suspicion remained to color the lives of all throughout the rest of the year.

Subsequent conversations I had with students turned again and again to the question of whether the administration had the legal or moral right to act on the contents of that diary (what if it had all been fantasy and lies?), much less read it in the first place. My mind was filled with all those questions I posed several pages ago. To my own way of thinking, such adult actions were indefensible, but what if I admitted my reservations to the students and the facade of the united front cracked wide open? On the other hand, what if I defended those actions before the students, or said something like, "Well, he shouldn't have written things in that diary that he would have been embarrassed for *anyone* to see or read in public," and in so doing became either one more member of what by now was seen as undeniably the enemy camp, or caused them to doubt their own growing sense of morality and fair play in an ostensibly Christian environment where Christian love and patience and forgiveness were preached as a daily dietary supplement?

I got pretty troubled by all that, sidestepped the students, and talked with the administration about the issue at some length. Not the least of my burden was the fact that in no small measure, I had contributed to the crisis by taking those students off campus in the first place. If some of them had to be kicked out in their senior year for smoking and holding hands, then I should be fired for allowing the chance to exist for them to break those rules.

The people I talked to were understanding, and they patiently explained to me that while the students were in their care, they had every right and obligation as in loco parentis adults to exercise the prerogatives of parents in monitoring and correcting improper behavior. Further, they affirmed the right of students to have private property, but only when it was beyond a shadow of a doubt that they deserved it. And further, they assured me that I was not wholly at fault but that the students sent home had broken numerous rules, had been given multiple opportunities to shape up, had emerged as bad influences on the rest of the students—especially powerful now that they were seniors—and that the diary had simply been the proverbial last straw.

And there the matter ended. But I could not shake the notion that something deeply wrong had been done, and I remain convinced of that today. Put in a similar situation now, I would probably resign. We could argue the point endlessly and to no avail, but the fact remains that even if the school officials acted completely within their rights (and it seems clear they were at least legally on firm ground), their actions served to convince the students that the school's vigilance was not motivated by love and concern but by deep suspicion and mistrust. And I can tell you from experience that the atmosphere under such conditions is absolutely poisonous. It's the old half-full or half-empty, optimist-versus-pessimist dialogue. Search for evil, sniff it out, and you will be rewarded on finding it not by less evil and more good but by the opposite. Search for good, exalt it, make it the focus of your life, and though evil will still exist, good becomes irresistible and triumphs.

Ah, I never was much of a preacher.

Meanwhile, when students asked me about the diary episode, the best I could do then, as a teacher, was to explain the legality of the school's position as accurately and as clearly as I could. I told them that I thought they were absolutely justified in asking such questions, however, and that I was proud of them for wrestling with such issues. I urged them to look at the whole incident apart from the question of whether or not someone had been "caught" because of it: "What would you think of the administrators reading the diary if it had contained nothing but harmless stories and praise for the school and its program?" And I asked them to look within themselves and question what they would do when faced by a closed diary written by one of their own children, or by an employee or a parent. And I asked them to examine what rights they thought they had as young people, and how they had come to have or deserve such rights.

And that's about the best I could do. I was determined, though, not to belittle their concerns. And that would have remained the case whether I had agreed with those concerns or not.

As the *Foxfire* project began to gather momentum and I found myself spending more and more time with students in out-of-classroom situations, a growing variety of student concerns was shared with me. Sometimes action was appropriate, sometimes not. There were times, for example, when a student just wanted to sound off about conditions in general and didn't have any specific grievance in mind. He'd just be blowing off a little normal steam from his adolescent engines—the kind of random, aimless griping I do sometimes after a bad day—and a sympathetic ear was all that was required to put everything in a different light. At other times, the student was angry about something quite specific: perhaps he had gotten caught doing something he obviously should not have done, had been punished appropriately, but was still mad at the world and ready to lash out again in some unpredictable way. Talking the whole thing through and giving the student a chance to defuse generally did the trick, and when I'd offer to go to the adult who administered the punishment to present the student's side, he'd usually say, "Naw. Don't worry about it. It was my fault and I guess I got what I deserved. I'm just madder at myself than anything else."

On other occasions, a student would have what sounded like a legitimate beef against some condition at the school or some adult, but when I'd offer to go, either with the student or alone, to talk it out with the adult responsible, he would begin to backpedal and stammer, either out of fear of repercussion, fear that I would discover he had only told me part of the story, or a realization that, after all, the situation wasn't worth raising any dust about. These were always the toughest cases, for they required so much reading between lines for which I had not been trained. That student who "lied," for example; did he tell me something false because he wanted my sympathy and couldn't think of another way to get it, or because he had misunderstood the situation completely or had heard only a portion of what was said, or for some other reason? The student who was afraid of repercussion; were his fears justified? Was the problem serious enough that something should be done about it anyway? Should the student's identity be kept secret? Could it?

Minor to major, the problems ran the gamut, and slowly I began to develop a working approach that seemed, at the time, at least, to do the job, the key being never to blithely dismiss the problem or put the student into destructively embarrassing or dangerous positions.

On one end of the scale, the solutions tended to be pretty simple, requiring only an adult ally to run a little interference or get a door opened, and, by example, show the student how to do the same. Several times students came to me convinced that something was wrong with their records: credit for a course had been left off, for example, or a grade was incorrect for some reason. When I'd tell them to go talk to the guidance counselor or the teacher, they'd freeze in fear, and so we'd go together, track down the source of the problem, and, if a mistake had been made, get it fixed, all in an atmosphere of good-natured, honestly concerned inquiry rather than accusatory anger. If no mistake had been made, we'd find out where the problem lay and figure out some strategy for dealing with it.

When a student came to me, angered that he had put in more time than a classmate on a term paper or assignment but had received a lower grade, I'd usually take the student with me to talk with the teacher if that teacher was a friend of mine, or someone I knew to be honest and concerned—someone, in short, who would talk with us and not land on the student later in some petty, vindictive way. We'd talk the whole thing out together, and I'd offer to help in whatever way I could, and I'd back up that promise with action, be it reading a draft of the student's term paper and making suggestions in advance of the deadline, or whatever, for as long as the student needed the help. With teachers who were capable of more petty reactions to our concern, I'd usually approach them myself with something like, "George seems really upset about how badly he's doing in your class, and I'd like to try to help out if I can. His concern seems genuine to me, and if you will show me how he's having trouble, I'll be glad to work with him." Usually they'd help me pinpoint the difficulty, be it behavioral or academic, and we'd work out a possible approach. Sometimes just the expression of my concern, coupled with the student's willingness to cooperate, was more than enough to turn things around both on the part of the teacher involved and of the student (who had sometimes decided without justification that the teacher was out to get him).

At the other end of the scale were the problems students brought that were more troublesome: the two-way intercom in the dorm recreation room, for example, or the suspicion that mail was being opened and read, both of which I talked about earlier. In such cases, one approach that often worked was to have the student get a group of three or four peers together who harbored the same suspicions, meet with those students, take a careful look at the evidence, and talk the problem through. Usually I'd take the point of view of the adult or adults in question and argue that position to help them see whether there were holes in their logic and their assumptions. Sometimes the whole concern simply fell apart under such scrutiny and was seen to have little or no basis in fact, or was seen in a completely different light when the adult point of view was revealed. At other times, the concern was real, and after going over the data and the arguments several times, I'd make an appointment with a houseparent or an administration official (sometimes requesting in advance that the identities of the students involved be kept confidential if the problem warranted that), and the whole group of us would go together to discuss things in a responsible, concerned manner. Often that resulted in action, for nearly always the administration appreciated the students bringing legitimate complaints out into the open in adult fashion rather than bickering and spreading rumor and dissent behind the scenes.

The intercom, for example, was disconnected. New rules were made governing the handling of student mail. When remedial action could not be taken, I found that the students were usually willing to accept that fact if they felt that they had had a fair hearing, that they had been treated as adults by those who had to explain the opposing point of view, and that they had been given good, solid, justifiable explanations for a policy or practice they disagreed with being continued. At the very least, student discussions about the problems usually were elevated to new levels, and the fact that their concerns had been treated with respect sometimes made a real difference in their attitudes toward both themselves and the school. (Since I began visiting other schools in earnest, I have heard the same conclusion reiterated many times. I recently spent an afternoon in the office of the principal of South Boston High, for example, once one of the meanest and most volatile of our inner-city high schools. Now, though the student population is basically the same as before racially and economically and socially, and though problems still remain, discipline is not nearly the predominant factor it once was. The walls are graffiti-free, the teachers open and confident and secure and self-assured, and the atmosphere is positive and exciting. As Jerry Kosberg, the principal, told me, "It took us over a year to turn the school around, but the important ingredients were the facts that we began to listen to the students, deal with their concerns [by bringing in more bilingual teachers, for example], and treat them like adults.")

At the risk of driving the point into the ground, I must go one step further because the point is too often misunderstood. Teachers and administration officials who decide to react to student concerns in serious fashion and give them the respect those concerns deserve sometimes take such a stance only in the interests of preserving order and control in the schools. There is a much bigger purpose that I am talking about serving, one that goes far beyond simply reacting when things heat up—and that is the active struggle to help young people evaluate all those forces that affect their movements and their activities and their beliefs and, if necessary, act in a *positive, responsible* way, being careful to scrutinize and weigh the arguments of all sides.

The first step, obviously, is to get beyond the stage at which adults and students are simply bitching unproductively with or about each other. The second step involves opening those lines of communication that may have gotten clogged. This is what I was attempting to do as I helped students look carefully at problems and then, if warranted, present their data and their conclusions to the administration—not out of anger but out of genuine concern. Such an act is usually a terribly intimidating one for teenagers who are not used to standing up to a figurehead such as a principal, and who are convinced they're either not going to be listened to or are going to be punished or embarrassed somehow. Thus I usually encouraged the students to form a small group so they could buttress and balance each other, and I usually went along to the meeting to make sure the adult gave them a fair and complete hearing.

The third step, and one we should covet for all our students, comes when those students have enough self-confidence and integrity to approach adults without our help, having looked closely at an issue and drafted some alternate stances or solutions. We, in turn, must be ready to listen as we are approached, knowing that we are helping young people do nothing less than gain the strength and wisdom they must have if they are to be adults themselves who are not cowed or convinced no one's going to listen so "what the hell, let it go"; who are not afraid to challenge the dominant point of view and fight to right obvious wrongs, and who will actively participate in the creation of a better society.

In class, I like to initiate this process myself, encouraging students to challenge my opinions, for example, sometimes seeding my remarks with obviously unworkable or unpopular stances to provoke discussion and argument and give them some exercise in this type of thinking. Sometimes I'll push them pretty hard, baiting them and making them angry to help them see how quickly logic goes out the window as anger takes over. As they get to the point at which they are scoring well-articulated points against me and the opinion I pretend to represent, I'll continue to challenge them, demanding evidence and proof, and when they don't know how to find it, I'll help them, congratulating them as their insight and self-confidence grow.

Having a project like *Foxfire* as part of our class fosters the process even more, for there will frequently be ideas students want to try relating to design or contents or promotion that I will be skeptical about, but if the students can present me with logical, well-thought-out reasons, I'll give in. Later we'll evaluate the results together, and if a mistake has been made, we'll all learn from that. No condemnation is ever in order. I want them to challenge my prejudices concerning the projects we do together and to fight with me in a good-natured, logical way and defend their stances. I don't want them to be dried up little wisps of human flesh who bow to my every opinion and refuse to challenge the status quo. I want them to be alive and eager and curious, searching constantly for a better way to accomplish any given task and committed enough to the quality of their own work that they'll fight to have it presented in the most effective way. At this point, my role simply becomes one of making sure they've double-checked all their bases and that failure would not be injurious to themselves or the project.

An issue of *Foxfire* devoted to the Betty's Creek community is a good example of what can happen as students gain this coveted self-confidence. The study, which was a seven-month examination of that community in terms of the changes it had gone through over time and how those changes had affected the quality of life, was planned originally as a series of centerfold inserts that would span four issues of *Foxfire*. The series was announced to the subscribers as something to look forward to.

When the series was completed and ready to run, the three girls who had worked so hard over it came to see me as a group, but without any adult support, and told me that they felt that to break up the study into installments spanning a year's worth of magazines would rob it of the considerable force it had as a complete whole. They wanted it to appear as one issue. I balked, not only because of promises already made to the subscribers, but also because of the amount of material other students had now completed. In fact, the rest of the issues for that school year were ready for press, minus the Betty's Creek inserts, and to print the study as a separate issue played havoc with our budget and put us one issue ahead for the following school year, meaning that the work of new students would have to be postponed an issue, and so forth. Such a scheme threw the whole train off the rails.

They went away, but two days later they were back to plead their case again. They had given what I had said serious thought, and they still could not accept the installment idea. It just wouldn't work.

At first I was irritated, but then I realized that they were doing exactly what I should be applauding and encouraging rather than squelching. They had weighed my position as objectively as they could, reevaluated theirs in light of what I had said, studied little else for several days, and had finally decided they had to stand up for their right to have seven months of genuine labor presented in what they believed to be the most powerful and effective form.

I relented, throwing out some comment like, "I hate people who stand up for their convictions," and we all laughed, and it was done. The issue was one of the best we've ever published. The subscribers reacted with nothing but praise, and the new students whose work was postponed took it all in stride, knowing that one day they might be in a similar situation.

And the girls *were* right. To have put more mechanical, mundane considerations—none of which was sacrosanct or inviolable—ahead of the remarkable growth and development that year of those girls, all in the interests of convenience and utility, would have violated some of the principal reasons for starting the magazine in the first place. (Nowadays, by the way, all such proposals are made by their authors to all the students involved with the magazine rather than to me. At that time, however, I did not have the confidence as a teacher in those students that I have now; and if you're starting at the beginning, as I had to, you will probably find yourself going through the same evolution, never turning your back completely on the students' work but taking a less and less dominant role.)

As the students got more and more comfortable about challenging me, I began to help them devise other avenues through which they could look at issues affecting their lives, and then act. In its earlier stages, the school newspaper the students and I founded became the primary vehicle. Students would identify an issue of general schoolwide concern (a rule, for example, or a type of activity or class conspicuously missing from the school scene). After drawing up a questionnaire that was carefully designed to get at the various aspects of the issue and make sure all sides were represented fairly, they'd mimeograph it, hand it out in home rooms (assuring respondents' anonymity), and then collect it and tabulate all the responses. At the same time, on-the-record interviews would be conducted with adults and students who represented various points of view, and these individuals would be allowed to check their interviews before publication to make sure their views had been accurately stated. Corrections, additions, and deletions were allowed at this point. Using this information, a major signed editorial would be drafted summarizing the findings and, as a consequence, either proposing changes of a positive, workable nature or explaining to the student body why no changes seemed warranted. If changes were called for and criticisms were either implied or stated directly, I followed the policy of the newspaper we ran at the prep school I attended, which allowed the criticism of school policy or of institutional flaws but demanded that before anything actually go into print, the editorial be shown in its entirety, by the author or authors, to the adult most directly responsible for the situation, so that that individual could either draft a response that would be printed alongside the editorial itself or could devise an acceptable remedy before the editorial went into print. I can remember several times at Hill when policy of some sort was changed simply on the strength of the student findings and the proposed remedies, and the original editorial was never printed at all—just an announcement of the policy change and the reasons for same.

Such a requirement virtually ensured that the students involved got all their facts straight, gave equal time to all parties, and, finally, discussed the matter at hand face to face with the appropriate adults, alone, without me being there to run interference. They had to stand on their own feet and present their points of view and their proposed solutions based on some solid homework and good sense—exactly the kind of stance that would give them the most credibility as adults involved in change; the kind of stance that assured them a respectful (even if an opposed) audience of the adults involved.

I still believe that this approach gave the best of our papers a seriousness and a tone of responsibility that many of the student newspapers of the sixties lacked. We had the Supreme Court on our side, anyway. (In 1969, in *Tinker* v. *Des Moines*, it ruled, for example, after students wore black armbands to protest the Vietnam War, that students do not "shed their constitutional rights to freedom of speech or expression at the school house gate," and are allowed spoken and written expressions of opinion, as well as dress and other symbolic gestures, as long as classroom activities are not disrupted.) But the tone of the student inquiries in our case was such that the issue never had to be brought up.

With increased confidence in their ability to successfully and responsibly deal with controversial issues, I and my staff members began to move the focus of such work beyond the school itself to the surrounding community. The Betty's Creek issue is an example of one such project, complete with charts, graphs, statistics, and lengthy interviews with adults who represented both sides of the question of whether the kind of change taking place in that valley was good or bad. The data in, the girls presented it all and then drew their own conclusions.

As introduced by Laurie Brunson, one of the editors, the magazine is "a cold sobering look at what pressing change and terrific increases on the pace of life can wreak on such a community. It is a look at how land, once essential for a family's existence, suddenly became a commodity with a price tag, and the new, confusing issue of land development moved in.

"It is a look at how outside forces and influences began to change social interaction within the community and force people to look outside the community for economic sustenance.

"Finally, perhaps, it is a penetrating look at the astonishing about-face progress can force the old values to contend with."

Sanctioning and encouraging such efforts, I'm convinced, is one of the most productive things we did—and do—not only in terms of the increased motivation that was brought to the acquisition of academic skills through looking at such issues, but also in terms of both personal growth and self-confidence and, sometimes, real results that bolstered the students tremendously.

As *Foxfire* achieved real fame, for example, outsiders who had moved into our area and started businesses began to use the word "Foxfire" in connection with those enterprises in an effort to stimulate sales. The first such instance was two men who moved from Florida and applied for a loan at a local bank to start a restaurant that would be called Foxfire and would feature reproductions of our magazine's covers on menus and place mats. A bank official called me to ask if I knew of these plans. I didn't, and I told him I'd call him back as soon as I had checked around a little. When I took the news to my classes, the students were furious. Each class, in turn, voted to stop them, some with the threat of use of extraordinary means, but the event placed in our laps the opportunity to examine the extent of the protection our name deserved (we had not, of course, invented the word, as was the case with such brand names as Cellophane, Xerox, Kleenex, and Exxon), the legal rights we had in the matter, and the various acceptable channels of action we could take to stop the restaurant owners. Because there was a clear intention on the part of those owners to mislead the public into believing that there was some sort of connection between their business and ours, John Viener, our lawyer in New York, assured us that we had firm legal rights. Bolstered by that news and by the unanimous student votes, the bank official was asked to tell the men (whose identities he could not reveal) that if they proceeded with their plans, they could count on being sued. The restaurant opened—but under a different name.

That event led to a whole series of discussions as to how we could protect ourselves in the future, the end result of which was, with our lawyer's help, the realization that even though we had not coined the word *Foxfire*, we had every legal right to trademark and thus prevent its use in association with any types of products or services we might be providing the public now or might want to provide in the foreseeable future, as long as someone else hadn't beaten us to those uses and trademarked that application of the word first. The students and staff and I drew up a list of services we wanted the rights to attach our name to, and Rich Bennett, a trademark attorney John Viener located for us, proceeded to establish our trademark successfully in connection with such things as magazines, television shows, record albums, Appalachian crafts and cultural affairs, and the like, thus reserving for us the right to use the word *Foxfire* in connection with such activities. When the trademark was actually awarded, a group of students (and I) knew a good deal more about legal recourse and protection than we had known before.

Good thing, for other instances of its use began to crop up with increasing frequency. Shortly after the restaurant episode, another pair of Florida businessmen opened a "Foxfire Crafts" shop on our county line and began marketing Appalachian crafts and antiques. Phone calls came in to our office from community residents before the paint was dry on the exterior sign, and a team of students and I drove to the establishment and explained the problem to the owners, who were visibly angered and promised to consult their own lawyers about the situation. The students and I left, waited a few days, and then checked back with the group. This time the mood was different, and the primary concern of the owners was the financial loss they would incur in changing the name, which would necessitate reprinting business cards, matchbooks, ads, and so on. We explained patiently that if they had just taken the time to give us a call before opening the business, all this could have been avoided quite easily, but since they had proceeded anyway, and since there was absolutely no way at all that we could allow them to selfishly trade off the credibility of a name we had worked for years to establish, they were just going to have to change the name. Assured that we would take legal action, and undoubtedly assured by their own lawyers of the precariousness of their stand, change it they did.

When "Foxfire Homes" opened for business locally and began marketing real estate and summer homes of rustic architecture, the students appointed a five-member student delegation to discuss the matter with the owners. The students left on their mission, and I remained behind. When they returned, they reported that not only were the owners also selling crafts and *Foxfire* books out of their sales office, but that they had also told the students in no uncertain terms rather precisely where they could stick their concerns. Nothing they could have told those young people could have done more to cement their resolve for what turned out to be a lengthy court contest, which we won, hands down; at which point the owners simply disappeared, leaving a list of creditors behind who, along with their lawyer, have not been paid to this date. We lost money, too, of course, due to the legal fees we had to pay, but the sight of those students disbursed throughout the school at every available phone, listening to our trademark attorney, Rich Bennett, explaining to them the procedures required and the evidence he would need from them in the form of photographs and documents, was worth the money it cost. And, of course, we received a court judgment in writing that has proved to be invaluable in the numerous subsequent attempts that have been made to trade off our credibility—attempts that have recently included marketing records and other products that we ourselves have been marketing for years.

Few things are more aggravating or ruin an otherwise good day faster than having to pursue unscrupulous, greedy types, knowing that the money invested in legal fees could be put to far better use, and knowing that—as in the case of Foxfire Homes—the money will probably be lost, and knowing that *not* to pursue and stop such abuses means ultimately the loss of our ability to protect our good name (as happened with cellophane and kleenex); but at least the students who have been involved in such cases so far and who will be involved in the future stand a better chance of being the kind of adults who will not be cowed in the face of clear abuses of rights, and who will not only know (or know how to find out) how to correct the abuses in responsible ways, but will also have the strength and willingness to do so. High school is a fine (and perhaps essential) place to begin building that knowledge and resolve, for there students can be trained early in the company of sensitive adults to act appropriately and wisely—to hook their brains and their consciences together—rather than the reverse.

They Are Constantly Engaged in the Process
of Professional Growth

The best teachers I know are always actively involved in the process of becoming better teachers. Knowing that they may never be as good as they should be; and knowing that despite all they do, there will always be those students who will fall between the cracks, never touched or influenced in a positive way by their efforts; and knowing that they are human and that there will always be some students they will like more than others, despite themselves; and knowing that they will continue to make mistakes they will regret—they persist, determined if not to become the best teachers around, then at least to become better, year by year, in the practice of their craft. They never stand still. They never stop dead in their tracks. They grow, and that growth is observable.

How do they grow?

First, they are reflective. Lillian Weber, a pioneer of the open-classroom movement, told me recently in New York, "I fear the static and unreflective nature of a teacher even more than I fear a static and unreflective child." She's right. The best teachers constantly ask themselves questions ("Why am I teaching this course in this way? How could I teach it differently? Would it be any better? Why is the course being taught at all? To what end? Do the materials I'm using actually *serve* that end, or are there other things we could do that would serve it more forcefully? What is the real reason I just punished that student? Did I do it correctly? How could I have done it differently? What function does punishment serve? How can it be made positive instead of negative? How do young people learn best? How did I learn best? What are my students' grades really telling me? To what extent do my own teaching practices contradict what I know about learning both from my own experiences as a learner and a teacher?"), and they constantly reevaluate their performance. They are their own harshest critics, anguishing over the gap between their goals and claims and the reality of their students' growth and performance.

The best of them are not intimidated or overwrought when things are not going well. They see such times as opportunities for learning and growth, not as excuses for giving up. They are prepared for failure, but they do not accept it with a shrug. They push on, convinced they are smart enough to find a better way, convinced an answer lies out there somewhere (or within themselves). They never accept the status quo.

Second, they encourage an open dialogue with their students, both past and present. As old students reappear, they ask them what they remember about the course: what classes transcended the ordinary, what aspects they took with them into the world that have since proved to be useful. They ask about teachers they've met since, and what methods and materials those teachers used that seemed to work. With current students, they constantly stop and reevaluate. "Is any of this making sense? Should we stop and try this a different way? Should we be using other activities? Are you with me, or are you bored stiff?"

And they are delighted, not insulted, when students give them positive feedback and criticism. I remember once, after a short unit on public speaking during which I had cautioned against the use of innumerable *ands* and *uhs*, I took a student with me to give a speech to a group of teachers, and afterward the student told me exactly how many times I had used *uh* in my speech and showed me the tally sheet he had kept while I was talking. I practiced my next speech with him, as he did with me, and I think both of us became better speakers as a result. Though numerous people must have noticed that habit of mine, that ninth-grader was the first to tell me about it.

Similarly, students have come to me and said, "That lesson didn't work at *all* for me," and if the verdict is the same from a majority of that student's classmates when I check with them the next day, we work together to figure out different ways to get the same points across, sometimes creating some of next year's classes in the process. I have two large notebooks filled with an ongoing flood tide of information about what works and doesn't work, and each summer those notebooks are used to help me restructure my classes for the upcoming school year.

Third, the best teachers are careful about getting their own egos inextricably tangled with those of their students. They don't use students to enhance their own professional reputations (a fatal mistake that leads far too many into taking a much too heavy hand with "student produced" products like magazines, scientific experiments destined for display at state fairs, and home ec projects) or feed off them to bolster their insecurities. They realize that former students represent the sum total of hundreds of experiences—of which they can lay claim to only a fraction—and that the most powerfully formative of the best of those experiences were those in which the teacher played a distinctly backseat role and allowed the student to act and learn independently.

The best do not work in the hope of being able to claim responsibility for the future success of students. I always cringe when former teachers whom I barely remember write saying, "How I wish I could believe I was partly responsible for your present success." Such teachers are searching for affirmation to feed fragile egos, and begging for reinforcement. That sounds perhaps unnecessarily cruel and heartless, but the point I am trying to make is sound: to claim credit for a former student's success belittles that student's efforts in his or her own life and all the learning experiences initiated independently, or drawn from, without our help. Our job is not to be these students' parents or their lifelong mentors or guardians but to help propel them into independence and sublimate our own egos completely. Some of them may give us credit later (as I have done to some of my former teachers), but to *work for* that credit is a terribly misplaced goal and skews our approach to students in bizarre ways.

Fourth, they welcome systematic evaluation of their courses and their teaching methodology rather than being intimidated by it—as long as the evaluation is based on a fair sampling of their work; and they welcome help in structuring pre- and post-tests of their students that are sensitively designed to get at whether or not they are meeting the goals of the course.

Concerning the former, I have been angered several times by evaluations of my work that were the result of one visit to one of my classes by someone supposedly trained in such things, and I can empathize with teachers who have had similar experiences and thus recoil at the word *evaluation*. On the other hand, I have also been involved in team-teaching situations over a semester-long period of time when all of us decided in advance that we would be openly curious about one another's styles, ask one another questions constantly, compare notes and techniques, and actively experiment together to create new approaches to the subject matter in association with some of our students; they turned into some of the best teaching experiences I've ever had. We buttressed each other, drew strength from each other, and felt free to experiment, knowing that we were all in the soup together and we would sink or swim as one.

I trusted the evaluations and critiques of my techniques by those peers far more than those that resulted from one-time observations. Several very real weaknesses I knew I had I admitted from the outset, as did the others, and we worked on those weaknesses as a team—and in many cases fixed them. It can be a great way to teach, as long as those involved aren't too defensive or territorial.

Though I have never seen this done at a public school, I believe that a solid evaluation system could also be set up by a positive, concerned principal and set of department heads whereby students would evaluate their teachers much in the way that is now common on many college campuses. I am convinced that the vast majority of students would participate conscientiously and thoughtfully if the program is initiated in the right way. I know that's going to bring howls of protest from many of my peers, but I stand behind the idea anyway. If the program were explained to the students in groups by a sensitive principal, and the students knew the evaluations could not affect their grades and would have no bearing (at least for the first few years) on whether a teacher was retained or not, and knew instead that the real purpose was to help each teacher come to some clearer understanding of his or her strengths and weaknesses, I think it could be enormously helpful and informative. If a majority of students affirmed, for example, that a certain teacher constantly put them to sleep, or spent too much time on activities that had no relation to the subject matter, or failed to help them see the utility or worth of the material being studied, or was constantly preoccupied or grouchy; or, conversely, that a certain teacher was always willing to change approaches when it became obvious something wasn't working, or was always willing to work in small groups with students who were lost or confused, or was unfailingly fair or courteous, or was always willing to listen to the students' points of view and treat them responsibly, or managed through a number of activities (and students might be asked to list the most powerful or useful of these activities) to bring the subject to life and make its worth crystal clear—if any of this could happen, then the teachers themselves, department heads, and principals would have material they could really work with.

The objections to such an evaluation (students wouldn't take it seriously, students might not realize the worth of a course *now* that will prove to be valuable to them in several years, students will favor the easy teachers over the hard ones, etc.) just don't hold water, in my experience. On trips with students, I often ask them about their other teachers, and I have been amazed at their objectivity. I have frequently had students say, for example, "Some of the kids don't like her very much because she's tough, but most of them will tell you they think it's good for them and they're glad she *is* working us hard. We know we're getting something out of that course."

Likewise, I have sat down with an entire class that has just been taught for a semester by one of my staff members, and I have tape-recorded the reactions of the students to that class so that both I and the staff member (who is always allowed to listen to the tape) can find holes in the course content, or can locate strengths of the course and/or the teaching style that we want to preserve in future courses, and I have found the students to be unfailingly helpful and serious.

If I were a department head, and the rest of the school was reluctant to try it, I'd think I'd do it just within my department, leaving out those teachers who objected strenuously, and I'd continue doing it each semester until either all the teachers in my department had come around and were willing to participate, or until we discovered that it just wasn't working and couldn't be made to work, at least by us. I doubt that the latter would happen, and I suspect several other departments would soon follow our lead when they observed how positively the results were being utilized by us and how close the interchanges thus generated had brought us as a team.

It's all part of that elusive package in which students participate more and more openly and responsibly in the life of the school and actively help us structure it to serve them better. I've seen the difference it can make when students honestly believe we're pulling out all the stops to make our school open and responsive and *worth attending,* and I can tell you it's something to see.

Besides, we evaluate students daily. It's time they had the same opportunity.

Fifth, the best teachers decry the growing tendency to push reforms on school systems through unions that can mitigate against what they know to be a vital part of good teaching. Look at this excerpt from an article in *Time*, for example:

"Medford [High in Medford, Massachusetts] teachers . . . won a limit of three evening appearances at the school per year (two for parent-teacher open houses). They are only required to remain thirty minutes after school twice a week to help students. Any supervision of student activities [such as yearbook, etc.] costs Medford extra."[11]

I am just as aware as you of the inequities of our salary situation, and I can even be persuaded that organized action is sometimes necessary and justifiable in remedying those inequities. Well and good (though I must confess that teachers' strikes in general are anathema to me and I think there are better ways to get the job done). I can even go along with a teachers' union demanding that teachers only be *required* to remain after school twice a week, and so on. It's the next step at which I draw the line—a step that is almost always forthcoming once the train begins to roll and gather momentum, and that is signaled by a subtle shift in wording, to wit: "Hereafter, teachers may only remain thirty minutes after school twice a week to help students," or "Hereafter, teachers may *only* supervise student activities if they get paid extra for same."

Teachers who make a practice of being available to students after school every day (and I've known lots of them) suddenly find peers regarding them in the same category as strikebreakers. Because the school cannot come up with the money, and teachers are not allowed to step into the breech and volunteer, numerous student activities vanish. Much of the work I and my staff members do with students takes place after school hours and on weekends, as well as the work a number of our peers do willingly as part of their jobs. The best teachers I know feel a decent annual salary is part of their due, but beyond that, the number of minutes and hours they spend in the interest of doing a fine job is no one's business but their own, and they refuse to have such matters legislated on their behalf. I know how much energy I have, for example, and how many hours there are in a day, and I won't be told how I may or may not use that time and that energy that are mine.

Sixth, the best teachers, like their counterparts in such professions as the law and medicine and pharmacology, read and compare notes in the interest of improving themselves and their profession.

When I was learning how to teach, I took several courses in educational psychology and methods. As far as I can determine now, little that I studied in those courses was of real use. Propelled into my first teaching job, it was sink or swim.

Over the next few years, I developed my own approach to teaching in direct response to my experiences and observations, and it served me well. As I was asked to explain to other groups of teachers what I was doing, a rough umbrella philosophy began to emerge that encompassed easily the sorts of things I was doing with students that seemed to be working and provided a rough road map—a set of educational generalizations, if you will—that not only seemed to help others but also gave me clues as to how the new courses *Foxfire* began to offer as new staff members were added should be set up and structured. Questions and challenges emerged constantly from both my staff, my administration, parents, other teachers, and from within myself; and the philosophy was added to and honed and refined in light of new evidence and new experiments and increased former and current student input and increased confidence in the fact that all of us were somehow on the right track. After some ten or twelve years of tinkering, I began to allow myself to believe that we really had something *worth* sharing with others.

At about that point, due to the growing number of requests for information we were getting from other teachers, I decided to write this book. At the urging of a number of Foxfire's board members who were involved in education, and out of a desire both to check my observations against those of others and to locate the best existing books available for teachers, I began to read. I had kept up with many of the sixties and early seventies proponents of liberal education anyway and had read books like *The Way It Spozed To Be, Death at an Early Age, What Do I Do Monday?* and *The Lives of Children,* but what I wanted was the real heavyweights, the real philosophers—the Whiteheads and the Deweys and the Piagets—those names I remembered so dimly from some of my college courses.

One paragraph into *Experience and Education* by John Dewey and things began to crystallize. By the time I finished it, I was shaking my head in amazement. On every one of its less than a hundred pages, insights had leaped out into the air and I had found myself pounding the arm of my chair and saying, "That's *right,* damnit, that's *exactly* right. That's just the way it is." All those discoveries I thought I had made about education, Dewey had elucidated into complete clarity fifty years and more before. . . . And he showed me how incomplete my own philosophy still was.

I read more, and the same thing happened over and over, to my chagrin and awe.

There are some who say it is good that we never learn from the past. Failing to learn the lessons of the past demands that we constantly reinvent the wheel, and in fields like education, our arriving at some of those universal laws of learning independently weds us to them in a way that will never be the case when they are handed to us by others. They become "our" discoveries, nurtured and protected and proselytized by us, and so we apply them with a verve and a degree of commitment that we simply would not have had otherwise.

When I'm in certain moods, I can be persuaded by that argument. Having to reinvent the wheel—making old discoveries independently through our own observation—has a nice, confirming sound.

But most of the time I don't buy it. Not anymore. Not after having seen what is happening in and has happened to so many public schools. Not after having watched buildings full of bored and restless students all over this country. Not after having seen teachers in the infant stages of projects ignoring completely the experimentation that has already been done and fully documented about similar attempts around the country from which they could learn so much. Not after having seen hundreds and hundreds of teachers using methods *known* to be counterproductive. Not after having watched textbooks literally take over and dominate nearly every classroom in the land. Not after having experienced the growing flood tide of criticism against our public schools that we have all experienced in the last ten years.

In short, I don't buy the argument anymore because I don't think we can afford the luxury of dabbling. We have built too many of our classes on philosophical quicksand, and we are reaping the results.

Why didn't I hear what Dewey et al. were saying when I was first introduced to them at Cornell? Well, Dewey, for example, struck me as being unreadable. And he wasn't the only one. Thus I skipped most of the readings. The professor certainly was precious little help in deciphering them. All this was combined with the fact that the courses in which philosophy and methods were taught happened to be among the most boring courses I've ever been part of. Most of us skipped class frequently —and passed anyway. Added to this was the vital fact that we had no experience base by which to judge or which to *apply* those readings. We were taught, in short, precisely as we were later to teach using those deadly high school texts. My high school students had no experience through which those texts could come to life, and thus they remained gray and lifeless in their hands.

The fact that it took years of teaching myself before I could hear what Dewey was saying does not, however, forgive that philosophy teacher any more than it forgives the high school teacher who fails to make his courses relevant. As a student, I had *been taught* for some sixteen years, but not once was I helped to analyze exactly what the philosophers were saying in light of the experiences I and my classmates had already had. I had also done a semester's worth of practice teaching, but not once during that time or subsequently was I helped to see the experiences I was having in light of what the philosophers were saying.

Not once did that college teacher stop in midstream and say, "Now. Do you *really hear* what this man is saying? I'm not going any further until I'm sure you know what's going on here and how it relates to what you've been through already and will undoubtedly go through next year. Do you *hear* him? For the next five minutes I want you to think about your old elementary school. Don't talk. Just think. At the end of five minutes, we're going to do some *real* talking."

I could have been saved a lot of trouble. And what of all those classmates who began with me as first-year teachers and dropped out of the field almost immediately, realizing how little they actually knew about teaching and believing themselves to be completely alone?

The fact is some schools of education with which I am familiar are about as close to being worthless as I can imagine. The very way their professors teach contradicts everything we know about the forceful acquisition of knowledge. Most of them, quite simply, should not be allowed to graduate teachers at the present time. And given the size of the job ahead of us, they should not be allowed to do so until education has been turned into one of the most rigorous, demanding, creative and respected majors on campus.

But that's another story.

After making the humbling discovery that not a single blessed one of my convictions about education was unique or new (only the precise *ways* in which I had applied some very old and universal truths—and not even a large number of those were radically different from much that had gone before), I began to talk to other teachers about the reading they had done in the field and found that virtually none of my colleagues was doing any *real* reading at all. Some of them affirmed that they scanned a teachers' journal of some sort or another on occasion, but virtually none ever went beyond that. Most admitted they had not read any educational philosophy since college, their reasons ranging from "I never could understand what any of those guys were saying then and I'm not about to try it again now" to "Look, I read those guys once. But every one of them drew his conclusions from work either in a free or an alternative school or an experimental lab–type elementary school, and none of them could imagine what I face on a day-to-day basis."

True, much of the research was done under conditions most public school teachers are not fortunate enough to have. But the best teachers read them anyway. They return to the Deweys and the Piagets the way Sierra Club members return to Thoreau, for they know from their own experience that those philosophers can bring meaning and breadth and light to the darkness of their individual struggles. They know these men and women are our allies and our mentors; and they know, through them, that they are not alone in their efforts to make schools work, but that they are merely new entries in a historic and honored thrust through time that they are helping to perpetuate and keep alive—a movement that gives them guidance, that fuels their fires, that gives them the patience that can only come when one sees oneself as being squarely in the mainstream of a long, continuing struggle that must never cease.

And they know, through their reading and their experiences, the bedrock of educational knowledge on which they must continue to build. They know, through their reading and their experience, the larger goals of education that must be served by everything we do with students. And knowing those goals keeps them focused in a way that their colleagues who drift like mindless cattle through the feed stores of one educational conference after another, and one stack of chattering journals after another, will never know until they are imbued with that guiding philosophy and its attendant goals. How else traverse the roaring Niagara Falls of information and projects and ideas and gimmicks and ads that threatens to wash us all away except we close our classroom doors determined to ignore it all?

The teachers that frighten me most say, "I don't read books like *Experience and Education*. They have nothing to say to me."

They couldn't be more wrong.

They Know How to Avoid Teacher Burnout

Finally, the great teachers I know are masters at avoiding a condition that has become widely known as teacher burnout. They do this in several ways.

First, they build relationships among their peers, fighting isolation with as much strength as they can muster, knowing that such networks are their life-support systems as well as their sources for new ideas and input. They are on softball teams together. They congratulate each other on accomplishments both small and large. They give each other silly presents. They gang up together to deal with the problems that particularly troublesome students pose. They trade tricks and strategies. They sometimes grade papers collaboratively, a science teacher grading a set of term papers for scientific content and a friend in the English department grading them for grammar. I'll never forget being invited to join an already well established underground of like-minded teachers during my semester of practice teaching. We were all in a bowling league together and bowled weekly. We also stumbled across a nearby Holiday Inn that offered a spectacular Friday happy hour, complete with free shrimp and oysters, which we began to patronize regularly. Each Friday an eighth-grader would appear at my classroom door with a note from the math teacher across the hall asking cryptically if I planned to attend the "teacher seminar" that afternoon. I'd initial the note in the affirmative, and the (presumably) unsuspecting eighth-grader would then take it to the other teachers in our clan. Thus alerted, we would finish the day with a flourish of good humor and regroup at that local den of iniquity to initiate the weekend with proper style and panache. Those activities dissolved my sense of being stranded without support in Binghamton and helped me get through a difficult time. In fact, I still remember that year as a definite high point, and I suspect that old gang is still together somewhere, carrying on in its inimitable and unflappable style, and I suspect they're still some of the finest public school teachers around.

Second, they tend to be involved in the community from which their students are drawn in ways other than teaching. They go to community meetings, they know numbers of parents on a personal basis, they have numerous friendships outside the teaching profession. Sometimes they work at completely different types of jobs during vacations and summers: as carpenters, salespersons, manual laborers, gas station attendants, photographers, fashion designers, horse trainers. Such relationships, by getting their minds off teaching, tend to give them a balance and stability that many teachers lack. They become somehow more "normal" in a funny way. They find other networks of support and friendship. They have balance. In an important way, these relationships not only help them cope with the sometimes unreal demands of teaching and give them a welcome respite but also go a long way toward helping them avert the adoption of the sometimes unreal and artificial air some lifetime teachers have about them. I have met veterans of elementary school positions, for example, who talk to me and exclaim over me as if I were a third-grader. And I have watched high school teachers, separated from the outside world and unbalanced by virtue of that separation, adopt absolutely stilted and artificial stances and behaviors when dealing with students and peers—stances and behaviors most people would never use in *real* situations in out-of-school contexts. They become mysteriously warped.

Third, they recognize that adults are not finished products. They welcome being in situations in which they can continue learning and growing, either as teachers or not; and they enjoy the sensation of mental exercise and the surprise and amazement that always come as one masters a new skill or becomes acquainted with a new philosophy or idea. It is in this role that the best often have so much fun with their own students, for together, they trek out into the unknown, exclaiming together over what they find, and youth and vigor are always in the eyes and smiles of such adults.

One of the best teacher-renewal centers I know about takes teachers into the out-of-doors and places them before obstacles that most feel they can never master—climbing a sheer rock cliff, for example, after years of being inside the classroom. Most balk, saying, "I'm sorry, I just can't do that; that's out of my league." After a week, with the help of supportive instruction, they've all done it successfully. Even the least talented and most insecure finds himself or herself, panting, at the top, surrounded by applauding peers.

Then the lesson is driven home: "One, never forget the sensation you had of foreboding and apprehension and failure as you faced this cliff; remember what it felt like. And remember that many of the students in your classes feel that way every day. Two, remember the sensation you now have of success, and accomplishment, and of a whole new realm of activity and learning and experience that has just been opened for you. You can still learn. You can still experience the exhilaration of success. You can still become as excited as a child at the prospect of the new horizons before you. Don't forget that. Continue to make it happen both for yourself and for your students, for therein is a fountainhead of renewal and energy that you must continue to tap."

In the face of such affirming experiences, the normal teacher in-service meetings and certificate-renewal courses pale as deadening burdens. The missing ingredients? The bolstering of self-esteem and pride, and the excitement of future growth and accomplishment. In their place is substituted a gray mush without texture or flavor that squats in the stomach like dead weight.

Fourth, they have become skillful at the art of sharing responsibilities with others to reduce their work loads and increase their effectiveness. They see a new class of thirty-seven youngsters, for example, not as thirty-seven albatrosses but as thirty-seven potential teachers. I haven't gotten as good at this as I hope to become someday, and consequently I don't regard myself yet as one of these master teachers, but I have had enough experience to know that much of what I teach quarter after quarter, from use of equipment to printing photos and transcribing tapes to recognizing and dealing with comma splices and misspellings, can be shifted onto the shoulders of students who can teach such skills at least as competently as I. Breaking the class up into small "needs" groups frees me completely both to wander among the groups giving input and encouragement and to plan new activities and exercises that will bring all those students to awarenesses that absolutely transcend the ordinary. They acquire the tools of the trade from themselves. I provide what I'm more excited by (and consequently better at) providing: the means and strategies by which all those tools and skills come together in harmonies none of us anticipated previously. I take them beyond themselves—beyond myself—and beyond the ordinary into the unexpected. As a result, I find myself constantly refueled.

Fifth, in balance, they are having enough fun with what they're doing that the temporary setbacks and disappointments and frustrations are seen in proper prospective—combined with the balance a solid relationship with the world outside the school can give. Again, I cannot lay claim to being a master teacher, but I can lay claim to the fact that after years of teaching, I still relish nothing more right now than starting a new school year. My work with education and with Foxfire keeps me so excited that I cannot imagine living any other way. For a time, I became pretty depressed not only about the way things were going in my own school, with students being kicked out and bounced around, but also about education in general. As always, contact with the real world outside, and the fact that our project was so much a part of that world, pulled me through. As I said in a letter to Howard of May 26, 1973:

[There are pressures here that are relentless.] It's a genuine bitch all around; but then you run into a guy like Vince who is a bartender on the Red Concourse in the St. Louis airport. He and the boys there spent a late, slow morning measuring the distance from the end of the Red Concourse to the end of the Blue Concourse, and found it to be exactly one measured mile. They did it with a baggage tractor, after which time Vince set up the house. A great moment in airport history. And when he tells the story, his eyes light up and you're consumed by his enthusiasm and everything else drains away and the world takes on a human perspective once again. Things are back in control.

I have heard terrifying stories of men who took the weight of the world on their shoulders and worried personally about every rumble and every fart the globe gave off. And they wound up killing themselves because they had no way to influence those happenings—no way to get a handle on them. They just wound up choking to death on their own frustration and their own very real grief for the world. And yet things went on. The sun came up again the next day. A new crisis supplanted the old. Nothing changed as everything continued to change.

I have gotten older. I find myself more and more drawn to a piece of land on which I am building a log house and growing a fine garden. My peas are now up almost two and a half feet in the air, and blooming like crazy. When kids and I are out there working, digging in the ground or nailing in a new window, everything falls away and there is just us and the land and a house. Everything somehow makes sense there. That, and *Foxfire*. Those things in my life remain honest, and allow me to deal honestly, as a human being, with my kids.

That was true in 1973, and it is no less true for me today.

27

How Do We Measure Up?

For years I have been listening to my students, my colleagues, and my friends describe their favorite teachers as well as those who seemingly had no measurable impact or influence whatsoever. I try to integrate this data into my own teaching, combine it with my own hunches, and then double-check myself as each school year passes, constantly weighing the utility and success or failure of lessons, projects, and various kinds of interactions with my kids.

Now I'll be the first to admit that all this inquiry and testing was never as consistent or as calculated as it might have been. It was never systematized or computerized or codified in the way a scientist, for example, might like. There were numerous times when I simply tried something just for the hell of it, or imposed a lesson or project on my students knowing in advance that only a minority of them would get anything out of it. In the heat of battle, as it were, or numbed by fatigue, or distracted by an event outside my classroom, or preoccupied by pressures other than the business at hand, or caught in the web of some strange mood or another, often I just taught, not really evaluating the quality of the activity of the day. I just did it to get through it. Period. And all that still happens to me today.

You know and I know that none of us will *ever* get to the point at which every lesson pushes all the right buttons with every one of those thirty disparate individuals in each of our classes. We aren't superhuman. And even knowing how to teach well is no guarantee that we will *do* so. Knowing in advance that certain methods don't work well is no guarantee that we will abandon those methods, any more than knowing that smoking is harmful to one's health causes all smokers to throw away their cigarettes forever. We are human beings, after all. That's the reason, of course, that the elusive seven cities of gold of the curriculum specialists is "teacher proof" learning materials (and if there were ever a phrase I've come to despise . . .)

But closing the gap between theory and practice is something lots of us strive for. We want to be better teachers, and so we listen and test and probe and experiment, and scratch and claw our way along toward that bottled water stand we see beckoning to us from the horizons of our individual deserts, hoping it's not a mirage.

How close does any average group of teachers in the real world come to matching that description? Hard to tell. There ought to be fairly systematic ways to get some indication, however.

While I was in Athens, the local Cooperative Educational Services group (Pioneer CESA) found out I was in town and invited me to speak to several groups of local teachers for whom they were conducting workshops. I jumped at the chance, for it gave me the opportunity to get away from the enforced isolation of my apartment and back into face-to-face contact with some living peers. It also presented me with the chance—if I could develop some sort of instrument—to see whether there was any "fit" between a group of working teachers and my list of qualities.

For several days, I worked to develop a questionnaire. When it was finished, it contained forty-one mostly multiple choice items. Never having taken a course in the fine art of developing this kind of testing instrument, I knew it was flawed, but I had made a conscious attempt to key many of the items to each other to make it as revealing as I could. A multiple choice item concerning the teaching techniques the respondent most often used, for example, was keyed with one several pages later in which the respondent was asked to check those teaching techniques that, looking back, had proved to have been the most memorable when he or she was a secondary school student. Pretty simple stuff, but I thought it might work.

The group with which I first tried it was made up of some twenty-five public middle and high school teachers from the Athens area. They seemed enthusiastic about helping me with this book and agreed to fill out the questionnaire. After about fifteen minutes, when they had finished, I showed them some slides I had brought along that illustrated our work in Rabun County.

When I got home that night, I was stunned by the results. The first teacher, for example, had seven years' experience as a public middle school social studies teacher. She considered herself "usually well pre-pared," "very popular," and "respected"; and she subscribed to and claimed she regularly read *Reading Teacher, Learning,* and *Instructor.* Later, however, she admitted that she did not try new teaching techniques since her subject allowed little "flexibility of approach," and she didn't have "enough time to develop new techniques and approaches," and she was "a little nervous about tinkering with the formula," these three being categories I provided that she checked.

She admitted to using texts in her course, rated them "poor," and when asked what she does when the students hate the text, wrote in the blank provided, "Make them use it anyway." She admitted that nearly 90 percent of her class activities were based closely on the text, even though, later, when asked to check off the activities that had been most useful and memorable to her when she was a student, she checked "lectures not based on text material," "class discussions," "laboratory periods," and "field trips."

When asked how often she was able to give her students individual personal attention, she checked "not very often/once a month," yet when asked how important that attention was, she checked "pretty important." When asked how well she knew her students personally, she checked "I know almost nothing of them other than what I've learned in class." When asked how important it was to know them well, she checked "It's essential."

She revealed her belief that none of her college education courses had been of any use to her, and when asked whether she had read any educa-tional philosophy since college, she checked "None."

Finally, on the question dealing with the possibility of finding applica-tions for her subject matter (social studies) in the outside world, she checked "Very difficult" and "I'm not sure how to do it."

I went through the rest, and a similar pattern emerged. A twenty-year teacher of math, for instance, who, when asked whether she tried new techniques, checked the category "My subject is such that there's not much room for flexibility of approach," said "It's essential" that we know our students well, but admitted "I know a few of them well"; character-ized her peers as "talented" but "burned out," "overwhelmed," and "isolated from each other"; and of the philosopher whose work she most agreed with (Piaget), said, "I am not able to apply [his philosophy] in the present situation"; and of the applicability of her course (math) to the outside world, checked "very difficult" and "I'm not sure how to do it."

An eight-year teacher of economics, law, psychology, and civics admit-ted she subscribed to no professional journals, only "occasionally" tried new techniques, checked "vital" when asked how important it was to give students individual attention, and "almost never" for the frequency with which she did it; and, when asked how often she applied her courses to the world outside the classroom, checked, "I don't do it very often."

An eight-year veteran of the language arts field, on the question concerning the applicability of the course to the community outside the classroom, circled the choice, "My course really doesn't apply to the outside world."

The responses overall were so completely contrary to what I would have expected from good teachers—professionals—that I wasn't sure how to react. Either none of these teachers was good, or they were good teachers whose particular situations made it impossible for them to teach as they knew they should, or my definition of *good* was badly flawed or too idealistic, or I had asked the questions incorrectly and the teachers had misunderstood them. Something.

As a first step, I got a friend in evaluation at the University of Georgia to critique the language I had used in the questionnaire and help me sharpen it as well as restructure some of the questions completely and add new ones.

Next, I began to take the revised questionnaire with me on speaking engagements around the country, giving it to teachers in workshops when the opportunity arose. In each case, they filled it out before I spoke so that nothing I would say about education could prejudice the results. In each case, I guaranteed anonymity, explained how the results would be used, and requested complete honesty.

I gave the questionnaire to hundreds of teachers over a six-month period. Then I divided the finished ones into piles, putting those from elementary teachers in one pile, college teachers in another, and so on. For purposes of this book, geared as it is to teachers of grades seven through twelve, I tabulated ninety-three from middle and high schools from four different states: Oklahoma, Alabama, Pennsylvania, and Tennessee. Seventy-three percent were teachers of English.

This time the results were more encouraging, though they still revealed what I would consider professional weaknesses. The questionnaires are most revealing when each is studied individually, giving the questions that are keyed to each other a chance to play off each other and paint a portrait of the respondent, and they would be even more revealing if the responses were computer coded so that one could see immediately if there were any statistical differences among history and math and English teachers, for example, or any statistically significant correlations in the way those who answered yes to one question then answered certain other questions. That is a project for another day, however, and with a much larger sampling. For this, and for now, what I wanted was some general trends, some indications of the state of things. And that's what I got.

In general, these secondary school teachers, randomly selected, claim to know their subject matter well—well enough to teach it without a text —but only a minority (11 percent) actively hook it up to the outside world; the methodology most of them employ has at its core the utilization of texts and lectures, despite the fact most do not hold the quality of the texts in high regard, and only 12 percent remembered their use as being effective when they were in school, and that most remembered from their own student days other types of methodology as being more effective. Most (85 percent) feel it is necessary to know their students as individuals, as well as to know the communities from which those students come, but most (62 percent) are unable to accomplish that. Most (91 percent) affirm the importance of individual attention for their students, but only a few (25 percent) manage to give their students that attention regularly. Most (61 percent) view their students as likable and cooperative, but few (28 percent) see them as having much in the way of talent or potential or enthusiasm. Since classroom activities that involve students around common goals that are perceived by all as worthwhile are not high on the list of teaching techniques, discipline and control are accomplished by most through such tactics as moving disruptive students to different seats (61 percent) or sending them to the administration. And most claim to stay abreast of new developments in the field and subscribe to professional journals and read books, but the evidence would indicate that little reading is actually taking place (or that the reading that is taking place is absolutely unmemorable), and certainly no commonly perceived leader in the field of education emerges at all. When asked to list favorite books, or books read recently about education, for example, only 29 percent listed any books at all. Those teachers listed a *total* of thirty-seven books, only two of which were listed by two separate teachers (Glasser's *School Without Failure* and Holt's *Why Children Fail*).

Compared with the list of ideal qualities I drew up several pages back, this sampling of teachers would appear to fall somewhat short. Is the list, then, flawed?

Well, I will admit that it *is* possible to do a competent job without reading the work of peers and mentors and without knowing the students individually and giving them individual attention, and without cranking up numerous activities and projects to supplement the text, and so forth. We *can* teach by ignoring many of the admonitions of that list. We can push on through the prescribed material and get most of our students successfully through the tests. We *can* do it. The *best* of us can even make the experience memorable for them through the force of our personalities and through our conviction and eloquence.

My concern, however, is for the quality of the experience the students have in the process at the hands of most of us, and for the long-lasting utility of the material covered (if it doesn't continue to inform and influence their lives long after they've left us, why bother?).

I continue to stand behind the list of ideals. I regard it as exactly that— ideals to which I aspire, but the accomplishment of which I never quite reach. But I never stop thinking about how to do the job better. I never stop asking questions of myself, my students, and my peers. I *do* reread Dewey and others, searching for clues and reminding myself that I still have a ways to go before I can regard myself as the teacher I'd like to be. I never stop caring. And though, in the end, I may be accused of many things, I hope I'll never be accused of simply stopping in my tracks and letting a predictable routine take over the life of my classroom.

Many of you feel the same way. I know you do. I meet you all the time, and I know I'm just as hard on you in this book as I am on myself—no harder—and just as unforgiving. But in our defense, and in conclusion, let me say that I also know that the burden for accomplishing these goals —for shooting for the ideals—had better not rest on our shoulders alone, because alone, we'll never do it.

To all those out there, for a moment, who aren't in our classrooms every day—parents, administrators, college professors, state legislators, school board members, and all the rest:

You like the sound of that list of ideals? Great. You applaud, for example, the ideal of giving each student quality attention? Fine. But know here and now that it will never be accomplished as long as you give us 135 to 180 students a day to deal with. Know that it cannot be done under present conditions, and stop shouting at us. We can acknowledge the importance of that goal (as did the teachers who answered my questionnaire), but we can only aspire to it—and never reach it—under present conditions.

You applaud our putting the texts into proper perspective and stretching all our students in important ways? Fine. So do I. But same as above.

You want professional teachers—teachers who make the profession their lives and never stop learning and never stop trying to do the job better? Fine. But you should be aware of some dangerous trends that have developed under your noses. When asked how they normally get their rewards, take note of the fact that the lowest response of all on the questionnaire (9 percent) was accorded to "Teaching gives me a certain status in the community that is a reward." Lower even than "I don't get many. It's the nature of the job. I've learned not to expect many." And when asked the kinds of rewards they *should* be able to expect, the highest response by far (58 percent) was given to "The community should hold teachers in much higher esteem."

And you should be aware of how little *quality* help we get in learning how to do the job better. Concerning the utility of college courses, the lowest response of all (9 percent) was given to "They really helped me with teaching strategies." All the others said the college courses didn't help at all. Most of us start from a position of basic ignorance and fly by the seats of our pants, hoping we can figure out how to teach in the process, and your toothless in-service sessions and the inane courses you make us take to remain certified just don't help much on the front lines.

And you should be aware of the fact that we all know now how inadequate the salaries are that you pay us for the work you expect us to do. We see the figures every day. We look at the 1983–84 Annual Edition of the

NEA's *Today's Education,* and we hear the editors when they say, on page 65, "Yeah, you're right: if college graduates chose their professions on the basis of salary alone, there wouldn't be any teachers. Well, maybe two or three." And we see the chart of average starting salaries on the same page, with education the lowest at $13,358, topped by accounting (at $18,233), computer science (at $24,485), and chemical engineering (at $27,025). Worse, I know that my students who don't even finish high school (much less college) can go to work in many jobs (the postal service, for example, or driving a city bus for MARTA in Atlanta) and start off at far more than $13,358. We know these things, and when stacked against the esteem with which we are regarded by our communities, I can tell you that you have a serious problem.

You want us to get those state and national test scores up? Fine. But be aware of one final thing. Most of what those instruments test is material that students can learn by rote and that we can cram down their throats through constant, unrelenting repetition. It's not that tough to do, and we'll make lots of workbook and computer software manufacturers wealthy in the process. The test scores will go up. But don't be deceived into thinking that any real learning has taken place. What has happened is that more students have acquired—perhaps—greater proficiency in some basic skills. That's all to the good, but those basic skills should be just a prelude to the education that *should* be taking place. When the test scores go up, and you relax your guard and sit back, know that you have settled for far less than our students deserve and for far less than our mission demands—if our mission, in fact, is *education.*

And if you want quality education, you'd better figure out a way to get us some relief and some competent help.

28

The Basic Skills, and . . . ?
What Are the Goals for Our Students?

I have thoroughly tried school-keeping, and found that my expenses were in proportion, or rather out of proportion, to my income, for I was obliged to dress and train, not to say think and believe, accordingly, and I lost my time into the bargain. As I did not teach for the good of my fellow-men, but simply for a livelihood, this was a failure.

Henry David Thoreau *(Walden)*

What I have concentrated on so far in Part II is us as teachers and what happens inside our classrooms when we close those doors between us and the hall. We carry certain burdens as individuals, and we have certain powers and opportunities, as individuals, that deserve special attention. As individuals, we can create oases of learning and growth even within schools that by almost any yardstick would be judged to be less than ideal.

Conversely, within the most ideal schools, as individuals, we can turn our own classrooms into teenagers' visions of hell.

Or we can even survive for a certain period of time, independent and alone, concentrating solely on ourselves and our students; accepting, but not being much influenced by, the daily intrusions into our lives from the larger whole. We do the required paperwork, and we listen to the intercom announcements; we silently endure the faculty meetings, and we stand in the halls as the classes change; and then we close our doors and get on with the business at hand, putting the irritations out of our minds. I have personally known teachers who survived this way for all the years I knew them. They defied Donne's famous quotation. They passed between the lives of the rest of us like ghosts, silent and eerie and unperturbed; cordial, but very nearly invisible. The rest of us wondered about them. But not much.

For many of the rest of us, however, if we genuinely care about our work, there usually comes a moment in time when we leave our classrooms mentally to think seriously about that larger whole, its overarching mission, and our place within that mission. Despite some inevitable overlap, then, between this chapter and the previous ones in Part II, I think it's important to talk about that larger whole: the purposes of our public schools.

All of us think about this to some extent, but too many of us think about it only in vague, mist-enshrouded, peripheral ways. Our principals may remind us of our larger goals at the first teachers' meeting of the year, or we may blurt out a set of halfhearted or ill-formed generalities when some parent or former college roommate asks a question like, "How come you went into teaching anyway?" But for most of us, as long as the specific content of our own courses occupies the majority of the space inside our brains set aside for occupational matters, our focus remains skewed and we run the risk of losing sight of what it is we as a group are supposed to be doing—and what larger ends our courses are supposed to serve. To lose sight of these ends can put us in a situation analogous to that of Mark Twain's rednecks who fought on with grim determination despite the fact that they had all forgotten what started the feud in the first place.

To be aware of these goals, though—constantly aware of them—can be a liberating and informing and crucial experience. Reconnected to the whole, I as an English teacher become just as concerned about my students' skills in math as I am about their communication skills, and I find myself teaching math and English together. Reconnected to the whole, I become a member of the English department, and those of us in that department who have had a similar moment of awakening find ourselves working as a team to bring all our talents to bear collectively for the benefit of all our students. Just as we try to stimulate activities in our classrooms that we hope will make the students feel part of something bigger than themselves, so, too, we become part of something bigger, something that transcends our individual daily agendas. Concerned as a group about the fact that we're making little progress as individuals on certain problems our students are having with grammar and mechanics, for example, not only do we all redouble our efforts to attack those problems collectively and simultaneously (as we have done in our school), but we also send out an SOS in the form of an appeal in a teachers' meeting and a Dittoed memo to all the other teachers in the school (as we have also done). Not all teachers respond, of course, but some do, knowing that we'll respond in kind to their requests, and suddenly a biology teacher and a math teacher are telling their students they can't get away with comma splices on biology or math term papers. The network grows, and when the principal, in another teachers' meeting, says, "Look, I was really concerned the other day to find that many of our students don't know what the county seat of this county is, or who runs the county, or how those people even got into those offices," he finds a ready audience, and the network takes it from there.

Soon pieces of subject matter that were blasted into separate little compartments by some curricular convulsion eons ago are coming together again. There is a strange mood—an unfamiliar camaraderie—infusing our lives. Things feel better somehow.

Look, I don't want to get carried away here and take this too far. Things like this happen, but only in schools in which a number of people are aware of and buy into the overarching goals of the institution for which they work. Thus I think those goals warrant review.

First, let me set the scene. According to the 1983–84 edition of *Today's Education*, the NEA journal, during the 1982–83 school year, there were 39,707,940 students enrolled in our public schools (p. 63). In 1980, 25,300 of those schools were public junior and senior high schools, checking in with nearly 17,000,000 students and more than a million teachers and administrators. The cost to keep this vast industry functioning is over $200 billion a year, with annual per-pupil expenditures ranging from a high of $6,301 in Alaska to a low of $1,546 in Alabama (*Today's Education*, p. 67). If you glance at some of the figures on page 74 of that same issue, you'll find that in two school districts, needed repairs and renovations to their buildings *alone* could account for nearly $1 billion worth of that total, with New York City estimating $680 million needed and Los Angeles estimating $315.5 million. That's a lot of money, granted, but it helps to remember that the cost of education is not an expense but an investment, people being this nation's most precious resource and so forth. (And if you don't believe that and you're a teacher, you're sure enough in the wrong occupation.)

There are lots of reasons I get caught up in the importance of these figures, and I'm not going to list them all, but I am going to mention one. Students acquire knowledge, skills, attitudes, and values from many sources. The family, obviously, is the premier source, followed, though

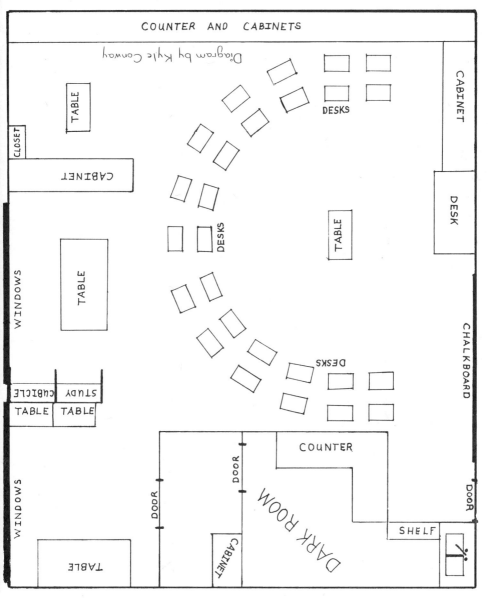

Room F-201—my classroom.

Just inside the door stands a Revolutionary War soldier, a near life-size piece of folk art, and one of a pair we now own that was carved by our late friend C. P. Ligon. Both have been exhibited in the Library of Congress. The second soldier, other examples of folk art, quilts, tools, and artifacts dominate every wall and every counter in the room, creating a purposeful mosaic of life and color.

WEEK FOUR

Composition: describe a person

	# development outlined	individ. grammar chart	class grammar sheet	good sentences noted	good papers read	reinforcement/skills
PRIMARY CBE						
– write neatly, accurately, legibly	X					X
– organize thoughts, details, ideas – logic		X			X	X
– control organizational pattern – thesis, central idea	X				X	X
– maintain unity & coherence in org. pattern	X				X	X
– select style, tone, diction for audience	X			X	X	X
– distinguish among feelings/opinions & facts	X			X	X	
– support opinions with logic, evidence, facts	X			X	X	X
ALLIED CBE						
– correct spelling, punctuation, & capitalization		X	X			X
– use basic English sentence patterns		X	X			X
– use standard English usage forms/agr. etc.		X	X			X
– paragraph structure	X					X

ACTIVITIES:

	Artifacts	process negatives	describing a person:	technique (+example)	rationale	exercise w/classmates	prepare for interview	set up class project	first interview	Composition	grammar sheets/charts	Offal list
CONTENT												
– some aspect of culture	X							X	X			
– history of county and/or region									X			
– government/politics of county and/or region									X			
– changes in county and/or region									X			
– what affects changes in region and/or county									X			
– goals/structure of Foxfire								X	X			
– specific community linkages/illustrations	X							X	X			
– skills useful outside class in real world	X	?						X	X			
METHODOLOGY												
– Lecture with class notes												
– discussion – lists on board – class notes					X	X		X			X	X
– demonstration alone or with students	X				X							
– individual work					X					X	X	
– small group work		X				X	X					
– class conducts activity on its own							X					
– peer teaching												
– chaos/break/fun					X	X						
– student evaluation and reflection								X				
– conscious attempt to build intrinsic motivation				X				X				
® culture, use of cameras, t.r.s	X	X					X	X				
OTHER CBE												
Speaking: phrase questions to obtain information							X		X			

A sample chart from the grammar/composition course (Foxfire I) described in this book. I do this weekly summary as a supplement to my lesson plans so that I can see at a glance whether or not I have varied the content and methodology sufficiently to keep the class fast-paced and active. This particular week was dominated by the first in-class interview and a composition in which the students were asked to describe the visitor.

Sometimes the person interviewed in class is a member of the school's faculty or support staff, like Jack Prince (top left), who was raised on a mountain farm near Fontana Dam in North Carolina. More often it is one or two of the community resource people with whom we have developed a longstanding friendship, or a grandparent of one of the students in the class whom we are meeting for the first time. Buck Carver (bottom left and facing page) has been a favorite for years, and often the thank-you note to him from the students generates another thank you in return.

You couldn't have been nicer—
You couldn't have been more thoughtful—
You couldn't have made me happier!

Thanks Again!

"Thanks a Million"
Forever your friend, Short "Buck"

Please make me Happy again, just as soon as you think that you can stand my presence for awhile

Sometimes a contact shows the students how to make something (in this case Harry Brown demonstrating how to bottom a chair with corn shucks) and the interview takes place on the school grounds instead of in the classroom.

In other cases the tables are turned, the students and I being interviewed by newspaper and television reporters. In these cases, the reporters simply become part of the class, which gives the students the chance to observe professionals at work and ask them questions about their techniques when the formal interview is finished.

Small group work with peer teachers is a regular feature of the grammar/composition course, with students breaking up into groups to do everything from learning how to load, unload, and operate a single lens reflex camera (left), transcribe tapes (below), use the dark room, to finally producing a publishable product.

BRUCE ROBERTS, *SOUTHERN LIVING*

A group of students visits a log home being restored by Foxfire, decides which architectural details to document, measures those details, and then turns their field notes into diagrams drawn in class for an issue of *Foxfire* devoted to the history of the building.

Students come to realize that photography is as important a means of communication as the written word, and even the work of young people who have never taken photographs before begins to reveal their struggles with the medium as they work to find the perfect portrait or the most expressive camera angle or the most forceful double exposure. Some of their photographs wind up on the covers of our books.

Even as beginners in our program, students write articles as a group for the local newspaper or help me conduct workshops for students and teachers in other schools. For part of each of these workshops, I stand aside and let the students face groups of teachers or students by themselves.

A Vote For David L. Mize
Coroner
Rabun County
August 5, 1980
Democratic Primary
Appriciated!

Qualified!

A constant feature of the grammar/composition course is the weekly theme. To help impress upon students the need for attention to grammar, I continue to build a collection of examples of mistakes made by others outside the classroom, asking the students as I show them examples, "How do these make the people responsible look?"

CARVERS CHAPLE BAPTIST CHURCH

ROAD CONSTRUNCTION 500 FT

LITERARY EVENTS BANQENT

In some cases, the examples are pretty embarrassing—the cover of the program reproduced here, for instance, that was printed for one of our school's annual events, a celebration of student competence in language-arts-related activities. In attendance at the banquet, along with the students, were parents, school administrators, and the members of our school board.

Comp 1

This is a good start. You have covered many of the points we made in class, but several important ones are missing. You'll see what they are in the class discussion —

B−/78

8

G22

Al Edwards

In Foxfire, we go on interviews with people throughout the community. On these interviews we need a way of recording what was said in the interview. Few people can write or even type as fast as someone talks, so an alternate method is need-ed. [So] (*Therefore*) we use tape-recorders.] This (*fragment*) enables the interview to go smoothly without having to stop the interview (*sp*) so you (*We*) can write everything down.

For a tape recorder you need tapes. These (tapes) should be a quality brand (Sony, Maxell, TDK etc.). Also (it) (*agr*) should be a C60s, which is (*are*) a sixty-minute cassettes. Nothing (*shorter than?*) below a sixty-minute tape should be used because you cannot get a whole interview on a thirty-minute tape. Also, nothing longer than a sixty-minute should be used because the tape tends to be thinner so (*that*) more tape can fit in the cassette.

A quality recorder should be

The weekly compositions receive one grade for content and one for grammar. Students can rewrite them as often as they wish. Composition topics generally flow from classroom activities, giving multiple opportunities for reinforcement. The first theme, for example, is usually about the use of the tape recorder.

1. (And) transcribing can give you alot of time to yourself.

2. If we (didn't) take a tape recorder, we would probably forget (alot) of the information.

3. There is no way to write down every thing a person says

4. Do not move the tape recorder at any time. Do not block the microphone.

5. The reason Foxfire uses tape recorders for (there) interviews. Because?

6. (Don't) move the recorder around (to) much.

7. It would be wise to take along a good tape recorder that you also know how to use. This is an absolute must.

8. Good tapes (is) another thing you need.

9. Keep the tape recorder still. (Don't) move it around, hit on it, etc.

10. (And) the last (2) things to remember (is) make sure....

11. (Don't) have them (to) far away.

12. (And) also point the microphone toward the person that is talking.

13. The good thing about the tape recorders (are) that....

14. Things that you should be careful about (is) never drop it, throw it around, or bang on it.

15. During the interview, check the tape and turn it over when (it's) finished. Then continue the interview.

16. (And) with a tape recorder you get the flow or magic of what the person is saying.

17. Good equipment is the most important thing. If (you've) got (an) old beatup recorder and sorry tape there ain't no need in even going.

18. Always be careful with your equipment. Don't be tossing it back and forth to each other and throwing it around. Take a little pride in it.

19. Always (know) how the particular recorder works.

20. (So) when you want to transcribe the tape all the words will be clear.

Good sentence:

   When using the equipment, be careful not to force any unwilling mechanism.

Each theme is returned accompanied by a grammar sheet made up of sentences from student papers that contain errors I want to see eliminated from their writing. Students correct the grammar sheets as we go over them in class.

Joseph

Nice statements from the "Beam" composition. Good work!

1. The hardest times were around Christmas because of all of the dancing
and the snow on the roof. It was very hard to hold up when the roof was
full of snow and the house was rattling from all of the dancing.

2. I was so depressed because I had not been cut yet. All my friends
had made something out of themselves, and me....

3. The furniture in the room was made out of my grandma. She almost had
a heart attack when they cut her feet off.

4. As I awoke, I saw the sun sneaking across the old injun trail atop
the centuries-old mountain. Then I heard the moans and groans of a horse-
pulled sled as it approached my standing site.... Then I took a terrible
plunge onto my ancestors' grounds.

5. Now I'm just here in this old building with nothing better to do than
talk to you. But now that's over and I'm going back to sleep. I'm awful
tired. It's not easy being a log!

6. The pine beam into which I was fitted was one of the Ranskins - the
trees that our family had been feuding with for years.... Everyone who
came into the room was usually happy although Ma and Pa often fussed about
something called "hard times." Son got older and changed his name to
Tommy. When Baby got older, he changed his name to Bill.

7. I have scars all over my beautiful form from these daily spats. What
once used to be beautiful to look at now looks like garbage. If my family
saw me now, they would hang their limbs in shame.

8. When he saw the bear, he raised one end of the stick to his shoulder
and a tremendous roar issued forth.... Several of my pine brothers had
already been rendered horizontal. That black fellow thought his ax was
a really nifty tool until I started to fall at which time I dropped a dead
branch on his head and knocked him out.

9. I started out as an acorn. That much I know because I am an oak tree.
... The valley I grew to saplinghood in was full of animals and there
were always birds and squirrels climbing and resting on me.

10. I remember when I was about four months old a black bear almost sat
on me, and another time a deer almost ate my leaves off.

11. There has to be something more exciting than just holding up two walls.

Often I will also type up a sheet of sentences or colorful details from their
papers that I feel represent fine work. These examples are from a composition where the students, using the first person, told the life story of a
hand-hewn beam that was taken from the kitchen wall of a hundred-year-
old log house. The beam now stands in a corner of my classroom.

September 26, 1983   Jay Vinson

Place
1. Size, shape, dimensions
2. Walls (what they are made of), colors, textures
   Ceiling, lighting
   Floor, carpet or concrete
3. Placement of windows, doors
   Things hanging on walls
4. What is in the room (furniture, etc.)
5. Accessories
6. Mood: sounds, smells, brightness/darkness
   (atmosphere)

For the room description assignment, students first make a list of the types of details they need to collect. They take this list with them to their assigned locations and make notes.

September 27, 1983   Jay Vinson

Place - downstairs area of library in front of magazine racks at one of the tables.

Walls - coarse, rough cement; speaker on wall, also thermostat. Glass is around on top of some cement. Intercom in one wall.

Ceiling - contains vents, lights, intercom systems, and has lines drawn in the ceiling. Five lights do not work.

Floor - carpet; red with purple and black designs.

Placement of windows, doors, and things hanging on walls - (refer to walls also). From where I sat, I saw two windows. Up above in media center, I saw four doors and a conference room. There is one room door for faculty members behind the fiction bookshelfs and one door by desk. Four pictures hanging on walls by bookshelves. There are two posters on windows.

What is in the room. Many book, six tables

G11 September 27, 1983 *How many details did you notice this time that you had never noticed before?*   Joy Vinson

In this quiet atmosphere, the
5 only noise you hear is the whispers
2 of voices maintaining their volume level.
2 It's not very busy, but there were students
doing research and looking at magazines.

This room has no desks. It has
tables to write on and chairs to sit
in. It also has glass above rough concrete
to provide walls. *→ Size and shape of room would help here*

Other walls are still as coarse as
the one below glass walls. On these *→ subjects?*
walls there are few pictures. There is *→ one thermostat and one speaker on each wall!?*
one thermostat and one speaker on these
walls.

Joy: watch tenses!
Present tense

Past tense

The ceiling contained many vents, *??*
lights, and intercom systems. It has *→ speakers?*
black lines drawn in the ceiling to
divide each square.

Present tense

Past tense

The floor was covered with
red carpet. In this carpet, there were
purple and black designs. It also
needed cleaning.

From where I sat, I saw a *→ the room had a large room.? Does that make sense?*
room above the one I was in. It
had four doors and a large room.

These notes are then used to write the two-page descriptions, and they are stapled to the composition and handed in as part of the assignment. The final step is the creation by students of the introduction to a publishable magazine article, which includes a description of both the person interviewed and his or her home environment.

Where You Came From

About a hundred years after_____invaded

and conquered England in_____, an Anglo-Norman invasion of_____

was begun. It was never completely successful, and the Irish and the

English have fought ever since.

After the invasion, the Irish fled to the Highlands into the northern

counties that make up the province of_____. English took Dublin.

During the reign of _____in the 16th century, things got

worse when he broke with the Catholic church over the numbers of wives

he could have. In retaliation, he confiscated church property - difficult in

England, but almost impossible in Ireland, stronghold of the_____.

For the Catholic monasteries were the storehouses of Celtic-Irish culture.

In_____,_____came to the English throne. He was

a Scot, and a Protestant. He decided to solve the Irish problem, and

imposed the English land division and tenure system upon Ireland. The

chiefs of_____rebelled, were defeated, their lands confiscated,

and in_____, these lands were given primarily to_____colonies,

all of whom were_____. These were the_____.

The three classes of land ownership were:

1. _____ - who leased to English and Scottish tenants.

2. _____ - (Scots who could take Irish tenants).

3. _____ - who got the poor land nobody else wanted.

In the 18th century, the children of the Scotch Irish began the migration

to _____, the New World. They entered through_____

and through_____. By 1763, Governor Tryon could

report that over a thousand immigrant wagons had passed through Salisbury, N.C.

The reasons for the continuing conflict in Northern Ireland between

the Protestants and Catholics should be obvious. Note that Irish Catholics

also come to this country (Boston, the Kennedys, etc.)

When we are studying the history of the Scotch Irish immigrants, students fill in the blanks on this handout as I lecture. They then keep the handout with their class notes.

KEVIN Fountain 1st

Any older Rabun County residents will immediately know the definitions of every one of these words. Define as many of them as you can.

Dutch oven

crane

fire dog used to elevate logs in a fireplace

pot hooks hooks used to support a pot over the fire

dasher

fire board

dough tray

piggin

white oak split

chair round

finial

corded bed

tick Feather BED

bed wrench

shucks The stuff wrapped

felloe

hub

dish

worm

slop arm

cap

bead

ginseng a plant used to c.

poultice

granny woman

thrash

glut

KEVIN Fountain 2nd

Any older Rabun County natives will immediately know the definitions of every one of these words. Define as many of them as you can.

Dutch oven A cooking pot used in a fireplace

crane A support for pots over a fireplace

fire dog A support for holding up logs in a fireplace

pot hooks a utensil used for putting and getting pots in+out of a fireplace

dasher The middle of a churn

fire board MANTLE PIECE

dough tray a Tray USED for ROLLING DOUGH

piggin A Handled Bucket

white oak split USED for MAKING chair Bottoms

chair round used for holding chair legs together

finial Things on top of chair

corded bed A BED MADE of ROPES

tick A MATTress

bed wrench A tool used to make a Beds rope tighter

shucks Corn LEAVES

felloe Outer part of A WAGON wheel (where spokes fit into)

hub Middle of the wagon wheel

dish Where the wheel curves in to Prevent Breaking

worm Part of A moonshine still (condinser)

slop arm Part of still used to clean out bottom of

cap Top part of moonshine still

head used in telling proof of white liquor Kettle

ginseng herb used in Remedies

poultice ———

granny woman WOMAN who goes door to door delivering babies

thrash a disease (caught usually by small Kids)

glut wooden wedge

The pre- and post-test of words familiar to Appalachian grandparents nearly always shows a huge difference in familiarity on the part of the students.

Stephen Bro[w...]

Correct any grammatical errors you find in the following compositio[..,]

The first impression I had on ~~c~~ Carl ~~w~~ Wilson was that he was a old man that was ~~sorta~~ sort of quite. He didn't speak to you until you spoke to him. Then he was friendly ~~&~~ and really had alot to say ~~once he got started~~ unnecessary. Now I think a lot of him. I like to ~~here~~ hear him talk. He must of lived a amazing life to know so much about well digging, dowsing, home remedies, trapping animals, etc.

Carl lives in a small shack in Mountain City, Ga. He lives a simple life and ~~he~~ He is very happy making his crafts. Some of the things he makes ~~is~~ are chairs out of ivy. ~~he~~ He also makes puzzles, rat traps, games, wooden rings, and belts. He sells some of these to ~~h~~ make money. ~~he~~ He gets by ~~that~~ ~~not needed~~ way. Maybe he's not the richest man in the world, for he don't have all the things that other people ~~has~~ have. But he has never ~~took~~ taken any handouts or welfare. Hes always supported himself. He is content

One problem is that it don't look like he takes very good care of ~~hisself~~ himself. His eyes look like there bloodshot, and it looks like he needs some good meals to fill him out. But if I had to cook ~~2~~ should be written or ~~3~~ times a day on a ~~w~~ Wood ~~s~~ Stove, I probabl[y] wouldn't eat to good ~~n~~ either.

~~Their is~~ There are lots of old people in ~~r~~ Rabun ~~c~~ County who were glad the students from ~~f~~ Foxfire ~~was~~ were interested in them and ~~there~~ their skills and customs. And ~~c~~ Carl is one of ~~them~~ those people. He likes to ~~b~~ visit us in ~~c~~ Class, and we like to visit him to ~~o~~ O because of what he can ~~learn~~ teach us how to do.

I hope we can have him come to our class again this year. I would ~~sorta~~ like for us to interview him ~~alot~~ a lot, ~~a~~ As many times as we can. Carl's knowledge is worth saving ~~bec~~ because he knows a whole lot about the way things use to be, and it should be recorded and wrote down so we don't loose track of it. Even after the ~~2nd~~ or ~~3rd~~ written interview, you get the feeling that you haven't even scratched the surface of what he knows. That can be ~~sorta~~ Sort of frustrating, but it also means we have a great opportunity before us.

The grammar and mechanics pre- and post-tests also routinely show significant improvement in the ability to find and correct errors.

Stephen

Correct any grammatical errors you find in the following composition:

Capital Letters

    The first impression I had (on)(Carl)(Wilson) was that he was a old man that

was (sorta)(quite.) *slang* *quiet* He (didn't) *did not* speak to you until you spoke to him. Then he was,

friendly (&) really had (alot) to say once he got started. Now I think (a lot of) him. *and* *never use* *a great deal*

I like to (here) him talk. He must (of) lived (a) amazing life to know so much about *hear* *have* *an*

well digging(,) dowsing(,) home remedies(,) trapping animals(,) etc.

    Carl lives in a small (shack) in Mountain City(,) (Ga.) He lives a simple life and *home* *Georgia*

and he is very happy making his crafts. Some of the things he makes (is) chairs out *are*

of ivy(.) (He) also makes puzzles(,) rat traps(,) games(,) wooden rings(,) belts. He sells *Capital* *capital*

some of these (too) make money. (He) gets by (thataway.) Maybe (hes) not the richest *to* *capital* *slang* *he is*

man in the world, (he don't) have all the things that other people (has.) (But) he has *or* *have* *but*

never (took) any handouts or welfare. (Hes) always supported himself(.) (He) is content. *taken* *He has* *and he*

    One problem is that it (don't) look like he takes very good care of (hisself.) *does not* *slang*

His eyes look like (there) bloodshot, and it looks like he needs some good meals to *they are*

fill him out. (If) I had to cook (2) or (3) times a day on a (wood) (stove), I probably *not needed* *spell out* *small* *Capitab*

(wouldn't) eat (too) good (neither.) *would not*

(There is lots of) old people in (rabun) (county) who were glad the students from *There are many* *R* *C* *were*

(Foxfire) (was) interested in them and (there) skills and customs. (And) (Carl) is one *F* *their* *not needed* *Carl*

of (them) people. He likes to(o) visit us in (class), and we like to visit him to *those* *small c*

because of what he can (learn) us how to do. *slang-teach*

    I hope we can have him(,) come to our class again this year, I would (sorta) like *don't use* *as*

for us to interview him (alot.) (As) many times as we can. Carl's knowledge is worth *Combine As one*

saving (cause) he knows a (hole) lot about the way things use to be(.) (It) should be *because* *whole* *It* *spell out*

recorded and (wrote) down so we (don't) loose track of it. Even after the (2nd) or (3rd) *written* *do not*

interview, you get the feeling that you (haven't) even scratched the surface of what *have not*

he knows. That can be (sorta) frustrating, but it also means we have a great *slang*

opportunity before us.

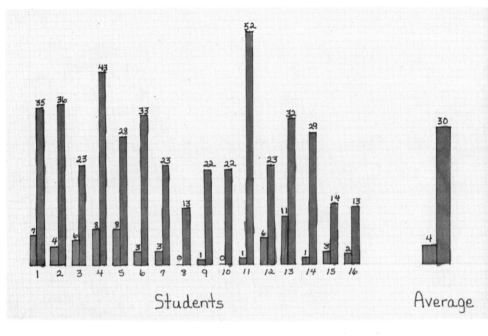

Charts of the pre- and post-test scores of a typical class show the difference graphically. The chart on top is for the terms test, the one on the
bottom, grammar and mechanics. Each pair of columns indicates the test
results, before and after the course, for one student.

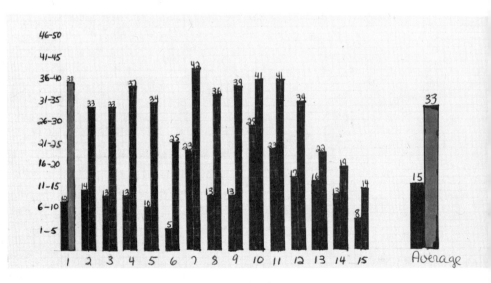

not necessarily in this order, by teachers, peers, preachers, and adult leaders, bosses, the media, and so on. During adolescence, however, when the influence of the family begins to wane, and when television and the pull of peers and part-time jobs exerts increasing influence, to say nothing of the dramatic escalation of self-doubt and paranoia that hits the more vulnerable young people with special force, things tend to get a little crazy. Most young people come out of the fire relatively intact, but during this period, for many of them, school may be the only place where steadying, stabilizing, and sane forward-looking forces have a chance to rule. After all, in a world where one's favorite television series may be on the air one week and canceled the next, and where one's after-school job in a fast-food restaurant depends on whether a buying public is hungry for Big Macs or Whoppers, and where one's family may be together one minute and split in half the next, and where one's boyfriend or girlfriend is here today and gone tomorrow, and where fashion designers and record promoters and gadget hustlers prey on kids with a shamelessness that would put many thieves to rout—in a world like that, schools have the potential, at least, of being places where students can find help in making sense out of what's happening around them.

The fact that schools don't often live up to that potential but merely contribute to the general craziness is well known, but tell me what other choice there is in the lives of young people (given the fact that the advice of families is temporarily discredited by many during adolescence) that has a greater opportunity to be a force for wisdom, perspective, and the acquisition of the necessary tools for self-determination in the lives of those young people. A preacher they may see once a week? The heroes of "Knight Rider" or "Dukes of Hazzard?" An exhausted parent?

It's schools. You know it and I know it.

Now, the point I want to make: of the seventeen million students in junior and senior high schools in 1980, it was predicted, based on past experience, that over four million would not graduate.[1] Four million. That's twice the size of Atlanta, Georgia—and Atlanta's a big town. Of those who graduate, it was predicted that over half would not go on to any form of higher education.[2] In other words, the school systems of this country were poised in 1980 to have their last shot at about ten million of those seventeen million students. Sure, many of those will go through some type of employee training program or some sort of instruction in the armed services, and many of them will do fine without us (Col. Harlan Sanders dropped out of public school in the sixth grade), but their exposure to much of the subject matter that public schools offer, except in cursory ways, ends with us.

The high school where I teach is, I think, a good case in point. Of the 1980 graduating class of 138, 25 went on to four-year colleges, 13 to junior colleges, and 22 to vocational technical schools; 60 out of 138. And

I know that several of those dropped out well before their first year was completed.

Over half, gone.

And that's the reason I get so dismayed when I read the results of an Institute for Development of Educational Activities (IDEA) study that polled 13,700 junior and senior high school students and found that when they were asked to pick the one best thing about their schools, only 7 percent chose "The classes I'm taking." Eight percent ticked off the choice, "Nothing."[3] The data in *A Place Called School,* John Goodlad's even broader study, revealed almost identical results.

Maybe that shouldn't bother me, but it does. Given the fact that most of our schools are having their last shot at over half their students, and given the fact 93 percent in a study like the IDEA one don't rate their classes very highly, and given the fact that my experience in schools would tend to support the findings of that study, I'd say it's time to get our act together. I can't help but agree with Ernest Boyer, the president of the Carnegie Foundation for the Advancement of Teaching, when he writes, "If the schools—especially the high schools—don't make dramatic reforms in the 1980s, the public school will become more and more rejected. It will lose constituency support.

"And if the traditional support of public schools is lost, there will be more alienation among young people, parents and the public than we have ever seen in this country—with disastrous consequences. We will be losing an essential resource at the very time it is needed most."[4]

Looking at the history of the public school system would be instructive at this point—why was it started, anyway?—and it's fascinating, but it does not expedite my getting to the core of this chapter: what are public secondary schools for *now?* What is the mission? What are we supposed to accomplish besides keeping the kids off the streets?

Let's turn to our teacher handbooks that await our arrival at the beginning of every school year. (The quotation marks indicate an approximation of the language most of us find in those handbooks.)

A Firm Grounding in the Basic Skills

First, "A firm grounding in the basic skills—the reading, writing and computation skills—that all students must have for success in school and the workplace and adult life."

Few of us would argue with this goal. We may argue about the means for achieving it but not about its importance, for the plain and simple fact is that young people that can't handle basic language arts and math skills are cripples. A failure to master basic skills does not lead, as *a* to *b*, to a life of antisocial or noncontributing behavior or crime, but to deny that it is a major factor is like saying the light that floods this planet comes from the moon instead of the sun. The Children's Defense Fund, for example, recently reported a survey done in Massachusetts that revealed that 98 percent of the young people incarcerated in that state (at a cost of at least $11,000 per person per year) had a history of problems in school; and we all know that the roots of many of those problems lie in an early and persistent failure to master the fundamentals. Students who can't function in school are usually so filled with alienation and frustration—even though they may feign an attitude of nonchalance or unconcern—that we can usually count on it boiling over somewhere. Those teachers who shake their heads and say "the problem with my students who haven't learned the basics is not frustration but just plain laziness" forget the root cause of much "laziness" is failure and frustration.

In the "My Turn" column of a 1980 issue of *Newsweek*, a fifteen-year-old black student named Deadrich Hunter found himself caught up in a Brooklyn high school environment where the student population was divided between the "hard rocks" (those who had essentially given up) and the "ducks" (those who still had hope and were still striving for a better life). He said, in part, in a column that had the ring of authenticity, "The hard rocks want revenge. They want revenge because they don't have any hope of changing their situation. Their teachers don't offer it, their parents have lost theirs, and their grandparents died with a heartful of hope but nothing to show for it."[5]

In an ABC television documentary entitled *Youth Terror: The View From Behind the Gun*, a street youth well on his way down a dead-end street says, "I wouldn't mind goin' to school if I knew how to read." Another echoes, "I can't do nothing. I can't function."[6]

Granted, other factors are causative in the making of antisocial behavior, and there may be little we can do to repair the damage done to students of ours who were abused by their families when they were three or four years old, but there is virtually no excuse for our schools to turn out students who cannot function at basic levels of competence. There is no excuse for the Continental Bank of Chicago having to run a school of its own for potential employees who happen to be high school graduates but are functionally illiterate in basic grammar and math (especially considering the fact that the students obviously learn the necessary skills quickly when faced with a real-life situation like Continental's training program. There's a lesson in there somewhere for all of us).

There is no excuse for a high school athlete being awarded inflated grades and being slipped through the system into college on scholarship, only to wake up one day and find that he's not pro material, that he can't do academic work either, and that he was sacrificed by his own schools on the altar of alumni loyalty and ticket sales. As an athlete in *Sports Illustrated* said pointedly:

[The old caricature of] the fullback whose neck is a size larger than the best grade he has ever received in math class . . . was always an exaggerated image, one that was more playfully than seriously advanced.

No more.

The "dumb jock" has now come into full flower in the American educational system. He is fast becoming a national catastrophe. He is already a national disgrace. About the only good thing one can say about him is that his blossoming has inadvertently exposed the larger failures of the educational process.

What happened? Why is it different after all these years?

It is different because the educational system is in chaos, its spirit preoccupied, its standards blunted to a point where almost anything that passes for curricula is permissible. High schools—many of them—do not educate; they graduate. Junior colleges—many of them—have such meager academic requirements that they are fertile ground for any angling coach who feels the need to do some academic cheating to keep his players eligible. . . . Only the terminally naive can deny the existence of a deliberate pervasive warping of the system.[7]

There has been some frantic work recently in response to the blizzard of attack, including suits brought by parents against schools because their children are so helpless academically. All sorts of options have been advanced, including magnet schools, optional schools, continuation schools, schools within schools, and all the rest. But the simple fact is there is no excuse for all our pupils not learning how to read and write and do math proficiently in our regular public schools, and *from us*. To fill that function is one of the main reasons public schools were set up and we were hired.

If we believe the predictions advanced in *Megatrends*, this job will become even more crucial as this country moves away from its role as an industrial giant (shifting the manufacturing of most goods to other countries) into its new role as a country where the majority of the work force is involved in the processing of data and information.

Though some would regard it as a separate goal, one that is so closely related as to almost defy being placed in a separate category is to ensure that all graduates have a firm grounding in basic life survival skills, including creation of a household budget; checkbook balancing, banking, and credit skills; wise shopping practices and consumer savvy; basic nutrition and health, including sex education; selection and application to an institution of higher learning; preparing a résumé and applying and interviewing for a job; choosing a career; and so on. This is especially important for girls who may still assume—even in today's world of the career woman—that many of these concerns (such as preparing a résumé) are things they will never have to worry about, but who may find themselves, through divorce or death or choice, alone in the world.

I am constantly amazed at how few of my students, even today, have never done simple tasks like writing a check or balancing a checkbook.

And so, even though I teach English, I make it a point to involve all my students in the mathematical side of running a business like *Foxfire* magazine before their time with me is over.

Similarly, I find out at the beginning of each quarter how many students there are in my classes who still—even though they may have been told before—do not know fundamental things like the fact that they can write to colleges for free catalogs and application forms, and that there is financial aid available; and then I make exercises in those areas part of our normal work together.

I just don't feel I have any choice.

How to do it?

The first step is to back up and examine again our methodology and our review of what clearly works and what doesn't. We must pay heed to the cautions advanced by educators such as the ones who, in 1985, released *Becoming a Nation of Readers: The Report of the Commission on Reading* (prepared for the U.S. Office of Education by the National Institute of Education), in which they say on page 80, for example, ". . . it is a mistake to suppose that instruction in grammar transfers readily to the actual uses of language. This may be the explanation for the fact that experiments over the last fifty years have shown negligible improvement in the quality of student writing as a result of grammar instruction. Research suggests that the finer points of writing, such as punctuation and subject-verb agreement, may be learned best while students are engaged in extended writing that has the purpose of communicating a message to an audience. Notice that no communicative purpose is served when children are asked to identify on a worksheet the parts of speech or the proper use of 'shall' and 'will.'

"Skillful teachers find ways to give children reasons to communicate to real audiences."

And I think we can celebrate the potential of computers, given the proper software, to assist us in this task of basic education. As students acquire certain fundamentals and skills, our role may then become to help them put those skills to work in real ways, and to become adults who are, as William Bennett said in an interview on page 20E in the February 17, 1985, issue of the New York *Times*, ". . . engaged in the architecture of the human soul."

In other words, the following:

An Understanding of How the World Works

A second stated goal of most public schools is to help young people "understand how the world works" and why many of the events that are happening out there are happening—and why we should attempt to understand them at all. Any person of reasonable intelligence and concern, upon listening to the questions of the audience during the average audience-participation television show, or talking with the average teenager or parent, cannot help but be struck by the astounding level of ignorance abroad in the land as to just what is going on in economics, the environment, politics, the sciences, or foreign affairs. We have a populace that makes knee-jerk responses to inflation, for example, but could no more describe to you how we got into that mess or the pros and cons of the various remedies than it could flap its collective arms and fly to Mars. We have a citizenry that may react angrily and briefly to a chemical spill or the depletion of a state's freshwater resources or a series of documented cases of fish kills because of acid rain, but that could no more explain the chemical or biological or geographical (or political) causes than it could walk on the empty waters of its lakes. We have a society that may cluck disparagingly over an assassination attempt here or abroad, or warfare in Ireland or El Salvador or Syria, but that too often knows no more of the roots of such crises and how they affect us and vice versa, than it knows of the history and background of America itself.

Public schools must shoulder a share of the blame for this kind of situation and must actively work to counter it in the future. Students must have a firm understanding of the contemporary institutions that shape our lives. They must know the inner workings and ultimate purposes of our political systems—local, regional, and national—and how, why, and by whom those systems were set up and who runs them now. They must have an understanding of themselves as members of a society with a history and a future—an understanding that includes not only the specifics of their own family's history and culture but also that of their own communities, their nation, and their nation's interactions with other cultures and nations. They must understand how social groups function both in isolation from and in contact with others, and how such interactions can work in both positive and negative ways. They must understand prejudice—its causes, its functions, its effects, its remedies. They should have a more than nodding acquaintance with psychology, philosophy, logic, linguistics, folklore—the humanities—not only to create an insatiable curiosity about and thrill with the act of life, but also to consider life's meaning and purpose.

They must have a firm acquaintance with the sciences and technology, including not only the mechanics of how things work but also the history of technology, the benefits and curses and opportunities with which it has presented us, and the implications for the future. They must have some perspective on where we are now and from whence this technological revolution came—a perspective that can be vastly aided, by the way, by simply spending some time with any of a number of people still alive and active who were nearly teenagers when the first airplane left the ground.

And they must understand the implications of all this on life itself. One of the more frightening aspects of the blizzard of condensed and dessicated information our new communications technology makes available to us is the speed with which people lose their capacity to become concerned or involved. They see only the end results of family conflicts, political struggles, criminal activity, environmental problems. A space shuttle appears, flickers briefly on the television screen, and is gone, simply absorbed somehow into the interstices of the brain. When the second one blasts off, no one watches. Someone shoots the President, and three days later, everyone's forgotten the assailant's name. A scientist warns again that we have the nuclear capacity to destroy all life on this globe, and people have heard it so many times they wander off to the kitchen to get another beer. Trout die in the Great Smokies from acid rain, and the public reaction is, "Oh, yeah, I read about that when it hit the Northeast. I've heard all this before."

The sense of numbness that many of us feel after our daily dose of news is understandable and forgivable. There is only so much we can absorb and react to at any given time. That's one of the reasons high schools are potentially so vital: we can help students understand that behind most of these events are living, breathing people just like themselves; we can help students understand roots and causes; we can help students learn how to sift through and react to those things that should most concern all of us. Certainly the environment should be at the top of the list of concerns, for without exquisite care we may well, as Paul Erlich so often says, "overshoot the carrying capacity of this planet."

We are in an age when everything moves so fast that we can no longer afford the luxury of making past mistakes over and over again. We can no longer afford the luxury of ignorance. We cannot afford to allow ourselves to become numb. We must recognize the inevitable interconnectedness of everything and everyone on this globe, memorizing that first picture of Earth from the moon—arguably the most important photograph of the twentieth century. We must realize that such things as cutting down a rain forest in Brazil *do* matter, in fact, like it or not; for such an act can change weather patterns to the point that wheat can no longer be raised on the Great Plains. And though the environmental offenses we commit in our own communities may have no consequences so dramatic, they each add to the cumulative whole of one of the most serious problems we've ever faced.

In short, we and our students must understand how the world works. A curriculum composed of a toothless excuse for a civics course, a deadly American history course, a biology class in which students never go outdoors, an English class in which students write about their summer vacations, and a couple of mindless, empty electives will simply not fill the bill. Not in an age like this one. It's stupid, and potentially catastrophic. As Carl Sagan said, "Any retreat from thinking is a prescription for disaster."[8]

An Appreciation for the Arts

A third goal of public schools generally is, to paraphrase numerous statements of purpose, "to foster an appreciation for creativity and the arts."

Of all aspects of a school's curriculum, this is the one, traditionally, that is most abused, and yet there are few offerings in our schools that can so well offer potentially *every* person involved a deeper sense of what it means to be magnificently, triumphantly human.

There are few offerings in our schools more forgiving of individual idiosyncrasy and ingenuity; few offerings in which so many "right answers" are possible.

The arts, in short, are the one piece of landscape where virtually every student can find a home, whether in an individual solitary act of creativity or as an integral part of a team making up a marching band, a stage crew, or a chorus. This fact, ultimately, rather than the myriad of final products, is the real beauty of the arts, for here as nowhere else, all can take part. There are no "bench warmers" or "dummies" in the arts.

From the beginning of intelligent life, as the first cave men attempted to gain some control over their world through cave paintings that still exist today, the arts have been an inseparable part of our lives whether we're whistling in our showers, singing along with a song playing on our car radios, relaxing near a fountain in a city park, mailing a greeting card or a postcard or a photograph to a friend, playing a musical instrument, purchasing a handmade quilt or piece of furniture or stoneware at a craft shop, experiencing the strange thrill of seeing our own children in a school play, watching a film in a theater or on television, or feeling a momentary shiver as a massive organ begins to play a favorite hymn in a church filled with the color and light from a dozen stained-glass windows. We insist that the arts decorate, embellish, and bring meaning, depth, significance, and mood to all our social rituals from birth to graduation to marriage to death. We cannot imagine—nor would we long tolerate—a world without spoken eloquence or color or music or literature. If all that were to disappear, we would simply remake it all and fill our lives with it once again as the means of elevating us beyond the drudgery and meanness our lives would otherwise have.

The arts often provide the most visible evidence that the atmosphere of our public schools supports life as we know it today. Visitors are shown immediately any murals or exhibits or photographs and paintings within or upon those walls. A tour of the art room and the theater is a must for most parents of prospective students—the administration's way of proving that "culture" is attended to sufficiently. At every formal function, the school's orchestra is asked to play or the chorus is asked to sing.

And despite all this, the arts budget is normally the first to feel the ax when the going gets tough financially.

I'm not going to dwell on the irony of that. For now, I'll just reiterate the importance of a solid arts program in all our schools. Handled properly, the arts become the means by which our students' emotions can be gathered into focused beams of light and energy. Through the arts, students can find solace, inspiration, a means by which—even if they are unpopular or shy or tongue-tied—they can communicate with others and forge alliances and friendships. Through the arts, the chance exists that their sensitivity to themselves and to others can be nourished and kept alive.

If we, as human beings, ever lose the capacity to move others emotionally and to be deeply moved ourselves, we cease to be human.

Personal Traits

A fourth major goal, code named in our handbooks something like "personal traits such as honesty, reliability, curiosity, self-confidence, etc. . . ." refers to individual characteristics nearly *everything* we do with students should foster, for it is these characteristics that will virtually guarantee them success no matter what careers they eventually enter or what life-styles they adopt. The best courses in our schools foster these traits as vigorously as any academic or artistic material they include. The two aspects are inseparable. The reason for the separate category, of course, is the fact that the majority of courses too often only incorporate attention to them incidentally, if at all. Let me begin to list them and you'll see what I mean:

• As a direct result of our work with them, students should acquire a rock-hard belief in their individual self-worth and potential. This does *not* mean that they should never experience failure or disappointment. It means, instead, that failures and disappointments should come honestly, not as a result of a teacher's punitive streak, and then, in an atmosphere of caring and concern, should be worked through to lead to that triumph that promotes the necessary willingness to take on something else without fear, and keeps alive and intact the student's sense of self-esteem and self-confidence. From the wellspring of such beliefs in self, our students acquire the courage they must have for tomorrow.

• Students should leave our schools with a sense of curiosity and wonder that propels them into an increasing dialogue with the outside world. Rather than being so disenchanted with the learning process that they shy from the active acquisition of knowledge ever after, they should not only have learned from us how to learn independently but they should have also acquired an active desire to do so. They should be eager to stretch themselves further, thanks to our sensitive initiation into the learning process. And sensitive it must be. As A. Bartlett Giamatti writes, "No good teacher ever wants to control the contour of another's mind. That would not be teaching, it would be a form of terrorism. But no good teacher wants the contour of another's mind to be blurred. Somehow the line between encouraging a design and imposing a specific stamp must be found and clarified."[9] In the process of finding this line, Giamatti continues, each teacher must ". . . feel what you think, do what you talk about: judge as you talk about judgment, proceed logically as you reveal logical structure, clarify as you talk about clarity, reveal as you show what nature reveals—all in the service of encouraging the student in imitation and then repetition of the process you have been summoning, all so that the student may turn himself not into you but into himself."[10] This, as opposed to the more typical classes in which students are simply presented a body of predigested material to master and regurgitate, and given little if any opportunity to analyze, problem solve, experiment, test, and draw their own conclusions in an atmosphere where those conclusions can be scrutinized, constructively criticized, and supported.

• As a corollary to this, students should have been aided by their work with us in their ability to analyze situations objectively, make decisions as to wise courses of action, and justify them. There is no good reason I can think of that they should not be immersed constantly in the decision-making and analysis process concerning individual projects, class projects and concerns, and issues concerning the school as a whole, all as prelude to being able to make wise decisions concerning their own lives and life-styles, and their roles in their careers and their communities. Such a process is touchy, for teachers can't simply throw decisions onto students' shoulders in an uncaring, "do whatever you want to do, I couldn't care less" manner, or try to trick them into thinking they're making a decision when in fact it has already been made and students are simply being asked to rubber stamp it. Students will ferret out the latter technique quickly, will know instinctively that they are being tricked, and no amount of teacher protestation to the contrary will convince them otherwise. They must be put into situations in which they make real decisions when all the possible options have been studied, the possible consequences weighed, and they are psychologically ready to move; all in an atmosphere in which they know the consequences of those decisions will be analyzed constructively.

• Students should have been involved in enough projects and activities to have developed a familiarity with the need for and the mechanics of planning ahead, and they should have the ability to see beyond today and immediate gratification into tomorrow. They should have a sense of patience combined with a sense of persistence, as well as the beginnings of a sense of vision of what their future could be and how to proceed toward it with the knowledge that has derived from their accumulated experiences. They should know the absolute futility of living only for the moment, having experienced the intense pleasure of seeing some major work come to fruition after months of effort and planning; and yet they should also know how to enjoy and get the most out of any present experience. They should be alive and forward-looking; excited, but tempered in the best sense by the beginnings of wisdom.

A letter I got recently from a former student, who had just finished college and spent several months on his first job in forest management, revealed that kind of lively self-confidence and questioning we should celebrate. It read, in part, "The temperature is not the only thing that is high [here]. My spirits are high also. I have begun a new phase in my life. Leaving Athens was the termination of college days. Now Life has interesting and new twists that I must deal with and put in perspective. Now I am free to say, 'Am I happy?' 'Is this right?' 'What do I want to be?' etc. This is the first time that [a series of] major goals have been completed in my life. Now is the time for me to decide new goals and manipulate my own future."

He may never find the answers to all the questions he's asking. Few of us do. But the important thing may be not so much finding the answers as continuing, throughout life, to ask the questions, and then having enough self-confidence and strength to change direction and continue the probing when a need for change is indicated.

• Students should leave our schools with their creative abilities burnished to a glow rather than darkened and tarnished by our constant imposition of our wills and our ideas and our directions upon them. The historian Arthur Schlesinger, Jr., says, "Creativity implies that leap of imagination and understanding which enables individuals to grow in dignity and purpose in a world where whirl is king. Creativity also implies the ability on the part of the creator to carry others with him in the endless quest for insight."[11]

Businesses and corporations are crying for creative employees who have the ability to study a problem, see it whole in all its parts, and, with that leap of imagination, propose workable solutions. Creativity is needed as never before in areas as diverse as politics, science, education, architecture, and agriculture. Those people who have it are prized for their ability to reconceptualize ideas and see beyond imagined obstacles to rethink and remake our reality in fine new ways. They are prized so highly that foundations like the MacArthur Foundation, the fourth largest private foundation in the nation (surpassing Rockefeller, Carnegie, and Sloan, with assets of $862 million), awards its huge grants only to truly creative individuals who, with their support, may make "discoveries or other significant contributions to society."[12] We very nearly worship creativity as a nation, and yet in many of our schools, we actively discourage it in favor of conformity and the status quo. No wonder truly creative people are in such short supply.

• We should strive to help students leave our schools with a sense of physical and mental wellness that springs from all the foregoing, in combination with knowledge of diet, the essential nature of exercise, stress management and the control of emotions—of *health*. Health as a total package that even includes a lack of greed and encompasses Socrates' statement, "I love to walk through the market place and see all the things I can live without." Health as an understanding, as never before, of self and potential and hope. Health as the growing conviction of independence in its best sense, and wholeness. To have our students be *whole*.

A Determination to Make a Contribution

All this is a prelude to what I consider the most important goal of all: the willingness of each student to move beyond himself and his new understandings, finally, into an active, caring relationship with others; to, as our handbooks say, "make the world a better place in which to live."

First things first. As I've said before, until our students are assured of the fact that they are whole, they cannot give of themselves in a healthy way to others or to their world, partly because they refuse to believe they have anything of worth to offer. If I feel I am useless, how can I be of use? If I feel I am helpless, how can I be of help? If I feel I am stupid, how can I contribute to knowledge or enlightenment? If I am frightened, how can I help others to stand fast? If I am discouraged, how can I offer hope? If I am a piece of a man, am I not justified in spending most of my time and energy trying to put myself together?

That's all oversimplified, because in the very act of being concerned about others, one can contribute to one's own wholeness and find additional sources of confirmation and worth. But since I have made a separate category of this goal, indulge me.

Giamatti again: Every classroom is an act of making citizens, and thus a political act; "a giving to others the gift of how to share their desire that humankind survive as it should, with dignity and moral purpose. At its best, teaching must lead us out of ourselves, into an understanding that our hope for a decent, civilized life depends for its very existence on others having the same hope."[13]

When we first begin to work with students, their natural hunger for self-esteem has led most of them to base their self-concept to a large extent on what their peers (and to a lesser extent on what we adults) think of them. They define themselves by others' yardsticks. Gradually we try to wean students from the conviction that their self-concept must necessarily be dependent on what others think and urge them toward a state of inner strength and a conviction of inner worth and innate ability that will allow them to slice through an umbilical cord that is potentially disabling, because we very much want them to be independent and self-confident and whole.

Fine.

Except for the fact that graduating an auditorium full of individuals jammed with self-confidence and independence can be something like igniting an arsenal of unguided missiles tipped with nuclear warheads. Nobody knows what direction they'll take or where they'll land. The people responsible for many of the problems our society faces were (and are) independent and self-confident too.

The public schools have frequently been viciously attacked for their failure to stimulate and nurture an active social conscience in their students. And the attacks have frequently been justified. When I was in elementary and junior high school in Athens, Georgia, for example, I am positive that there was not a single instance—not one—when any of my teachers initiated, or even allowed, a discussion about racism. In that nine-year period, it was not even mentioned, and that was in a town where I can distinctly remember, even today, years later, separate, clearly marked water fountains for whites and blacks, separate bathrooms in the downtown five-and-dime (one for white women, one for white men, and one for all blacks), separate waiting rooms in the train and bus station, a balcony area in our Presbyterian church set aside for blacks, none of whom were ever allowed on the main floor (in fact, when some African students attending the University of Georgia came to a service once with some of their white friends in the early sixties and sat on the main floor, it precipitated one of the biggest crises in the history of that church), a separate ticket window and balcony seating area for blacks at the movie theater, no admission for blacks at all in the local hotels, and absolute and total separation of blacks and whites in terms of schools, neighborhoods, and so on. And because it was never talked about, my classmates and I really never even asked ourselves why the town was set up that way. That was just the way things were, had always been, and always would be. It would have done as much good to ask why there was grass or why there were mockingbirds. They just *were*.

Likewise we were taught how Columbus discovered America and found Indians here, and, by the simple act of sticking a flagstaff in the ground, took possession for his country. The Indians, like the rocks and trees, simply came with the territory.

And we never asked why. That was just the way things were.

And we were taught there was one God (I even remember when they stuck the words *under God* into the Pledge of Allegiance we recited every day, hands over our little hearts, facing the flag) and that He was a light-skinned male with a long beard who sat on a golden throne up in heaven and watched each of us and took note of our every transgression and tallied the fall of every sparrow. And though other peoples in other distant lands held other gods before them—briefly mentioned, to be sure —there was no question as to the fact that ours was the *real* one; and when missionaries came to talk to us about their work in darkest Africa and asked us for our lunch money in order that they might continue to lead these people out of darkness and the threat of eternal damnation into light, we gave it willingly and felt sanctified for having done so, and never questioned what our reaction might have been to an African missionary who might have visited our school and handed out some songbooks and taught us some native hymns and tried to woo us away from our god to his. Ours was the only righteous cause on the globe.

And we never asked why. That was just the way it was.

Not once were we led to a hint of a question as to the justification for the particular and special arrogance of the white Anglo-Saxon race. We were simply reminded again and again of how wonderfully we had been blessed. I don't remember feeling an overwhelming sense of gratitude, because I had had no personal experiences with any other race or culture or life-style with which to compare mine, but I do remember being basically content and happy with my lot, my life revolving around such concerns as whether or not the chickens I was raising were laying eggs, whether or not there was enough air in my bicycle's tires, whether or not I had any friends, and whether or not my dog was raising hell in the neighborhood and if so, what consequences would be awaiting me when I got home.

We lived in a self-contained airtight capsule, and as far as public schools were concerned, whatever went on outside that container was best left to those unfortunate enough, or stupid enough, to be out there. What went on inside the black public schools was anybody's guess and was certainly no concern of ours. And so we didn't think about it. Had we known those black kids were being taught to read out of our used Dick and Jane readers, the tattered pages of which featured a middle-class white family, we probably wouldn't have thought about that, either, there being no one to encourage us to look at that situation more carefully.

During the sixties, when I was in college and then began to teach school myself, attacks on the public schools intensified sharply, and I became aware of those shortcomings for the first time. A whole generation of eloquent critics emerged. Some of them then and well into the seventies charged that there was an active conspiracy on the part of the leaders of our capitalist society to use the public schools as tools of that society to perpetuate the capitalist philosophy. Naturally they were correct. Those in charge of the schools used different language—something along the lines of "The purpose of our schools is to keep alive and strong the American way of life," or something like that—but the meaning was the same. Public school leaders simply shrugged and said, "Of course that's what we're doing. You think we're going to advocate and teach socialism in a capitalist nation? Do socialists teach and advocate capitalism in their nations' schools?" Or as Paolo Freire said in a seminar I was lucky enough to be allowed to attend in Chicago in 1977, "To expect the bourgeoise society to create a new kind of education to fight the bourgeoise society is incredible."

The point being, obviously, that the entire makeup of our society would have to be changed before the schools would alter their devotion to the present one. Though that may happen someday, the delight with which many people welcomed the election of Ronald Reagan and embraced his cabinet and his programs convinces me that such a revolution is a long way off.

Others charged that the real conspiracy of the public school system was not so much to make the students buy into the capitalist system as it was purposely to keep the majority of them ignorant and unquestioning, so that they could continue to be led like passive sheep and used by the leaders of the ruling class (America's only true minority), whose children all attended exclusive private schools.

Well, maybe. But after the Supreme Court decision that separate school facilities were inherently unequal, and the subsequent integration of all such facilities with a great national belch and a lingering case of heartburn (and an ugly rash of private "Christian" schools that blistered up on the magnolia-white skin of the South), it began to look more as though the main agenda was to get as many people as possible into the middle class as quickly as possible. Some critics, snorting at the stated goals to "ensure the comfort and economic well-being of all Americans," said that was just a less offensive way of saying, "to make sure the morally bankrupt capitalist system stays intact by making everyone equally greedy"; and they had, and have, a point. People are basically self-centered, and I've seen poor people manage to start businesses of their own and then become just as selfish and tyrannical where their employees are concerned as the worst of any of their former employers. I have friends at Cornell who, accustomed to the comforts of home, would no more walk away from that comfort to struggle for a cause than they would try to eat bricks. (That's like the old parable sometimes used to illustrate the difference between contribution and commitment, in which the old man and old woman who have only hard bread want to provide a good breakfast for their guest. They ask a chicken and a pig for help. The chicken responds immediately, for all that is required of her is an egg. The pig hesitates, for a contribution from him means a piece of his butt.)

The fires set by the left have all pretty much burned out. The shouting has stopped. Temporarily. Everyone's distracted now by the fires set by the right while their backs were turned, lit by torches into the handles of which had been carved the letters *B-A-S-I-C-S*, whatever that spells.

There's always smoke somewhere.

Through it all, however, the public school system seems to make its stately, quiet way like some huge rust-encrusted steel Flying Dutchman, largely uninterrupted by the shouts and darts and stones from the pygmies on the shore. And the old questions remain. Is there an active conspiracy to *keep* people insulated and passive and accepting of their lot as fodder for the rich? Or an active conspiracy to *make* people greedy and soulless?

I doubt it. Not on a national scale, at any rate. Nationally such things tend to happen by default. Students don't learn the basics *not* because someone higher up tells us not to teach them well for fear that once they master the basics, they'll have within reach the tools of power, but because too many teachers simply don't teach them well, either out of laziness or ignorance as to how, or fatigue, or whatever. And our capitalist system doesn't really need to enlist the aid of the public schools in promoting or maintaining or feeding itself. Most people come by their self-interest honestly, without a hell of a lot of prodding. There have been various localized regional conspiracies that utilized their public school systems as a means of keeping one race or another from getting a piece of the pie, but nationally, in a country hammered together by the flotsam and jetsam of the world—immigrants who often had been denied their piece of the action back home—the slogan has always been Land of Opportunity, which, roughly translated, means, "Grab as much as you can" as opposed to "Take only what you need." It's been that way since our socialistic hunting and gathering ancestors discovered agriculture and realized land was power and wealth. Come the big revolution, without a parallel moral revolution, the world will probably turn capitalist, not socialist or communist—not so much because we exported the system as because of the realization that in such a system, virtually anyone can become rich. The American Dream.

What's wrong with that is the fact that so many people get stepped on in the process. Individualism makes for competition and division, and that tends to be a very shaky foundation on which to build a society.

In such a society, people tend to be so preoccupied with their own concerns that they have little time for those of others or for the greater good. In the face of clear injustices, the public schools tend to remain serenely uninvolved, not so much because of an active national conspiracy as because the adults within them tend to say to themselves, "If I say something about that, someone will get mad at me," or "If I do something, I may get fired," or "That's their problem, not mine," or "It's none of my business," or "I got mine the hard way. They can too," or "That's not my job. That's all." Or, having been kept in ignorance by the failure of their own education, they may say, innocently, "Hey, look, I really don't know what you're talking about." Or they may just acquiesce.

In a regular column he used to write for *Esquire* entitled "Ethics," Harry Stein wrote, ". . . the accommodation so many individuals have [been able to reach] with their own most selfish impulses [is], I think, the principal reason the Reagan program has been so seductive: the policymakers have made it easy, even respectable, for us to abide by our basest instincts; all one has to do is acquiesce.

"Of course, acquiescence is something of a tradition in this country.

From the time of the Mexican War through the Indian campaigns and the Palmer raids, right on into the McCarthy era, the weight of the vast silent majority was so great that those few who stood up against it appear, in retrospect, to have been heroic."[14]

Later in the same column, he quotes Ed Asner's comments about his colleagues who refused to take a stand during 1980's bitter actors' strike: "Most of them aren't bad people. In terms of morality, they're just asleep at the switch."

America. In many ways, it's a wonderful, wonderful country. If I were to list the Americans I know of who have invested entire careers in pioneering medical and technological and agricultural and cultural advances for the good of all mankind, the list would go on for pages. And their contributions were, and are, *real*, not trumped up or faked. You will never convince me that people like Jonas Salk, to name one example, didn't have the welfare of all humankind squarely at the heart of his lonely fight to develop an effective polio vaccine; or that the impulse for the creation of organizations like the Sierra Club came out of purely selfish motivations.

And before I would believe it, you would have to show me another country that protects the rights guaranteed in constitutional amendments like the first more vigorously, or is more willing (some would say too willing) to let those who want to fight for those rights (or for causes like civil rights or the ERA or socialism or the KKK or nazism) do so. A Satanic church in a county adjacent to ours is tax exempt, for God's sake —no pun intended. There are more causes being fought for in this country than you could count in ten years of Sundays.

And before I would give in to arguments to the contrary, you would have to show me another country more filled with gratifying paradoxes (such as the fact that Septima Clark, the elderly black woman who helped organize the citizenship schools that taught blacks to read so they could register to vote in the then incredibly hostile environment of Charleston, South Carolina, at this moment sits on the school board for that city's public schools).

Sure, those people fought for the victories they ultimately achieved. But that's just the point. They were allowed to fight. This very country was birthed in revolution and political protest, and the right to carry that tradition forward has been protected. And I can't think of a place in the world where I'd rather live or for which I would more willingly fight. This country is one of the more noble and most exciting social experiments going on in this world. I believe that. And I believe in the inherent generosity and kindness and potential of the American people. I am still moved when I go to a Braves game in Atlanta and hear the national anthem.

But I cannot shake my dismay at the amount of ignorance abroad in this country as to how the world works. I cannot help but be discouraged at the myriad ways in which the opportunities this country gives its citizens are abused or cheapened. I cannot help but be saddened by the amount of greed and selfishness that exists.

And I am convinced that the public schools in this country should be at the forefront of the battle to create a more sensitive, responsive, and responsible society.

At the national meeting of the Progressive Education Association in 1932, George Counts said, "That the existing school is leading the way to a better social order is a thesis which few informed persons would care to defend. Except as it is forced to fight for its own life during times of depression, its course is too serene and untroubled. Only in the rarest of instances does it wage war on behalf of a principle or idea. Almost everywhere it is in the grip of conservative forces and is serving the cause of perpetuating ideas and institutions suited to an age that is gone."[15]

And that is just as true today as it was then.

Should the schools be blamed for the problems of society? Of course not; not entirely. There are too many other forces at work on our citizens' opinions: churches, the military, the workplace, pressure groups, unions, and so on. By the time they graduate, many teenagers, (and this is well documented) will have spent several thousand more hours in front of television sets than they have spent so far in school.

But given the fact I posed earlier—that over half of the young people who enter first grade will receive no other formal academic training beyond the twelfth—and given our potential to *educate* in the best sense of that word (as opposed to *indoctrinate* or *baby-sit* or *coddle* or *maintain the status quo* or whatever phrase comes to your mind, depending in which observer's corner you happen to sit), it is inexcusable for us to continue to graduate young people who don't know how our President gets elected, who never heard of Zimbabwe, who think that the only feature of Argentina worth remembering is that there are gauchos there, who can't explain the First Amendment (or even tell you how amendments are passed), who think that genetic engineering has something to do with exercise equipment, and who, on hearing the names Rubenstein, Pavarotti, or Cezanne, think you are talking about dress shops or a new line of perfumes.

It is inexcusable for us not to be fully aware of the other educational forces going on in young peoples' lives, and then, while we have them, not to work to counteract all the influences on them that are misleading, degrading, mean-spirited, immoral, and cheap.

It is inexcusable for us to not even try to build within our students a sense of social consciousness and conscience; an understanding, through the study of the civil rights movement, for example, of the means by which unjust and unconstitutional laws like those enforcing segregation can and must be changed and new, more morally sound ones implemented; or an understanding of the way certain groups of people are allowed to fall between the cracks of our consciousness or are exploited indefensibly by those in positions of power; and what must be done to redress those imbalances.

It is inexcusable for us not to confront head-on with our students the paramount issue confronting all humankind now and in the future: the awesome, throat-gripping specter of a nuclear war that would render any discussion by any of us as to how to move into the future moot and pointless.

So what should we do?

Do what we would be ideally equipped to do if we cared enough:

First, we should attempt to move students beyond concern with self and self-indulgence as their primary future orientation. We must unbuckle ourselves and our students from the love of things and money over people and the environment.

Second, we should attempt to help students acquire a world view, perspective, and a realization that the United States of America, though it is a great country, is not the navel of the universe. We must counteract the arrogance with which our citizens regard the rest of the world and help them appreciate and accept cultures and values and philosophies that are different from our own rather than trying to make the whole world a carbon copy of Times Square.

Third, we should attempt to help students understand just what is meant by a "better society" or a "better world," and to recognize actions or policies that are likely to run counter to or be destructive of that aim, whether on an international, a national, or a local level. We should try to help them recognize right from wrong where the welfare of human life is concerned. Though many people would give many different definitions of "better society," there are certain overarching truths within which nearly all these definitions would fit, and it is these truths we must recognize ourselves and help our students recognize. Under the umbrella of these truths, certain things going on now can immediately be seen as wrong.

It is clearly wrong, for example, for our society, making up as it does 6 percent of the world's population, to consume one third of the world's resources and generate two thirds of the world's garbage. Where does a sense of global responsibility fit within such statistics?

It is clearly wrong, similarly, for any industry to be allowed to back away from environmental safeguards and standards in the interest of cost efficiency. Economic arguments notwithstanding, actions that jeopardize the future of life itself on this planet are clearly and irrefutably indefensible. Period.

Likewise, it is clearly wrong for industries, like the infant-formula conglomerates, to put their own economic well-being above the well-being of babies in third-world countries who are dying or becoming malnourished as a result of the use of their products. When employees of such companies dress up as medical personnel, as they did in the early 1980s, and go from village to village promoting their products, someone's sense of morality is clearly and unquestionably awry. When the members of the World Health Organization meet in Geneva to vote on a resolution governing the marketing of such products, after years of study, and of the 119 members voting, 118 vote in favor of the controls, and only the United States votes no, it makes a mockery and a sham of our national rhetoric about doing good in the world.[16]

Closer to home, it is clearly wrong for self-interested, selfish individuals to destroy public resources like parks and natural wonders for their own thrills. It is clearly wrong for fools to be allowed to ride roughshod over archaeological monuments on motorcycles. It is clearly wrong to infringe upon another's freedoms or put another's life in jeopardy through crime.

And so on.

Without getting caught in the rhetoric surrounding fuzzier issues, it is a realistic goal to help students identify an entire pantheon of abuses that undermine the quality of life and the "better society" or "better world" we all should so fervently seek. Such work is as clearly part of our job as the teaching of addition and subtraction.

Fourth, as they develop a yardstick for determining right and wrong, we should attempt to help them in the act of deciding what their response is going to be both to clear-cut instances of and general trends toward both right and wrong.

There are lots of ways to go here, including:

• Observing, acknowledging, thanking, rewarding, emulating good decisions and moral actions, which can be just as educationally valuable as focusing on the opposite kinds of decisions and actions—and certainly those with the strength and determination to act morally in the world and stand up for the right deserve some thanks and recognition and support.

• Observing dangerous trends (environmental, for example) or immoral actions (putting corporate profits above human welfare, for example) and deciding, at the very least, never to contribute to or exacerbate such problems.

• Finding needs that exist in the community and figuring out ways to address them. Working as a group to build a park or a playground or lay out a nature trail or create a volunteer service of some sort for the community, or creating a RIF program, or getting involved in adult illiteracy campaigns, or any of scores of other forms of action are all ways of giving a sometimes neglected side of students' personalities some valuable exercise.

• Speaking out in some way, or taking some kind of clear-cut action, either alone or in the company of others, to confront and correct some ill or to push the proper authorities off dead center. Learning *how* to take corrective action that is responsible and reasoned and morally right (as opposed to irresponsible harangues against "the establishment" with only half the needed facts and no solid, well-thought-out remedies, or accusations that turn out to be based on half-truths and misunderstandings that damage reputations and create a climate of hostility and just make things worse instead of better) is one of the most sensitive—and yet one of the vital—aspects of the work of all teachers who really care.

Students should know *how* things get done. They should realize that one of the seemingly universal truths of responsible change is that the passage of a law by the Supreme Court or an environmental standard by the EPA is often a step in the right direction, but only a first step, for usually concerned and continual public pressure of some sort is needed to guarantee enforcement.

During the civil rights struggles of the fifties and sixties, laws were passed in the highest courts of the land guaranteeing blacks the rights to such simple American freedoms as voting, access to a decent education, and equal access to public facilities such as bus stations and restaurants, but until direct, nonviolent action was employed to make sure those laws would be obeyed, nothing happened. John Kennedy, as good a President as he was, did not move on these laws and their enforcement until pushed.

The simple fact is that sometimes positive reform requires direct action, and students should understand from close examination of past events how such action takes place, when it works, when it fails, and why.

And ideally, they and their teachers should then become involved in positive, direct, appropriate action of some sort in their own communities to put into effect and cement what they've learned, for *knowing how to act* and *acting* are two separate realities. This, followed by a period of reflection and analysis to digest the lessons and analyze the consequences; education to preparation for action to action to reflection; that's the ideal process.

I am just as aware of the political realities of the public school system as you are, and you must not be misled into thinking that I am advocating that all of us walk into the fiery furnace of hugely controversial local issues and get ourselves thrown out on our ears. That's just as counterproductive as sitting behind our desks and completely ignoring the world outside. Neither is the answer.

What I am saying is that we *cannot* separate education from the political and social realities our students have to deal with every day and will have to continue to deal with as adults. Failure to examine such realities in our classes simply increases the distance and the isolation between school and the real world.

And no matter where or under what conditions you're teaching, on that huge spectrum between the extremes of simply understanding inequity or wrong so they'll know how to act as *adults*, and taking direct action as *students* inside their communities in any of hundreds of different ways (many of which are acceptable and laudable by even the most conservative school board members), there *are* openings of which you can take advantage to lead them into positive involvement around community needs and/or change. All you have to do is watch for them—and move.

The important thing is that in the face of clear wrongs or needs, we cannot acquiesce and sink into the lobotomized safety of our television sets. All of us are defined by the choices we make in this world.

The heroes many of us have are usually those men and women—some famous and some not—who did just that. Rather than remaining silent and uninvolved, they stood and took the blows for us while the rest of us hid. They were the cutting edge. Others of us got involved later, but only after they had softened the resistance. They were our consciences, doing what we might have done had we been less intimidated. At the same time I was working on this book, I interviewed many of them for a second book that I was writing simultaneously, the royalties from which go to benefit the Highlander Center, an adult education school involved in social change that celebrated its fiftieth birthday in 1982. The people I interviewed included Pete Seeger, Studs Terkel, Rosa Parks, Andrew Young— about thirty adults who had the strength and the conviction to stand up for unpopular causes, knowing they were right, and we have since acknowledged that fact. E. D. Nixon, for example, the Montgomery, Alabama, sleeping car porter who recruited Martin Luther King, Jr., into the civil rights movement, was hated then, and his house was burned down by local rednecks, but he has since been honored with over two hundred plaques and honorary degrees and certificates and keys to cities. People like that.

And one of the questions I asked them all was where they got the strength to take such stands, against what must have seemed insurmountable opposition. Did any of it come as a result of public school experiences? Did any teachers foster or nourish their courage?

In every case, the answer was negative. The schools they attended played no role at all. And I think that is a tragic, damning indictment.

We must foster that kind of courage in our young people, not with the idea that they will eventually emerge as heroes, but with the prayer and the hope that wherever they settle, they will be part of the solution and not part of the problem.

At the same Chicago meeting I mentioned earlier, Myles Horton, the founder of the Highlander School (with which all the adults I interviewed were once connected), said, "You can't just look at the problems of this world and wring your hands. You can talk yourself into a state of utter pessimism in which you believe all is lost and there's no way out. You have to *act* instead of talking. Act your way out of pessimism. . . . Those of us living with the dream of a more humane world know that work—*whatever* it is—can have meaning if that work has to do with laying the groundwork for a society that's worth living in. It may not be everything we want to see happen, but there is some satisfaction in trying to create little pockets, little seeds of a better society. A revolution isn't going to come out of the sky or come winging in from the clouds. That's obvious. So we carve out islands of decency—little units that are contagious and can spread. And then work becomes fun and life becomes interesting again."

Each of us must work to help our students become committed to other people and to the triumphant, humane survival of life in the world. We must help them see that real meaning in life comes in direct proportion to the extent we serve others, and that otherwise it is hollow. We must help them learn about persistence and patience and humility and sensitivity to suffering. We must help them shape ideals. We must help them have the courage that comes from realizing that many have struggled before them and that they are not alone. And we must help them have the strength to move from understanding to action. As they work with others who are afraid, we must help them understand the advice of Ralph Helstein, a labor leader I interviewed in Chicago for the Highlander book, who said, "Look, man doesn't automatically come with courage. Courage is something that grows on him as he learns how to use it. He has to learn *first*, however, what it is to be a human being." We have to help them go surefooted into the world, determined that the world will be a better place for their having been here. We have to help them see that their goal *must* be to enhance life rather than demean it, and that they *must* be people who "enlarge other people's happiness rather than contract it."[17]

Too big a task? Sometimes I think so. But usually when I'm low, a letter comes in from a former student that picks me up again. As I was writing this chapter, for example, a letter arrived from a former student of mine who was just finishing his freshman year in college. I can't take credit for the philosophy he's developing now, but as one of his high school teachers, I can hope fervently that at least I did not retard or discourage the feelings he expressed as follows:

"I've done a lot of thinking about my major. . . . Always before it was, 'What can *I* do to become rich,' and 'How can I support *myself* and have luxury?' Whenever I thought about it, everything seemed fruitless and I was just working on ambition alone. I didn't really have a purpose except the direct purpose of doing it to get it done. And even now I don't claim to have seen any real light, but I don't look at it the same way either. I think that after completing college, I'm going to return home and see if I can do something where I'm really needed. And if not to [my home town of Clayton], I sort of want to work somewhere in Appalachia. I want to make a contribution. I want to put something back into life. What other use is there? Wig, I know that's a far cry from what I have been, but until I started looking at things on those terms, things just didn't fit."

Exactly.

Whose Job Is It?

Teaching basic skills and life survival skills, showing how the world works, fostering involvement in and appreciation for the arts, building personal traits such as curiosity, self-confidence, independence, and self-esteem, and simultaneously moving the student beyond self into a caring relationship with humanity and the environment and a sense of the inter-dependence of all life—a big job indeed. But those *are* our stated goals. Look at your school's statement of purpose. Look at your handbook. There they are. Are they in black and white as window dressing? Are they saying, "Well, we say this but we don't *really* mean it?" Is the message, "Read these but don't *act* on them." Come on. There it is. That's our *job*.

Whose job is it? Well, ideally, the job of everyone from whom young people gain knowledge: parents, teachers, television actors, youth leaders, neighbors, employers. Realistically, since we have most of them captive in an educational environment for twelve years, and since the information they receive from the outside world is so scattershot and contradictory and uneven in terms of quality, a large share of the opportunity *must* rest on our shoulders.

It is for this reason that the best teachers, realizing the limitations on their time and energy, make sure that all the projects and lessons that take place in their classes serve double and triple functions; and they constantly strive to find activities that are so compelling and so rich that they go even beyond that. They are, in short, activities that serve nearly all the goals simultaneously, with no real increase in time or energy required.

Such teachers are a far cry from the one-dimensional types that exist in all our schools. They are the types of teachers all of us should strive to become. They are the types of teachers who have yanked off the blinders that so long have so constricted their views of their particular courses and so limited their range of vision. Suddenly, rather than being narrow and pinched, they see things whole.

The monochromatic ones look at *Foxfire* magazine and see it in black and white. They say, "Oh, look at this. These youngsters are recording and preserving the past. What a nice idea. But where does it fit in the curriculum? How do they learn the basics? What's going to happen when they run into state competency tests?"

The polychromatic ones look at the same product and, keeping our school goals in mind, say, "Take a look at this. *If* this project is being run properly in Georgia, these youngsters are learning a number of very specific language arts skills. They're also gaining a rich, real historical matrix within which they can fit (and appreciate) their other history courses. In addition, they should be learning some math skills, and through their photography and design, they should be coming to an appreciation of the role of the arts in their lives. A whole range of career objectives is being fulfilled through the fact that they're actually running a business, with all that that entails. They're probably acquiring some un-derstanding of culture and what culture means, and through understand-ing and celebrating and criticizing their own, they're probably also more receptive to interactions with other cultures. And on top of all that, they're probably acquiring a good dose of self-confidence and self-es-teem, and the ability to make and weigh the consequences of decisions; and if things are really working properly, as members of a team that must, of necessity, work closely with other people, they're probably learning to care about others besides themselves. And probably a whole lot more than that."

The monochromatic ones may begin such a project, but they will con-strict its focus and its function to the extent that the other potential benefits, if they happen at all, happen only serendipitously to the young-sters involved. The polychromatic ones automatically see all the poten-tial, and they structure the project in such a way that it does double duty, without impossibly increasing their work load.

And so it should be with everything we do.

Book III

Foxfire I: A Grammar/ Composition Course

I never sleep very well the night before the first day of school. My pillow, which I haven't noticed for months, now seems thin and flat, and beneath it, I can feel the fingers of my hand against my ear. For some mysterious reason, I don't know where to put my knees. Every time I begin to drift away, I say to myself, "Good. At last I am falling asleep," and instantly, with the sound of the words so distinct inside my head, I am wide awake again.

When I do sleep at last, it is in the belief that I am still awake. Two of my car's tires are flat. I need a haircut. I don't have any clean socks to wear. Lunch today, our first day back, is a burrito, french fries, peanut butter, a carrot stick and a roll. The ink has completely faded on the lesson plans I wrote last week. There aren't enough desks in my room, so Dennis and Suzanne are sitting together on a counter in the back of the room. My chalk is gone already. I am lecturing about comma splices, but my mouth is dry and no sounds are coming out. Everyone is smiling. A voice on my classroom intercom is calling me to the office, where the assistant principal is sitting on the floor with his legs crossed, surrounded by eleven cartons filled with yellow mimeographed hall passes, which he is counting, two by two, mouthing the numbers silently. I can hear the students in the room next to mine laughing. The guard at the gate has just pulled his pistol and fired at a kid on a bicycle. The bell is ringing to change classes. It's still ringing. Fire drill. No, an alarm clock. I'm still at home and school is about to start. I'm going to be late if I don't move. Outside my bedroom window I hear Jimmy Law's schoolbus go by on Hellcat Creek Road. Move. No time for coffee.

The first few hours of school are sacrificed on the altar of routine. Students assemble in the gym, are divided into homerooms, report to homerooms, fill out information cards, listen to a recitation of school policies. I get a cup of coffee in the lunchroom during break, dropping a dime, as instructed by the sign, into the coffee can beside the urn. The urn, full at the beginning of the day, is almost empty now, but my coin hits the metal in the bottom of the can. Futile business, this wringing coins out of teachers. Why even bother? Don't we at least deserve a free cup of coffee? Looks like we're getting it anyway . . . A bell. My room is filling with students. My class roll calls for twenty-six. Good number. Certain groups are scrambling to get desks together. Business as usual. Looks like Chris has grown at least a foot taller over the summer. His voice has changed. The laughing and talking stops. They are watching me. Waiting. Here we are. What do we do first? Silence.

What we do first and second and third, and why, is curriculum. *Curriculum.* The word resonates with a heavy, important tone. All it really means, however, is what happens to students in school as a result of what teachers do. It is the program of studies, the planned learning experiences for which we are responsible. For each of our courses, it is our road map, listing the towns ("activities") we will pass through on the way to our destination. It anticipates the results of our instruction ("objectives") and outlines our methods of checking our progress ("evaluation").

It all looks so simple and clean and logical when it's written out on paper over a quiet weekend. All the businesslike little blocks and grids: activities, objectives, materials; one, two, three. It's all so precise and ordered, a neat little world beyond the looking glass unto itself, oblivious to the sights and sounds and smells and realities of twenty-five to thirty adolescent brains and bodies, tensed and wired.

It does not (cannot) take into account all the serendipitous, unplanned moments when true learning unexpectedly takes place; the numerous daily variables ranging from teacher and student moods to fire drills that will assault it; the classes that do not even convene because of club meetings or assemblies or snow or films shown in school over a two- or three-day period to raise money for one cause or another; or those times when we simply throw a piece of it away because it is not working, and presumably replace it with some other activity we believe will do the job better.

For the above reasons and more, many teachers despise wrestling with a written plan of attack (or curriculum outline) in advance of the fact. Those on one end of the spectrum say they rely on a free, spontaneous approach to the subject matter that guarantees them maximum flexibility in responding to their students' needs, and thus the effort they put into creating anything more than the briefest outline is a waste of time or, worse, an imposition laid on them by a principal or department head who does not trust them to know what they are doing. They say that since it's an exercise in futility, they never use a plan of attack and have never needed one. I believe they are telling the truth. I also believe they are not very good at their jobs. I would not want one of them on my staff. At the other end of the spectrum are those who claim it is an absolutely pointless exercise, since their courses follow a textbook precisely, and the text itself, with its study hints and relevant questions following each chapter, dictates those courses from beginning to end; there is no need to plan other supplementary activities since there will be no time for them anyway. Most of the rest of us fall somewhere in between those poles.

I used to. Since largely abandoning my textbooks, however, and subsequently finding that I was pretty uncomfortable walking into class without some knowledge of what I wanted to see accomplished before the class was over (sorry, folks, that's the kind of teacher I am); and since moving into a style of teaching that almost demands advance preparation (community visitors to class don't just appear automatically when you want them available for a class interview), I have found that a curriculum outline is not only useful but very nearly as essential to me as wings on a plane. Best of all, once I am able to develop a good one, I can fine-tune it and alter it and play with it with relatively little effort. As I think of new activities, or students suggest changes or shifts, I can lift old pieces out and drop new ones into their places almost as easily as if the curriculum were a board game. When major changes are called for, I just grit my teeth and start rewriting. That is not to say my courses are planned to the point that they are inflexible or refuse to allow for the unexpected or for student input, for a curriculum plan must not be static. It must be a living thing, constantly being altered as we grow and learn and constantly being reworked to fit the circumstances. It *is* to say, however, that rather than just flying by the seat of my pants, I think long and hard about every activity that is going to go on in my classroom, the rationale behind it, and how it fits into the scheme of things when I get up into the sky above the fray, shut out all the noise, and look down upon the world from that much-needed perspective to make sure, to the extent possible, I know what I'm doing.

For those of you who are interested, then, let me take one of my courses and dissect it. In our school's course guides, it is called Foxfire I. It was developed several years ago after our school adopted the quarter system and demanded that in order to graduate, each senior must have completed at least three quarter-long composition courses, three grammar courses, and three literature courses. Foxfire I is one of several courses a student can elect to earn a composition credit toward graduation. A student can take it only once.

Students register for the courses they will take in any upcoming quarter two weeks before the current quarter ends. They register by homerooms, seniors first, in the cafeteria, where each department in the school has a table set up with sign-up sheets for the courses it offers. It is first come, first served, and when a course is full, it is closed until the following quarter. To guarantee an age mix in Foxfire I, I usually save a certain number of slots for eighth-, ninth-, and tenth-graders so that the older students cannot fill the course completely. One selfish reason for holding slots for younger students is that Foxfire I is a required prerequisite for Foxfire II—the course in which students produce *Foxfire* magazine—and I want to be able to start identifying (and hopefully holding) promising talent earlier than the eleventh and twelfth grades. Another reason is that I enjoy working with an age and ability mixture because of the possibilities it opens up for peer teaching situations.

[Note: As this book was going into production, several major changes were put into effect in our school starting with the 1984–85 school year: we reverted to the old eighteen-week semester system, and we began to schedule students by computer. Students now must have a combination of eight eighteen-week-long grammar/composition courses, literature courses, speech, and English electives to graduate. Despite the new scheduling system, I have been able to retain the age and ability mix I want; the course now counts as one of the grammar/composition offerings from which students may select, and they still may take it only once. The addition of six weeks opens a host of new opportunities for the twelve-week course described here. I suspect that what will happen is that I will lengthen the amount of time spent on portions of the course that were treated too superficially before and add some new units to broaden the course's scope, but I will not be able to tell you what actually happened until the end of this school year.]

Foxfire I, like the other courses in the school, is a daily fifty-five-minute course. It is composed of twenty-four students that meet in my classroom during fifth period (1:10–2:05). The classroom itself is filled with the tools of my trade: books, traditional tools, pieces of pottery and furniture, and equipment like cameras and tape recorders. Since we were allowed to hang nothing from the cement block walls, the students lifted the ceiling tiles, attached wires to the girders above, and suspended bamboo poles horizontally against the ceiling, from which we then hung quilts and other artifacts. On balance, the room is bright, colorful, and, above all, interesting. It draws spectators. It says, "Serious, real work goes on in this room, but it's fascinating stuff. You'll probably like it. It's different." Furniture in the room is rearranged on an average of once a year by student vote and student labor. I like the room. I always get a little lift of spirit when I walk in the door—and that's important. A teacher cannot function properly in an unfriendly space.

There are scores of methodological approaches to any course: the course may be taught by the lecture method, the stick-to-the-text method, the self-paced study guide and workbook method, the modular instruction method (self-study packages with audio and visual media), the simulation method (where students do reading and personal research, and enact, utilizing their findings, situations involving issues like women's rights or the nuclear arms buildup or the battles between environmentalists and industrialists and factory workers), the contract method, the tutorial method, the class discussion method, the peer teaching method, the hands-on experiential method—or a combination of any or all of the above, and more. The method we choose for instruction in any course depends, to get embarrassingly basic, on such things as the material to be taught and the course objectives, the class size, the characteristics of the students in the class, the teaching resources available, the nature of the school and its flexibility or inflexibility, parental desires, and our own personalities and needs and insecurities and strengths as teachers.

When I first designed my Foxfire I course in 1978, for example, I knew going in that certain methods were out, either because of a lack of materials (modular instruction), or inappropriateness to the course objectives (workbooks, to my way of thinking, at least). I also knew, from years of experience with students in this school system, that the *majority* of my students would be below national averages in language arts skills, would come to me having already decided they did not like English for whatever reasons, would be almost completely resistant to the "what are the elements of a paragraph" didactic approach to writing, and would be as restless as a roomful of weasels. They would know already that the rules of English make no sense (give me the past tenses of *bake, take, make,* and *break* and tell me how logical our language is), and that the Emily Post propriety of "It is I" and "This is he" is stupid and perhaps even dangerous given their belief that any person who uses such language should be branded forever and cast into darkness.

[I can already see some readers nodding their heads and saying to themselves, "What he just said contradicts completely his earlier statements about not making negative assumptions concerning student potential." Not quite. I am never negative about student *potential.* I never allow myself to fall into the trap of saying that because my students are behind in terms of skills they should have mastered by the time they enter high school, they therefore cannot catch up and therefore do not deserve my best energy, do not deserve the finest class that we can create together, and do not deserve to be trusted or to be given real responsibility. In fact, the moments in my teaching career of which I am proudest are those when I have seen students who were assumed by others to be lost turn completely around. What I am saying, and I want to be clear here, is that based on years of real observation (not speculation), I knew that most of the students I received would still be writing at the *kinda, sorta* and *alot* level, and that that fact dictated a certain teaching style that might not otherwise have been necessary.]

Knowing all that—knowing, in other words, that I would not have a room full of young people who had already decided they wanted to be professional authors and playwrights and were consequently starved for instruction as to the finer points of the craft, and knowing that a substantial portion of the students would be right-brain types who would not easily internalize verbal instruction and lecture, I knew, for starters, that I would have to employ almost all the other teaching methods and materials left to me to make the class fast-paced, full of variety, unpredictable, and infused with energy. I would have to keep things moving or I would lose them. (I prefer this method anyway, for the ultimate advantage of the experience-rich, fast-moving approach is that it gives me numerous opportunities to get to a reluctant student and engage his or her interest.) In addition, I knew that some few of the students would *not* fit the normal pattern mold and would come to me already comfortable with written expression. Our agenda would have to be flexible enough to allow and encourage those to take in all the work they could handle to guarantee their growth also. In other words, there would have to be ample opportunity for me to give quality attention to individual efforts that went beyond what was required.

I knew in advance that the mood I would have to project would be not, "I know you come to me severely lacking in skills and my job is to fix your inadequacies," but rather, "I know you can do good work in language arts and my job is to prove it to you, and have you prove it to yourselves. Before this class is over, you will be amazed at what you can create." I knew I would have to try to build intrinsic rather than extrinsic motivations for learning the material. I knew the mood in the classroom would largely have to be one of celebration, amazement, surprise, adventure—a series of constantly unfolding experiences that would have them exclaiming to their peers over lunch about what they were doing. I wanted them coming into class every day ready for action.

Whew. Big order. Probably more than I could fill. But worth the attempt. I wanted it, in short, to be one of the best English courses in the school—and one of my favorites.

To specifics: in the state of Georgia, as in most other states, I have a mandate to get a certain number of skills and concepts into students' brains, and the *methodology* and content I use are largely up to me and what my superiors will accept. If I don't do crazy, outrageous, and destructive things, I have a certain amount of flexibility as a responsible, caring, professional teacher, as long as I can demonstrate results and prove that I am more than a hired teen-sitter.

Setting aside methodology for the moment, I must be able to answer the questions, "Exactly what am I expected to accomplish in a twelve-week composition course?" "What skills and concepts are the students supposed to learn?" "What is my job, as defined by the state and local school boards?"

I must answer the question "Why?" Why should my students be able to do these things? What good will these skills be to them? How will they be able to use them? What are they for? I have to be able to answer that universal student question, "Why are you making us sit here and do this?"

Third, reminding myself of the school goal that insists that all our subjects serve the betterment of the larger society, and reminding myself that everything we teach must be an entry into that bigger picture, I ask myself what the content of my course is going to be—at least for now, until I and my students know each other well enough that we can make alterations together.

Fourth, I have to ask, "Are the materials I currently have available adequate to do the job?" Are there other, more appropriate materials I can scrounge, beg, or borrow that will do the job more efficiently? Can students create their own learning materials and get the job done as well? Or better?

Last, I ask not, "Can I do the job?" but, "Will I do the job?" Yes or no? For I believe what I do as a teacher is important. As Hugh Keener said in the November, 1977, issue of *Johns Hopkins Magazine* (p. 19), "Someone's life may be changed by a suggestion you never meant to implant, by a casual word. . . . What we do [as teachers] matters. And what we do therefore deserves all the attention we can muster."

In Georgia, we have a Competency Based Education (CBE) program leading to graduation. Students who fail to pass the Basic Skills Test (BST) do not graduate with a diploma but with a certificate of attendance, regardless of their high school grades.

Here's what the CBE program tells me to teach: there are five "learner" competencies for which students will be tested through a 100- to 120-item multiple choice Basic Skills Test before graduation: mathematics, problem solving, reading, writing, and speaking/listening.

As a teacher putting a new composition course together, I knew I was responsible for *at least* teaching directly and successfully the following state-mandated writing "Enabling Skills":

> Write neatly, accurately, legibly.
> Organize thoughts, details, ideas in logical pattern or sequence.
> Control organizational pattern with thesis stating central idea.
> Maintain unity and coherence within organizational pattern.
> Select writing style, tone, diction appropriately for purpose, audience, occasion.
> Distinguish among feelings, opinions, ideas and factual information.
> Support written opinions with logic, evidence or factual details.

That was the bottom line—the academic mandate for the course. Answers to all the other questions—the methodology, the content, the why, the materials used—were left up to me as a professional. What I knew was not negotiable, however, was a dimension of academic rigor—certain standards of excellence and academic responsibility that would be unassailable. I decided, at that point, on at least one major (300- to 500-word minimum) composition a week from my students, to be graded immediately, rigorously, and with substantial attention to content, style, and organization. Some might call that oppressive. Fine. I didn't then, and I don't now. I insist on the best my students can give me for their own self-respect, and I've never been sorry.

Then I took the next step: as long as I was going to be teaching composition, weren't there other allied state-mandated skills that I could address simultaneously with little or no extra effort on my part and that could naturally be wedded to the work that was going on anyway? I went back to the state guidelines: "Use correct spelling, punctuation, and capitalization." "Use basic English sentence patterns." "Use standard English usage forms including subject-verb agreement, antecedent agreement, verb forms." Given our department's composition/grammar/literature format, I wasn't *responsible* for grammar in my Foxfire I course, but it was difficult for me to divorce the two skills and put them in separate boxes, especially considering the fact that I believed I could deal with them together and that to split them up was pointless. [Note: as I mentioned earlier, under the new semester system, grammar and composition are now back together again, taught as one course.] The only argument, in fact, that I could find for separating them was one advanced by a colleague of mine who said, "Fine, but remember that if students have to pay attention to grammar and mechanics at the same time they write compositions, their writing will be timid and constricted and tentative out of fear of making grammatical mistakes that will bring their grades down."

For this reason, I decided to give each composition two grades—one for content and one for grammar—and to allow students to rewrite their compositions as often as they wanted in order to improve either or both grades. To divorce the two skills, however, seemed artificial and silly. I began from that premise and I maintain it today, for clear, logical thinking and writing and accurate use of the language seem to me to be very closely allied. How can one write three or four clear, expository paragraphs, for example, without also paying attention to the basics of syntax, sentence structure, pronoun usage, agreement, tense, and all the other allied skills? It just doesn't work.

Fine. At this point I stopped to look at the course again: Foxfire I. Composition. Twelve weeks—twelve compositions—grammar included. Now, what would I have them write *about?* At this point in my career, I had the undeniable advantage of having already worked with hundreds of students in numerous different types of activities, from writing scripts for and filming satirical television commercials through writing the standard papers around topics like alcoholism and teenage pregnancy. The feedback I continually received from former students told me that those things we did together that concerned the culture from which they came had turned out, in retrospect, hands down, to have been the most beneficial, the most interesting, and hence the most memorable. Since I had never had an introductory course that concentrated on the overall culture and was a prerequisite to the Foxfire II classes that produced our magazine, I couldn't shake the notion that a solid twelve-week preparatory course would not only result in my having students in my magazine classes who were operating with a much higher level of sophistication and understanding vis-à-vis their own culture and the importance of the magazine's work, but could also give them an opportunity, before they were plunged into the work, to see whether they wanted to take a magazine class at all. At the same time, I could give those students a solid enough composition course that even if they did not go on to Foxfire II, they would have acquired some real skills in writing, would not have lost any ground academically, and would presumably walk away with a deeper understanding of their roots and traditions—an understanding that would go far beyond the gratuitous, false, "one log cabin plus one log cabin equals two log cabins" attention some teachers pay to culture in the mistaken notion that they are making their courses somehow more relevant.

I had come to the firm belief that this understanding was vital partly through former student feedback, partly through my knowledge that not a single other teacher or course in the entire school was paying any attention to it at all, partly through observing the almost complete and needless ignorance of my students regarding their own culture, partly through my realization that almost nothing in their lives was at work to counteract the negative national stereotype of the ignorant Southern Appalachian hick—and the effect of that stereotype on other people's opinions about them and their potential—partly through watching the astonishment and the grins on the faces of students I had had as they became caught up by and immersed in some traditional custom—and the joy and satisfaction with which some older person had introduced them to it—partly through my conviction that pride in background and roots has much to do with pride in self and with mental health and with never again having to feel apologetic for origins, and on and on for enough pages to fill another chapter. If some of the compositions dealt directly with culture and others dealt with the means of exploring and presenting certain aspects of culture as well as the carriers of the traditions themselves, that should give me enough leeway in terms of types of compositions to hit all the various CBE objectives several times apiece.

How would I build in other aspects that I knew to be important to keep the course fast-paced and varied? Taking each week as a distinct unit or block of time, I decided to try as best I could to structure into *each* block, above and beyond times when I would probably have to do a certain amount of lecturing, times for discussion, a certain number of hands-on activities and experiences, opportunities for peer teaching, opportunities for small-group work, and times of "planned chaos," when everyone could take a break and relax for a moment and just enjoy being with each other in my room. Recognizing that aside from prior student input, I was putting this new course together myself ("I decided," "I determined," etc.—and I do not believe that that is inappropriate in a situation like this, by the way, where a teacher is drawing on all his or her past experiences to create an outline for an experimental course offering that will go beyond anything he or she has ever offered previously), I consciously built in times when student input and evaluation would determine absolutely the changes and mutations the course would undergo. I also drew up a list of activities for use in emergency situations (films, videotapes, etc.), when either the students or I or all of us were having a bad day and just couldn't make the planned agenda work. That happens.

Knowing the danger of fragmentation inherent in splitting the course into twelve distinct units, I also began to structure in ways to build on themes or skills initiated previously and reinforce them and/or lead the students on to new levels of understanding or competence. I knew I had to try to make sure that each unit, though it was distinct, was linked to the last, giving that sense of forward motion and growth and momentum I so wanted the students to experience.

Last, I became familiar with the rest of the CBE objectives so that, as natural unforced opportunities arose, I could experiment with them out of my own curiosity, out of my own conviction that as long as I was teaching the course, anyway, I ought to make it do double duty when I could without adding extra work to my load, and out of a genuine desire to perhaps reinforce what some of the other teachers in the school were doing. There had to be opportunities for interdisciplinary linkages, for example, that would help the students see certain important connections they might otherwise have missed.

How I addressed the needs (not always successfully) articulated earlier for usable class projects, intrinsic motivation, and forceful real-world linkages will be revealed, I think, as you look at the course itself. Here's what the course looked like during the 1983–84 school year:

Week One—Tape Recorders

Now an adult who has never been in this situation cannot fully appreciate the range of emotions that well up inside a teacher facing a room full of teenage strangers. There's an intensity there that is unique and, despite all preparation, instantly disarming. I need time to look at them, watch them, get used to having them in the room. Therefore, on the first day, rather than giving them lists of rules and a description of the course and so forth, I give them three pretests, one at a time, emphasizing that the results will not affect their grades at all but rather are my means of testing myself. The first is a list of words any of their grandparents would recognize, which I ask them to define. The second is a piece of writing filled with the kinds of errors our English department is trying to eliminate from student compositions. They correct any errors they can find. Last, I ask them to write a composition pretending that I am a stranger to the mountains and know nothing about the Appalachian region, its geographical location, its history, its people and their origins, their culture, and their traditions. I know nothing, in short, about what makes the region unique or different from other parts of the country except what they can tell me. While they write, I walk around the room memorizing names and just feeling the pulse. It gives me breathing room and a chance to become oriented.

As they finish (and depending on the group, the pretests may take a full day or a day and a half), I collect their work, give each student a clean manila folder and a copy of the newest issue of *Foxfire* to look through. Students put their names on the folder tabs, and at the end of class, when they return them to me, I construct my class roll. I keep all the pretests in a drawer in my room, and students do not see them again until the end of the quarter.

When all the students have put their names on their folders and have flipped through the magazine, I explain that the folders are for all the work we will do in class together, and that their final grade will be based largely on their contents, which will include all their compositions and revisions, class notes, diagrams, progress charts, and the like. If they have questions about the course or how they will be graded, they can ask them at this point.

Under normal circumstances, I am by now about halfway through the second day. I take the next five minutes to show them one of the artifacts I have in the room that came from this or a nearby county (one that was named on the first pretest) and demonstrate its use, emphasizing the ingenuity of the settlers who developed it and the skill of those who used it. It is a custom I follow every day for the first few weeks and every two or three days thereafter, beginning the class each time with a new item and its purpose. At various times interspersed between activities throughout the rest of the quarter, I also introduce them to terms on the pretest list that refer not to artifacts but to customs, types of legendary animals, diseases, and so on. By the time the quarter ends, we have covered the entire list and more, and the activity provides an interesting way to begin a day or break up a class period; it is always a time when the students are focused, attentive, and curious. As they mention words at home that they were not familiar with until my class, family members tend to reinforce the activity by their responses and provide the students with stories they bring to class ("My grandmother said that one time she was making some white oak splits for a chair bottom and . . .").

If the second day's period is almost over, I show them a second artifact. If I have at least twenty minues left before the bell, I read them, without explanation, a very short story transcribed from a tape recording made of one of our contacts. One they seem to like is "The Buzzard and the Dog" from *The Foxfire Book* (pp. 228–29), which, coincidentally, includes some information about early fertilizers. There are hundreds of others I could choose, however. Then I ask them to take out a piece of paper and come as close as they can to reproducing the story. They usually stare at me as though I have lost my mind, and I say, "Come as close as you can. If you can't reproduce it exactly, tell it in your own words." When they have worked for about five minutes, I stop them and ask for two volunteers to read their versions. If I can't find any volunteers, I ask for two students to allow me to read theirs for them, promising that we're not going to make fun of what they wrote. After reading, the students invariably agree that the version from the book that is in the contact's own words is the better one, and they can usually be pretty specific about why, since the student versions rarely come close to the lively, rich tone of the original.

I say, "Okay. Pretend I'm the contact who's telling the story. Turn your papers over and try to keep up with me so you can get the story in my words." I begin to read the story again, slowly. Even though I'm going slowly, however, by the time I reach the third sentence, students are already yelling at me to wait or slow down. I say, "If you keep asking me to stop, I'm going to get pretty tired of this. There *has* to be a better way. What do we do?"

Usually someone will suggest using a tape recorder. Whether or not this happens, I reach into a desk drawer and pull one out. Continuing to use the backs of their papers, we make a list of reasons together for using recorders, such as, "You remember the *story* but you forget the exact adjectives and descriptive words and phrases"—and "You can't listen and write at the same time."

Finally I make several concluding points, such as the fact that the contact who told us the story is dead and, had we not taped it, we could never have heard him tell it in his own words again; and I introduce the point to them that writing, in a sense, is speech, and that when we write a composition, we are actually talking to an imagined person or audience on paper. We use a different format, but the intent is the same—lively, interesting, or informative communication. Picking up one of the *Foxfires* from a student's desk, I note, "Much of the writing in here is from tape-recorded interviews. Take these home and read." Their papers go into their folders at the end of class.

By the third day, we are working. Moving fast, I ask, "How did we get that story off the tape?" The process of transcribing word for word suddenly becomes a skill to be reckoned with. More paper. "Let's make a list. Why do we want to use good-quality tape like TDK or BASF or Scotch or Memorex?"

"Because cheap tapes break." "Cheap tapes get tangled up in the recorder," "Cheap tapes don't last."

"Why do we want only high-quality recordings?"

"Because you can't transcribe them if you can't hear them." "Because someone might want copies for the family after the person interviewed has died." "Because as long as you're recording *anyway*, you might as well go ahead and get the best you can." "Because you might want to play it to our class and we wouldn't be able to understand it." "Because it won't *sound* like the person if it's not good." And so forth.

"How do we get good quality?" I ask for two volunteers who know how to use cassette tape recorders already. Grabbing an inexpensive one, a reasonably high quality one (something like a Superscope by Marantz) and two tapes, I ask the students to set both up on a small table in front of the class and get ready to record. There's always good-natured laughter and anticipation here, and the class is completely centered. I check what the volunteers have done, make any corrections necessary out loud ("This is really a common mistake. No criticism is in order. Try to remember . . ."), and ask the student to start the machines recording. Standing directly over the recorders, I say, "Now I am talking in a normal tone of voice from about three feet away and presumably these recorders are working." Continuing to talk nonstop in a normal tone of voice (asking the class to keep quiet for now so the recorders will pick up only the sound of my voice), I move around the room, sometimes facing completely away from the recorders, always describing my distance from them and my position; and then I return to the table, still talking. As I continue, I ask the students first to fiddle with the machines, moving the volume and tone dials back and forth to see if that has any effect at all, then to tap on the built-in microphones, bump the machines up and down, place their hands over the microphones, and the like. Then, still talking, I ask the whole class, on a signal from me, to begin murmuring together ("banana, banana" or some such) and laughing; and then I ask for questions from various parts of the room. When finished, I play each of the tapes back. The class is frozen, listening, comparing their quality, my position during periods of highest, clearest fidelity, and so on. "Now, what have you learned about the limitations of the equipment, the placement of the recorder/microphone?" and so on. To build anticipation and interest, I now tell them that by the third week, we will divide into small working groups, each of which will conduct an interview in class, using a recorder. "When that happens, where should the group conducting the interview sit? Where should the contact sit?" Notes are optional here. They'll remember.

Two more important points to make now, everyone listening: record something on tape with the recorder you plan to use *before* you start interviewing, and play it back. Record, for example, your names, the date, and who you're about to interview. Why?

They brainstorm again, making notes. "To make sure everything is working." "To make sure you haven't forgotten a tape!" "To make sure you have a cord." I embellish accurate points as the students volunteer them with horror stories of things that have happened in the past on interviews in the community to drive the point home; then move on to the second:

"Do you ever tape in secret or without permission?"

Confusion.

"Never. Why?" I lead them through a quick but forceful discussion of the ethics of the situation, possible lawsuits and libel cases, and Watergate stories (a situation with which many are not familiar. Has it been *that* long ago?).

Now, still moving fast, I divide the class into five convenient groups, get a volunteer from each, give each volunteer a recorder and tape, and instruct each group to make sure *every* member knows how the machine works. This always turns into the beginnings of what will emerge as some solid peer teaching activities. With the groups preoccupied, I can visit each and double-check, often having each student in the group show me which buttons to press to record. When they're all ready, I ask each group to designate a narrator and have that narrator tell a quick joke (no racial jokes allowed) or story about something that happened on the way to school that day, and after about two minutes I stop them, have the narrators rewind the tapes while everyone else is getting their paper and pens ready, and then I have them figure out how to transcribe. I leave them alone at this point. They'll figure it out. When they've transcribed for a few minutes, I have the narrators, who have been operating the recorders according to their groups' shouted instructions ("Wait!" "Stop!" "Go back!" "Slow it down!") play the piece they transcribed over again so the others in their group can check what they wrote.

Ten minutes left. (Unless we had to hold the buzzard story until today. If so, parts of this get postponed. You know how to deal with this situation.) Someone in each group puts the recorders and tapes away. All class members now know where they are stored.

I wrap the day with a caution about making sure transcriptions are accurate ("We don't want to put words in people's mouths or distort what they said") and a statement about using permission slips. "We show the interviewee what we want to print *before* we print it in *Foxfire*, so he or she will have a chance to correct it, and we *must* have their signed permission —*not forged*—in order to print." The day ends with a discussion of why.

Notes into folders. Bell.

By Thursday, they are ready for their first compositions. The assignment is for them to pretend that I know nothing about the reasons for using tape recorders, the means of or rationale behind ensuring quality, the necessary preparations for an interview, the placement of the equipment during the interview, the skills of transcribing, or the ethics of the situation. Though I do not ask them to explain precisely how to use the equipment itself (which buttons to press to record, for example), I do ask them to explain in detail what they can remember of the rest of what we talked about, as well as what they learned from (as opposed to how to repeat) the in-class demonstrations. To help them with their paragraph structure and sequence, we usually make a list together on the board of one- and two-word hints, in some logical sequence, each standing for the contents of one paragraph (why tape at all/why use quality tape and quality equipment/placement/initial check/treatment of equipment/ transcribing, etc.). They write for most of the period, using their class notes if they wish, and their compositions tell me immediately where they are in terms of skills, how much they have remembered of the important points I have covered, whether there are misunderstandings I must clear up at once, and whether or not I am moving them too fast.

Thursday evening I begin a ritual that will continue for the entire twelve weeks. As I read their papers for content, I place a check in the right-hand margin for every important point they make. I also make a quick master list of each point, adding to the list whenever a composition notes one that the previous papers have missed. The total number of checks on each paper (totaled in the upper right hand corner) gives me a means of assigning a relatively objective content grade.

Then I read over the papers a second time, marking mechanical and grammatical errors. I label each error, using standard proofreaders' marks, and, in the left-hand margin opposite the error, subtract a certain number of points for each (15 points for every fragment, comma splice, and fused sentence; 5 for each agreement problem and each impersonal use of *you;* 3 for spelling, misuse of apostrophes, capitalization errors, punctuation, and so forth). I resisted this system for several years, feeling that negative grammar grades would destroy some of the more fragile students, but with my careful explanation of *why* I'm doing it, and with the option all the students have of rewriting their papers as often as they want, it seems to be working. (And when a student is so far behind in skills that he or she makes multiple errors in each line of the composition, I am usually more selective about the number of errors I mark, concentrating instead on five or six errors of the same type on each of his or her papers.)

I total the number of points in the upper left hand corner, subtract that total from 100, and place the result in the fraction.

I also note problems with style or paragraph structure in the margins and note good paragraphs or especially well stated observations. I always try to find several things in every paper that I congratulate, and I often share excerpts from some with the whole class.

Next, I go to my typewriter and type what I call a Grammar Sheet,

which is, quite simply, a page of sentences lifted directly and anonymously from their papers, each of which contains one or more errors I do
not want to see in their writing. I try to use at least one sentence from
every single paper, so that each student will experience that shock of
recognition and no student will have grounds for ridiculing any other.
They're all in the same boat.

Last, I make a chart that shows me the total number of As, A minuses, B
pluses, Bs, and so on, in content and the range of grades in grammar so
that I can copy it onto the board the next day and show the students how
they ranked in relation to the rest of their class.

Though this process sounds rather lengthy and cumbersome, with
experience, it really goes more quickly than one might imagine. With
twenty-four students, I can usually complete the entire job in two and one
half hours—or an average of approximately five to six minutes per paper.
In addition, it absolutely sets me up for the next day. I'm ready. I'm
infused with that sense of anticipation I feel only when I'm really prepared for the next day. I *want* them to be in that Friday class. I feel like a
prizefighter who's completely in control. I'm primed to say to them, "I'm
going to make this the best composition class you've ever had."

On Friday, before returning the papers, I copy the grade chart onto the
board. Next I ask each to take a clean sheet of paper and draw a grid that
has the list of proofreaders' marks I use *(sp, cs, frag, agr,* and so forth, and
the numerical weight of each) in the left margin, one per line, and the
numbers 1 through 12, indicating the composition number, in a horizontal row across the top. Then I return the papers and ask them, under the
number 1 on their charts, to place a number beside each appropriate
proofreaders' mark indicating the number of times they made a mistake
in, say, spelling. This chart becomes their own individual progress report,
kept up to date weekly, as well as an extremely useful tool for me.

Now I explain how I arrived at each content grade (I copy my abbreviated "points covered" list onto the board, which gives me a chance to
quickly reinforce the things I want them to remember about using tape
recorders, and gives them a chance to check their papers' contents
against the master list), and I clear up any serious misunderstandings that
I feel need immediate attention—usually only one or two, if any. Reminding them that they can rewrite their papers as often as they wish, I
then pass out the duplicated grammar sheets, and we spend the remainder of the period going over the sentences one by one, finding and
circling or correcting the errors (at the end of the quarter, they get an
extra half-point added to their final grade for every grammar sheet that is
completely corrected). At the end of the period, their papers and grammar sheets go into their folders.

At some point during the weekend, I evaluate the first week and fill out my first activity chart.* Did things move quickly enough? Too quickly? Are students above or below my expectations in terms of skills? Are some so far behind or so far ahead of the others that they need special attention or a special program of some sort? Can I identify any students now as promising peer teachers? Are there potential discipline problems building that I need to watch closely and perhaps deal with on Monday? Are there students in the class whose families I already know and, consequently, can think of some way of involving? Do I know the grandparents of one of the students, for example, and would I want to try to get one or both of those grandparents into class to demonstrate some skill before the quarter is over? What am I going to do, starting next week, to find out what resources the other students represent of which I am currently ignorant? Did I involve students enough in discussion and small-group activity, or did I lecture too much? What mid-course corrections are necessary? What am I forgetting? Like that.

(Now the absolutely frustrating part about writing this course description, for me, is the number of variables I encounter with each sentence I write that could be expounded upon for pages. Leading discussions, for example. Or the various methods of helping students understand paragraph structure. Look at the peer teaching sentence for a moment. Each of us might use a different method for identifying such students. Some teachers would choose only the best and brightest for such roles. Others might choose the most articulate. Others might shy from the practice entirely. We could talk about the pros and cons and the means endlessly. Sometimes I'll use a bright older student to teach certain skills to other students, matching them with each other according to my own set of guidelines, which have grown out of my own sometimes successful and sometimes calamitous experiences. At other times, I'll take a student who may be failing and badly in need of a boost, train that student myself in a certain skill, and then match that student with two or three others who need to learn it; and I choose that student not because he or she is either bright or articulate, necessarily, but just simply because he or she needs that ego boost. At other times, I'll have a younger one train an older one for some special reason. Or I'll enlist the help of an older one privately, as a special favor to me, to give me a hand with a younger one who is floundering—not because the older one is particularly bright necessarily, but because he or she is a certain personality type I want to put to use. This could go on, with examples, but Lord, this book would never end. All I know how to do, for now, is remind you that Part II and this part go together, even though they're separated; to assume that you already know or will remember that positive energy and commitment to young people

---

* Though it seemed rather pointless and cumbersome at first, I soon got caught up in this weekly ritual of analyzing the days just completed, and trying as honestly as I could to plot my methodology and content to ensure variety. It's like a game.

nearly always points us in the appropriate directions once it is part of our mind set; and to plunge on in this shamefully abbreviated—but necessary —fashion with the skeleton of the rest of this course. There are still eleven weeks to cover.)

Week Two—Cameras

Monday of the second week. After looking at an artifact (something we will do together at the beginning of every day this week), I spend ten to fifteen minutes talking about grammar and mechanics. I explain that I see no use for using grammar texts together as a class and that I don't intend to do it (sigh of relief, usually), though I have a classroom set available if needed. I believe that at this point in their lives, they are generally immune to grammar books; that many exercises I would assign to the class would be a waste of time for at least half its members; that what we need to work on rather is specific skills with which each, individually, is having problems; and that after all have written several compositions, I will be able to see from the charts in their folders which problems keep recurring each week with each student and will be able to tailor special activities—which may or may not employ texts—for all who, for example, still do not understand subject-verb agreement. I say to them, "Look, let's just fix this kind of error now, once and for all, so you won't ever have to worry about it again."

Then we brainstorm for a few minutes about the need for writing accurately. When someone volunteers, "Because it makes you look dumb if your writing is full of mistakes," I pull a handful of examples that I have been collecting for years out of a notebook on my desk, and to which I constantly add new examples as I run across them. (One of my favorites is a full-page ad for Federal Express that ran in the September 5, 1977, issue of *Newsweek*, part of which stated, ". . . we're the only people who will come to your office, pick up the package, fly it overnight in our own planes, and deliver it to you before noon the next day." Do I really want this company to pick up a package from me, fly it around all night, and then bring it back to me the next day?) I try to make it a high-spirited session, full of laughter and noise, but with a serious message that will be repeated often: "It is *not* that hard to gain control over your problems; I will help you as much as I can; many times the first impression a potential employer has of you is through your résumé, and if it is full of errors, it makes you look stupid, and I don't want you to look stupid." I show them examples of résumés I have received from people who have wanted to work for me—résumés full of grammatical mistakes—and explain that I know, sight unseen, that these résumés represent people I would not want on my staff. I don't even grant them interviews.

Then we move into the use of single-lens-reflex cameras. Sometimes I hand out a drawing of one first and ask them to label any parts they can identify as a pretest. My idea was that when they took the posttest at the end of the week, they would be able to see immediately how much they had learned and get some instant, positive feedback. More recently, however, I have abandoned that. They seem to realize without comparing pre- and post-test results that they know far more at the end of the week than they did at the beginning, and the use of the test seems somehow contrived. I may go back to it later. I have mixed feelings as to its use.

At any rate, I begin by taking a Pentax K1000 out of my desk drawer and explaining that every student in the class will be using it before the quarter is over (most have not used one before), that they will also print photographs they have taken themselves in our darkroom, and that the camera is a precision piece of equipment that is expensive and, though sturdy, can be broken, and it deserves their respect. I say that they need to listen to me very closely, even though it usually seems unnecessary to say it. They are watching every move I make.

First I caution them about removing the front flap of the case, explaining that the fastening system in the back may be a half-moon device, a snap, or any of several other designs, and if they pull too hard without thinking, they can tear the flap.

Then, carefully cradling the camera in my hands, I talk about basic care (the need for keeping one's fingers off the lens, for example) and the absolute necessity of *never* forcing any mechanism. ("When you feel yourself forcing something, stop and think. Your camera is shouting at you, saying, 'Wait. Something's fouled up here. Don't push me. Take a look.' ")

Now we talk about the viewfinding system that makes a single-lens-reflex camera unique. I explain how it works, cautioning, "Remember. What you see is what you get. If you look through the viewfinder and the image you see inside has someone's feet cut off, that's the picture you'll get. Is that what you want? Check the background. If there's a power line going across the corner, you'll have it in your photograph too. Is that what you want? How much wasted space is there on either side of the subject? Should you turn the camera up and make a vertical rather than a horizontal composition?" And I explain focus.

Now I split them up into groups again, have one person from each group get a camera from me, open the case, and focus on something in the classroom. As each finishes, I check to make sure he or she has focused properly, giving extra help where needed. Then in each group, I have that student take the camera out of focus, pass it to the next student in the group, have that next student focus on something and then let the first check what he or she has done, and so on around each group's tight circle until each student has handled the camera, focused on something, and been checked by the student from whom he or she got the camera. In this way, each person in the group is momentarily a peer teacher, and, watching the activity, I can continue to identify students I am going to want to use in this role later.

Despite my cautions, by now each camera will probably have finger-prints on its lens. It happens inadvertently as cameras pass from hand to hand. There is no cause for anger or criticism, just an opportunity to reinforce an important point gently. I hand out lens cleaning paper to each group, demonstrate its use to the class, have each group clean its camera's lens, replace its case, and return the cameras to the desk drawer.

On Tuesday, we review briefly points made on the previous day, and then I show the class the photographs selected for the covers of *Foxfire 6* to *8*. We talk about their composition, noting especially such things as the need for a relatively uncluttered area at the top or corner for the book's title. Then I put on a carousel of slides of potters taken by students in the cover competition for *Foxfire 8* that were rejected because of poor focus or poor composition, and we discuss each. I reiterate, "Remember, what you see is what you get." The slides are arranged in a sequence from making a piece of ware through building a kiln and firing a kiln, so that at the same time we are talking about composition, I can also point out the process of making the ware that is on display in the classroom and introduce the students not only to the potters but also to the concept of folk art. Whenever possible, I try to accomplish three or four goals with each activity (in this case, the book-cover competition and how it works, the composition of good photographs, and the introduction of a cultural tradition that was once essential in this area—those three things at least), and this process of doubling up on goals I find to be the most efficient and powerful use of our short time together. You will notice the principle at work throughout the course without my drawing undue attention to it.

The slides finished, I hold up a copy of our current magazine, which they each have, and I point out certain portraits and their strengths and fine points. I explain the technique of setting up a portrait shot in terms of focus and composition and then simply holding the camera, ready to shoot, for as long as necessary to catch that perfect gesture or facial expression. Then I split them up into small groups again, hand each student an index card with a rectangular hole cut out of its center, explain where to hold the card to approximate what they would see in a camera's viewfinder, have each group choose a portrait subject, and then move around that subject choosing possible angles for shots. If there is time, we may go outdoors and do related activities to keep the students moving around and active. This period is normally a bit chaotic and noisy, but that's acceptable. At the end, I ask for quiet, ask each to show the rest of the class his or her favorite angle, and have the others in the class critique it. The critiques may not be overly strong, but at least all the students are thinking about the difference between a photograph and a snapshot—many for the first time—and they know that, as with using a rifle in the woods, one never just points and shoots but composes the shot carefully and squeezes the trigger at a precise moment, and I can build on that. It's one more brick in the foundation.

By Wednesday, I am ready to introduce them to ISO, shutter speed, aperture and use of the light meter, and depth of field. I keep it short and simple at this point, giving them enough information to enable them to take a photograph that is properly exposed and not blurred, but I don't want to drown them in technical data. We will continue to work with cameras all quarter long, each time adding a new layer of understanding; and for those who want to grow even further, there is Foxfire II. After this brief introduction, I ask them to split up into the groups with which they would like to remain for the rest of the quarter. Having had several small group experiences by now (often sampling different combinations in the process), they can group themselves into compatible teams of five or six students each with a minimum of confusion. If I have students who might, for some reason, find themselves left out of a group, I will already have spotted them before now and will have taken care of the situation in some appropriate way behind the scenes and before the fact (either by enlisting the help of several students upon whom I know I can rely, or by any of a number of other strategies that are available, which you know as well as I).

The groups formed, I announce a field trip scheduled for the following week and tell them we'll be taking cameras along and that those who want to use them may. The combination of the anticipation of the field trip and the actual use of the cameras propels us into the activities that take up the last half of the period; one student in each group focusing on an object and setting the ISO, shutter speed, and aperture opening. As before, I check the first in each group, make any necessary corrections, and that person then scrambles all the settings, passes it on to the next, and checks his or her work. It goes quickly, leaving enough time for a final exercise involving opening and loading film into the camera. Each student, in turn, tries it, loading the camera, closing the back, advancing the film twice to "0" on the exposure counter, and then pressing the clutch and carefully rewinding the film to the point where the film end pops free of the takeup spool but does not disappear into the canister. Then each opens the back of the camera, removes the film, closes the camera, and passes film and camera on to the next. Inevitably a student or two will rewind the tail of the film completely back into the canister, causing loud laughing and consternation all around, but I've already told them in advance that it will probably happen and not to worry if it does. We can teach the students how to get the tail back out fairly easily, or simply reload the film into a new canister, thus teaching a new and useful skill.

On Thursday, the writing assignment is the same as the week before, except this time it deals with what they've learned about cameras instead of tape recorders. As before, they are to regard me as the audience and pretend that I am basically ignorant. As before, we brainstorm about the various paragraphs and a suitable sequence. If there were major areas of confusion or structural problems in the first paper, I clear those up to the best of my ability before the second. What I am after here is, as before, a solid process analysis paper: clear, precise, well-organized thought and explanations of such things as the care of the equipment, the act of composing a decent photograph, the settings that must be made on the camera (without getting overly technical and struggling for half an hour trying to figure out a way to tell me in words the exact location of the ISO dial on the camera itself), and cautions regarding its use.

Friday the usual grade summary is posted, papers are returned, error charts are brought up to date, grammar sheets are gone over and errors corrected, and the content of the compositions is discussed. Nearly every Friday, work that is exemplary is read and analyzed for its particular strengths. Each student's paper, as before, also contains written comments of mine pointing out certain specific flaws as well as commendably clear sentences or paragraphs. Then the new work is added to their folders. By now, the folders are beginning to acquire some satisfying heft.

Week Three—A Field Trip

Monday, new artifacts introduced.

The momentum at this point usually feels good. The students are comfortable in the classroom, and we are settling into a workable balance between small-group work, intense class concentration, writing, and frequent laughter and good-natured kidding. Students are beginning to become individuals, and their personalities are clearer. I am making mental notes about certain students in relation to upcoming activities ("Be sure to watch Susan this week and see that she's not cowed by the group around her. Don't take her on the field trip at the same time the football players go." "As soon as possible, get John aside and see if he'll try to get that grandfather he talks about to come to class." "Get Joy and Dale and Dawn some instruction in darkroom work soon. They'll be perfect as teachers with about half the students in here.")

To keep the energy going, I pass around two sign-up sheets for the upcoming field trip. One is for Tuesday, fourth and fifth periods, and one is for Wednesday, fifth and sixth periods. I ask the students to choose one of the two days, depending on whether it will be easier for them to miss fourth or sixth period. Hopefully there will be a roughly equal number going each day. If not, I can get some students who can miss either period easily to shift from one day to the other. That done, I take the last three quarters of the period to get them ready. For ten minutes, as they make notes, I give them a brief lecture about the Cherokee Indian removal, the first white settlers into this area, the lottery by which they acquired their tracts of land, and the fact that there were no roads, no stores, no electricity, no plumbing, no television, no cars, no airplanes, no telephones, no refrigerators or freezers—in short, none of the amenities we're used to today. That situation is nearly impossible to imagine, and the facts probably don't register very strongly, but they introduce what the students are about to see firsthand.

To end the lecture before it reaches the point of no comprehension, and to stir things up again, I move to another carousel of slides. A student sets up the projector while the others stretch and visit, and when the projector is ready, I run through the slides showing one of our staff members and some students dismantling and reconstructing a huge log house from beginning to end—a house that was built originally by an early settler shortly following the land lottery. The slides reveal many of the construction details and distinctive architectural features I want students to look for, recognize, and appreciate during the field trip. Since many of the artifacts we have been studying in class include the types of axes and adzes and augers used to do such construction, an additional tie-in has been consciously established.

Tuesday I take the first group out for a two-period block, and Wednesday I take the second. While I am gone, our bookkeeper shares letters from our subscribers with those left in the classroom, so that they begin to get a feel for the national audience of readers of *Foxfire* that is out there waiting for their work. Hopefully this will add to any intrinsic motivation the students may be developing for wanting to write well. She also shares the magazine's budget with them so they can appreciate the amount of money involved in producing the magazine and the necessity of keeping the subscribers satisfied to assure that the magazine continues paying for itself. At the same time she hits the state CBE objective that students be able to "estimate income, costs, expenditures in financial management." Suddenly they realize it is a very real business and not an artificial exercise, and that its success depends upon the work of students like themselves.

Meanwhile, I have taken my group to our center, holding the number at about twelve because that is the most I can fit comfortably inside many of the spaces and ensure that all can hear and see what I am demonstrating. Before we start walking, we discuss as a group the kinds of photographs that would be fun to try to get, and those who want to take pictures while we walk trade the two cameras back and forth. One of the places we visit is a log building, furnished just as it would have been over a hundred years ago. On its porch, I try to help them imagine a family of early settlers arriving in a wagon (they have just seen the three in our collection), cutting trees for the house, and pulling up the stumps to create their garden plot. Then I ask them to move inside, find a place to sit, and just be quiet and observant. There is always some good-natured giggling and pinching anyway, but as eyes adjust to the darkness, the students begin to notice things that strike them: no windows, no light except what the two open doors admit, no interior partitions, beds and dining and living-room furniture all in the same room, the fireplace set up for cooking, the absence of a bathroom, the lack of space. I explain to them that the room is as authentic as we can make it, the placement of the furnishings having been dictated by Betty Crane, the grandmother of a former student, who was raised in just such a house. (See *Foxfire 6*, pp. 442–48.) As I show them the items their own grandparents had to make and use to survive both in the furnished house and throughout the complex, I emphasize again the astounding amount of ingenuity these people displayed, as evidenced by the construction of a wagon wheel, the design of a corded bed with its shuck and feather ticks, and the operation of a wooden lock or a pottery chicken watering jug. My hope is that as we talk together, I can lead them to the beginning of an understanding of the incredible task basic survival became when people were almost completely dependent on their own skills, determination, and raw materials from the environment.

Thursday's composition assignment—partly description and partly argumentation—is to write at least one paragraph dealing with each of the following, in order:

•Describe the overall setting of the Foxfire center, and the placement of roads and fences and buildings, clearly enough that someone who had never visited could see it in his or her mind.

•Talk about items you saw there that you had never seen before, and realizations you came to for the first time while on the property.

•Propose some ideas for other ways the property and resources there could be used during this quarter that you think would be of interest or benefit to the class.

•Analyze the experience overall. Was it useful and/or informative or largely a waste of time? Should the same field trip be made with a new class next quarter? Why or why not? If you're in favor of the field trip being continued, justify it to a skeptical parent who thinks field trips are a waste of time—or support that parent's point of view.

The next day, before going over the grammar sheets, I summarize the results of the compositions, reading some of the more thoughtful ones aloud. Then I make a list of the suggestions for the center's use by this class, and we discuss them. Sometimes suggestions are received so enthusiastically that we go ahead and try them, asking the student who made the suggestion to enlist the help of some classmates to organize the proposed activity. On one occasion, for example, community craftspeople were invited to come to the center on a Saturday to meet with interested students and teach them how to repair some of the artifacts in the museum or make replacements. On the designated day, craftspeople arrived and cut down several tulip poplar saplings the inside bark from which, with the help of the students, was cut into long strips and used to replace the bottoms in three handmade chairs we owned. Another craftsperson made and replaced the wooden wheels on a child's wagon. Another taught students how to make several new brooms out of broomcorn he brought with him. Meanwhile, other students helped several community friends cook dinner for everyone in Dutch ovens and pans in the museum fireplace. The event lasted some eight hours, and it was so enjoyed that it will undoubtedly be repeated.

Week Four—An In-Class Interview

Negatives from the field trip have been processed, and so the photographers cut them up, slide them into glassine negative sheaths, label them as to date and photographers, and pass them around for all to see after scrutinizing them themselves. So many kibitzers and critics were close by while the photographs were being taken that most of them have turned out, but whether good or not, all will be used soon for teaching purposes and darkroom work. If the student photographers are particularly eager and excited, they can come into the classroom during a free period or after school and learn how to print immediately.

Now, for the first time, I begin to get them ready for this week's composition immediately. The topic? To describe a person so accurately that the reader could stand on the sidewalk in town and recognize the person from the paper alone if he or she walked by. To illustrate, I read examples from the work of an author who does this particularly well, usually concentrating on writers like Thomas Wolfe, who were or are natives of this area.

As they take notes, we make a list together of the features such writers emphasize: overall physical size and shape; hair and eye color and complexion; placement and shape of features; physical abnormalities such as scars or warts; clothing, shoes, and accessories such as a scarf, pins, watch, or jewelry; mannerisms, body language (I have lots of fun here demonstrating with students the various signals we send unconsciously through carriage and stance and gesture); use of hands and eyes and head; the overall attitude of confidence or nervousness or relaxation; tone of voice; and so on. We begin to exercise such skills as making our verbs more descriptive. (Look at the difference in the visual impression one gets from "He walked into the room" versus, "He lumbered into the room.") Two student volunteers go to the board, and as the class shouts out options for *walk*, they put them up. Sometimes the list numbers almost a hundred. As we work, more outgoing students demonstrate and get the others to guess which verb they're acting out. We begin to work on figurative language, such as similes ("He has eyes like a snake). Fill in the blank as many ways as you can: "Her gaze was as _____," etc. I get them to list similes that people use in our county ("Ugly as a mud fence," "Mean as a striped snake," "Steep as a horse's face," "Straight as a rifle barrel") that they often are surprised to learn are unique to this area. I then point out the loss of much of the colorful flavor of our language as we shift to hopelessly inadequate substitutes: "Nice as hell," "Hard as hell," "Mad as hell," "Cold as hell," "Hot as hell," "Ugly as hell," and so on.

Before the class ends, I have them take another sheet of paper and in five minutes observe and describe an unidentified classmate (using no negative figurative language) for practice. I read several of these to see how quickly the class can identify the subject. It's an exercise that's fun and harmless (as I read, I leave out any references to features that might embarrass the subject) and drives the point home.

On Tuesday, I reveal that their first interview will be the following day, and they should make enough brief notes during the experience to be able to describe the person who was interviewed. Holding up a black-and-white portrait of a contact interviewed for *Foxfire*, I ask them what's missing. They immediately note things we talked about the day before, such as colors, tone of voice, mannerisms, and gestures. "Exactly. What you have to remember as a writer for *Foxfire*, or any other publication, is that photographs alone leave too much out. You must, as a writer, be the eyes and ears of the audience." I read examples from student-written articles to enforce the message.

Now I ask for one group to volunteer to conduct, tape, and photograph the interview. When I have a group, I say, "Okay, you have two minutes to get and set up all the equipment you'll need." On my signal, with the rest of the class laughing and timing them, they run through a drill. Even though they usually can't do it in two minutes, they soon decide who needs to do what to set up the situation at the beginning of tomorrow's class.

That done, I get the class to figure out the physical setup. Where should the group conducting the interview sit? Directly in front of the contact as a group? Scattered in the audience? To either side, facing the class? Where should the tape recorder be placed? Should the other students in the class sit in any special configuration? How can members of the group get photographs without disturbing the interview when they get up to move around the room? What happens if the members of the group run out of questions halfway through the period? Should the rest of the class help or leave them dangling in the wind?

Those questions answered to everyone's satisfaction (and they may be answered differently from quarter to quarter), we move to: "But what questions do we ask?" As the class makes notes, I suggest they start by using a chronological format, taking the person whose identity I have not yet revealed, on purpose, to heighten the suspense—"It's someone you all know . . ."—step by step from ancestry to birth to the present. That is usually enough to get them going on a collaborative list: ancestry as far back as you know; grandparents' identity, occupation, and life-style; parents' identity, occupation, and life-style; childhood (an exercise I often encourage the students to try is to get the contact to draw a floor plan of the house in which he or she was raised, relating it mentally to the floor plan of the log house at our center, and the layout of the surrounding farm); early chores, games, and recreation; school; first paying job, other occupations, periods of history remembered, such as the Depression; marriage; changes they have noted over time in customs, the town, or values, and so on. A good session with students can produce a surprisingly full—even intimidating—list of possibilities. I get them to look at the difference between various styles of questions. ("Did you like school?" versus "What was your school like?" versus "What were the things you liked and disliked most about your school?") Then I explain that this first interview should be an example of a "preinterview"—the kind of forty-five-minute exploration we so often do that reveals what kinds of things a contact obviously loves talking about and is full of information concerning; the kinds of things we would interview the person about *in depth* on a second interview, for example. I also encourage them, as they ask about the person's childhood or young adult life, to remember artifacts they have seen so far in class and things they observed at our center and use them as a source of questions. All this, incidentally, begins to accomplish yet another state CBE objective, that students be able to "phrase questions to obtain information."

With about fifteen minutes left in the period, I initiate the idea of a class collection project through which each individual group would be responsible for the publishable documentation of several items or customs indigenous to the culture, results of which *will* be published in *Foxfire*. Normally the whole class concentrates on a single subject (like toys, or games, or a type of furniture, such as chairs, or the set of diagrams one class produced detailing the various kinds of notches and mortise and tenon joints in the log house featured in the slides during week three, reproductions of which were then made in shop for classroom demonstration purposes). Each group is responsible for the documentation of several different examples. The reason for initiating the idea now, of course, is so that the group conducting the upcoming interview can be sure to determine whether their interviewee could be of help to them in a subsequent interview. If the class chooses to document traditional toys, for instance (as they did in the spring quarter of 1984), and the group conducting the interview finds out that their subject can show them how to make several kinds, they are well on their way to getting their contribution to the overall topic started. I run through a list of a few possibilities, encourage additions, add to the list, and through class vote, we make a decision. I am careful to make sure that the class project selected deals with a simple enough topic that it can be completed easily and no group will get swamped or discouraged.

With two or three minutes to go, I hit the class with one of my very few inviolable rules: if any class member, during a time when we have a guest in the room, does anything to cause that guest to be embarrassed (such as talking in the back of the room, passing notes, yawning repeatedly, etc.), that class member will be transferred into either a study hall or some other class the following day. I will meet the student at the door of my classroom that day with a note from the guidance office detailing his or her schedule change, and I will not discuss it. To date, in the years I have been teaching, I have never had to take that step, but my students are invited to test me. I will not have one of our visitors embarrassed.*

On Wednesday, the group that has volunteered to conduct the in-class interview often shows up with uncharacteristic promptness. The members quickly set up the equipment, test the recorder, load a camera, and retrieve their lists of questions from their folders. As the final bell rings, the subject arrives (it has been explained in advance to the person that the students may be nervous, since this is their first interview; that they may need his or her help; and that they will be making some notes and he or she should not be concerned), the class settles in, I go to the back of the room to watch, and the interview begins.

The person invited is always someone who has been raised in the kind of self-sufficient circumstances that are illustrated at the center. Often it is a member of our faculty, our administration, or our support staff (a custodian or a lunchroom worker, for instance). Though the interview itself is not always as dramatic or gripping as one might like, it is always a powerful experience, and it accomplishes a number of goals simultaneously:

•It puts what the students have learned about the use of cameras and tape recorders to use in a real situation, and reinforces and adds to that knowledge.

•It adds important new material to our archive ("What you preserved on tape and film was not preserved until you made the effort to do it") and gives the students a vital feeling of accomplishment.

•It brings a real-life dimension to the artifacts and the museum buildings studied so far that puts them in a new perspective.

•It illustrates the forty-five-minute preinterview format they can then initiate with any of their relatives or older neighbors on their own.

•It shows them a different side of an adult with whom they have been familiar but about whom they have usually known little; instantly the relationship changes. I'll never forget the time it was discovered that one of the men who worked in the lunchroom mopping up and wiping tables once served in CCC camps in Rabun County; he became a priceless source of information about those days in a series of in-class interviews in which his granddaughter, who was a member of my class, participated,

---

* I try to make sure that any class rules I enforce have a logical, real basis in my class. It is a school rule, for example, that students not bring soft drinks into class. Students resent that, and they test me. In our case, however, that rule makes real sense because of the danger of getting the sticky liquid on the photographs, layout boards, and diagrams lying on every flat surface of the room. They understand, and they do not break the rule.

and suddenly was seen by students as something more than a "custodian."

•And it gives them a flesh-and-blood subject to study and describe in a composition.

Not bad for one forty-five-minute interview.

On Thursday, using the notes they made Wednesday, the students create their descriptions. I suggest that they start with overall physical dimensions first and then work gradually into the more subtle details of presence and attitude, but that is optional. They can use any format they like. If they finish before the bell rings, I encourage them to add an additional paragraph or two either analyzing the interview itself or summarizing the most important and interesting subjects about which the person talked. They hand their compositions in with the notes they made in class stapled to them so that I can see both, and so that they can later have a visual reminder of the process of going from notes to composition.

Friday the compositions are returned after I have shared the better ones with the class. When we have finished the grammar sheets, I make the first entries in magic marker on a large sheet of poster paper I title the Offal List. The first four or five entries are simple stylistic offenses that I have almost eliminated from their work (*alot, a lot, kinda, sorta;* incorrect use of numerals; confusion of *there, their,* and *they're;* and so on) that I never want to see in their work again. I help them with memory tricks (*there* shows location, and it includes the word *here,* which also shows location, which, in turn, is different from hear, which contains an *ear; their* means ownership and it includes the word *heir,* etc.), and I encourage them to invent their own tricks and share them with all of us, at the same time warning them that each time I see the offenses repeated once they are listed on the chart, I will subtract an additional five points per offense from their grammar grades. The chart remains in front of them even as they write the subsequent compositions, and new offenses that I think are close to being under control are added each week until the chart finally includes even serious errors such as fragments or fused sentences.

It is effective, by the way.

Week Five—Describing a Place

By the first day of week five, another set of negatives has been processed and the student photographers cut them up, label them, and pass them around for the students who, by now, are crowded in close asking to see what they've got. I find this is a good time to get an opaque projector and project a proof sheet of their negatives onto a screen to critique the angles, focus, exposure, and so on.

During the entire interview the previous Wednesday, I sat in the back of the room behind the students and let them run with it. At regular intervals, the student photographers would pass in front of me and let me take a quick look at their camera, check their settings, and ask about the possibility of getting a certain kind of shot that would be interesting. With each, I'd ask that he or she take a photograph from the approximate area where I was sitting and then advance the film while sitting beside me so I could see (and demonstrate) that as they advanced it, the rewind lever was also spinning backward a half-turn (a sure sign that the film was advancing properly). If there was a problem—and there has been in the past—the two of us could usually get it straightened out quickly or change cameras and continue. I enjoy these brief "strategy sessions," because there is an air of tension and urgency about them, and because they give me a chance to give each photographer some individual encouragement and a squeeze on the shoulder. They also allow me to virtually guarantee that we'll have negatives we can work with as opposed to a blank roll or, worse, a series of shots taken with a camera that was never loaded at all, and several needlessly embarrassed students.

Now we analyze Wednesday's interview in terms of the more technical details (for example, did the students label the tape at the end of the interview to prevent its being used by someone else?) and the questions asked and the pacing. Did the students in the group jerk the guest around through time with questions that jumped too quickly from subject to subject, with no connection whatsoever to a previous answer, or was there a natural pace and flow and progression through time that was comfortable and logical? Did they ask questions too quickly, forcing the guest to give unnecessarily abbreviated answers, or was there enough spacing to allow some development of response? If the visitor obviously wanted to and began to go into some detail about a topic (which should almost always be allowed even though there may be a different planned agenda), did they cut the answer off and ask an unrelated question?

What subjects did the contact obviously enjoy talking about that we could develop fruitfully in a subsequent interview? How about school, for example? How can we pick that subject apart and develop a list of thirty or so questions *just* related to school? "Let's make a list. Can you all see how to do the same thing with any of the other subjects touched on? Can you see how to come at one subject from different angles?"

Did the group get a good-quality tape? A member of the group sets it up and plays part of it back, not only to answer that question but also to get the class to listen to part of the interview with the previous inquiries in mind, concentrating on the questions asked as well as the responses. While we have the recorder set up, I then take them through a transcribing exercise. As I operate the recorder, all the students in the class transcribe half to three-quarters of a page of material. Then I play that piece over again intact so they can check their work. Next I go to the board and lead them into a short discussion about dialect and phonetic spelling. ("Is it 'goin'' or 'going'? Is it 'wuz' or 'was'? Is it 'far'—which spells a new word and just confuses the reader—or 'fire'?") Then we listen to the piece they've transcribed again with dialect in mind, and I stop the tape at certain words or phrases and ask how they think they should be handled. The exercise also gives me a chance to reinforce what they know about contractions and quotation marks.

By this time the bell is about to ring, so we stop for the day. Tuesday I review any areas shortchanged by the frenetic pace of the previous day. Then I try to make several points, all of which will be hit again during the quarter and then greatly developed with those who go on to Foxfire II:

•Use of contractions is fine in dialogue, inside quotation marks, but it is slang speech and thus not usually appropriate in formal compositions unless you are doing it for a special, justifiable reason and you know what you are doing.

•Use of extreme phonetic spelling in dialogue often makes the work unreadable, and use of spellings like "wuz" for "was" makes the speaker look ignorant and foolish. If that is your intent, fine, but use caution.

•Stories you write in the future can be enlivened greatly by the use of natural-sounding dialogue. Stick this in the back of your minds for future reference, and we'll hit it again later.

Last point: You *must* listen closely and transcribe accurately. To drive this point home, I pass out a xerographed sheet showing transcription errors that have been made in the past that have completely changed the tone and meaning of what was actually said. We read over it together, at the same time looking for examples of eloquence that could be used as chapter titles—times when words bump against each other in powerful ways.

To conclude the unit, I ask each student to write a brief thank-you letter to the person interviewed. These letters are collected by a student, folded, and put into a manila envelope to be either hand-delivered later in the day by a volunteer (there's an opportunity here to give one or more students a boost) or mailed.

Now we stand and stretch, and after a break of several minutes, we start again, this time to begin to get ready to describe a place. As when getting ready to describe a person, I read several examples, hold up a black-and-white photograph of a room from *Foxfire*, and ask them to tell me what is missing (colors, smells, sounds, temperature, the atmosphere, etc.). As before, I make the point, "When you are writing for *any* reader, you must *be* that reader's senses to allow him or her to participate as fully in the experience as you did. Otherwise the reader gets shortchanged." The examples of good descriptions I use in class come not only from literature but often from newspapers and magazines. This page 28 introduction to *Time*'s January 24, 1981, cover story about the death penalty is a good example:

The chair is bolted to the floor near the back of a 12-ft. by 18-ft. room. You sit on a seat of cracked rubber secured by rows of copper tacks. Your ankles are strapped into half-moon-shaped foot cuffs lined with canvas. A 2-in.-wide greasy leather belt with 28 buckle holes and worn grooves where it has been pulled very tight many times is secured around your waist just above the hips. A cool metal cone encircles your head. You are now only moments away from death.

But you still have a few seconds left. Time becomes stretched to the outermost limits. To your right you see the mahogany floor divider that separates four brown church-type pews from the rest of the room. They look odd in this beige Zen-like chamber. There is another door at the back through which the witnesses arrive and sit in the pews. You stare up at two groups of fluorescent lights on the ceiling. They are on. The paint on the ceiling is peeling.

You fit in neat and snug. Behind the chair's back leg on your right is a cable wrapped in gray tape. It will sluice the electrical current to three other wires: two going to each of your feet, and the third to the cone on top of your head. The room is very quiet. During your brief walk, you looked over your shoulder and saw early morning light creeping over the Berkshire hills. Then into this silent tomb.

The air vent above your head in the ceiling begins to hum. This means the executioner has turned on the fan to suck up the smell of burning flesh. There is little time left. On your right you can see the waist-high, one-way mirror in the wall. Behind the mirror is the executioner, standing before a gray marble control panel with gauges, switches and a foot-long lever of wood and metal at hip level.

The executioner will pull this lever four times. Each time 2,000 volts will course through your body, making your eyeballs first bulge, then burst, and then broiling your brains. . . .

On Wednesday, we make a list of categories any complete description of a place would have to include—overall shape and size, building materials, colors and textures, placement of windows, doors and furnishings, tiny details or personal touches that would have gone unnoticed by the casual observer, mood. "Every room has its own personality and mood and presence caused by————?", and so on.

When their list of important categories is developed, I take a stack of envelopes out of my desk. "Inside each of these envelopes is a card stating a specific location in this school such as a janitor's closet, the in-school detention room, the greenhouse, a shop, the art room, the little theater, etc. There is also a xerographed letter to any school official who might stop you in the halls or challenge your being out of class. The letter explains what you are doing. If anyone gives you a problem, send them to me. The teachers whose classrooms I've designated have given me permission to have you visit. They won't challenge you. Just ease inside and sit quietly out of the way. When you're in place, make a comprehensive list of all the details necessary to describe the space, and then return to this room with that list before the bell rings." Every student gets up laughing and talking, grabs an envelope from me, and disappears out the door, leaving the classroom suddenly, deafeningly silent. Within a few moments, some return. "The door's locked. I can't get in!" I give each a different envelope. By the end of the period, all have returned (usually), and I have had a chance to check over, then collect their notes for tomorrow.

Thursday they write. I take five minutes at the beginning of the period to remind them of the use of strong descriptive words and figures of speech. Sometimes I'll have them all write a sentence describing the mood of a room in, say, an abandoned house, and, copying one sentence onto the board, we'll brainstorm together about adjectives or verbs or similes or details we could add to enrich it. Usually we go hopelessly and gleefully overboard (allowing me to make a point about "too much" and "purple prose" versus "not enough"). Then, as with the description of a person, I encourage them to start with the overall dimensions and gradually focus down to the smaller details and more intangible, elusive qualities, though they may use another format if they wish, and I turn them loose to write for thirty-five to forty minutes. As they finish, they hand in their papers with the notes they made in the location they visited stapled to the final composition.

On Friday, I read a number of the papers (leaving out truly obvious details like automobile bodies that would give the place away instantly), and the class tries to guess the location. It's a good game—fun for ten or fifteen minutes. Then grammar sheets and the usual routine. Usually now, as I will do for the remainder of the quarter, I add several new offenses to the Offal List.

Week Six—Process Analysis and Evaluation

So far students have been introduced to the skills of describing both a person and a place. I feel this is an appropriate time to reinforce the need for acute observation and use of precise language and extend it to the skill of being able to give a set of directions for doing or making something that are accurate enough that the average reader can follow them correctly (a skill that is essential for those who go on to help produce our magazine and create the "how to do it" articles many of our readers favor, as well as a skill that hits state CBE objectives such as "Recognize units of customary and metric measurement"). I begin with a pretest designed to see whether they can even read a ruler (many cannot) and whether they can convert measurements and draw something to scale.

That done, I place a handmade, traditional ladderback chair on a table in front of the group. It is the artifact for the day, and as I talk about it, I emphasize features that illustrate the ingenuity of its construction in days before glue was available (the use of seasoned hardwood chair rounds, for example, shaped with a drawknife and shaving horse, two artifacts we studied previously, and driven into the holes made in the green chair posts, which, as they seasoned and shrank, gripped the rounds so tightly that no glue was necessary). Gripping one of the rounds of this eighty-year-old chair, I try as hard as I can to twist it loose, unsuccessfully, and invite students to try also. I point out the two lone wooden pins that help hold the chair together, and the decorative finial atop each back post—the maker's mark.

Now I ask each student to get a sheet of paper and draw a rough, freehand diagram of the back of the chair, making it big enough that we can add measurements. As they draw, I draw the same thing on the board in chalk. Though this activity is usually accompanied by some groans, those who are most apprehensive can simply follow along with the one I draw and can come up with something reasonably acceptable. When they're finished, I ask two students who can read a tape measure to come up front and give us all the measurements we need to complete the diagrams. As I point to distances on my diagram, the students call off the measurements and all of us fill them in. There are opportunities here for several good activities (do the numbers on the left side of the diagram, for example, add up exactly to the overall height of the chair itself; how does one add fractions, etc.).

I end the day by holding up examples of good work from desks around the room, emphasizing all the while that though a diagram done for publication would have to be done much more neatly, the art of doing a publishable one requires patience more than great artistic skill, and that any student in the class can do it. I then hold up examples of student-drawn diagrams from our magazine.

On Tuesday we break out of the accustomed routine and write the weekly composition. Its topic: write a clear, step-by-step set of directions in complete sentences for making something (a hat, an airplane, an envelope, etc.) out of paper. If they wish, they can also draw a set of diagrams on a separate sheet of paper to accompany the instructions. They usually finish within thirty minutes, and I take the last half of the period, after I have collected the compositions and diagrams, to remind them of the need for precision. On thumbing through the papers, for example, I can usually find several that begin, "Take a piece of paper." Pretending that I am going to follow the directions and make the item in class, I take a sheet of notebook paper and tear from one corner a piece of paper so tiny that it would be virtually impossible to complete the job. Students who started their papers with that sentence, meanwhile, as I go to step two and attempt to follow it, are squirming and moaning in their seats, the point made. Now, keeping the diagrams, I pass out the written directions to students other than the authors with the instructions, "Take a sheet of notebook paper and follow the directions on the composition I've given you exactly. When you're finished, return the composition and the item you made following its directions to the author." This is usually a time of good-natured laughter and suspense, and toward the end of the class, it always erupts in chaos as completed paper airplanes sail back and forth across the room. That's fine. We all enjoy it together, the points I wanted to make having long since been accomplished; and just before the bell rings, holding a trash can up at the front of the room, I ask everyone to throw their various missiles and constructions at the can I'm holding, thus filling the can and cleaning the room simultaneously.

On Wednesday, I begin by reminding them that their small-group projects (the documentation of certain toys or games, say) require good clear directions and diagrams. Then I hand back the compositions and diagrams, have them bring their grammar charts up to date, go over the new set of grammar sheets, and add to the Offal List in the now familiar sequence of events.

Thursday is set aside for mid-term evaluation. I begin by handing each student his or her folder. The instructions are to remove the compositions and arrange them in the order in which they were written, do the same with the grammar sheets, set the grammar chart aside for me to collect separately, and place anything else in the folders, such as the chair diagram, in a separate pile. Next the students list each of their compositions and the two grades each received on the inside front cover of the folder, in order. They convert letter grades to numbers (B+ equals 88, B equals 85, B— equals 82, etc.), add the resulting twelve numbers and divide by twelve (there are always several calculators floating around the room, which simplifies this process). Next they add to this total a half-point for each grammar sheet on which they have corrected every mistake. Grammar sheets that have not been corrected may not be counted. The result is their mid-term grade. Each returns his or her folder to me, shows me the work, and I enter the grade in my grade book. Some have been keeping up with their progress carefully and have rewritten papers the grades on which were lower than they wanted. The new versions have all been graded and stapled to the old, and students use the new grades to figure their averages. Other students have been drifting and, shocked at their grades, begin to gear up for the last six weeks. All, however, can see in the act of figuring their own grades exactly how those grades were derived, and all are welcome to challenge or discuss any confusion or perceived mistreatment.

Going over the contents of the folders has served as an effective review of the work of the past six weeks, and so we spend the rest of the period evaluating what we've done together and brainstorming about ways to revise any activities to make them more effective. Have they had an effective and interesting composition course thus far? The response is almost always unanimously in the affirmative, even from those whose grades were less than they had hoped.

On Friday I break the class up into small groups that are different from the interview-project groups. I have had a chance to go over the measurement pretests by now, and so one of the groups I have created is composed of students who obviously cannot use a ruler. It is sometimes taught by a student I have borrowed for the period through our school's drafting teacher. I have also gone over the students' grammar charts, and a second group is composed of students who are still having problems with certain aspects of usage and mechanics. I teach this group, and supplement what we do together with assigned workbook or textbook exercises. A third group goes into the darkroom with a peer teacher. This group is always composed of *at least* one member from each of the groups that has taken pictures so far, and the negatives that are printed represent their own work—and in the process give me peer teachers for at least two groups and often more, depending on how the class breaks down. A fourth group, paired with another peer teacher, begins to transcribe that portion of the in-class interview that relates to the upcoming small-group projects. That transcribing group always includes at least one student from the group that conducted the interview.

It is always a confusing day, but at the end, I can almost always see progress: a couple of students emerging from the darkroom with their first prints, grinning like Cheshire cats; several others bragging about their newfound skills with rulers, smiles of relief on their faces at another mystery that has burdened and embarrassed them finally solved; two or three pages of fresh, competent transcription moving one small group well along on completing its project; and some students hopefully reassured about their ability to confront and beat some problems with writing that have always confused them. The idea is forward motion and a sense of overall accomplishment strong enough that even the most reluctant find themselves being dragged along. Usually it works; sometimes it doesn't. Even when it doesn't work, however, an observer would simply conclude that I had given my students a break on the last day of the midterm and let them relax for one period. And I would have some useful information to digest before breaking them down into small groups again.

At the same time that I am going over student grammar charts and looking at the contents of their folders with them and listening to their comments and woes and suggestions, I am also evaluating my own performance over the first six weeks and setting the stage for the next. Am I moving students too quickly, or is the pace about right? Are skills I introduced earlier in the quarter being reinforced often enough that they are being mastered, despite the fact they were introduced quickly (a style in which I believe, experience having shown me that after ten to fifteen minutes on any one topic, most students have absorbed almost all they can take at that time, and another fifteen minutes added to the first is just wasted time and an exercise in futility). Are the activities cumulative, each adding an additional layer of sophistication and competence, so that we are moving upward in a spiral rather than around and around in a circle? Are compositions improving in terms of both mechanics and content, or are the students stalled and making the same mistakes again and again? Am I moving all students toward involvement in projects, or are some hiding from me? Which ones? Why? Am I staying sharp, or am I exhausted? If the latter, what can I do about that? Am I getting enough sleep? Am I having enough fun? Am I rolling with the punches and bobbing like a cork or am I flailing in the water, the students like weights around my legs?

Get up in the air above it all and look down. Much of what we have done together has seemed fragmented and noisy. Look again. On command, can a group materialize out of what was once twenty-four individuals and set up and load equipment and conduct a competent interview? Are students alive and interested—focused—when we're talking about a new artifact? Am I asking the right questions? Is a collective sense of accomplishment and pride emerging? A sense of surprise at becoming comfortable with once-foreign skills? Look at the eyes. Is a collective class consciousness emerging—a sense of "We are the Foxfire I class and we're hot." Are compositions tighter, cleaner, better? Look in the folders. The answers are all there. There, and in the eyes.

Week Seven—Small Groups, Project Work

Time is ripping by. Where does it go? Students bring their report cards in and I enter their mid-term grades. Since we have already figured them, this formality takes about five minutes and we are back at work.

Now I introduce a new schedule we will follow for the next two to three weeks: activities Monday and Tuesday, composition Wednesday, analysis and evaluation Thursday, and small-group work on projects Friday. We review the topic chosen to research—let's say, for purposes of this discussion, toys. Each small group is responsible for the documentation (background and history, if available; directions for making and using, complete with photographs and diagrams; and tape-recorded recollections of personal experience) of at least two simple toys or one more complex one (like a jointed toy, or a wooden-wheeled wagon). One group has already started, thanks to the first in-class interview. They now have a contact with whom they can do additional work. A second group will have the same boost with this week's interview. Other students have or will shortly identify older family members or neighbors who can help. Any student who wishes can check out a tape recorder and camera to take home for a prearranged interview, and members of his or her group can arrange to meet after school at the interview location to help out if they can find transportation, or, if they cannot, I can usually help out.

Again, I go over the information each group needs to collect. For practice, I split them into their groups and give each a traditional toy from the classroom collection. They themselves decide whether one member will be responsible for diagrams, one for photographs, and so on, or whether each will help in all areas, trading jobs among themselves. Either way is fine with me, just as long as each group figures out its own way to come up with its own final contribution to the whole class effort.

Toward the end of the period, I get them ready for tomorrow's interview. We talk about how to take one subject, like toys, and ask questions about it from a number of different angles (advantages or disadvantages of storebought versus homemade, where and how each toy discussed was used, experiences with, etc.), listing these on the board. I also remind them of the other topics they may get the contact talking about if there is time. Then I give them Wednesday's composition assignment: to write an effective summary of the content of the interview. They can make notes during the interview if they like, but what I want them to do is listen carefully enough to what is said that they can summarize all the main thoughts for an imaginary audience that was not present. Here, again, state CBE objectives are addressed ("Listen effectively to summarize contents;" "Paraphrase thoughts, details, ideas;" "Classify, categorize thoughts, details or ideas;" "Follow patterns of thought, details or ideas;" etc.). Again, an attempt to accomplish several goals simultaneously.

On Tuesday, the second group sets up the equipment and the interview situation and begins. Members of the group take the visitor through his or her ancestry and childhood, and then they focus on toys. As they talk about the various types and their uses, I begin to make a master list of all the ones mentioned—a list that will be posted on the classroom wall and added to continually so that the students in each group can see the variety of examples available from which they can pick their final project. (To begin to get an idea of the number of types, you may wish to look at *Foxfire 6*, in which some fifty are documented.) If the group wishes to get the contact to show how to make one of the items discussed, arrangements for a future interview may also be made at this point.

On Wednesday, the students write a composition, using the notes they made the previous day. As usual, we brainstorm together in advance about a possible paragraph sequence (moving from the contact's background to specific toys—one in each paragraph—to an overall summary of the relative importance of toys and play and the differences between turn-of-the-century and today's types of and attitudes toward toys in general, for example). If they finish early, I encourage them to add a paragraph at the end critiquing the overall interview in terms of the questions asked, and so on.

Thursday begins with thank-you notes to the person interviewed and then moves into the regular routine of reading the better papers (as always, trying to make sure the same students' papers are not selected each week), correcting grammar sheets, filling out charts, and paying special note to additional points that were subtracted from some students' papers because of errors made that had been posted on the offal list.

Friday begins the small-group-work days, for which I have been trying to prepare the class all quarter. Despite the amount of preparation and practice we have had, there is still some confusion, but I push on, gripping the belief that the nature and the reality of the work going on will impose its own order on the activities with time. I am usually—but not always—right, and I find I must constantly be on the lookout for those students who are slipping between the cracks or drifting away unnoticed.

This kind of work takes a bit of advance preparation, especially given the fact that any particular class can be subdivided in so many ways. A typical arrangement for this class, at this point in the quarter, and depending on the students and their abilities, might look like this:

Two different groups have taken interview photographs now, as well as several different students who took pictures on our field trip. (The negatives and tapes and transcriptions and diagrams for each group are kept on separate shelves in a cabinet in the back of my room.) Using a peer teacher, I send two new representatives of each of these three groups into the darkroom to make proof sheets of their negatives and several prints. The ideal, of course, is to have them printing actual shots they took themselves. The results of this work are posted on the classroom bulletin board for all the students to see and evaluate toward the end of the period (and presumably, at the end, I have six more potential peer teachers).

Two interviews have been done in class. I set up two transcribing groups to either begin or continue transcribing the portions of those interviews having to do with the toys their groups are documenting. (One usually operates the recorder, one writes, and the others listen to the tape and check the work of the one writing. Every ten minutes, they rotate jobs.) Assisting may be members from groups who have not yet done an interview but want some additional practice in the skill.

A fourth group (composed, ideally, of at least one student from each of the class project groups) gathers around the back table with a peer teacher to actually diagram a toy I have in class, thus getting some valuable practice. This toy, from our collection, may actually be the one documented by one of the groups. This is permissible, as long as the group also gets some tape-recorded documentation from a contact as to its use, variations on the theme, if any, as well as photographs of the contact with the toy, to round out their project.

A fifth group (the members of which I have selected in advance by going over the grammar charts) is made up of individuals who are continuing to have certain problems with sentence structure or mechanics that I think I can fix. Depending upon the specific problems, I may have identified new workbook or Harbrace exercises, which, after explanation, I assign; or I may just take the group through a sequence of activities I have designed myself. The activities may revolve around specific compositions the members have written in the last two weeks, portions of which I want them to rethink, rewrite, and staple to the original. It all depends.

I may also have identified a student or two I want to use during this time in some special way. Prior to one of these Fridays, for example, one of the ninth-grade girls in my class confessed to me very quietly that she hadn't taken any photographs yet, was afraid of the camera, and didn't think she was going to be able to use it. The next time we broke down into small groups, I called her quietly to the front of the room, put my arm around her, and with the two of us facing the class, said very gently and good-naturedly so as not to embarrass her at all, "Dawn here thinks she needs a little additional help in using a camera. I'm sure there are several others of you who feel the same way. I've got something I really need some help with that I'm going to use Dawn on that will give her a little extra practice and make life a lot easier for me at the same time. If there are a couple of others of you who want to get in on this, come on up here." Two other girls came forward, and hooking them up with a peer teacher, I had them take and then print many of the in-class photographs of the fall, 1983, Foxfire I group that I have used to illustrate this chapter.

Week Eight—Creating a Culture

Now I shift gears. I warn the class in advance that there is a piece of material I want to introduce them to, and that the most efficient way to do it is through a straight lecture, and that I'll hold it to fifteen minutes if they'll just stick with me. A student is chosen to time the lecture, warn me a minute before my time is up, and stop me a minute later. Before I begin, I hand out a one-page outline of the talk, containing blanks for them to fill in as I go. I also draw a rough map of the British Isles and the eastern coast of the United States on the blackboard. When I'm ready, the student timing gives me a signal and I start. Since the majority of my students are of English, Scotch, and Irish descent, I concentrate on those selected portions of history that provide part of the backdrop for their ancestors' immigration to this country—especially those who call themselves Scotch-Irish. I concentrate on trying to make sure they understand the roots of the Catholic-Protestant conflict in Ireland, the reasons that conflict continues today, and I use any current newspaper or magazine articles about the conflict there to illustrate the struggle's unabated virulence. Some students had no idea that immigration was the universal experience for all but American Indian families, and this section gives me the opportunity to make that important point. Others had heard, either from their own families or from an interview in class, that the majority of Appalachian families had come here from the British Isles, but they didn't know when, or why, or the ports of entry; most had not thought about the fact that some families here were of African or German descent, also. Here I have the opportunity to get them thinking about a whole new aspect of their backgrounds and, as my time runs out, point them toward a stack of reference materials they may borrow and some sections in their history books to which they might want to pay special attention in their history classes.

Now they stand and stretch and take a break. Some come up and say, "That wasn't so bad. That was interesting." Others share some piece of family background that has suddenly made sense. Others flip through the reference materials and choose a few to take home.

After five minutes, we get back together and go again. I take the first sixty seconds to remind them of the covered wagon we looked at in the field trip—the method by which nearly all their ancestors first came to our part of the mountains—and the conversation we had in a previous week about the Cherokee Indian removal, which opened this land for the lottery by which many of their ancestors acquired the farms on portions of which these students still live.

That done, I pass out examples of original deeds and plats that the people who run the state archives in Atlanta have copied for me and which I have laminated for classroom use. We have a large copy of the 1820 survey made that subdivided a section of our county into land lots, and we locate the plats I have on the large map and talk about how those pieces of land are being used now and what families live on them.

Last, we tie the whole picture together by drawing a rough time line on the board, which they copy for their folders. Dates from the lottery and the plats are located first. Then we add the dates from the fifteen-minute lecture, followed by dates of the Indian removal (along with the president's name), the creation of Rabun County (along with the governor's name), and points in history such as the Civil War, World War I, the Great Depression, World War II, the introduction of the airplane, automobile, electricity, radio and television, telephone, and the like. At the end of the period, I end by drawing a bracket over that portion of the time line represented by people we can still interview in our county who are ninety years old. It is usually a dramatic revelation with which to end the period.

On Tuesday, we switch back to culture, my intent being, as on Monday, to reinforce and tie up a number of loose ends. I ask them to define culture, and I put our definition on the board. Beneath it, we brainstorm about and list all the various needs—the universal human themes—any group of people anywhere would have to meet in order to survive in some comfort and a minimum of chaos. The list usually includes at least thirty items (food, food preservation, housing, supplementary structures, building tools, other tools and implements, water systems, clothing—ordinary and formal, furniture and cooking devices, transportation, means of exchange, weapons, government, laws, entertainment and music, means of communication, the arts, education, religion, mind-altering substances, fashion, and so forth).

I help them make the connection between the aspects of our culture we have talked about so far and the list on the board, and I remind them that the immigrants into this part of the southern Appalachians (reinforcing that often-unfamiliar term again and again—reinforcement that also includes a map of the United States that hangs on the classroom wall with the area outlined) represented several *different* cultures and thus the one that developed here was an amalgam. Most don't know, for example, that the banjo, which they hold in such high regard, was not invented here but was brought to this country by Africans. Thrown together in a survival situation here, settlers shared what they had and knew with each other, and new customs appropriate to the situation arose.

Now, halfway through the period, I throw them a curve ball that is completely unexpected and have them invent a creature. "How tall is it?"

"Ten feet," one shouts. I write it on the board.

"What kind of skin does it have?"

"Scaly!" "Blue!" "Orange stripes!" I write it down.

"How many eyes, and where are they?" And so on.

When we've finished, wanting to make the point that environment has a powerful influence over any cultures (how can one build a log cabin on a desert where there are no trees?), I ask them to tell me what specific environment this being inhabits, and I put that on the board.

"What is its name? What is it called?" I put choices on the board, and we vote.

"Now," I say, "pick one of the areas I've listed—housing, entertainment, whatever—as your specialty."

As a student volunteers to take one, I erase it from the master list. "It's yours." Then another grabs one. As the students see what is happening and see the more interesting items on the list being claimed and erased, they begin to panic and shout out their choices, and I work as fast as I can to keep ahead of them, not wanting to say, "Quiet! One at a time," but to preserve the atmosphere of urgency. At the end, if some students are disappointed that they did not get their first choice, I'll let them double up and have two students, for instance, with the same topic. It's no problem. I want them all to have topics they're intrigued by.

Now I assign their next paper: each student, keeping in mind the creature and its environment, and keeping in mind what we've learned about describing and explaining, is to write a full two- to three-page composition that tells how our creature deals with the need the student has selected. I ask them to invent as much as possible (not saying, for example, that the creature travels in an automobile and eats at familiar fast food joints and wears jeans), so the papers will be unique and interesting. They may use dialogue and dialect if they wish, and they may use diagrams, but I want at least two pages of solid descriptive writing that do *not* include a description of the being and its environment, since that has already been established.

If there is time left at the end of the period, they begin to make notes. They may also work on their papers at home, though this is not assigned.

On Wednesday, they write all period, checking against the Offal List for errors at the end. That night, along with a grammar chart, I also type a composite description of the culture they've invented, making certain that I use at least one paragraph from every student's paper. I try to arrange the paragraphs in some logical sequence, and I may make some changes as I type to keep tense consistent and to eliminate any glaring contradictions in content (a student who describes the kinds of meat the creature eats, for example, versus another who says the creature is a vegetarian), but otherwise the work is completely that of the students.

On Thursday, I begin by reading what I've typed. Except for moments of hilarity or groans of disgust, the class is always spellbound, amazed at what it has created. At the end, the reaction is always, "We actually wrote *that? That's good!*" Now I can lead them into a discussion about what anthropologists do and show them that if one lived among us and wrote a letter to a colleague about us, its form would be similar. Then we move on to grammar sheets, and so forth.

One example from a dozen I could have shared with you:

SMAUGS

Smaugs are four-legged creatures that stand about twenty feet tall and weigh anywhere from 450 to 1,000 pounds. They have beards and bald heads, horns, one eye, a large mouth, and each has a pair of wings. They were originally brought to this country by the mayor of Atlanta who located them and hired them to fly through the sewer systems of the city and keep them clean. They are very good at this, and very conscientious, except for the weekends when they have a tendency to buy Smaug lightning, play sewer ball in the pipes, and get drunk as dogs.

Since they have to be in the sewers most of the time anyway, the Smaugs have become largely isolated from the world above and have adapted their own civilization to fit their underworld circumstance. They live, for example, in big round holes cut into the earth behind the sewer pipes, and they get to their homes through tunnels cut into the sides of these pipes, but ten feet off their floor to keep the water in the sewers from flooding their homes. The homes have four rooms each: a living room (where the entrance tunnel comes out), two bedrooms, and a kitchen. The living rooms are brown because of the dirt; the bedrooms have tree branches for beds; and the kitchens have a supply of wood to cook with and holes in the wall for food storage. Smaugs relax in their living rooms on top of cars, and in some of the homes there is an extra room about 7,854 square feet large with twenty-five cars in it for times when large groups of friends gather to relax.

Smaug children have two mothers and one father. When the father marries the first mother, they have two children, keep the children until they are nine months old, and then go off by themselves to spend three months together and get married. The second mother watches the children while the first couple is gone, and when it returns, the father has two more children by the second mother. The father has sayso over the house, and punishes his children by beating them with his wings. He lives ten years, and then the mothers have sayso.

Smaugs kill cats, dogs and rats to make their clothing out of. They make socks out of rat hides, pants out of the hides of little dogs, and shirts out of the hides of large dogs. They make special water bottles out of cat hides for when they travel from village to village. They also raise an animal that is a cross between a frog and a bear. The hides of these animals are used to make waterproof coats. They do not have to feed them because they eat the trash in the water. They make thread out of scraps of cat hide for sewing their clothing together.

Since they have feathers, they have unusual beauty problems. They use round brushes to curl their feathers, and then someone else fans them to dry their feathers. Female Smaugs enjoy wearing lipstick.

Smaugs often raise gardens, growing lettuce, cabbage, beans and other vegetables. They also gather nuts sometimes in a nearby forest. They have invented a vine that is a great help because it grows easily up the sides of the sewer pipes, lives only in that environment, and yields a fruit that is part fruit and part vegetable. They never overcook their food, being very health-oriented. For meat, they concentrate on the animals like alligators, bats, rats, lizards, fish and dills which are common in the sewers where they live. Dills are rotten dill pickles that have been flushed away and have come to life, turned green, grown hair, wings, a mouth and eyes, and can travel at speeds of eighty miles an hour. The Smaug is the only creature that can catch the incredible dill. Smaugs kill rats and lizards with their pop shots which are hollow sticks that they blow rabbit droppings through. They eat fish rarely, considering them a gourmet treat. They catch them by spotting them with their x-ray eyes, swimming up beside them, and stabbing them with their horns. When they use utensils to eat with, they carve them out of wood themselves.

Smaugs do many things for entertainment. They play hoofball, which is like our football, and they make very good tackles. Sometimes they have leg wrestling matches, or water ski on all fours holding the ski ropes in their mouths. Their favorite pastimes, though, are those that are destructive. They like to steal video games from arcades—not to play them, since they have trouble getting money—but to throw them at children and watch the children blow up. This game came originally from Rome, where the ancient Smaug race began, and where they used to take Roman columns and throw them at Christian invaders. They also had their own colosseum in Rome and had mock air battles where they flew around until they could get a good shot with their flingers, which are similar to our slingshots.

For entertainment, they also play with a breed of pet they have developed called a horseopotamus, which is as tall as a horse, has legs like a hippo, and a back as broad as a hippo. These creatures have antennae on their heads, and ears with shields over them which serve as protective covers to keep out sounds that they don't want to hear. They have either purple or orange fur during the warm months and brown or black fur during the cold months. They mate during the summer, making drum sounds; one beat means they are looking for a mate and two beats means a mate has been found. Before they mate, the male grooms. Afterward, the male lays eggs and the female sits on them for thirty minutes for each of two days. These animals are active pets, running at least twenty-five miles a day and playing from the time they wake up until they wear themselves completely out. They are also protective, and won't let anything hurt the Smaugs that feed them six times a day.

The Smaugs have developed a fairly sophisticated set of values based loosely on those of their new host country. They have a Declaration of Independence, for example, that begins: "We, the creatures of the earth, in order to form a more perfect society, hereby demand the garbage of the world and demand protection of our siblings if attacked. Fourscore and seventy creatures ago, we began a new culture, and we believe that this culture shall endure and finally dominate the world . . ." They also have Ten Commandments:

1. Thou shalt eat regular garbage.
2. Thou shalt not steal from thy fellow creatures.
3. Thou shalt destroy all invaders of privacy.
4. Thou shalt not lust after thy fellow creatures.
5. Thou shalt not harm worms.
6. Thou shalt have thy own football league.
7. Thou shall be painters of garbage.
8. Thou shalt not devour thy fellow Smaugs.
9. Thou shalt not insult fellow creatures.
10. Honor thy garbage man.

They have five branches of government. The president is elected by the rest of the Smaugs, lives in the biggest tunnel, and has cabinet officials that help him rule. He is usually the biggest, oldest creature. When in session, they abide by three simple rules of conduct: No drinking sewage water, no smoking paper, and no fishing for cans. When someone in the society breaks a serious rule, he is punished by being made to put his head under water three times, but lift it out only twice. . . .

Smaugs also are somewhat religious, in their own fashion. Since it is hard to fit them all in a room, they meet to worship in an outdoor arena which is a stone stadium without seats. In the center is a monument to their god which they stand around and chant to. The main philosophy of their religion is mischief, and the more unorganized the proceedings, the better. Thus when they are chanting to their god, they all chant at different speeds and different tempos. It is like a three-ring circus. Their god is basically a good fellow, but he has one flaw, which is playing football and spending all of his followers' hard-earned tithes. Smaugs are generally loyal to their religion, but they have been known on occasion to have wild sewer parties, which their god, Shnoe, frowns upon since he is never invited.

Smaugs are largely indestructible, but when they do need to defend themselves, they can project a laser beam from their eye. They can also call up help from friendly laser beam snakes which live on energy alone. The only thing they fear is astro rocks, which, when they are hit by them, put them back in time eleven million years.

Smaugs have a high regard for education. Smaug children have to be in school by 6:30 every morning of the week. They go to elementary and high school and then are finished. They have three classes a day:

One teaches them how to get around in the sewer system of Atlanta.

The second teaches them how to find food (during the first three weeks, the teachers feed the students, but from then on they have to find their own).

The third teaches them how to defend themselves from the other creatures in the sewage system.

In order to graduate, one of the requirements is that the Smaug children go from one side of Atlanta to the other side in the sewage system while blindfolded.

Smaugs can find a job working at the school teaching if they wish, but if they don't want to teach, they may be put to work in the school anyway cleaning sewage off the little ones.

So all in all, the culture is a rich and fascinating one—and well worth further examination by the students in the Foxfire I class.

On Friday, we break into small groups again. By now, students in each group, as one of my rare homework assignments, should have collected the information they need by borrowing our equipment or using their own to complete their group's project. I have done what I can in class to speed things up, and on several afternoons, I have taken students on interviews myself. Some groups, unable to meet after school, have gotten me to help them get excused from a certain period for one day to interview someone on campus, such as one of the women in the lunchroom, a custodian, or a faculty member who is free that period. Setting it up in advance ensures that the person who is going to be interviewed has either brought a toy to school on the appointed day or has brought the materials (or requested that we round up the materials) with which to make it. Groups break themselves down in my class into the various task categories and go to work rotating people through the darkroom and through transcribing stations as desired. New photographs are beginning to be posted on the board regularly now, some students having stayed after school to work. Students in each group can rotate taking a tape recorder and their tape home to work on as homework, or they can stay after school to transcribe. I meet with any group that is in trouble during this

Friday class to plan emergency measures to get it caught up with the rest. Projects are beginning to take shape.

Week Nine—Cultural Stereotypes

On Monday, I write the word *nigger* on the board. There is some nervous laughter in the room, a few loud snorts. Some students squirm uncomfortably. I ask them to help me make a list of supposed traits, both physical and cultural. They do. I write them on the board.

Now I hand out to them two quotations from a book by Margaret W. Morley, copyrighted in 1913, called *The Carolina Mountains*. The two quotations:

> You know the approach of the melon season from the vanguard of empty rinds lying along the roadside. There is no trouble getting at a melon. All you need to do is to "bust it open," root into the crisp, pink, and juicy interior with your hands, and go ahead. This the negro children do, lacking a knife, and you will see them, tears of pure delight, as it were, streaming from the corners of their happy mouths. The Southern watermelon! What other fruit ever bestowed such joy on humankind. To see a Carolina negro camped down before a big watermelon is to see what the philosophers try to make us believe does not exist,—a perfectly happy mortal.[1]

> Inseparably connected with the persimmon in one's mind is the 'possum. For the 'possum loves the 'simmon as the nightingale loves the rose. Of a dark night they may be found sitting in the tree among the ripe fruit. He gets fat on 'simmons, and acquires that peculiarly rich and delicate flavor so highly appreciated by the negro. All through the hunting season you are wakened by the excited bark of the 'possum dog, accompanied by the wild yells of the negroes and an occasional gunshot. . . .

> Baked 'possum is the Christmas goose of the epicurean negro, and as the season moves on, the voice of the 'possum dog is heard in the woods assisting in the preparations for that season of high living and neglect of work which is the negro's perquisite, inherited by him from the days of slavery.[2]

"Do you agree with those? Is what she's saying true?" There are some hesitant nods, a few guffaws, but mostly silence. The two foods are already listed on the board, having been volunteered by students previously.

"Fine," I say. "Now let's look at these." I hand them sheets bearing several more selected quotations. A sampling:

> The Southern sun that floods the mountains and beautifies the landscape has an irresistible influence over the people as well. No native thinks of disobeying its implicit command—"Thou shalt not hurry"; therefore the native-born of the Blue Ridge, no matter what else he may lack, is rich in time, a possession denied to the foreign invader who keeps his hoe in the tool-house where he can find it when he wants it. The mountain man leaves

his in the field, and when he wants it, if he cannot find it, he drops the subject. That the ancient and honorable art of "setting around" has been cultivated until it has grown into an integral part of life, you discover upon asking a mountain woman, who has waited in town half a day for some one to come, what she did with her time, and receive the illuminating reply, "Oh, I jest sot. . . ."

When a mountaineer unexpectedly completes a piece of work or makes some unwonted exertion, you may be tempted to think it the result of forethought, but if you ask him about it he will probably tell you it was because he "tuk-a-notion." Life has many consolations run on the "tuk-a-notion" principle.[3]

In our drives about the country we soon discover why the people dread the winter. It does not take very cold weather to make one shiver over an open fire, when the house walls are open to every breeze that blows and one's clothes are not winter-proof. One never sees a winter wood-pile in this country, and as to "filling the cellar," with the ant-like thrift of the New Englander, it is undreamed of. There are no cellars, neither the quality of the land nor the climate lending itself favorably to cellars: one reason, perhaps, for dreading the winter. Corn-pone, dried beans, and salt pork must get somewhat monotonous, even to those who love them. Store-houses are almost as rare as cellars, and is one to deprecate or envy a state of mind that enables people cheerfully to sell their corn in the autumn at thirty cents a bushel, with the certainty that they will have to buy it in the spring at eighty cents?[4]

"Now, those came from a book written about your grandparents. Do you agree with those?" There is usually furious disagreement, since all students, if they didn't know earlier, know by now that in an age when one's very survival depended upon hard work and the storage of ample food and wood for the winter, there was no room for cultivation of the art of "settin' around" or preparing for days of snow and ice on the "tuk-a-notion" principle. It is patently, blatantly false.

"Well," I continue, "if you agree with the lines about watermelons and possums, you have to agree with these, too, because they came from the same book."

Next I put the words *hick* and *hillbilly* on the board. "Now that's you," I say. "Let's make a list of all the traits people away from here think you have. I'll start you off." I put *lazy, shiftless, ignorant, rotten teeth, moonshine liquor,* and a few others on the board. The students add to the list readily enough, but the tone in the classroom has usually shifted a bit.

Next I write the word *stereotype* on the board and lead them into a short discussion of what it means, ending with the question, "Where do these attitudes *come* from?"

Someone usually ventures, "People who don't know us," and I put that on the board too. "And how true are these stereotypes?"

"Maybe a little bit, but not much. They aren't universal. They aren't fair."

Niggers and hicks side by side on the board. For some students, the wheels are turning.

"After your ancestors were established here, when did the first tourists or outsiders begin coming in and buying up land and building summer homes?"

The answers are usually lodged somewhere around 1970, most students believing that tourism and second-home development in the mountains began in their lifetimes. I hand them two more quotations from the same book:

> Long before a train had surmounted the barrier wall of the Blue Ridge [which happened in 1876], the beauty, and salubrity of the high mountains had called up from the eastern lowlands people of wealth and refinement to make here and there their summer homes. The first and most important of these patrician settlements was at Flat Rock, the people coming from Charleston, the centre of civilization in the Far South, and choosing Flat Rock because of its accessibility, and because the level nature of the country offered opportunity for the development of beautiful estates and the making of pleasure roads through the primeval forest that in those days had not been disturbed. Into the great, sweet wilderness, now quite safe from Indians, these children of fortune brought their servants and their laborers, and selecting the finest sites, whence were extensive views of the not too distant mountains, surrounded by the charming growths of the region, in a land emblazoned and carpeted with flowers, built their homes of refuge from the burning heat and the equally burning mosquitoes of the coast land.[5]

Now I put on the board, "Before 1876." We look at the time line, a large copy of which is now posted, and we add this new fact to it.

"Were the people that came in here *like* us? Were they the same?" Another quotation, same book:

> To the romance of this old [1827 turnpike] road was added a charming touch when, with the spring flowers, there came every year that migration from Charleston, like a flock of birds winging their way over the blue mountains in search of their summer homes.
>
> One can imagine these processions of young and old starting out . . . a procession that makes one think of the stories of far-away times, when queens and princesses traveled from one city to another over roads as bad as these. This procession up the mountains had fewer trappings on the horses and less gayly attired escort than did those of the olden time; but we may be sure that the carriages of the gentlefolk of the nineteenth century were pleasanter conveyances than the mule litters of the Middle Ages, and we may also be sure that no lovelier faces looked out from the gorgeous retinue on its way across the hills of the past than could be seen in the carriages where sat the ladies of the New World, with their patrician beauty and their gracious manners. And although the escort of the New World travelers did not number a thousand gayly dressed cavaliers, it consisted of a retinue of those ebony children of the sun, who loved the pleasant journey, and loved their gentle lords and ladies—for all this happened in those

halcyon days "before the war" when the angel of wrath had not yet righted the wrong of holding even a black man in subjection to the will of another, and when the real "quality" cherished their slaves and were greatly loved by them.[6]

"Pretty obvious they weren't like the people we've been studying, isn't it?" Now I lead them through a conversation about wealthy visitors and their homes and what kinds of resources they must have to be able to own and maintain two or three residences. This blends into a discussion of the culture they represent, how it is basically different from ours—and why; and, most important, what happens when cultures collide. Two more short quotations, same book:

> The spectacle is on a grand scale; one can wander over thousands of square miles encompassed by flowers;—beyond the limits of North Carolina these unconsuming flames have spread over hundreds of miles of the ridges and spurs of the Southern Appalachians, so that one seems to get lost even in thinking of it. The [mountain] people call these azaleas "yellow honeysuckles," and get tired of them. The azaleas flaming throughout the forest are like great music, great poetry, great pictures; they strike too high a note for the lives of the people. Such fervor wearies their unaccustomed nerves, and they turn for consolation to a calmer expression of the great renewal.[7]

> To the mountaineer all things are admissible that serve his ends, and one is horrified upon first coming to find him burning rhododendron and laurel wood because, he says, they make a hot fire good for cooking. Think of cutting down for such a purpose a rhododendron or a laurel tree with a trunk thick enough to be split into four sticks of wood![8]

Now I add to the board, beside *hicks, Florida tourists,* and we create a list about them ("Lincoln Continentals and Mercedeses with windows rolled up," "poodles," "flowered shirts and Bermuda shorts," "cameras," etc.).

I end with the question, "When we run into each other, and we represent different cultures and traditions and values, what happens?"

On Tuesday, we continue the same theme. We talk, again, about cultures in conflict, why conflicts erupt, and what kinds of compromises must be made by each group if there is ever to be any common ground for understanding, for coexisting side by side, and even for celebrating and learning from the culture of others as well as the impulse that leads us to share ours with them. We talk about hatred and suspicion and its roots. We talk about how dominant cultures, in clearly immoral ways, sometimes nearly destroy other cultures for their own ends ("Are there any parallels between what the dominant white ruling culture did to the Cherokee Indians and what we, in this century, tried to do to blacks?") and what can be done about that.

I circle back around to stereotypes again, reminding them that when people believe and accept certain stereotypes about, say, blacks, and they become prejudiced against them, it then allows them to do things *to* blacks without feeling guilty about it. How can one feel remorse upon exercising power over something subhuman?

We talk about ridicule and humor directed at certain cultures (Polish or black or whatever) and its consequences. Now I direct a barrage of derogatory humor about Appalachian hicks at them. I show them place mats collected from area restaurants that serve tourists. One of my favorites, which all the students have seen but which I cannot reproduce here because of copyright restrictions, has colored-line drawings of farm shacks, barefoot children, liquor stills, hogs, and mules surrounding a center section, in which are listed examples of supposed mountain dialect with definitions for the ignorant traveler about to enter a strange land: "Et—Eaten—'Have they et?' " and so on. I also show them comic strips that feature hillbillies. I end by showing them a booklet written by a Florida native who now lives less than twenty miles from our school. Called *Thangs Yankees Don' Know,* and intended to be humorous, we wonder together just how funny it really is. Is its tone "just in fun," or is there an element of ridicule?

On Wednesday, we continue to study the booklet, and we make a list on the board of those elements we find most objectionable. When finished, I ask them to write a letter to the author as this week's composition, giving a paragraph to each objectionable element listed on the board. The students are, quite frankly, more than a little angered by this creation of a Florida transplant, but I remind them that the tone in their letter should be reasoned and logical—that shouting and haranguing will accomplish nothing.

That night I take the letters home, grade them as this week's composition, and type a composite version made up of a number of paragraphs taken from their papers, as well as the regular grammar sheet.

The next day I read the composite letter and, if they like it, have them all sign it. We put it in the mail to the author. (We have done this a number of times now, and so far there has been no response. No matter. It is still a good exercise.) Then I return the papers, asking, "If your letter contains grammatical mistakes, and we put it in an envelope and send it to him, what happens?"

The immediate and obvious response: "It just makes him look right when he says we're stupid." Grammar sheets that day take on a slightly different cast. We close discussing their own personal prejudices, and the stereotypes of others they carry, and what they plan to do about that.

Friday, small groups again, the projects continue to move toward completion. With the end of the quarter approaching and all groups now well aware of what remains to be done with each of their projects, I tell them that during the next two weeks, rather than having small-group-activity days, we will have two interviews in their place, thus giving the last two groups a chance to conduct an in-class interview. If the projects require after-school work for completion, each group will have to figure out how it will deal with that fact. [Note: with the move to the semester system, this problem may be solved.]

Week Ten—Cultures in Change

On Monday, continuing the discussions initiated the previous week, with each student making notes, I lead them through a discussion about why cultures change. First, I ask if ours *is* changing. I point to the pretest that was composed of a list of cultural terms, reminding them that their own grandparents would have scored 100. I ask them how much they still see of people plowing with mules or living in log houses or making lye soap. "Is the culture changing?"

"Yes," they answer. No question. I put *yes* on the board.

Now I ask them to brainstorm with me as we make a list designed to answer the question "Why?"

Immediately they come up with, "Because we don't need to know how to do that stuff anymore. There's no *reason* to make lye soap when you can buy it at Winn Dixie and save yourself a whole day's work."

"Right. What else?" Gradually the list lengthens: electricity; automobiles and roads and mobility; teachers from outside who "correct" cultural speech patterns like the common use of double negatives or introduce new customs that are judged superior; missionaries who move in and condemn and change certain religious practices; industries that relocate to areas like our own and make the conversion from a barter to a cash economy not only possible but, for many, desirable; government programs like VISTA, the Appalachian Regional Commission, welfare, food stamps, health clinics, various highway programs; doctors and nurses who relocate here and end the days of home remedies; familiarity with other cultures and values via the media; the wars that drain the mountains of men and women and then return them home from abroad; and the new residents who demand different types of restaurants and clothing stores and entertainment; ridicule directed at the culture and its carriers, which leads them, through embarrassment, to change; and on and on almost endlessly.

Now we make two lists and tally the positive and negative aspects of change. Under one we list such things as "Ending the unending grind of dawn-to-dark daily survival at subsistence levels," and words that note the advantages of better health care, more comfortable housing, more enlightened educational practices, increased leisure time, and the like. Under the other we note such things as the introduction of greed and acquisitiveness, the loss of self-reliance and community interdependence, the loss of the genuine humanity and concern associated with the rich customs and traditions once surrounding the rituals of birth and marriage and death (I remain unconvinced that the digging of a grave by backhoe is somehow better than the old custom of a grave dug collectively and then filled in by those neighborhood residents who knew and truly cared about the deceased), and—the point I hit the hardest—the loss of distinctiveness. I ask them to give me their priorities in terms of clothing, cars, music, food, entertainment. And when the list is complete, I say, "Do you realize that if I went to Montana or Texas or Maine and asked teenagers there to make a similar list, it would look almost identical? What's the point of traveling to Japan to stay in a Holiday Inn and drink Coke and watch American movies on television? What's the point of *anyone* visiting Rabun County when it looks the same as their hometown? What happens when we all look the same?"

Leaving them with, "Every time you eat at a Pizza Hut or a Hardees you cast your vote," I move on to a reminder of the story behind the creation of *Roots,* and a reminder of the fate of the Cherokee when their cultural base was exploded, to the equally interesting discussion that arises when we ask the question, "To what extent do we have any control over these trends? To what extent *should* we? Who is making all this happen? Who benefits? Really? Who are the beneficiaries of our unquestioning acceptance of the designer label? To what extent have we become totally dependent on others for our own definitions of style and custom?"

I try to end the day by making the point that cultures and their differences—whether they be black or Polish or whatever—all add wonderfully different patterns to the quilt of life; patterns that we should celebrate and rejoice over rather than condemn or regard as anachronistic or "quaint" or irrelevant.

On Tuesday, we continue the same theme, this time focusing with even more vigor on the changes that are happening in our county. Using graphs and charts they copy off the board (and, at the same time, hitting the mathematics CBE objective, "Use maps, charts, graphs, tables to illustrate information"), I can show them specifically how things like the number of farms in our county, or the ownership of land, or the number of homes occupied by full-time as opposed to part-time residents, has changed and how that has affected the county's tax income, and how that income is used. I take them through a typical sequence of events (self-sufficiency via natural resources to the takeover of natural resources by government—66% of the land in our county is owned by the U.S. Forest Service—and industry, to the breakdown of farms and the movement into blue-collar, minimum-wage employment, to the trend to seize on tourism as an alternate economy, to eventual powerlessness and total dependence of all but a few of the members of the culture if the forces are allowed to run their normal course to, ultimately, the abandonment of the culture's home turf by all but the hardiest and weakest of the survivors). Acknowledging that it is fruitless—even wrong and anti-American—to insist that the young stay on in their home cultures rather than moving out into the world beyond to accept new challenges, we wrestle with the extent to which it is desirable to preserve some semblance, at least, of the parent culture (if only to give the tourists something "interesting" to look at). And acknowledging the dangers inherent in romanticizing the past, we search for some appropriate blend of present trends and past values that might make sense in the future.

With their heads filled with more questions than answers (but, hopefully by now, with a sense at least of "hillbilly pride" and a new perspective on their backgrounds), I begin to get them ready for an interview tomorrow with someone who may be able to shed more light than fog on the situation.

The next day, depending on the class, the person being interviewed is either a member of the business establishment, or a local person who has some well-reasoned perspective on the whole question of change, or an articulate outsider who has seen his or her own town change dramatically and has fled to Rabun County because of it, and for pretty specific reasons. Interviews with all these, and more, would be ideal at this point, but the limitations of a twelve-week course begin to pinch in the tenth week. The best I can do is summarize, before the interview, what others have said and turn the students loose on this new subject to gain some new insights and perspectives on the situation. It is always thought-provoking, at any rate. And selections from the resulting tape recording can fuel the next week's discussions.

On Thursday, they write what has proved to be one of the most interesting and enlightening compositions of all. Depending on the group, I'll pass around the battered, nearly destroyed front half of a plastic doll's head I found at a construction site, or I'll show them a worn, hand-hewn beam from a log house we have dismantled and moved, or some other similar item that has obviously been through a long, dramatic ordeal of some sort. Asking them to assume a first-person stance and pretend they *are* the object, I instruct them to tell me their life story from their creation in the mountains through the changes they've witnessed and their reactions to those changes, to the present (being stared at by strangers and written about in the Foxfire classroom). Being largely unable to influence events, they must be relatively helpless observers of the changes that happen all around them, assuming the kind of stance, in other words, that many of their friends and acquaintances assume in the face of the bewildering events they see going on about them.

I also ask them to create, within the composition, at least one good description of a place and one of a person, drawing on what they've learned. Indicated by brackets the author places around them, I grade each of these separately, thus giving the paper four grades (and double weight) instead of the usual two. Dialogue and dialect are also permissible.

On Friday, they write thank-you letters to the person interviewed on

Wednesday, I read a selection of compositions and then return them along with grammar sheets.

Week Eleven—County Government

The next to the last week. I spend part of Monday tying up loose ends and driving home, again, points I've tried to make about stereotypes, prejudice, cultures in conflict, the inevitability of change (even among cultures like the Amish), and our reactions to that. I remind them of the purposes of Foxfire, the fact that every tape and photograph they have made goes into our archive for future use, and the fact that even though we do not advocate a return to the days of outdoor toilets and kerosene lamps, we certainly do advocate the need for an understanding of and pride in the parent culture, and a concomitant respect for and interest in the cultures of others.

Then I ease into a series of activities designed to pick up on their eighth-grade Georgia history course and remind them of the history of our county—the date of its creation, for whom it was named and why, and so on. We review county politics (who is elected, who is appointed, and the nature of their jobs) and the ideal candidates in terms of their honesty, sensitivity to cultural values, and knowledge of how to guide change to the advantage of all concerned. We talk about the possibility that students in this class may someday run for office, and the procedure involved. We talk about tax money and where it comes from, and, making a chart, show how it is allocated in our own county and in what amounts. We make a list of the county's elected and appointed offices and who holds them, and we talk about how ordinary citizens can have some impact on the local (and national) scene by virtue of making themselves heard as concerned citizens.

On Tuesday, we continue, focusing at first on copies of our county's economic-development profile—a four-page summary of vital facts about our county (population, per capita income, county retail sales for the past years, average weekly manufacturing wage, the ten largest manufacturers and the number of people they employ, property tax structure, sanitation facilities and their capacity, etc.) that is completed each year by our Chamber of Commerce and filed with the Georgia Department of Industry and Trade. (The fact that such documents are readily available and free for the asking was a real revelation to me some years ago as I first began to ponder the task of ever getting much data together and keeping it up to date.) Looking at the statistics from previous years, we can chart growth and change on the board. This leads us into a discussion of the nature of the jobs currently available, the future picture, the growth of population and tourism in our county and the need for some sort of control over that growth, our own county's zoning policies and the difficulties involved in enforcing them and the means by which existing policies are sometimes challenged and/or changed (for good or ill) through public hearings before the zoning board. Obviously the discussion can go in a number of different directions and could easily, in fact, become the content for an entire twelve-week course, and I cannot predict in advance what directions it will take. It usually depends upon factors such as an issue that happens to be hot in the county at the time, or certain personal concerns the students may have. I rarely know. One thing that does tend to be of abiding interest quarter after quarter, however, is the future job picture in our county and the fact that many of the students in my classroom will wind up leaving the area to find the kind of work they want. One of the more interesting wall charts we concentrate on and add to at this point shows a list of businesses the county will need in the future as the population grows and changes (a bakery, a travel agency, an interior design firm, etc.). Added to quarter after quarter, a dimension of reality is brought to the exercise as we put a check beside businesses we predicted in previous classes that actually get established, and put the names of their owners (and whether local or from outside the area) beside them. (A continuing question, of course, concerns whether or not any students in the class will be responsible for one of those predicted businesses starting up.)

On Wednesday, we have the final interview of the quarter. Depending on the students' interests, it may be with a former student at our high school who has started a business and is fighting for survival or a county official such as a member of the city council or the zoning board. Like the previous interview, the subject varies from quarter to quarter.

On Thursday, the students write a composition in which they reflect upon the changes that they see around them and talk about changes they'd like to see. Unlike the previous composition, for which they had to be passive observers, this time they take the role of someone who would actively work for certain kinds of change. They talk about strategies for action and what they themselves can do to influence the course of events positively and in a way appropriate to the basic culture and values of the area.

On Friday I read the more thoughtful papers, we talk about them, and then we move into the familiar routine.

Week Twelve—Evaluation and Review

The end. For the first two days, the students are broken down into their project groups to complete their work. At some point, I do an exercise with them that shows them how to take a raw chunk of transcription and edit it into something readable. Usually they need additional help editing their rough tape transcriptions and inking their diagrams, and with the class broken down into groups, I have the freedom to roam the classroom, giving whatever assistance is needed. By the end of class on Tuesday, the projects are usually completed and publishable, and the grades I give the projects constitute the students' final composition grade. If a project is not completed by the end of the quarter, the students involved receive an incomplete for the course, and when the project is finished, they receive their grade and credit.

On Wednesday, I hand their folders out and we spend the period organizing their contents, reviewing what we've done together the past eleven weeks, and brainstorming about ways the course could be improved. Toward the end of the period, they list all their compositions and the grades they received (listing the better of the grades if they rewrote any compositions) on the inside front cover of their folders so that I can average their grades quickly and efficiently. They also add the number of grammar sheets they have, the errors on which they actually corrected as we went over the sheets in class. Finally, though I keep the folders for several weeks in case a parent or administrator wants to question a grade, I tell them I will return their folders to them if they write something like "I want this back" on the front. I discard the contents of the other folders.

On Thursday, I get out their pretests. Keeping them at my desk, I hand each student a fresh, blank copy of the words pretest and, assuring them that the results will have no bearing whatsoever on their grades, ask them to take it again. As they finish and raise their hands, I return their original pretest to them along with a clean copy of the grammar pretest, which they then complete. Passing back their original grammar pretests as they finish, I ask them to compare both sets of tests carefully and see if there is any difference. This is always one of my favorite exercises, for by now the students have completely forgotten the answers they gave on their pretests when they took them the first week of the quarter, and the differences in the scores are nearly always dramatic and startling. I like to remember the comment of one of my eighth-graders, who exclaimed, "God, I really *did* learn something this quarter!" That sentiment is virtually unanimous. Stapling the pairs of tests together, I retain them for my files.

On Friday, the students write for the last time, taking what is usually a two-question exam. First I ask them to summarize any new insights they have gained during the course about their culture and their background. I compare these with their third pretest, and again the results are nearly always dramatic, most of the students having moved from not even knowing where the southern Appalachians are, much less how to spell it, to some pretty strong insights.

The topic I give them for the second question varies from quarter to quarter, but usually it has something to do with the course itself and what aspects of it they would keep, and why, and what aspects they would change, and how and why; or some aspect of education in general: teaching styles or class activities they hate and ones they love and why; ways they would change the school if they were suddenly placed in charge, and so on. The topic for the spring, 1984, class posed a situation in which critics were saying that an English course where students used tape recorders and cameras and went on field trips was not a course that paid proper attention to the basics. I asked them to draft a formal response to be read at a school board meeting. Whatever the topic, I ask them to be completely honest and thoughtful, and, if I fail to receive any specific ideas I can use, at the very least I have a chance to check their writing skills.

So what is this course anyway?

Well, basically it's a composition course. The students, in twelve weeks, make demonstrable gains in terms of skills—organizational, grammatical, and mechanical—and I can document that fact not only to my own satisfaction but also to the satisfaction of a department head or an administrator. I can rest secure in the knowledge that at least the state academic mandate is fulfilled.

Why do they make gains? Partially because of the amount of writing we do. Partially because of the frequent repetition and reinforcement of some of the tricks of the trade that they should be able to carry with them and utilize later (the emphasis, for example, on first gaining control of the material before writing begins, through deciding in advance what each paragraph is going to do and what sequence the paragraphs are going to follow, and then making a quick checklist or road map of one- and two-word reminders to guide the paper's development; or the trick, in description, of observing carefully and making lists of details that can be employed when writing begins). Partially because of the emphasis paid to individual problems of grammar and mechanics that the students are having (grammar sheets, check lists, folder reviews, the revision of compositions, etc.) rather than grammar and mechanics in general. Partially because of the atmosphere in the room and the fact that the course doesn't "feel" like a composition course because the composition topics, rather than being artificial and contrived, seem to flow naturally out of the other activities going on in the room, which are rich and varied and fast-paced. Nearly every day is different. Partially because we are working together throughout the quarter on a class project that is actually going to be utilized and seen by an audience beyond my classroom.

And partially because the subject matter about which the students are writing is, for most of them, interesting. It's the old "unit" or "theme" approach we learned about in college; nothing new. I can remember in college, for example, developing a complete English unit around the theme of westward expansion that could be dovetailed with a social studies class in a team-teaching situation. Somehow, though, our units never got much beyond finding a few appropriate short stories and poems and composition topics, locating a poster or two for the bulletin board, and perhaps even a few folk songs and a film. The units were surface illustrations of the theme that were often forced and somewhat unnatural. We weren't *immersed* in them. They weren't vital and living and breathing. The Foxfire I course, I think, has gradually evolved over time into one that comes closer to the mark, and certainly one that is culturally appropriate to my students and their backgrounds.

In addition, I think the students make gains partly because I want them to so much and because I care so much about the course and its content and its mission, and partly because they sense that the course is like a living organism undergoing a process of evolution over which they can have some influence if they choose. Much of what I've just said is speculation, but I've thought about it a good bit and I believe it's the combination of all those factors that makes the students feel generally positive about the course and influences the amount of energy they give it.

There are aspects of the course with which I am still unhappy. I think we try to cover too much material too quickly, and thus the students only get introductions to some material—county politics and government, for example—that I feel they need to understand in more depth. Our reversion to the semester system opens up a whole new cabinetful of possibilities.

As much as I would like to be able to say that I have developed a composition course that is largely experiential in the best sense, I don't feel I can make that claim yet—though I hope to be able to someday. Certainly it is experience rich, and the acts of interviewing, and working in small groups to create a useful—even important—project fall squarely within the definition advanced by the Association of Experiential Education, which reads in part, "[It] occurs when newly acquired skills are applied through direct and active personal experience in order to illuminate, reinforce and internalize cognitive learning. . . ." But there is still too much emphasis on the kind of class discussion that is not internalized by the students to the degree I'd like. There are moments for most of the students, however—peak experiences—when there is that sudden flash of insight about oneself or the surrounding world, or that sudden new understanding, or that moment of self-confidence that arrives as one masters a skill he or she had perhaps feared or shied from previously, and I want to make more of that happen.

Likewise the matter of intrinsic versus extrinsic motivation. I've gotten the course to the point, I think, at which the students work for more reasons than just the external one of grades. Is the use of a numerical grammar grade, however, a step in the wrong direction? Maybe. It makes the grammar grade far less subjective, and that's an advantage. It's therefore a fairer system. But those first papers are sometimes an awful shock.

Recently, however, I was talking with a student in class who was virtually immune to the threat of failing grades and who had just conquered the habit of writing the days of the week with an initial lower-case instead of a capital letter. I wasn't scolding him. I was just curious. "Hadn't anyone told you that rule before?" I asked. "Did you just miss it some-where back there in grade school?"

"I don't know," he said. "I must have heard it before. I just didn't have a good enough reason to use it until now."

That's what I want more of, somehow.

So the course is still not all I want it to be. It still doesn't match the philosophy as closely as I am determined it will one day. I've shared it with you in its unfinished state *not* so you'll duplicate it, Lord knows, but in the hope that you may get some ideas from it that will make your life easier and your job more fun and rewarding.

I can hear a teacher now, somewhere, as I've already heard so many times before, saying, "Easier? It looks like that kind of course takes more energy and time than less." Actually, it doesn't. That's the beauty of it. The energy is expended more in the planning than the execution.

Let me show you what I mean. On the days when there is an interview in class, I sit in the back of the room. One phone call to set it up, and I have the day off. The next day when the students write, I have the day off again (as well as on those days when they're working in small groups). I walk around the room giving help where it's needed, but that's so casual and relaxed and enjoyable an activity that I hardly consider it work. That evening I have some compositions to grade and a grammar sheet to type, but the grammar sheet only takes an extra fifteen minutes (fifteen minutes I would have spent planning the next day anyway if I didn't type one, and now that it's typed, the activity for the next day is also completed), and I would have had to grade that set of compositions no matter what method-ology I used to teach the course (unless I intend to teach it, as some people do, without grading and returning the papers at all—a policy that strikes me, at least, as being indefensible and irresponsible). In other words, I haven't added to my work load; I've actually reduced it, and I've gotten smarter about how I use that energy I do have. As I get better and better about making all the class activities do double duty, and as I get smarter about shifting the load increasingly to the students without abdi-cating any of my responsibility as a teacher, I get more and more "time off." And because the students are doing more work themselves, learning increases. The trick is getting that time off by having them involved in *meaningful* work instead of text and workbook exercises. And that just takes planning, the subject of the next chapter.

Before I leave this one, let me answer, again, that teacher I just heard in the back of my mind saying, "Why does he keep picking on texts and workbooks?" One more time, and then I'll shut up about it. A group of students has just been assigned a chapter in an American history text and told to answer the questions at the back for homework or as an in-class assignment (read teacher time off). As long as the students are on task and quiet, all's well. Right? Let's be honest. You know and I know what's going on with most of them. Half are not reading the chapter at all but have started with the questions instead. Using the chapter subheads, they quickly locate the section where each question's answer lies, find several sentences in each that look like the correct answers, copy them onto their papers, and, when finished, hand them in knowing that most teachers are simply going to glance over the papers and put a check in the grade book indicating a completed assignment. Some of the others are actually reading the chapter, but in most cases their minds are wandering. They're replaying Michael Jackson's new video in their heads. They're thinking about Friday night. When they finally get to the questions, they can no more answer them without help than I can fly, so now they repeat the process their more clever peers used. Some of the others are reading, genuinely trying to understand the material, and they make an honest effort to complete the assignment as we intended it to be done. I'll bet I can take this *latter* group, though (the best of the lot), and two days later lead them in a discussion about that chapter and find that what little they remember, they can't talk about with any degree of comprehension or understanding.

We know this. That's why we go over the chapter with the students before we move on to the next—usually. But if that's all we do, the amount of understanding is still primitive at best, and the amount of retention over time is almost nil.

Likewise, those students keeping notebooks for an assignment in biology. I see them in my classes frequently, copying sections out of their texts frantically because they have "ten pages due fifth period." I already talked about how much learning is going on in that situation—or even when the same thing is happening in the evening quiet of the student's room—earlier in this book.

Same with workbooks. We have now made learning the basics our first priority, and we've created tests to determine whether that mission has been fulfilled. Because of the tests and the fact that they determine whether a senior receives a diploma, we use more and more workbooks and study sheets that ask questions like those on the tests, and the students get better and better at answering them accurately and the scores go up. Fine.

But with those tests and the kind of information they are designed to check as our first priority, we run the risk of forgetting—or downplaying —some pretty important things. Remember Douglas Heath's study at Haverford? That's the one that uncovered the fact that there was little or no direct correlation between high test scores and adult success. What most of the tests measure is recall and skills levels, when the traits essential for future occupational success and happiness are such things as intellectual curiosity; the ability to analyze problems, think logically, and learn from experience; the ability to get along with others and work successfully in teams; the internalization of certain moral values, and so on. In other words, if we spend most of our time and energy getting students ready for the tests they must take to prove to their communities that they have learned the basics, we may forget that we are also supposed to be helping them learn how to be fulfilled and healthy and successful adults.

We may also forget that although a student can answer multiple choice test questions correctly, it does not necessarily follow that he can *apply* the basic skills those questions checked in real-life situations.

Things get out of balance fast. It's too easy for a teacher to get away with just covering the material in the text. It's too easy for a school to convince its school board and itself that it has done its job if student test scores rise, when in fact it may not have accomplished some of its other major—and arguably more important—functions at all.

That's not to say texts should not be used or students should not be tested for basic skills. I use texts in my college English course. I emphasize basic skills in all my courses, and I test for them. It is, rather, an appeal for balance. One teacher teaches botany exclusively from texts and workbooks. Another—equally misguided—teaches it exclusively out of doors without the use of reference materials and study guides at all. The better one teaches its specifics through the combined use of texts and study guides, the out-of-doors hands-on face-to-face confrontation with the subject matter, supplementary reference materials, the process of data collection, and the results of individual and small-group student research projects. The best uses this latter approach but is *also* skillful enough to go far beyond the study of the specifics of botany itself and help guide his or her students to some genuine understanding of what botany can tell us, by extension and generalization, about the forces that shape culture, about the wise uses of the information for the future well-being of all, and about ourselves. He or she constantly asks, "Now that we can collect and identify fifty plants apiece, and name their parts and explain their life cycles, so what? What's it good for? Why bother?"

Texts alone, whether in the form of printed pages or computer software, simply are not adequate to the real task at hand.

30

Making Courses
Do Double Duty

The course just described is one of twenty that our organization sponsors within our public high school's curriculum. I could include a complete description of each, but if I did, you would have to carry this book in a wheelbarrow. Those of you who are interested in course guides to the others will find information about them in the Bibliography.

Let's move on. Hopefully some of the information that follows will be even more useful to you than those descriptions. I include it, at least, in that hope.

At the end of every weekly staff meeting, I and the other staff members who teach at the school remain behind to talk about our courses in a session that usually lasts until about seven P.M. Over coffee and fruit, we look at one another's lesson plans for the preceding and the upcoming weeks. Each of us will share at least one proposed activity and its objectives and solicit ideas from the group for ways to tighten it, make it more effective, and evaluate it. Activities that were tried during the previous week are shared and discussed. Did they work? How? Why? Why not?

How do you know? Would they have served different objectives more effectively? Should they be retained as part of the course next semester, or should they be discarded as bankrupt or too cumbersome and replaced with something else?

Sometimes one of us will have a community resource person coming to our class in the next few days, and some of the other staff members will want to share that person with their classes while he or she is on campus. Sometimes one of us will have developed a pre/post testing instrument that others like and want to try also. This is encouraged, and we always compare results, examining the reasons for any differences we find: "What did you do with this activity that I didn't do?" "What did I leave out?"

This weekly debriefing and planning session, despite the fact that we are all a little tired since it comes at the tail end of a long day, is one of the most valuable things we do together. It keeps all of us on our toes, and it gives us the opportunity to fuel each other and keep the engines running. (If you don't have a similar support group in your school, I would recommend without hesitation that you start one. And don't let it slide because of headaches or exhaustion or bad days. The members of the group, going in, should make a commitment to each other to be there every week for at least one whole semester before voting as to whether or not to disband. Give it a chance to work and see what happens.)

In addition, at the end of each school year, we have a three-day staff retreat away from the school and the phones and the messages and the kids partly to decide which courses to drop from the curriculum, which ones to retain with revisions, and to plan new, hopefully more effective ones to take the place of those we have dropped.

It is this process of retaining/revising existing courses and planning brand new ones that I want to discuss more fully.

Revising an Existing Course

Before any of us can revise old courses or plan new ones, we have to have those lists of purposes and objectives. Without them, we're stumbling over mental furniture in the darkness of our assumptions. I used not to believe that, preferring instead to trust my gut feelings. Now I believe it. I'll show you why in a moment.

The charts I and my staff members use are not entirely of our own making, of course. One is the state list of Competency Based Education/ Basic Skills Test (CBE/BST) objectives I referred to frequently in the previous chapter. The only real argument I have with that list is that the objectives are sometimes stated in such vague terms ("The student makes generalizations and draws conclusions in the context of academic, everyday or employment materials") that it is difficult to tell just what it is the state expects students to be able to do. Looking at sample questions from the BST that test those objectives helps, but the questions are often so simpleminded and the answers so obvious that we find ourselves asking, "Wait a minute. Is this all they want? This is it? *This* is all we're required to do with that objective?"

In other words, we find ourselves facing pits of lime Jell-O. We misunderstand the objectives, or get lazy, or construct activities that we think sort of address the mission; but the activities are so off the mark or so toothless that they are bogus. A teacher brings someone in from the community to be interviewed and assumes that activity addresses the objective of helping to develop student listening skills. But did it? Really? Probably not. Certainly not by itself, in isolation, and without some active teacher intervention before and after—and I mean intervention by a teacher who has finally fought through all the muck and come to an understanding of what that objective is truly and why it's there in the first place.

Over the course of several years, my staff and I have developed a supplementary list of objectives that has helped us flesh out and give additional substance to the latter. Over the course of numerous meetings, we asked ourselves questions like, "What survival skills will students have to have when they get to college, not only to pass but also to wring out of that experience all that it can offer?" and, "What skills, aside from those specifically outlined in a job description, would make any students, college graduates or not, so valuable to a future employer that, as employees, they would be the absolute *last* ones to be laid off in a financial crunch?" The answers to questions like those—and you can do this work yourself without too much trouble—keyed to state objectives, form the second list we work with, a list that is five pages long.

The last two lists are ones I've already talked about: the school goals (developing responsible citizens, etc.), and goals specific to our own organization's priorities (making sure all the students have a firm understanding of their own culture and the Appalachian region, etc.).

Each of the four lists is different, but those of you who are already retreating in confusion should take another look before you throw up your hands. The first two lists are really one and the same; they're just different ways of stating and helping to understand and flesh out the same basic skills agenda, and they tend to be subject specific, with some skills for math, some for language arts, and so forth. The last two lists have more to do with content than basic skills and should be used to inform the kinds of activities that take place in the classroom, no matter what the subject area. And, as I have said before, with careful planning, almost every activity in the classroom can hit items on all four lists *simultaneously*. It just takes planning.

Using these lists to steer us from the swamps, I and my staff members evaluate our existing courses as *delivery systems* designed to implement the mandate. If a course, as it is being taught, is not fulfilling that mandate, we drop it and replace it with another, or we put it through a pretty extensive redesigning process.

I promised that I would return to an illustration of what happened to me when I trusted my gut instincts too completely. It's a lesson I learned while Margie and I evaluated the magazine course, our imperatives in the form of those ubiquitous lists in hand. In terms of the basics, I assumed students were mastering a number of writing skills, organizing skills, research skills, and bookkeeping and accounting skills. They had to be. The nature of the activity of putting out a magazine and being in a room where print and communication infused the environment and represented important, real work *should* have guaranteed it. Same with such things as learning about the region and its history. On closer examination, however, Margie and I had to admit that though some students were advancing in those areas, many were not. It made perfect sense on paper that all of them should have been posting measurable gains, but in reality, because of the way the course was being taught, it was too often affective instead of cognitive. The course had been going on for years, and we had fallen into a comfortable production routine, and the magazines were coming out on time, and they looked good; but we had a promising six-cylinder vehicle that was running on two.

For example, one summer we decided to move a magnificent log house and document the process for the summer, 1984, issue of *Foxfire*. Scott, one of the students on the construction crew, photographed the dismantling of the structure step by step; and that fall, in the magazine class, he began to process those negatives at the same time that he was photographing the phases of reconstruction that went on all fall with a crew of community adults hired to take the place of the students who were now back in school. He was buried in photographs and diagrams. Before the class ended, he finished most of those and much of the layout, and he had started work on the captions. Too late, I realized the captions were a disaster; Scott left our course still spelling *chimney* "chimbley." He had learned a few valuable things, granted, but as a student in a magazine class who was producing a publishable article, he fell through the cracks in terms of some of the things he should have learned—*could* have learned if I had been more attentive. He left us writing not one whit better than when he came to us. And he knew it. And although Scott learned a great deal about one type of traditional log structure, he learned nothing about the other types or about the broader picture of Appalachian culture in general. His knowledge of Appalachia was fragmentary and episodic, all based on one tiny tile in a huge mosaic he never saw whole and entire. He knew a good bit about that one tile, but he knew little of the overall picture to which it contributed its tiny spot of color. He was immersed completely in a project to which I never successfully added context. We were all too busy, too distracted by the pressures of deadlines.

In addition, within the magazine class, Margie and I found that we often violated Dewey's principle of spiral growth—a principle we believed in and knew the vehicle of a magazine should be able to serve. We violated it not on purpose but by default.

For example, after one article, Allison saw the process whole. She was bright enough to be able to conduct a competent interview, take and process good photographs, transcribe and edit her tapes, write a grammatically correct and reasonably informative introduction, and lay out and design the final pages. She was on her own. She had the necessary skills. She did not disrupt the class. We could move on to other students, secure in the knowledge that Allison could take care of herself with little interference from us. She continued to produce articles, all publishable. When we examined her work with Dewey in mind, however, we found that her articles all looked very much the same. She had gotten comfortable. She had mastered a process, and it was rewarding to her because she did it well, and so she did it over and over, producing articles that in terms of length and complexity and sophistication were no different from her first. She was moving in a circle, not a spiral. She was not being stretched and challenged. There was no growth.

With other students, we were coming close to having real impact, and there were many of those. But closer examination, in hindsight, even revealed flaws there when the work the students did was stacked up against those core objectives.

Another example: during the 1979–80 school year, I had a student named Kim. He would be the first to admit that he wasn't the most enthusiastic student who ever attended Rabun County High School, but he was personable and cooperative and unfailingly polite, and he plugged right along, and graduated.

As I remember it now, I had told the students in my magazine class, Kim included, that I preferred they find their own subjects to research and write about for *Foxfire*, but if they couldn't come up with anything, I'd let them go through a thick folder I had containing subjects that had been suggested by others that we had not yet had time to get to.

Shortly thereafter, Kim walked into class and told me that his father had what he thought might be an interesting story about working during the Depression for a man named Colonel Joe Gray to build a road by hand, using picks and shovels and dynamite and one mule named Old Doc, up the side of Black Rock Mountain. Colonel Gray's motivation for building the road had been largely unselfish: a number of men in the county were out of work, despite the presence of several WPA projects in the area; there was a magnificent site for a picnic area on top of the mountain, but because of the lack of a good road, it was virtually inaccessible to the general public; and he had enough money himself that he could afford to share that which he did have with others. Years later, at the urging of Colonel Gray and a number of other county residents—most of whom donated the land to the State of Georgia for the purposes of creating a public park on top of the mountain—Black Rock State Park was born, and Colonel Gray's road was paved to the top of the mountain by the state and named Talmadge Trail in honor of the governor. Colonel Gray died, was buried in the county, and was largely forgotten. The seven-foot-high marble marker at the entrance to his road carried the names of Talmadge and a number of state and county officials, but neither Gray nor the men who had labored on the original road were mentioned. And no tombstone was erected on Colonel Gray's grave.

I told Kim to grab the story and run.

With the help of his father, Kim located the name and address of one of Colonel Gray's nieces and, in class, struggled through several drafts of a letter to her, explaining his interest in Colonel Gray and asking permission to come and tape record her. She wrote back immediately and enthusiastically. Kim called her and made an appointment, and he and I drove into South Carolina one afternoon, found her, and Kim conducted an hour-long interview that was a real gem, filled with the memories Margaret Adams had of Colonel Gray when their family would spend summers with him in Rabun County.

When we got back home that evening, we stopped in the little tavern Kim's father owned, and his mother and father gathered around one of the tables and listened to Kim's interview from beginning to end, grinning with delight. As the project gathered momentum and the word spread around the county, old photographs and maps and documents began to appear. Kim interviewed and photographed his father, who, in a sudden burst of inspired enthusiasm, gathered as many of the survivors of the experience together as he could find for a group portrait, taken by Kim, at Colonel Gray's old cabin. The grave was found, and Kim photographed the faded marker that had been placed there years earlier by the funeral home that had been in charge of his arrangements.

Kim worked for weeks putting it all together and writing his introduction, which read as follows:

J. F. GRAY
A Forgotten Man

I had heard my father, Ellison Wall, talk about Mr. J. F. Gray and how much he had done for Rabun County, like for instance Mr. Gray had Black Rock Road built. But he did not only build it because he wanted the road to lead to somewhere, but also so that a lot of people could work on it and make a little money. And my dad was telling me that when he was about seven or eight, Mr. Gray used to hire him and Silas Giles to bust rock with a clawhammer and spread it around his driveway, not that he wanted a rock driveway, but just to let them work and earn a little money.

But something that has always bothered my father is that Mr. Gray hasn't even got a tombstone on his grave, but many people in the county that remember him are going to pitch in and buy him a tombstone just for appreciation.

There is a granite marker at the beginning of Black Rock Road, but it is a marker for Talmadge because he was the Governor at the time the road was being built, although Mr. Gray was the one who had the road built, so I think he should have a little credit for it, too. My father and I were talking that there should be some kind of marker for Mr. Gray. So I thought it might be good to have this man's life story in a *Foxfire* magazine, so I interviewed my father about him.

Then I asked him about some people who might be some kin to Mr. Gray, and he said, yes, that there was somebody still around that he knew right offhand, and he told me her name was Mrs. James Adams, and he said she might know a little bit about him and may even have some documents or pictures of them working on the road. We found how we could get in touch with her. She lives in Easley, South Carolina. I wrote her what I was trying to do, and she was pleased with it. So I called on the phone and asked her if Wig and I could come over and talk with her. She told us to come over anytime, so we set a date to go to Easley.

Wig and I arrived at Easley, and called to tell her where we were. We waited in a parking lot talking for a minute until she and her husband arrived and took us out to eat, and we got pretty well acquainted.

After lunch, we went to their house and we all got situated and we interviewed her. She had a lot of information about Mr. Gray. When I asked her about some documents or pictures, she told us that everything they had like pictures and things are all in Augusta locked up in a chest, but next time she was there, she would look for them.

I got to talking to Mrs. Adams about a tombstone for his grave, and why wasn't there one. She told us that the family never got around to doing it. So I told her my dad was going to get a bunch of people who knew and liked Joe Gray to buy a tombstone for his grave up at Taylor's Chapel, and she told us whenever he was going to do that to call her and she would help out.

When this article finally gets printed and in the magazine, Dad and I are going to round up all the people that are willing to donate a little. Then we will find out how much we have collected and buy him some kind of tombstone. That would help out a lot more for remembering him than what he has now. I am glad I took my time to do this article because I think this man should be remembered and not forgotten.

KIM WALL

The magazine that featured the article on its cover was an instant hit. One of the survivors took over a hundred issues himself to give to all his friends and relatives. For a number of weeks, Kim was a very popular young man.

Now, remember for a moment the lists outlined previously. With this particular project, a number of basic—and some not so basic—language arts skills were given a workout, among them reading, composition and grammar, asking good questions to elicit solid informative answers, listening carefully, and organizing a body of raw information into coherent form. Language arts became an essential vehicle through which to communicate to others a human story, recorded permanently now for others to appreciate; Kim himself received a welcome dose of self-confidence and praise; Kim and his father entered into a somewhat different kind of relationship from that they had been used to, with his father's knowledge that if this story were to be told correctly, Kim would have to be the agent by which that happened; and Kim stepped beyond himself to help correct what many in the county perceived as a wrong. Colonel Gray was given some measure of the recognition many thought was long overdue and much deserved (as were the survivors of one of Rabun County's bigger civil engineering projects); and the family got together to put a permanent marker on Gray's grave. And maybe Kim learned something, too, from Colonel Gray's unselfish desire to make a contribution in time of need.

And so the project fulfilled a number of objectives simultaneously, and it certainly beat, hands down, that perfunctory composition I could have assigned as an English teacher about the four seasons. (The latter would have taken less of my time and energy, but, in truth, the Black Rock project didn't take *that* much more effort on my part. Kim did most of the work. I did some chauffeuring, which someone else could have done, and some one-on-one consulting and editing, which I regard as part of my job anyway and not an imposition on my time.)

So what's the problem? The introduction represented one of the longest pieces of writing Kim had ever undertaken, and it went through several revisions, a process Kim would only have put up with in a situation like this with its panoply of motivational ingredients; but it is still flat and unemotional and without passion. Each paragraph of the narration has equal weight; there is no figurative language or color or sense of pace or momentum. It is a travelogue, and one that wouldn't be *that* hard to fix. In addition, though Kim learned about one event that happened during the Great Depression, he learned virtually nothing about the causes of that depression or its impact on all of Rabun County or the Appalachian region as a whole, or the role of government in bringing it to an end. The event was not connected in any way to the larger whole. In addition, because Kim worked largely alone, the rest of the class, which could have made some real contributions to the work by helping Kim find other informants (or by adding supplementary interviews themselves to round out the story as a class activity) was not involved. And so forth. None of these failings was Kim's fault. I only use this article as an illustration of the fact that with a bit more imagination on my part, and not that much more work, the project could have come closer, not only for Kim but also for the rest of the class, to delivering all it had the potential to deliver. It was a gold mine, half the gold in which was left in the ground.

Last, Margie and I also found that we had often fallen into one of the most insidious traps of all: that of allowing the production of an issue of the magazine to be sufficient as an end in and of itself. "The students have produced another magazine. They have accomplished the ultimate goal, the finished product toward which we have been striving all these weeks. It is complete. Fine. End of lesson."

And it was not fine, for we sometimes forgot the most elemental rule of all: the goal is *not* just the production of another issue of a magazine (or the memorization of another rule of grammar, or a list of names and dates, or a series of mathematical formulas, or a set of reasons for the causes of soil erosion), but the acquisition of skills and knowledge that can be applied in different ways, in different situations, and can lead to further growth. "The student can take and print pictures? Fine. But so what? What's that for? What does that lead to? What ramification does that skill have for other tasks?" "The student can write an introduction? Okay. But so what? What's next? How can the skills required to accomplish that task be applied in other ways in the real world? What has been learned? To what end?" "The student can ask perceptive questions in an interview? Fine. So what? What's next? What's that skill good for outside this room?" And so on.

Operating on the assumption that students would be able to answer those questions automatically for themselves, by themselves, I found that as a result, I had some students who had not even equated in a primitive way the process they had just gone through to produce an article with the process of writing a research paper for another teacher. There was almost no transfer of acquired skills to other tasks or classes.

The finished product (whether a magazine or a term paper for history or a science or math project or a play or a work of art or a video show) must be a transparent gauze veil, not a cement wall—a veil that we grope toward and reach, but once there, see *through* to the other side.

There are two workable approaches to redesigning any course, be it chemistry, math, or whatever. Margie and I are using both in the redesign of the magazine class. The first is to take an existing activity and rework it so that it better serves the objectives that are most appropriate to it. And I don't mean forcing a square peg into a round hole and trying to make an activity serve an objective it can't. I mean maximizing the natural potential of an activity already in place. The second is to start with an objective the course *could* address but isn't and design appropriate activities, keeping that objective foremost in mind. Margie and I are now trying a number of things that seem to be doing the job better.

For example, one of the existing activities in the magazine course is to write an introduction for an article. In the past, students often went on an interview, made no notes, and some weeks later drafted a half-page "We went to see Mr. Gillespie and he told us about his general store and he was a nice man and we liked him" introduction that Margie or I would help the students expand slightly and then approve. The students had completed a piece of writing, it was grammatically and factually correct, and though short of all it could have been, it was deemed sufficient.

No more. Building on some of the Foxfire I lessons, students on interviews now must also make notes that will help them describe the person being interviewed and his or her environment in graphic detail. Using those notes, and inserting appropriate figurative language and insights, they then draft introductions that are much fuller and richer than the old norms allowed.

In addition, students must now also conduct library research, the results of which help set at least one main topic of the interview in its proper historical or cultural context. In some cases, the results of this research demand additional interviews with the same informant to fill in gaps resulting from questions the student allowed the informant to answer incompletely, or questions the student simply did not know to ask at all. On one interview, for example, a contact revealed that he had served in a CCC camp in our county. Later library research concerning the CCC camps led to a whole list of topics that students then questioned not only the same but also other community informants about—topics they hadn't thought of before the interview and that the informants hadn't volunteered information concerning, simply assuming from the questions being asked that the students weren't interested. At the same time that the students are researching their topics, they are also searching for answers to questions like, "Is this a skill or experience unique to the Appalachian region?" or "If this skill or experience is widespread, was it altered or made distinctive in some way within the Appalachian region, either by mountain people in general or the individual being interviewed? How? Why?"

As first drafts of each introduction are completed, as well as drafts summarizing the fruits of the research, the students are all called together as a group to read and critique copies of the drafts and ask questions concerning areas that confuse them and make suggestions for revision. The scrutiny of the whole class, combined with some personal knowledge of the existing written record and the mechanics of information retrieval, elevates the production of an article to a whole new level, helps the students understand that they are adding vital, firsthand, previously unpublished material *to* that written record in the form of the informant's knowledge, and gives them a new understanding of the methods and purposes of research projects in general, both in school and in the outside world.

As the subsequent drafts near completion, I examine them in the same way I would papers from my college English class, marking grammatical and mechanical errors and circling awkward or clumsy or trite language, with the student present. Future drafts must incorporate the corrections in order to prepare the work for a much larger audience than the class itself. Then if I see a student is having continuing problems with the same kind of error, I can give positive one-on-one help as required. Basic skills, knowledge of the region, and several school goals are all addressed simultaneously, and cognitive and affective objectives come together.

Example: another existing activity is the drive to help students analyze the Appalachian experience. Addressed cursorily before, now, rather than working in isolated teams with students never seeing or discussing the work of the others until it is published, I am much more rigorous about the discussions we have as a class concerning each article that is in production, and the lessons to be learned from each. One of my most vital tasks as students begin to wrestle with their own culture is to lead them toward objectivity; to help them see that it would not necessarily be desirable to go back to the 1880s and duplicate their culture intact in Rabun County; to help them see that some aspects of Appalachian value systems and beliefs are not necessarily appropriate today; to help them understand that culture is not artifact but is a living, breathing, changing organism that has no end product per se but constantly evolves over time; to help them understand that they're part of a thrust into the future—not a stopping point, or a beginning, but a continuation; to help them evaluate Appalachian value systems in light of those of the dominant society and in light of the needs and pressures of the 1980s; to help them, for example, look objectively at the traditional Appalachian conception of the woman's role in the home and community, or the role of education or religion or justice, and evaluate that in light of today's needs.

And to help them, nearly above all, evaluate their own—and their culture's—attitudes about *other* cultures and deal with those, to help them see that just as they have often been wrongly stereotyped, so too have they wrongly stereotyped others, and to help them see that great men and women refuse to be contained by the tradition in which they were raised. They draw strength and pride from that but remain open to the full range of options and refuse to be squashed backward into outdated molds. When kids make some lye soap or string a few beads and that's the end of it, the study of the culture becomes episodic and fragmented, and it is never seen whole. The potential of the project is never fulfilled. It's like reading the first chapter of a book and then putting it down and moving on to other things.

It becomes easier now to see the role of in-class work and the teacher's perspective as an adult. Students have compelling experiences outside class and then put them into perspective inside. From the documentation and appreciation of a particular skill, like making a pair of shoes or a quilt, they are helped to learn *not* that we should necessarily go back to making our own shoes but that there is something else going on there that we should learn from: the value of self-reliance, for example, or the value and satisfaction inherent in the creation of a whole product that bears an individual's stamp. Now what place can those values play in the 1980s in each of our lives? How do we integrate them into our own lives? Does the Appalachian tradition of community interdependence (everyone pitching in to build someone's barn or house, or everyone gathering to plant or cultivate or harvest the crop of a sick neighbor) have any place in today's world? What form would it take? Is it in conflict with the other tradition of self-reliance? What appropriate form does *that* take today? And what about the traditional Appalachian views on family and the belief in a strong family unit?

And as questions are raised in class, the students return to the community and the culture itself for further exploration and experience—but now on a different plane. Now with focus. Now with purpose. The best teachers thrive on this ebb and flow between experience and analysis, and the resultant growth in their students.

Example: one of the objectives my staff and I identified as one that would make our students more valuable to their employers was not only the ability to determine accurately how much each of the projects they were assigned cost their employers, but also to be able to figure out ways to reduce those costs effectively. Several state math objectives easily and naturally keyed to this exercise. Though math skills were not part of our language arts mandate, and though we previously did nothing to hit these objectives in any systematic way, on looking at the objectives closely, Margie and I saw a way to address some of these skills as a natural, unforced extension of the ongoing work. Keeping the objectives in mind, and with the help of the class, we figured out the costs of every aspect of the production of an average twelve-page article, from the cost of every photograph (including film, processing, chemicals, paper, test strips, etc.) to the per-mile costs involved in gathering the information, to the number of hours required to process the information, to the printing and mailing costs of every issue and the portion of those printing and mailing costs that twelve-page article was responsible for. We even looked at the costs of rubber cement and tape and layout boards, finally estimating that the average article of that length rings up a tab of just over $900 in actual cash outlay if labor costs at minimum wage are included (which they must be during the summer, when students are hired by us to produce the summer issue).

Next we drew up a chart on which all students could keep a running record of every expense and every hour of time expended in the production of their own articles. As the articles are completed, we tally the costs and compare them against the average, figuring both what the article would have cost were the students being paid and what it cost during the school year without those labor charges.

When we come together as a class for budget meetings, we examine the production expenses, and I continually make the points:

•Those of you who can get a quality job done most efficiently without wasting an inordinate amount of time or supplies are the ones high on my list for summer jobs with us.

•All of you should be able, using the same system, to figure out what each project you are given by a future employer has cost, and you should be able to figure out ways to save the employer money without sacrificing quality. Those of you who can do that, whether you're pumping gas or fixing cars or designing ad campaigns, will probably be among that employer's most valued employees.

The specific math problems involved ("If a tray of developer will yield fifty prints and the cost of that tray of chemicals is x number of cents; and the cost of the fixer is added, what is the cost of the chemicals involved per print, exclusive of the price of the printing paper?") address specific math CBEs. In addition, there is the sobering realization of how quickly the hours melt away when the meter is running and how impressive the totals can become as pennies here and pennies there turn into dollars. The dimension of reality added to the project is valid and vital, for we are spending real money, not Monopoly money, and the important lesson learned for application in the real world is undeniable. And those students who are naturally distractible and slow moving can be helped, in a positive atmosphere, by their peers to plan ways of using their time and energy more efficiently and not letting their minds wander. This new activity, added in an easy, gentle way to an existing activity, accomplished several new objectives simultaneously with very little extra work on my part.

Every one of my staff members, whether in video, music, environmental education, or whatever, is doing and will continue to do the same revision process in the interests of making all our courses the effective delivery systems they can be when taught to their full potential.

Do you need to do the same thing? I don't know. Look at each of the assignments and projects in each of your courses and ask, "So what? What's this for? Really." Be hard on yourself. If you're like us, you'll get stuck once in a while, unable to answer yourself with any conviction. Wherever you get stuck, there's a place that's ripe for revision.

Designing a New Course

During the current school year, I and my staff have added four new courses to the curriculum, replacing four that we dropped. All the new ones were carefully designed and seem to be working. Based on a continuing series of such experiences, for those of you who are curious, let me take you through the process I would use were I asked tomorrow to design a course in a subject I had never taught before—say in math or

physics or history. There will be some repetition here, but bear with me.
I'll try to make it painless and brief. Here's my checklist:

The first thing I would do, to keep myself from getting discouraged,
would be to remind myself that my Foxfire I course has taken a good five
years to develop so far (that's fifteen different entrances and exits in the
quarter system), and it still isn't finished and it probably won't ever be.
That's the nature of this work, and I just have to accept that. Evolution is
part of the package whenever a teacher is growing, experimenting, and
asking hard questions. It's when we think we've reached the end of that
process that we need to ask the hardest question of all—the one having to
do with retirement.

Next, as a starting point, I would take the text for the course and read it
from cover to cover. I would make sure I knew the material cold, and as I
went through the text, I would probably mark it up pretty badly. I would
read it with one part of my brain continually asking, "Which of these parts
can I illustrate, either by bringing something into the classroom from
outside or by taking the students out of the classroom to another location?" I would circle those parts or make notes in the margin. If activities
were suggested at the back of each chapter, I'd read those, check the ones
that appealed to me, and make notes beside them if activities came to
mind that I could either add to or replace them with.

During times when I was not reading the text, I would continue to think
about its contents, watching for illustrations and applications in the world
around me. Even as I read the morning paper or drove to the grocery
store, I would look for linkages.

At the same time, I would search for another book or two. I would look
for one, at least, that summarized the best and most current thinking of
the professionals in that field. And I would search for one by a philoso-
pher/advocate who had looked at my field from the point of view of its
importance or its utility. Why should people study it? What contribution
can it make to their lives? In what ways can or do those who care about it
make contributions to all of us and to the general welfare of people, the
natural world, or both? Where does the field fit in the scheme of things?
What's it *for*? If I could find such books, I would read them, keeping
constantly in mind that image of a classroom full of teenagers who probably couldn't care less. I would make notes. I would mark up the books. I
would internalize them completely. I would eat them for dinner. They
would become part of me.

I would also attend to the students' culture and backgrounds and watch
for appropriate ways to use them.

At this point, if I did not find myself getting excited about the course,
and if ideas for teaching it weren't flowing, and if I found I was having a
hard time seeing much point in mastering the material, I would know I
was in big trouble and I would begin to try to find a way to get out of the
obligation of teaching it gracefully. I mean, life's pretty short, and there

are other things I could be doing that I would at least enjoy and care about. And though I don't teach math, I know enough math to be aware of one equation: bored teacher equals bored class. Where there's no smoke, there's probably no fire.

Assuming the opposite has happened and I'm getting excited, I would remind myself that a number of my students, despite all I do, will probably not emerge sharing my interest in the subject. But a number of them *will*, and I remind myself that I'm going to turn those on to something in a way they've never been turned on before, and that's going to make all this work worth it. Don't misunderstand me here. I didn't say that if I turn one on it will all be worth it. I don't believe that. Again, life's pretty short. I said "a number of them." I'm shooting for half. I mean if the subject's *important*, let's get serious and stop wasting time and messing around.

Now I'd start making lists. I'd begin with the state requirements, looking for three things: the specific *facts* my students should internalize (I'm talking one- and two-word reminders here, now, not pages of sentences); the specific *skills* my students should master as a result of the course; and the specific *concepts* and *understandings* and *awarenesses* they should have through taking it. Those guidelines and requirements, such as they are, reflect what I've been hired to do, and so I'd better deal with them first. I want this to be not only a good course but one that's virtually unassailable in terms of content. Then I'd round off the lists by adding what I'd found in the text that I judged important and what I'd found from my extra reading.

Now I would order the three lists in some way. Which is more important: facts, skills, or concepts? Which, if any, should be emphasized? The extra reading I have done should help here. And this is a time for more hard questions. With history, for example, is it more important that students memorize names and dates and places—facts—or that they understand concepts that flow from those facts and inform the present and the future? That's a question that needs to be dealt with, or we risk getting lost in minutia. And I'm not talking about dropping one of the lists or getting into conflict over state goals versus other goals my readings might have indicated were more important. I can serve *both* adequately. I'm just talking about being clear about which gets top priority and which, therefore, I am going to be most concerned about my students possessing when they leave me. Next, I would examine those lists to see whether or not, in each, any particular order, chronological or otherwise, needs to be followed. Does history, for example, have to be taught chronologically or, with the help of a good time line in the classroom to help keep things straight, can it be taught thematically? The texts follow a certain sequence, but that does not mean that order is necessarily inviolable. There may be far more appropriate ways of organizing the material. We are not, after all, dealing with a Holy Bible; we are dealing with a mass of information that can often be presented in any number of ways in terms of sequence.

What's going to come first? Maybe I'll want to start with my favorite chunk of information. Is there any compelling reason I shouldn't? If not, so be it. That's where I'll start. Maybe, for example, in American history, I'll want to begin with a favorite theme and go from there.

Okay. Next I would take that chunk of material I intended to begin the year with and deal just with that, leaving all the rest alone for the moment. I would rewrite the fact/skills/concept lists so they reflected an appropriate order—an order dictated by the material itself—and I would study and determine how the three aspects were related. Should the students learn a group of facts first and then draw a conclusion from them that becomes a working concept, and is the drawing of that conclusion a skill I want them to have, and if so, is this a pattern I need to follow continuously, or . . . ? I would get control over that piece of material, in other words, and prepare to present it whole, hopefully in the service of facts, skills, and concepts simultaneously.

Now, still dealing with the same chunk of material (let's say, for the sake of discussion, organized labor and the rise of the labor movement), I would make another list. This one would be a list of all the ways I can think of that that material shows its presence in or manifests itself in the school and/or the community from which my students come. Is there a teachers' union? If not, why not? Is there a mill in town? Is it organized? If not, why not? There may be very good reasons. What are they? If it is organized, how and when did that happen? Are any of my students' parents members of a union? And so forth.

Then I look at the ways the material shows itself statewide or nationally. What are the trends? What illustrations can I use that my students will understand and relate to?

Now I determine the means I can use to take those examples that are forceful and appropriate illustrations of the material at work in the real world and use them to bring the material to life and make it meaningful and memorable. To carry this one step further, in my community, I would find a parent or grandparent—hopefully of one of my students—who had moved to Detroit with his family to find work in the automobile plants, who had joined a union in his plant, who had later moved back home as conditions improved here (there are students who represent such a situation in every one of my classes), and who would be willing to come into my class and talk about that experience. I list all such usable options.

Now I would look at the text and ask myself the extent to which the text needs to dominate the material. Are there pages in the text I could literally tear out and throw away, illustrating the material on them through some more powerful means? If not, fine. There often are, however, and as I get better at replacing those pages with other materials, the text begins to assume a more appropriate position in the scheme of things and, rather than going from text to illustration, I sometimes find myself being able to go from illustrations and activities to text or not using the text for certain things at all.

I would also begin to look for other materials, perhaps essays or other readings, that I could either substitute for some portion of the text because they simply do the job better, or use to amplify or expand or enrich some portion of the text.

One note of caution: I am reminded of the English teacher in Rockville, Maryland, who was suspended in 1980 for teaching Machiavelli's *The Prince* and Aristotle's *Poetics* to his tenth-graders in conjunction with *Julius Caesar* (see *Time*, 12/15/80, p. 77). The record shows that he was suspended because the two supplementary works he used were not on the approved curriculum list for tenth-graders, but he used them anyway because they were so appropriate. The more probable reason for the suspension was not the nature of the two books (I taught *The Prince* to my Rabun Gap students several times with no problems) but the teacher's outright defiance of the system. In most cases, when we go to department heads or principals first and explain our rationale for using supplementary materials that may cause someone a problem, and justify their use, we can get permission. At least we've covered our butts. And if we can't get permission, we can usually find some other acceptable means of doing the job (using a summary of the books, for example, with selected quotations to give the students a feel for the authors' styles). When we consciously buck the system, however, and purposely try to make it look impotent and stupid to make a point, however valid the point is, we must expect the confrontation and accept the consequences. The system doesn't intend to be whipped by a teacher; it can't afford to be. And though we may win in the end through litigation or publicity or compromise, we ultimately lose, I think, because we virtually destroy our ability to work creatively and somewhat harmoniously within that system for the benefit of our students.

Now I would construct pre- and post-tests as a means of measuring whether the students understood the material—whether the plan "worked." I might want to teach the second chunk of material using the text/lecture method *only*, pre- and post-testing it, too, to see, for my own personal information, whether there was any difference. I would spend some time, in other words, thinking about how I intended to evaluate. At this point, I might want to sit down with a peer or a department head, or a professor in the education department of a local college, show him or her what I had done so far, and get some feedback for possible revision.

Still with me? This is not as cumbersome a process as it sounds, by the way, especially if, at this stage, we are dealing with the material in manageable, bite-size chunks. If we know the material well, we can do most of this fairly easily and quickly. It's the process of asking different questions of the material than we have asked before that takes a bit of getting used to.

Now I would construct a list of school goals similar to the ones I have talked about already ("how the world works," etc.). It might be the actual school list, or one of my own derived from my readings, or a combination of both. Then I would try to determine how the chunk of material I was about to teach could serve one or more of those goals, and I would make a conscious attempt to ensure that that happened simultaneously.

At the same time, I would begin to look at methodology, knowing that some of those school goals (self-confidence, etc.) are influenced as much by the *way* I teach as by *what* I teach. I would reread John Dewey's *Experience and Education,* and I would try to listen closely as he talked, making notes and reminders to myself. I would ask myself still more questions. How can I make this material *stick?* How can I bring it to life? What is the bag of tricks from which I can choose? How do I do it? Is it repetition? Is it drill? Is it action and experience? Is it discussion? Is it projects and real end products? Is it a field trip? Are there other tools at my disposal—not things, necessarily, that I'm going to have to find money for but things close at hand—that I can use? (I use equipment like cameras and tape recorders in my composition class, but if they weren't available, I'd just figure out some other way to accomplish the goals they serve.)

I would also, here, do some serious thinking about my own high school experiences—those things that remained with me as powerful moments of learning and those that didn't and why. I would analyze the best of them, and distill out their common ingredients, and use them in my own work.

Now I would overlay the material with the methodology. My own inclination would probably be—depending, of course, on the material—to employ a variety of techniques, knowing that some of my students are going to be left-brain learners and some right-brain, and knowing the value of mixing methods in the classroom to keep things moving and to avoid the deadliness of routine. If the material itself is not routine and deadly but alive and relevant, then the methodology must serve that fact and not squash the material backward into an inappropriate mold.

I would remind myself of how young people learn. I would review "process methodology" versus "content methodology" (learning to think clearly and problem solve versus memorizing lecture notes; learning by discovery and induction versus depending on information from the teacher and books; free discussion and small-group work to search for answers to larger questions versus recitation in class, etc.) and study the appropriateness of each in my particular situation. I would review Benjamin Bloom's work and the process of true cognitive learning (memory to translation to interpretation, to application to analysis to synthesis to evaluation) and strive not to short-circuit that process.

I would search for "fit." What are the most appropriate means—and at the same time the most forceful means—for not only teaching this material specifically but at the same time enhancing the very process of education itself?

Last, I would remind myself of the traits I must have as an individual teacher—traits I have already outlined at some length but of which I can always stand to be reminded—and I try, as I teach, to get to the point at which they become an absolutely automatic and integral part of my approach. Watching students as individuals. Reinforcing. Winning reluctant or hostile students to me as opposed to reacting in anger or plotting some form of petty revenge (it's almost like a game of chess with some of them —move, countermove, plan . . .).

Content and methodology joined, hopefully in appropriate, natural, vital ways, not artificial marriages. Theory and practice joined, ditto.

Now the acid test. Suddenly there they are and I am taking the roll. They sit watching me, waiting. The honeymoon will last two days. Then what?

What I do now is charge on through that first chunk of material. As we go, I watch them. What things seem to be working? Which are not? Which are disasters? Why? What happened? As we begin to know each other, and they know I'm as serious as a heart attack about wanting to make this one of the best courses they've ever had, I begin to ask *them* those same questions. Why didn't it work? What could we have done differently? At the end of each week, I fill out a chart similar to the ones I use for Foxfire I. I look at the content. I look at the methodology. I pre- and post-test each unit. I evaluate constantly. How could I have done that better? Why did I forget that simple fact? I make notes as to things that worked blissfully well and things that didn't. All this becomes material that not only informs the method by which the subsequent pieces of the same course are taught, but also the revision that must come.

I don't tear things up all at once and lunge into totally unfamiliar techniques and methods, but one step at a time, as I am comfortable and confident, and as the kids are with me, I *act*. As Bob Taylor said at an American Camping Association conference in Dearborn, Michigan, in March of 1977, "We have to act our way into a new way of thinking rather than think our way into a new way of acting."

Up until now, my domination of this course would have been pretty complete. As a teacher new to the course, I'd probably be like some of you: a bit nervous about swinging out too far. At first, I'd be concerned about control and concerned about my potential inability to stay on top of too much activity in a course I'd never taught before. I think that's natural, and I'm not going to apologize for that tendency within myself.

But once I was several weeks into the course, and I was becoming more and more familiar with the human and physical resources available to me outside, and with my students and their needs and interests, I would begin to watch for an opportunity to try one classwide project (perhaps with only one class at first) that seemed appropriate to the subject material and the students. In an attempt to find that project, I'd list suggestions of my own and of students, together on a sheet of paper in the room. At some point, as a class, we would discuss the options and vote. That's the way our magazine started: one of a number of suggested projects, it was chosen as a six-week experiment, after which we would very probably move on to something else. Keeping Dewey's notion of a spiral curriculum in mind, I would probably not kick off such a project until several months had passed and the students had some necessary background (such as that provided by Foxfire I) and we had a good working relationship.

Ideally, no matter what the subject area I was teaching, the project would culminate in an end product of some sort (an exhibition, a play, a slide-tape show, an experimental model, whatever) that would provide closure and a sense of accomplishment for the class, and that an audience would see.

The end product should stand as an illustration of how the subject matter being covered in the class can be utilized, should involve the use of resources—human and physical—from the real world, and should be broad enough in scope to allow for:

•Participation by all students in the class either individually or in small groups (where cooperation and consensus is emphasized).

•Peer teaching and small-group work, so that I am free to help students through that grueling period in the middle of any project at which energy begins to flag or hurdles are met that they can't leap over alone, such as times when one student is dominating the group's work so completely (as teachers often do in a class) that the other members have retreated into submission or rebelled; or when some members have simply gotten lazy and are letting the others carry the load, expecting all the while to receive the same grade; or when they simply do not have all the information they need to complete the task.

•Numerous approaches to the problem so that there is not just one "right" answer that only I know, but, as with magazine design and layout, enough right ways to do it that many student ideas can be accepted and used, leading each student into the realization that "my values matter and my ideas count."

•Questions for which I do not have the answers (in the magazine class, for example, students frequently have to track down pieces of information that they share with the rest of us, and all of us learn together).

•Class decision making, and plenty of opportunities to help them organize and achieve what they want rather than what I want them to do for me (ideally they get so caught up in the importance of the work at hand that they forget about the student personalities involved and make decisions together that are for the good of the project rather than for the recertification of any single student's power or influence).

•And, most important, the utilization of other academic disciplines, so that students can see their interdependence and the necessity of having a variety of interests and strengths and talents represented on any team. When George and his students produce a record album as one of their projects, a knowledge of music itself is just barely enough to get them started. Suddenly they realize the need for information or expertise (which they must develop) in technical and recording skills, photography, design, marketing and cost analysis, the ability to research the histories of songs and present those in readable form in the booklet of liner notes each album contains, etc.

One of these days, I'm going to take one of my magazine classes and push that idea as far as I can push it. If I could have a group of students for an entire year, and we could agree on one important cultural tradition or artifact we wanted to feature, turning what we discovered into an entire issue of the magazine (or even into a small book), I think it could be truly exciting. Take, for example, a grist mill. Since it's a language arts class, the bottom line would be that each group would have to explain its findings in a clear, clean, grammatically correct, publishable document. Taking that as a given, the class would then divide itself into groups according to special interests or skills, one each for: an oral history (through interviews with owners, customers, etc.) and a factual history (through documents such as courthouse records and deeds) of the mill; a technical description of the actual machinery inside the mill, including the wheel, that would require the utilization of physics and mechanics; a series of diagrams documenting both the mechanics and the architecture (with the construction of the sluices, gates, dams, rock walls, etc.); the folklore surrounding the mill, including such things as the game Fox and Geese, which customers played on the front porch while waiting for the meal to be ground, and customs that were common in association with the activity of taking grain or corn to the mill to have it processed, and legends surrounding the building, etc.; the business aspects of the operation and its contribution to the economic life of the community; and so forth. Taking it one step further, each group might also work in association with a willing teacher who represented expertise in the group's chosen focus (physics, business ed, social studies, drafting), and the students in each group might get credit not only in my class, for English, but also at the same time get credit for doing a special project in that cooperating teacher's class (the students with the history focus, for example, might also be able to use their work for my class as their term paper in American history). Final presentation might even extend beyond a magazine or book to include a slide-tape show, a public exhibition of some sort, a scale model of the building, or a television show involving Mike's video students and my own.

Jumping ahead another step, what if each of the cooperating teachers decided, instead of having only one group of students in one of their classes doing a project in association with mine, to have all their students in one class, instead of doing a more standard term paper, divided into groups to do similar work? In that way, a grist mill, a pottery operation, a general store, and a sawmill might all be documented at the same time, not as the sum total of the students' work in physics or history or whatever but as one part of their work within those disciplines. Okay, organization and scheduling are a problem (something's *always* a problem), and obviously I haven't got this figured out yet, but I will. I'll try it on a small scale first with a teacher or two I know, and we'll see where it goes. Maybe nowhere. But it's fun to think about, and I honestly believe it would work. And look what happens as every area of knowledge and expertise that can shed light and understanding on the subject is brought to bear, and finally brought together, in one unified, competent, academically sound presentation. Look at the number of entry points there are into the overall project through which almost any student, no matter what his or her interest, can become engaged, wrestle toward solutions independently, and make an essential contribution to the finished product—a contribution the absence of which would render it incomplete.

In the end, the projects finished, that essential period of time would pass in which we'd get some distance from the project and analyze together what it was that just happened to us—that period of reflection that is the means by which one really learns from experience—and then we'd try to figure out how the lessons we had all learned could apply to later life and work.

Then, while I had the class pulled back and regrouped, I'd initiate the next body of material to cover, and, following the same general sequence of events, move again through the material, working toward another class project of some sort and another illustration of that material at work and its utility in the world beyond our classroom.

Ebb and flow. Back and forth. Lecture and text to project and application and reflection. In what percentages? How is the time split among the various methodologies? What is the breakdown between student input and teacher control? I honestly don't know. It all depends. It will take years of working with this one course and its typical student population to be able to answer that question with anything resembling certainty. There are so many variables. At some point, however, I *would* figure it all out. At some point, it would all come together. I know it would.

Again, planning is all. Though there are times when random play and experimentation without guidance are appropriate, little of consequence gets accomplished when it dominates. We must study a potential educational vehicle carefully and *make* it accomplish those goals that lead us to select it as an educational tool. Serendipitous learning is wonderful when it happens, but it is too random and too occasional to be relied on. It's rather like taking an unprepared group of youngsters on a field trip and turning them loose in an environment, assuming they will absorb important insights by osmosis as they career off the walls. I've seen this happen too often as teachers turn their students loose in museum environments filled with objects to be manipulated and buttons to be pushed, and the kids rush from station to station pushing buttons and flipping switches and shrieking with laughter as mysterious objects buzz and whir and slides flash on a screen nobody is watching and a disembodied voice to which no one is listening runs its futile tape loop course. Museum directors and board members nod with satisfaction at the yellow school buses parked at their entrances, but far too often no learning is taking place within the building. It is recess on a neighbor's playground, that's all. We must plan.

Second, as we lead students into realms of increasingly serious responsibility, we will inevitably encounter those critics who will say to us, "Look, this business of placing students in adultlike roles is entirely misguided at the high school level. These are children, and they must be allowed to be children during this time in their lives. They'll have plenty of time for adult responsibilities and concerns later. You're making them grow up too fast."

I would agree if we were talking about the days of child labor and the Dickensian environments in which many children were routinely and completely immersed. Most students I meet, however, are sick unto death of being regarded as children, and of being robbed of all decision-making opportunities and all responsibility. For too many of them, schools are like Buster Brown shoes that are several sizes too small. As Natalie Rogers, one of my seniors, wrote in a composition recently, "We have been taught how to make responsible decisions, but we do not have any to make." The hunger that most of my students feel comes from a deep well of insecurity that leads them to questions like, "What's going to happen to me when I get out of here? What am I going to do? Will I be able to function in that world out there? Will I make it? How do I start? Where do I go? Whom do I ask?" Moreover, as I've said before, until those insecurities are resolved—and they can only be resolved by putting students into situations in which mistakes can be accepted and are not life- or job-threatening, and in which they can prove to themselves through trial and error that they can function responsibly—we have no hope of leading them on to the next set of equally important questions: "How can I make a contribution in this world? Why should I? Where do I start? What are the needs? How do I find them? How can one person make any difference at all?" Those are adult questions, resoundingly important for teenagers to wrestle with, and they do not get dealt with satisfactorily in a play-school environment. The kids I know want red meat, not a mirage—the

real world, not fantasy. And the reason the majority of them hold school
in such low esteem is that its connection to that real world they are about
to enter seems so tenuous to them as to be nearly illusory.

I can already hear some of you yelling, "Wait a minute. I have five
classes a day. I haven't got time to do that with all five."

Okay. Let's talk about that for a moment. First of all, both you and I are
going to have to determine how we juggle that fact and our energy, given
our specific situations.

In general, however, I'd say the best place to begin looking for answers
is with our peers. All of us develop our own tricks of dealing responsibly
with the load. Composition teachers, for example, know that if they're
going to ask all their students to write compositions, they have those from
each class due on a different day so they only have one set a night to
correct. My Foxfire I compositions, for example, are due on a Wednesday
or a Thursday, so that I can get them returned before my college English
class compositions come in on Friday, giving me whatever portion of the
weekend I wish to choose to deal with them. That scheme makes sense for
me, because the younger students in Foxfire I want and need immediate
next-day feedback. The older students are content to wait over the weekend, knowing not only that I need more time with their papers but also
that getting papers back on Monday and starting a new composition topic
the same day—with the mistakes of the old one in mind—makes perfect
sense in that sort of class. We get smart about scheduling and organizing
so we don't bury ourselves under work. That just takes practice, and the
skill of stealing other teachers' secrets.

Second, *most* of us are dealing with the same basic subject matter in all
our courses (you don't find many teachers teaching a math, a history, an
English, a physics, and a PE), and so most of the steps I've outlined in
creating or revising a course can apply to several courses at once. We're
not talking about going through the process five or six separate times for
five or six different courses. Even if we were, any number of those steps
(school goals, methodology, etc.) would only have to be done once. The
same results apply to all.

But if it's still too overwhelming a thought, here's what I'd suggest:

Forget the process for all but one of your courses. Continue teaching
the others as you always have. Take one—perhaps your favorite or the
one with which you feel most confident—and choose one portion of it
(one unit within it) and try the process on that. See how it feels. If it works,
see if there's another course you have for which you can use exactly the
same materials and activities and methodology you've just used once.
Again, the secret is in doubling up, making everything serve several ends.
If it doesn't work, try something else. But try. Get off dead center. Tinker
with one part of one course and see if, as you learn, the process can be
extended into other parts of the same course, and even at the same time
into others of your courses. For example, a person from the community

being interviewed by students in one of your classes will often agree to stay for two or three classes if you ask. See what happens.

Above all, stay ever vigilant, always watching. Always thinking about the subject matter. Always trying to figure out more forceful ways of teaching it. Involving the students more and more frequently in analysis and help. Experimenting as you have the nerve. Laughing with the students at the lessons you blow. It's not the end of the world. You'll do better tomorrow. Always caring about the material. Always caring about them.

That's what I try to do, because I *like* them. They're basically interesting, decent people. I enjoy trying to figure them out and I enjoy the game of trying to figure out how best to teach the material. It makes my day when they react with surprise and excitement to something we accomplish together.

I really like them. That makes all the difference.

31

Standing on Higher Ground

And so, the end. There's so much more to say. I look back over what I've written and the three hundred typed pages I've cut from the manuscript, and I know that any number of chapters in this volume could be turned into separate volumes themselves. But that's for another time, perhaps. Not now.

Today I came home from school and I was so tired I could not talk. I dumped my homework on my desk, went to the refrigerator and got a beer, opened it, and sat in a chair on the porch and watched the leaves moving on the tulip poplar trees in my yard. I knew I should try to fix supper. I didn't. I watched the movement of leaves.

Sometimes I'm tired because it's been a great day, and the excitement of one fine moment after another collapses me at the end of the day, with a grin on my face, into that chair on my porch. "It all worked today. It really worked. I hit them right between the eyes."

Sometimes I'm tired for the opposite reasons, and I find myself slipping, despite my convictions, into the pearls-before-swine syndrome. I spend hours setting up a great activity and only two students want to participate. I devote an entire Saturday to grading the compositions from my college-level English class, and then on Monday the students refuse to give some of that energy back by making a conscious attempt to understand and internalize my comments and master the stylistic and grammatical problems; and I find myself on the verge of shouting, "Look, I gave those creations of yours a day out of my weekend—a day out of my life. That's a day, gone forever, that I could have spent differently. I can't get that day back. You've just stolen it from me and spit on it, and I'm not at all sure you had the right to do that." I covet some signal from those I want to please that they acknowledge and appreciate the fact that I am giving this egg-sucking, no-win job every ounce of my strength and creativity and will, and the signal never comes. Nobody cares.

Then I sit and watch leaves.

It was a revelation early in my teaching life to find that those solid, competent, unruffled peers I passed in the halls had similar emotional highs and lows and had the same sulking gremlin of misgiving living in one of their closets. The earliest inkling came not from my peers, however, but from the fact that my school district sometimes thought it necessary to bring in to the county motivational in-service speakers who talked about such "epidemic problems" as emotional drain and lack of positive reinforcement and isolation and burnout.

And I listened to them in wonder. I studied these glowing specimens with their well-scrubbed faces and manicured nails and their "Is the glass half full or half empty" pop psychology; and their "Repeat after me, all together now, 'I Feel Great!' " imperatives; and their "Turn to your neighbor and tell her how terrific she looks today" exhortations; and their "Remember that what you sow, you shall also reap tenfold, and that if you give compliments you will not only receive compliments but also feel better about yourself" predictions; and their "You hold the future of the world in your hands through your students" pieties. And as I listened to their eternally, unflappably upbeat lingo—these professional purveyors of optimism who give their stock speeches all year long to captive audiences like us—I realized not only that I was not alone in my frustrations, but that these manipulative, sanitized cardboard cutout representations of perfect human beings were at least half full of shit and were not the solution.

Neither, I have found, are the inane night courses I have had to take to keep my certification current. Nor are the teachers' conferences I've been to where speakers who do not teach in the public schools—but who paradoxically know more than us about teaching—proffer bankrupt, stupid ideas or stand before us and harangue us about our shortcomings and accomplish nothing short of turning the mood in the room sullen and angry at best, or sending us on to the next session dispirited, with our tails between our legs, at worst. And we do not do things any differently because of them. We just retreat.

There's little help there. So where?

I have been around awhile now, and I have learned something about those highs and lows. Remembering the following helps me. Perhaps it will be equally useful to you.

Teachers tend to be ranged across a wide spectrum of attitudes about and stances toward this job. Leaving aside those for whom it is just a job, period, and nothing more, and concentrating on those who care, at one end of the spectrum we find those who have discovered that they can minimize the damage from discouragement by minimizing the passion they invest. They scale down their expectations of their students, they learn not to expect praise or encouragement from others, and they simply do what they can to be competent. They are not irresponsible; neither are they bad teachers. They are simply teachers who have learned to preserve their own sanity and their emotional well-being through the protective device of being basically numb. They are on automatic pilot.

At the other end of the spectrum are those young teachers who come roaring into the field with their ideals aflame and with their determination to permanently heal every wound, reverse every intellectual deficiency, correct every injustice and every abuse of power flapping like a multicolored banner above their heads. Because their passions are so ignited and their expectations are so high, their failures are legion; their few successes, though sometimes dramatic and inspiring, are not enough to offset the self-condemnation and depression that accompany the growing awareness of the numerous lost causes that litter their landscapes; and they retreat in dismay.

As always, there is high ground in the middle. On this knoll gather those teachers who are determined to preserve their spirit and their love for the field. Most of these individuals, myself included, have a credo that goes something like this:

The profession of teaching is exactly that—a *profession*, not an avocation or a hobby or a marriage of convenience. Because of its goals and its potential to achieve those goals, I *selected* it. It did not come knocking on my door. I was searching for a way to be of real service, and I found and chose this field; I believed then, as I believe now, that it is a profession of honor and true merit, and though I may not remain in it for all of my working days, as long as I *do* continue to teach, it will continue to deserve and receive my best.

It is hardly a perfect way to make a living. As in other professions, like law or medicine, there are daily disappointments. Guilty felons go free; children with leukemia die; students drop out or fail or turn against me or my course for some injustice, real or imagined. I will not—cannot—let my failures with students lead to a suicide of the spirit.

As with law or medicine, the profession is attacked—from outside by those who are ignorant, and from inside by those who should know better. It is also attacked by those who have legitimate grievances. Just as the attacks do not diminish the essential worth of the fields of law or medicine, neither do they diminish the essential worth of the profession of teaching or cause its beacon to burn less brightly. I acknowledge those criticisms that are informed and valid, and I take onto my shoulders my fair individual share of the responsibility for correcting, as a professional, any of my own practices that may be exacerbating the problem; and I acknowledge my obligation, as a working member of a larger team, to do all I can to make our own school an institution with which all of us are proud to be affiliated. I will do this rather than becoming defensive and sullen. Neither will I allow attacks from the uninformed to diminish my enthusiasm for the work at hand. People shouting in the wind are simply that.

And to prevent myself from getting stale or discouraged or impatient or exhausted—or to turn that mood around when it strikes and I find myself walking through the days—I head for a congenial tavern with friends; or go to a teachers' conference on the chance that lightning will strike, searching for colleagues who have had experiences that seem valid and who are engaged daily in the process of making it all work; or I go to a Braves game in Atlanta; or I watch tulip poplar leaves and think it through, one step at a time.

And lest I become like Santayana's fanatic, I try to remember our goals. I try to remember what it's like to be thirteen, sitting at a desk. I try to stay on high ground and not get caught up in the negative.

And I remind myself that though I don't necessarily love these students, I do *like* them as people and as individuals. And I do *like* the challenge of the metaphorical game of chess I play with them every day, plotting strategies and moves and countermoves and experimenting with the formulas. And I am often touched by their loyalty and by the way they adopt my classroom and some of the projects we try together proudly—almost haughtily—as *ours*.

Finally, I remind myself that there *are* young adults out there in the world who remember me. Some of them remember me as a caring individual who added to rather than subtracted from the quality of their lives, and they are passing that energy on.

My job—no, my desire—is to increase those numbers.

Notes

CHAPTER 24

1. National Public Radio, "Options in Education—The Critics Revisited," July 4, 1977.
2. *Newsweek*, September 12, 1977, p. 67.

CHAPTER 25

1. A. Bartlett Giamatti, "The American Teacher," *Harpers*, July 1980, pp. 28–29.

CHAPTER 26

1. Alfred North Whitehead, *The Aims of Education* (New York: Macmillan Publishing Co., Inc., A Free Press Paperback, 1967), p. 16.
2. George Dennison, *The Lives of Children* (New York: Vintage, 1969), pp. 92–93.
3. Mara Wolynski, "Confessions of a Misspent Youth," *Newsweek*, August 30, 1976, p. 11.
4. Harper Lee, *To Kill A Mockingbird* (New York: Lippincott, 1960), p. 21.
5. Ibid., p. 24.
6. Ibid., p. 31.
7. "Programs for the Gifted—Insults and Injuries?", *Psychology Today*, March 1981, p. 20.
8. Herroy E. Garrett, *Great Experiments in Psychology* (New York: Appleton-Century-Crofts, 1941), p. 273.
9. Seymore Fisher, "Experiencing Your Body: You Are What You Feel," *Saturday Review of Science*, July 8, 1972, p. 30.
10. Ibid., p. 29.
11. *Time*, November 14, 1977, p. 65.

CHAPTER 28

1. *U.S. News and World Report*, September 8, 1980.
2. *Time*, November 14, 1977, p. 63.
3. *U.S. News and World Report*, September 8, 1980, p. 47.

4. Ibid., p. 50.
5. Deadrich Hunter, "My Turn," *Newsweek,* August 18, 1980, pp. 14–15.
6. ABC-TV, *Youth Terror: The View From Behind the Gun,* June 28, 1978.
7. *Sports Illustrated,* May 19, 1980, pp. 39–42.
8. "The Phil Donahue Show," June 3, 1981.
9. A. Bartlett Giamatti, "The American Teacher," *Harpers,* July 1980, p. 24.
10. Ibid., p. 25.
11. Fred Heckinger, *New York Times,* December 12, 1980.
12. *Time,* June 1, 1981, p. 63.
13. A. Bartlett Giamatti, "The American Teacher," *Harpers,* July 1980, p. 25.
14. Harry Stein, "The Indifferent American," *Esquire,* June 1981, p. 20.
15. George S. Counts, *Dare the Schools Build a New Social Order?* (London: Feffer and Simons, Inc., 1932), pp. 2–3.
16. "The Battle of the Bottle," *Time,* June 1, 1981, p. 26.
17. Robert Shnayerson, *Quest,* January 1980.

CHAPTER 29

1. Margaret W. Morley, *The Carolina Mountains* (Boston and New York: Houghton Mifflin Company, 1913), p. 67.
2. Ibid., pp. 76–78.
3. Ibid., pp. 10–11.
4. Ibid., pp. 80–81.
5. Ibid., p. 112.
6. Ibid., pp. 113–114.
7. Ibid., p. 54.
8. Ibid., p. 60.

Bibliography

FOUR CLASSICS

BAYLES, ERNEST E. *Pragmatism in Education.* New York: Harper & Row, 1966. Many feel this is the most readable volume on John Dewey, clearly explaining not only the major tenets of the philosophy, but also providing a set of "illustrative units" that show the classroom applications of the philosophy in grammar, literature, math, history, and science.

COLLINGS, ELLSWORTH. *An Experiment with a Project Curriculum.* New York: Macmillan, 1923. This book is now out of print, but if you can find a copy, it's worth the trouble. It is Ellsworth Collings's account of his attempt to put into practice with his nine-, ten-, and eleven-year-old students the philosophies of his teachers, John Dewey and William H. Kilpatrick (who wrote the introduction to this book).

Especially fascinating is Collings's account of several complete learning experiences (or the "complete act of thought" explained by John Dewey in Chapters 10–12 of *Democracy and Education*) he conducted with his class. In one, for example, the class investigated the causes of typhoid fever in a neighbor's home, explored various means of preventing the disease, and then drafted a written report to the neighbor explaining its findings.

CREMIN, LAWRENCE A. *The Transformation of the School: Progressivism in American Education, 1876–1957.* New York: Knopf, 1961. This book is widely regarded as the definitive study of the progressive education movement. Its greatest contribution lies in Cremin's critique of Dewey's disciples, who tended to substitute the interests and whims of the students for the social and academic agenda Dewey urged. The result was predictable: an unfortunate and widespread discrediting of progressive education as "soft pedagogy." Cremin details the necessary solutions.

DEWEY, JOHN. *Experience and Education.* New York: Collier-Macmillan, 1963. In 1938, toward the end of his life, and after his experiences with the progressive schools, John Dewey wrote this short (91 pages) volume. Designed both to answer the critics of his philosophy and to restate the essence of that philosophy in the clearest terms possible, it stands as his most concise and readable statement. In it he contrasts the traditional method of education with the progressive method and argues that neither, alone, is the answer; what we must seek, instead, is a blend of the two. It makes especially provocative reading today as schools across the country shift to the wholly traditional approach that Dewey warns us so convincingly against in this volume.

RECENT BOOKS OF SPECIAL SIGNIFICANCE

BOYER, ERNEST L. *High School: A Report on Secondary Education in America.* New York: Harper & Row; 1983. This comprehensive look at teachers, students, and subject matter finds most schooling to be dull and routine—to no one's surprise. The beauty of the extensive recommendations is that they are mostly implementable within current institutional structures.

Child & Youth Services 4 (1982). The entire issue of this journal is given over to descriptions of innovative experiential programs that exist within school situations. One of the best-known of those discussed is the brave and now almost famous consumer action class in St. Paul, Minnesota. There's plenty of food for thought here.

CUSICK, PHILIP A. *The Egalitarian Ideal and the American High School.* New York: Longman, 1983. Through in-depth studies of three high schools in a northeastern industrial city, Cusick concludes that some of the problems our schools are having are the result of our too-lofty goal to "attract, retain, instruct everyone regardless of inclinations, predilections or abilities."

DARLING-HAMMOND, LINDA. *Beyond the Commission Reports: The Coming Crisis in Education.* Santa Monica, Cal.: Rand Corporation, 1984. The frightening conclusion that the author reaches in this report is that experienced, effective teachers are leaving the profession in large numbers partly because of the increasing control over their professional lives being taken by "the authorities." They are being replaced in large part by new teachers drawn from the lower ranks of college graduates.

GOODLAD, JOHN I. *A Place Called School.* New York: McGraw-Hill, 1984. Ineffective schooling often results from an oil-water mixture of the youth culture on the one hand and the orientation of teachers and the conduct of schools on the other. Two sets of recommendations accompany this penetrating study.

LIGHTFOOT, SARA LAURENCE. *The Good High School: Portraits of Character and Culture.* New York: Basic Books, 1983. Lightfoot searches for the characteristics that six supposedly "good" schools share. Her extensive observations were made in two urban, two suburban, and two private schools.

LIPSITZ, JOAN. *Successful Schools for Young Adolescents.* New Brunswick, N.J.: Transaction Books, 1984. Four successful middle schools are studied, culminating in documented ways to improve schools from within.

MUUS, ROLF E. *Theories of Adolescence,* 4th ed. New York: Random House, 1982. Finally, a *readable* introduction and summary of the research and theories of leading adolescent psychologists such as Jean Piaget, Erik Erikson, Lawrence Kohlberg, and David Elkind. Muus has done our homework for us, and we shouldn't feel guilty about taking advantage of his labors.

RAVITCH, DIANE. *The Troubled Crusade: American Education, 1945–1980.* New York: Basic Books, 1983. Since World War II, events such as the G.I. Bill and the *Brown* decision have left their mark on American education. This examination of these events provides historical perspective for the current surge of reforms.

RUTTER, MICHAEL, BARBARA MAUGHAN, PETER MONTIMORE, and JANET OUSTON. *Fifteen Thousand Hours: Secondary Schools and Effects on Children.* Cambridge, Mass.: Harvard University Press, 1979. In their study of twelve inner-city schools in London, the authors find that certain common practices definitely contribute to the academic effectiveness of a school. These factors include high teacher expectations of academic competence, field trips, trusting student-teacher relationships, positive reinforcement through the display of quality student products, and numerous opportunities for students to take on leadership roles and responsibility. Boy, does this sound familiar.

SARASON, SEYMOUR B. *The Culture of the School and the Problem of Change,* 2nd ed. Newton, Mass.: Allyn and Bacon, 1982. Any changes planned for schools must take into account the "regularities" of everyday activities of the schools and the cultural context into which the changes are about to be thrust, or be doomed to failure.

————. *Schooling in America.* New York: Free Press, 1983. This is one of the most provocative of the new studies, presenting the case for a new paradigm of schooling to guide badly needed changes. One of the paradigms calls for getting outside the school itself for most education. But will it ever happen?

SIZER, THEODORE R. *Horace's Compromise: The Dilemma of the American High School.* Boston: Houghton Mifflin, 1984. Horace, a composite character who symbolizes the conscientious and able teacher, is forced to compromise between what he knows students *should* get from schooling and what he is able to provide given the strictures and limitations of the schooling situation. Sizer draws his portrait, and his recommendations, from observations and interviews in eighty schools.

TURNBULL, COLIN. *The Human Cycle.* New York: Simon & Schuster, 1983. In many non-Western cultures, both adolescents and the elderly play constructive—if not vital—roles in the society. This fact should cause us to reexamine the roots of our own pervasive Western cultural myths of adolescent irresponsibility and elderly ineptitude. This book is a must.

COURSE GUIDES

Foxfire Course Guides. The staff members who teach the Foxfire-sponsored courses at Rabun County High School are in the process now of creating descriptions of their courses. By the time this book is published, the first of these guides should be available for use by interested teachers.

Most of the guides will include a narrative day-by-day description of class activities similar to the description of the Foxfire I grammar and composition course included in this book. In addition, each will include analysis of various special projects that either succeeded or failed, photographs of the students at work, samples of student work, a discussion of the philosophical underpinnings of the course, and more.

The first three guides to be published will be those detailing our work in videotape and television, in music, and in magazine production. The latter will include examples from the work of other cultural journalism projects.

Later guides are planned that will feature environmental studies, Appalachian literature, photography, folklore, etc.

The guides will be available through our publishing division at prices yet to be determined. If interested, let us know and we'll send you announcements with further details as each is completed: The Foxfire Fund, Inc., P.O. Box B, Rabun Gap, Ga. 30568.

MANUALS

IVES, EDWARD D. *The Tape-Recorded Interview.* University of Tennessee Press, Knoxville, 37916. This manual was written by Sandy Ives, the professional folklorist who for over twenty years has directed the work of the Northeast Archives of Folklore and Oral History at the University of Maine at Orono. It goes far beyond *You and Aunt Arie* in terms of other, vital information concerning such things as how the tape recorder actually works and the proper processing and archiving of tapes. If you're going to conduct tape-recorded interviews, a manual like this one by a real professional is a must. Save yourself the misery of having to learn the lessons included here through bitter experience.

SITTON, THAD, GEORGE MEHAFFY, and O. L. DAVIS. *Oral History: A Guide for Teachers and Others.* University of Texas Press, Austin, 78712. Thad Sitton's Ph.D. dissertation was the first comprehensive study of the spread of student-produced magazines like *Foxfire.* A supporter of this sort of effort ever since, Thad continues to work closely with advisors like Lincoln King *(Loblolly,* Gary, Texas) from his post on the Texas Sesquicentennial Commission in Austin.

Here, Thad and his colleagues offer solid advice to those about to collect oral history, advice based on their wide personal experience in the field and their observations of the work, and trials, of others.

STARR, LOUIS M. In this country, the proper systematic collection and archiving of tape recorded interviews started in the late 1940s at Columbia University. As the number of oral history efforts has grown nationwide, Professor Louis M. Starr, the director of Columbia University's Oral History Office, and his staff have responded to the flood of questions from the field by designing a special informational kit, the contents of which are constantly being revised and updated as new information becomes available.

For a description of the current package, write: Box 20, Butler Library, Columbia University, New York, N.Y. 10027.

WOOD, PAMELA. *You and Aunt Arie.* IDEAS, Nederland, Colo. 80466. This is a manual written by the teacher who, with her high school students, began the *Salt* magazine project in Kennebunk, Maine. It is designed specifically for teachers who want to start a magazine like *Foxfire* but who have had almost no training at all in interviewing techniques, transcribing and editing tapes, photography, layout and design, marketing, etc. Drawing on examples from *Salt* and several other student projects, clearly written and profusely illustrated, this is a fine initiation for the beginner.

NEWSLETTERS, MAGAZINES, AND NEWSPAPERS

Education Week, P.O. Box 1939, Marion, Ohio 43305. For teachers who are serious about staying abreast of new developments in the field, as well as news, book reviews, thoughtful commentary, etc., there's only one publication that appears frequently enough to be genuinely *timely,* and that's this weekly newspaper. If you can set aside some time each week to catch up with our field, this is your paper.

Foxfire, The Foxfire Fund, Rabun Gap, Ga. 30568 (quarterly: $9 per year). The original *Foxfire* magazine described in this book. Still going after twenty years, still student-produced. Each issue averages sixty-four pages and some fifty photos. Back issues are available.

Hands On, Foxfire Fund, Rabun Gap, Ga. 30568 ($5 for four issues). This newsletter is published specifically for public school teachers whose students are involved in experiential, community-based projects like cultural journalism magazines, community festivals, etc. It is the only forum that exists at the moment through which these teachers can exchange news, ideas, and descriptions of current projects—and can solicit help and information from their peers. Lengthy articles of interest to most subscribers are interspersed with letters, magazine and book reviews, and news.

We try to publish quarterly, but we often don't make that goal. Patience is requested. Back issues are available, as are the names and addresses of the other projects with which we are in touch.

NEA Today, 1201 16th St. NW, Washington, D.C. 20036. If you're a member of the National Education Association (NEA), you'll get this monthly publication (tabloid-size, newspaper format) and the annual magazine describing the state of the profession automatically with your membership. Because it is the largest teachers' organization we have, membership—and access to the related services for members—is recommended.

FILMS, VIDEOTAPES, AND SLIDE/TAPE SHOWS

Appalshop, Box 743, Whitesburg, Ky. 41858. If you're interested in films and videotapes that emerge from and are true to an indigenous culture, you should look at these. They're among the best. Write for catalogue.

"Aunt Arie." Encyclopedia Britannica Films, Chicago, Ill. 60611. This film features Aunt Arie in a fifteen-minute monologue about her life and her philosophy. Aunt Arie was one of the most compelling individuals we ever interviewed, and she was the woman on whom Jessica Tandy based her character in the play *Foxfire*, which was the Broadway hit that earned her a Tony award in 1983.

"Foxfire." McGraw Hill Films, Hights Town, N.J. 08520. Made in 1972, this twenty-one-minute film shows students at the Rabun Gap–Nacoochee School in the process of interviewing several local contacts and preparing those interviews for publication. Though outdated now, the film (which is available for purchase or rental) is useful in stimulating classroom discussions about local heritage and culture, and about whether or not a magazine project would make any sense in the location in which the film is shown. It's old, but we're still proud of it.

We are now in the process of preparing a slide/tape show, as well as several videotape shows, about the Foxfire project as it looks today. If interested, let us know and we'll forward to you information about the status of these efforts. (The Foxfire Fund, Inc., P.O. Box B, Rabun Gap, Ga. 30568.)

ORGANIZATIONS

Association for Experiential Education (AEE), Box 249-CU, Boulder, Colo. 80309. This organization, once dominated by outdoor education groups like Outward Bound, has been striving successfully for several years to achieve a membership balance that includes all types of experiential projects. Membership includes a subscription to the *AEE Journal*, a job placement service, and an excellent annual conference. There are also regional conferences and networking services available. It's definitely worth a look. We at Foxfire are members.

NEA. (See *NEA Today* under *Newsletters, Magazines, and Newspapers.*)

Oral History Association, NT Box 13734, Denton, Tex. 76203. This is the professional association for oral historians, but those of us who aren't university trained can join, too—and take advantage of the membership's accumulated wisdom. The biggest boon of membership is access to the annual conference, which is well worth the price of admission.

Teachers and Writers Collaborative, 5 Union Square West, New York, N.Y. 10003. For twenty years now, this group of poets, playwrights, and novelists has hung out in New York City through fat times and lean, working as visiting artists in the New York public schools. Out of the project have come wonderful books (Kenneth Koch's *Wishes, Lies, Dreams* and Philip Lopate's *Being with Children*, to name two) and a regular newsletter that details the strategies these folks have tried—not always successfully—in their classes. The publication is warm, always honest, and always provocative if you're a teacher of language arts/drama and looking for fresh ideas.

EXAMPLES OF BOOKS FROM OTHER PROJECTS

A number of other projects have, like Foxfire, published books that are compilations of the best student articles from the parent magazines. Because of its success with *The Foxfire Book* through *Foxfire 9*, Doubleday has published many of them.

Bittersweet Country, edited by Ellen Gray Massey. Anchor Press/Doubleday, 1978. How to build an Ozark johnboat, perform traditional square dances, and make rag rugs, and stories of such Ozark institutions as the general store, country kitchen, grain mill, and bluegrass music. Recipes and old-time cures, moonshining and shape-note singing, and appreciations of mules and the Ozark foxtrotter.

The Cama-I Book, edited by Ann Vick. Anchor Press/Doubleday, 1983. Kayaks, dogsleds, bear hunting, bush pilots, smoked fish, mukluks, and other traditions of southwestern Alaska.

The Loblolly Book, edited by Thad Sitton. Texas Monthly Press, Austin, Texas, 1983. Water witching, wild hog hunting, home remedies, Grandma's moral tales, and other affairs of plain Texas living.

The Salt Book, edited by Pamela Wood. Anchor Press/Doubleday, 1977. Lobstering, sea moss pudding, stone walls, rum running, maple syrup, snowshoes, and other Yankee doings.

Index